Sex, Drugs and Rock 'n' Roll in the Dutch Golden Age

Sex, Drugs and Rock 'n' Roll in the Dutch Golden Age

Benjamin B. Roberts

AUP

Cover illustration: Adriaen Brouwer, *The Smokers* (c. 1636), The Friedsam Collection, Metropolitan Museum of Art, New York

Cover design: Studio Jan de Boer
Lay-out: Crius Group, Hulshout

Amsterdam University Press English-language titles are distributed in the US and Canada by the University of Chicago Press.

ISBN	978 94 6298 302 1
e-ISBN	978 90 4853 299 5 (pdf)
e-ISBN	978 90 4853 300 8 (ePub)
NUR	694

Originally published as *Seks, Drugs en Rock 'n' Roll in de Gouden Eeuw,* Benjamin B. Roberts, Amsterdam University Press, 2014 [ISBN 978 90 8964 699 6]

Table of Contents

1. The Dutch Republic in the Seventeenth Century

Amsterdam, 2017

These days, arriving at Amsterdam's Central Station, many tourists will be overwhelmed by the distinctly sweet, herbal scent of marijuana or hash. Since the late 1960s and the Flower Power days, Amsterdam has been known the world over for its Red Light District and hash bars or coffee shops, where patrons can 'legally' purchase marijuana and hash in small amounts. In the last forty years, the city has become known as a modern-day 'Sodom and Gomorra' for its toleration of prostitution and use of cannabis. In Quentin Tarantino's Oscar-winning *Pulp Fiction* (1994), one of the many eclectic dialogues between mobsters John Travolta and Samuel L. Jackson captures Amsterdam's liberal drug policy in a nutshell.

> Jackson: *'Tell me about those hash bars again. It's legal now, right?'*
> Travolta: *'Yeah, it's legal now, but not 100% legal. You just can't walk into a restaurant, roll a joint and start puffing away. They want you to smoke at home or in certain designated places.'*
> Jackson: *'And those places are... hash bars?'*
> Travolta: *'Yeah, it breaks down like this: it's legal to buy it, it's legal to own it, and if you are a proprietor of a hash bar, it's legal to sell it. It's legal to carry it, but that doesn't matter, now get a load of this. If you get stopped by a cop in Amsterdam, it's illegal for them to search you. Now that's the right cops in Amsterdam don't have.'*
> Jackson: *'Oh man, I'm going, that's all there is to it. I'm fuckin' going.'*

Otto Copes, 1629

More than twenty years since *Pulp Fiction* was released, a growing number of states in the United States are legalizing the use of cannabis. No doubt, Amsterdam and the Netherlands' liberal policy on drug use have played some role in this development. In the Netherlands, toleration of the use of drugs and other vices, including legalized prostitution, has a longer history; a history that is embedded in the way in which Dutch municipal authorities, schoolteachers, moralists, and parents raised their adolescent children in the Golden Age, in the heyday of abundance and affluence, an era when moderation was a necessity, not an option.

Let us start our story with Otto Copes in December 1629. Otto came from a decent family. They belonged to the elite of the town of Den Bosch, in the Generality Lands of the Dutch Republic. Members of the family held high-ranking public offices as town administrators and mayors. His parents died when he was young, and so Otto was taken in and raised by his paternal uncle, who was a member of Den Bosch's magistrate. By now, Otto was 18 years old and his behavior could hardly be termed appropriate for someone from his background. On a winter's night in 1629, he met up with two friends in a pub in Groningen for a drink that turned into a drinking binge. Earlier that year, Otto had enrolled as a law student at the University of Groningen, a medium-sized town 200 kilometers away from Den Bosch. Groningen took Otto far away from the watchful eye of his uncle, and he felt at liberty to do as he pleased and threw himself into college life. That day in 1629, Otto and his friends started drinking early in the afternoon and by evening they were completely wasted. After they left the pub, things went awfully wrong for them. During their walk home, they became aggressive and started to attack people. The city guard came to the rescue soon afterwards, but by then Otto and his friends had worked themselves into a frenzy of violence, and they started to fire their pistols at the city guard. Miraculously, no one was injured.

Today, the mere thought of drunken students staggering down the street in the middle of night carrying firearms would cause immediate public outrage. Bystanders would call the emergency services and the police would become involved, as well as politicians. The media would have a field day and the newspapers would be filled with moral panic. Commentators would complain about the violence of today's youth. Lawmakers would likely call for an increase in the legal age for alcohol consumption, and the media would speculate about how young people were able to buy weapons.

In the seventeenth century, however, municipal authorities made little fuss about juvenile delinquency. Neither did the media, as in the seventeenth century there were no newspapers as we know them today. And it is unlikely the incident would have been cause for moral panic. This *laissez-faire* attitude tells us much about seventeenth-century society and how young people were regarded at that time. It immediately raises the question: if drunken young people and violence were commonplace, what was considered 'normal behavior' for young people in the Dutch Golden Age?

When I was sixteen years old, my older brother and I traveled through Europe together on a Eurail Pass. We were young Americans who wanted to know everything about European culture and civilization. We wanted to immerse ourselves in the culture of Rembrandt, Bach, and Goethe. We walked along the canals of Amsterdam, admiring the seventeenth-century buildings and feats of urban planning, while cyclists whizzed past and cursed at us as we unknowingly used their bike lane as a sidewalk. We marveled at the masterpieces of Rembrandt, Jan Steen, and Vermeer in the Rijksmuseum. In Paris we were awestruck by the nineteenth-century planning of Haussmann, and in the Louvre we got lost because we wanted to take our picture next to the Venus de Milo.

In picturesque Heidelberg, we relished walking around the medieval castle. At the city's university, founded in 1386, we were amazed by the *Studentenkarzer*, or student prison, where students were incarcerated and given a night to reflect on their inappropriate behavior. To my surprise, the walls of the cells were clad with profanities and obscenities. It reminded me of the toilet stalls at my high school in the United States, where the walls were covered with lewd texts, drawings of joints, and depictions of oversized male genitals. At that point, I started to question my lofty presumption of 'European civilization'. Were those young men the same Europeans who had created the fine art hanging in the museums I had just visited, the literary classics in the world's libraries, and the world's great musical compositions? Could it be true that young students in the early modern period were no better than myself and all those other pimple-faced teenagers in my school? Since that day, I have been wondering what we have in common with our ancestors, as well as how we differ from them. That question runs through this book as well.

The richest country in the world

What was it like to be a teenager and living under different economic and social conditions? During the Golden Age, the Netherlands had an exceptionally large child and adolescent population. How to educate and raise children as decent citizens was one of the main concerns of the early part of the seventeenth century. At that time, the Dutch Republic was the richest country in the world, and with nearly two million inhabitants, the most densely populated country in Europe. It was the most urbanized region in northern Europe, and it was one of the youngest nations, engaged in a fierce battle for independence from Spain and the Roman Catholic Church. The country was itself a teenager, seeking independence and desperately in search of its own identity.

With the eclipse of the Roman Catholic Church in the Dutch Republic, there was no predominant religion to take its place. The Protestant Church tried to gain the former's position as the state church, but failed. The religious landscape of the new country was fragmented, divided up among different religions, which lived side by side and were obliged to tolerate each other.

After the fall of Antwerp in 1585 and the blockade of the Scheldt River, which closed off the city's main source of trade, commercial trade in northern Europe was diverted overnight from Antwerp to Amsterdam. From one day to the next, Amsterdam became the new staple market of Europe. The sealing off of Antwerp's harbor created a large influx of immigrants, who fled the city and resettled in the north. They brought their knowledge, money, and trade contacts with them. The influx of immigrants from the Southern Netherlands unleashed a wave of economic prosperity and a building boom, and generated unprecedented employment. In 1602, the Dutch East Indies Company (VOC) was founded. It became the world's first multinational, winning exclusive rights to trade with today's Indonesia, India, China and Japan. In 1621, the Dutch West Indies Company (WIC) was established and went on to trade in North America, the Caribbean, and Brazil. With its large trading companies, the Republic straddled the globe like a giant octopus, collecting goods from the eastern and western hemispheres. During this period, many merchant families amassed large fortunes and were able to climb the social ladder. Many times, these families ascended from the merchant class within one or two generations and became members of the ruling elite.

In the seventeenth century, the young Republic covered an area that only partially corresponds to the current boundaries of the Netherlands. The country was divided into seven provinces: Holland, Zeeland, Utrecht, Friesland, Groningen, Overijssel, and Gelderland. The province of Holland with its major trading cities, including Amsterdam, Leiden, Haarlem, Hoorn, Enkhuizen, Dordrecht, Rotterdam, Delft and Schiedam, stood at the helm of the Republic. Among the cities of Holland, Amsterdam quickly emerged as the cultural and economic epicenter of the province and hence of the Republic. The worldwide demand for luxury goods such as porcelain, furniture, books, and paintings transformed the city into a commercial and manufacturing center.

Without the wealth that came from these industries, the artistic achievements of painters such as Rembrandt, poets such as P.C. Hooft, and writers such as Vondel would not have been possible. The new elite wanted to be portrayed and immortalized by the country's most prominent painters. In Amsterdam, the painter Bartholomeus van der Helst was the Annie Leibowitz of the Golden Age, painting the country's rich and famous.

The new wealth of the Republic allowed parents to focus on the education of their children. During the Dutch Golden Age, many books of advice were published on how children should be educated and molded into decent citizens of the new country. Numerous schools were founded and several universities were established. It was as though the country had been swept by a wave of optimism about the future, and was full of hope about the younger generation. According to the Dutch sociologist Henk Becker, in his book *Generaties en hun kansen* [Generations and their chances] (1992), generations of young people growing up during economic hardship and crisis, war, or times of disease, are more likely to be pessimistic and have a negative view of the future. They often see hurdles ahead.

Young people who grow up during times of economic prosperity and peace, by contrast, often have an optimistic outlook on life. They are hopeful and see opportunities everywhere, even during difficult times. The baby boomers of the twentieth century are a good example of a generation that grew up in an era of economic prosperity. On the contrary, Generation X grew up in the 1980s when there was economic downturn, overshadowed by the threat of nuclear annihilation at the height of the Cold War. They grew up seeing the future as a grim place with few opportunities, if any at all.

For the early modern period, it is impossible (and unthinkable) to divide generations into categories as sociologists and marketing agencies have done for the twentieth century. That does not mean, however, that there were no differences between the generations in the seventeenth century. This book will focus on young men in the early seventeenth century and examine how they became adults during an economic, cultural, and scientific golden age. Because sources on people in the lower classes are relatively scarce, this book will primarily be concerned with young people from the middle and upper classes. These were young men who were either enrolled at a university or had an apprenticeship, where they learned a craft or trade.

The sources on young people in the Dutch Golden Age used for this book include diaries, paintings, engravings, books on childrearing, educational treatises, police reports, reports from the academic court (the university's own court), and the entertainment books that were produced for young people in the Golden Age. These sources provide us with a glimpse of what it was like to be young in the seventeenth century.

During the Golden Age, a young man was considered a youth until he married; that is, until he was financially independent and had the resources to marry and start a family. In general, this included most men until their late twenties and sometimes as old as their early thirties. In comparison to neighboring countries, the Republic had a large population of young people. They were mostly young laborers or students who had immigrated to the Northern Netherlands. The influx of immigrants had many causes. In the Southern Netherlands, there was heavy fighting during the Revolt against the Spaniards, which disrupted the economy and unleashed social upheaval. This was a major reason for young people to emigrate and seek refuge in the Northern Netherlands.

In the early seventeenth century, there was similar social turmoil in parts of present-day Germany, where a bloody conflict was fought between Roman Catholics and Protestants. During the Thirty Years War (1618-1648), entire towns and villages were destroyed. The countryside was looted and reduced to ashes, crops were destroyed, and livestock were indiscriminately slaughtered. If the inhabitants did not perish from the sword, then they were likely to die from famine and plague. There was little future for the young people in these regions. For them, moving to the flourishing cities of the Northern Netherlands was often the only option to build a new life. They were like the young men from Syria, Iraq, Iran, and countries in Northern Africa today, who risk the dangerous sea crossing from Turkey to Europe in rickety boats. There was no other possibility for them than to leave everything behind and hope for a better life elsewhere. Staying was not an option, because the future that awaited them in their own country was one of violence and famine.

Although seventeenth-century sources do not provide exact statistics about specific age groups, as modern demographic bureaus can do today, we can assume that early modern cities were inhabited primarily by unmarried young people under the age of thirty. They flocked to the cities of the Northern Netherlands in the early seventeenth century. They gave a boost to the economy and stimulated demand for housing, foodstuffs, and household goods. At the same time, they found work in the flourishing trade sector, and in the emerging textile industry and other industries. They were the driving motor of the economic and cultural boom that was known as the Dutch Golden Age.

A country full of young people

Many of the young immigrant men found work in the shipping industry. One could earn good money working on board one of the many VOC or WIC ships. Such a job provided a young man with at least six to nine months of work, with fixed wages. In addition, he could see parts of the world that he could have only dreamt of as a child. Exact data on how many foreigners were employed by the VOC and the WIC during the early seventeenth century are unfortunately unknown. However, we do know that approximately 475,000 foreigners were employed by the VOC during the seventeenth and eighteenth centuries. For a country with a total population of two million inhabitants, the proportion of foreigners must have been considerable. The loading and unloading of ships alone required a workforce of 35,000. Most of these men were not born in the Republic and today they would be called ethnic minorities or guest workers.

The second largest group of young men that came to the country found employment in the army. At least half of the soldiers were foreigners, and sometimes entire regiments came from the same country or region. The Scots, Southern Germans, and the Swiss in particular had a reputation for providing mercenary troops. There are no exact data on the numbers of young men and the regions from which they came. A rough estimate suggests that the Dutch State Army employed one million men during the seventeenth and eighteenth centuries, half of whom were foreigners.

The third group consisted of 'journeymen', or apprentices learning a craft. They included many Germans, known as *Wanderburschen,* who had internships as craftsmen in the cities of the Republic. There were also many journeymen from the Southern Netherlands who, after the blockade of the Scheldt River, had little or no chance of finding an internship in any of the Flemish cities. In this period, many people from the Southern Netherlands sought refuge in the Republic. During the Dutch Revolt, approximately 150,000 people migrated from the South to the North. Many were wealthy merchants who chose Amsterdam as the new destination in which to continue their trade throughout Europe. Other immigrants in the Republic found work in the growing textile industries of Leiden and Haarlem, or were employed as seasonal workers in the bleaching industry outside Haarlem and Zandvoort, where linens were sun-bleached in the fields along the coast. Every town or village in the Republic had local factories where beer was brewed, or glue and straw were processed. In short, there were plenty of jobs for both skilled and unskilled laborers.

The growing economy also instigated a migration of students to the universities in the Republic. University towns such as Leiden, Groningen, Utrecht, Amsterdam and Franeker attracted many foreign students who wanted to study at a Protestant university. In Europe, with the exception of England, the Republic was the only country with a Protestant university. Leiden, for example, had a large student population with many foreigners. They made up a considerable proportion of the city's population and were usually responsible for disturbing the peace after sunset. The continuous 'pull factor' of young people searching for economic prosperity in the Dutch Republic unleashed an unprecedented golden age, while at the same time creating a country that bustled with a young and rambunctious population.

Amsterdam, center of the world

In the late sixteenth and early seventeenth centuries, Amsterdam inherited Antwerp's crown as the center of world trade. The city experienced a population explosion, similar to those that would occur in London and Paris in the nineteenth century. In 1568, at the beginning of the Dutch Revolt against Spain, Amsterdam was home to barely 30,000 inhabitants. By 1600, the population had more than doubled to 65,000. Fifty years later, it had grown to 140,000 residents. In the course of the seventeenth century, Amsterdam became the third most populated city in Europe.

In the early seventeenth century, there was a high degree of social upward mobility. Merchants who amassed large fortunes in a relatively short period were able to climb the social ladder. During the economic boom they acquired not only wealth, but they also sought political influence, and pursued key administrative positions in town magistrates. Some went further, and gained key national offices. Within one or two generations, this group of merchants had worked their way up the ladder and become the new rulers of the country. The new members of the elite also wanted to flaunt their newfound wealth and position. They built large patrician-style palaces along the canals, spent their summers at extravagant country estates, and acquired aristocratic titles from the impoverished old nobility to consolidate their status. They also raised their children in accordance with their new lifestyle, and provided them with an education that was similar to that of the nobility. Their sons attended Latin school and university, their education culminating with a grand tour of France, and Italy, sometimes England, which could last for months, if not years. The sons of the new elite were taught about classical civilization, which was considered appropriate for their new status in society.

The wedding party

One tier below the new elite lay the rising middle class, whose members also profited from the Golden Age. Unlike the *nouveau riche* with their large houses on the main canals and children at university, these were the members of the economic class that earned enough money to buy luxury goods, such as entertaining books and fashionable clothing. It was also a new class whose social power and influence were taken seriously. Its members included young men such as Manuel Colyn, who, together with his elder brother Michiel, ran a publishing and printing house on Damrak quay in Amsterdam. Today, Damrak is the first street that most visitors to the city encounter. It is the stretch from Amsterdam's main railway station to Dam Square, with its neon-lite fast-food joints, tacky souvenir shops, and seedy gambling houses. In the seventeenth century, Damrak was the hub of Amsterdam's publishing industry. Books and other publications could easily be loaded into the moored vessels only a few meters across the quay and shipped elsewhere. From the quay of Damrak, the forbidden works of the philosopher Descartes and pedagogue Comenius were published and distributed throughout Europe.

Manuel's parents had died in 1603, during an outbreak of the plague. Manuel, eight years old at the time, was raised together with his siblings by his eldest brother Claes Colyn, who at the age of 23 had become responsible for his younger brothers and sisters. They lived in a small alleyway named Teerketelsteeg, 'Tar Kettle Alley', that veered off into Amsterdam's main Singel canal. Claes was like a father to Manuel, and when he married 24-year-old

Catharina Cloppenburgh on Sunday 7 August 1622, Claes was his witness. Catharina's father, Jan Evertsz Cloppenburgh, was also a witness. Cloppenburgh ran a well-known publishing house that was located on Damrak next to that of Manuel's brother, Michiel. In Amsterdam's publishing world, the union between Manuel and Catherina must have been considered a merger between two leading publishing houses. After the church ceremony in the Nieuwe Kerk on Amsterdam's Dam Square, the couple hosted a wedding party where their guests played music, sang, danced, and drank.

Jeunesse dorée

At Manuel and Catharina's wedding party, there were many young people from the same social background. In the seventeenth century, these youngsters were known as *jeunesse dorée,* or gilded youth, because they were a generation of young people who were growing up in conditions of affluence and trying to distinguish themselves from the previous generation. With their optimism and energy, they were innovative and willing to take risks. One of the guests at Manuel and Catharina's wedding party was the 26-year-old Jacomo Pauw, the son of Reinier Adriaensz Pauw, a wealthy mayor of Amsterdam. In 1602 the latter had been one of the initial founders of the VOC, and in 1619 had been directly involved with the trial and execution of Johan van Oldenbarnevelt, the statesman accused of treason. Despite his extreme wealth, Reinier Pauw was also a pious and frugal man.

That was apparent in 1631, when the city of Amsterdam had to levy an extra tax on its wealthy citizens. All those with a personal fortune of more than a 1,000 guilders were required to pay a tax of half a percent. Pauw's private wealth was estimated at 200,000 guilders, which was probably on the conservative side, considering that he most likely played down the actual amount to avoid paying too much tax. Other members of the Pauw family tried to gain political power after they had amassed great fortunes. Jacomo's eldest brother, Adriaan Pauw, became *raadpensionaris* or Grand Pensionary of Holland. This was the highest-ranking public office in the country, and made Pauw the most powerful man in the Republic. He held the position until 1636, and was re-elected to the office a few years later.

Hendrick Hoochkamer was another guest at the wedding party who had moved up the social ladder. In 1601 his father, Jacob Pietersz Hoochkamer, had started a business importing silk from Italy, which he resold throughout Europe. In 1622, his 21-year-old son Hendrick was a silk merchant with a shop in Warmoesstraat, the most expensive shopping street in Amsterdam, where he sold silk cloth and other luxury goods. In 1631, the city taxed his father on a private fortune of 150,000 guilders. In the early seventeenth century, the economy was growing by leaps and bounds. This shaped the prevailing mindset; economically speaking, the sky was the limit. Everybody could become rich and move up the social ladder.

While climbing the social ladder was not difficult at this time, the real challenge was remaining at the top of the ladder and not falling back down. Some were unfortunate and fell faster than they had climbed. That happened to the father of Hendrick Hoochkamer. In 1638, his economic standing and social position collapsed when he was declared bankrupt. Hoochkamer was forced to step down from the city council and resign his position as captain of the city guard. To save face and avoid complete destitution, he was made porter of the municipal militia of crossbowmen.

Guilliaem van den Broeck was also invited to the wedding of Manuel and Catharina. When his father, Hans van den Bergh, went bankrupt a few years later, he was forced to sell all of his personal belongings, including his furniture and clothing and the inventory from his sugar factory, to pay his creditors. Behind closed doors, people gossiped about Van den Bergh's bankruptcy. Some claimed that he had lived an immoral life and had squandered his money on a mistress and alcohol – which was why the Amsterdam church consistory denied him the holy sacrament in 1628.

Consumer goods

At the beginning of the seventeenth century, massive fortunes could easily be made, but also quickly lost. The fear of losing everything hung over the new elite of the Dutch Golden Age, and it influenced their consumption. They tended to be frugal in their daily lives. Nevertheless, the early seventeenth century witnessed a sharp rise in material prosperity and the quantity and quality of consumer goods.

The middle classes and wealthy farmers profited from increased demand for consumer goods, and were simultaneously active participants in the emerging consumer economy. The furnishings in most homes in the late sixteenth century were usually modest, for example: simple wooden tables and plain chairs, rudimentary wooden boxes, and primitive bowls made from tin or wood. By the mid-seventeenth century, Dutch interiors looked quite different. Household inventories and wills reveal that people's homes were elaborately decorated with mirrors, paintings, books, and clocks. Homes were furnished with octagonal or round tables topped with expensive porcelain bowls, the chairs had comfortable armrests, and linen cabinets were made from oak wood and lavishly decorated. This new affluence was also reflected in everyday items, including clothing, dishes, and utensils. In less than half a century, both the quantity and quality of goods had substantially increased. In Europe, demand for such consumer goods originated in Northern Italy during the Renaissance and spread north through Germany and the Southern Netherlands, and finally to the Dutch Republic. The clearest indication of this new wealth in the Dutch Republic lay in the number of paintings that decorated the homes of the urban elite, the rising middle classes, and even those of farmers.

A fascination with children

In the early seventeenth century, the Republic was literally and figuratively a young nation. Not only was the Republic still establishing its political and geographical boundaries, but it was also a country with many young people. The political and religious twists and turns of the new nation resembled the growth spurts and mood swings of an adolescent. In the seventeenth century, the different stages of life were associated with specific character traits. Old people, for example, were known for their calmness, benign character, and tendency not to become overly upset about things. On the downside, they were known for their melancholy, their frugality, and for the fact that they usually felt the cold (hence old age was often associated with the season of winter). Youth, on the other hand, was associated with passion and love. The sanguine character of young people symbolized the warmest season of the year. The young Republic and its young people oscillated between play and learning, between freedom and obedience, and between independence and security.

In the Republic, almost all of the cohesive elements that the Roman Catholic faith had brought to society had been abolished from the country's religious and cultural life. Moreover, the Protestant Reformed Church failed to assume the old church's role as a state church and work to unify the new state. The country was religiously divided and embroiled in a long, drawn-out war for independence from Spain. Whereas most countries that declare independence from a mother country are involved in a quick war where they cut the umbilical cord, the Dutch Republic needed eighty years to free itself from Spain. In those fourscore years, there was only one period of peace, the Twelve-Year Truce, between 1609 and 1621. For the rest of that time, the Republic was caught up in a continuous war from which there seemed to be no end in sight. One of the consequences of being at war for over four generations was the fact that young people were infatuated with everything that had to do with war and the military. Both adults and young people became obsessed with news about military campaigns. The war propaganda machine produced pamphlets and history books about battles, and prints portraying heroic soldiers engaged in war.

After the Iconoclastic Fury of 1566 and the long war for independence against Spain, younger generations in the Dutch Republic developed an aversion to everything that was Spanish and Roman Catholic. During the Iconoclastic Fury, icons and saints in churches had literally been removed from their pedestals. A didactical vacuum opened up where the empty pedestals now stood. The young people of the New Republic had to find new role models in a society without one common faith and that was slowly becoming more secular. With the exception of new economic-political structures and free-market liberalism, there was little cohesion in society. Against this backdrop, a new secular and urban culture developed in which children and adolescents were raised.

One of the defining traits of the Dutch Golden Age, and the reason why the period fascinates me, is that it was the first time in Dutch history when great interest was shown in children and the education of young people. There was an outpouring of publications, including moralistic treatises, songbooks for young people, and child-rearing manuals books, which were either produced for a young audience or their parents. It was as though the country had become fascinated with the young people who would define its future. In part, this publishing boom was also due to the fact that new forms of media, such as books, had become more affordable, as well as the fact that more people were able to read in the early seventeenth century.

Moreover, it was also fueled by the widely accepted notion that youth were the future of the country. This is evident from the great number of portraits of children that were painted. Nowhere in the world in the seventeenth century were so many children portrayed with attributes such as birds and dogs, which symbolized and emphasized the importance of a good education. Children, like pets, were supposed to be well trained and educated. In the Golden Age, a good education was praiseworthy. It was an asset not only for the family, but also for the new nation.

Founding fathers of a new society

Another striking aspect of the Dutch Golden Age was the fact that the Republic was a nation in the making. The young people of the period were the founding fathers of a new state. When they grew up, they became the bedrock of a new society in the seventeenth century, one that is still recognizable today. Young people were allocated a central role in society and considered an investment in the future of the country. With the attention paid to young people, a rich youth culture emerged during the Dutch Golden Age.

These circumstances had a fundamental impact on how the youth of the early seventeenth century perceived the future. Historically, major societal changes have occurred when there is a substantial young population. In today's society young people are the motor of the economy, and the elderly, who require healthcare and depend on retirement benefits, are often considered a burden for society. In sixteenth-century Germany, the Reformation was driven by a large population of young people who were demanding social and religious changes. At this time, Europe's population had started to grow again after the drastic decline of fourteenth and fifteenth centuries and the Black Death, in which a third of Europe's population died.

In the first decades of the sixteenth century, a new generation of young leaders came to the fore. Martin Luther published his famous 95 theses at the age of 34. In the 1520s, many members of the academic staff at the University of Wittenberg were quite young, aged between twenty and thirty. The historian Matthew Aurogallus, for example, was only thirty years old when he was made a professor. John Hainpol and Philipp Melanchthon, professors and Lutheran intellectual reformers, were even younger than some of the students they taught. The intellectual innovators of the new generation were the movers and shakers of the sixteenth century, who initiated the Reformation and changed Europe and the course of history forever.

We can find other examples in history of times where young people took the lead in changing society. It was mostly young people who stormed the Bastille in 1789 and started the French Revolution. And almost two hundred years later, in 1968, it was the students of Paris who took to the streets and demanded more democracy. In the same year, young people made up the majority of demonstrators in Prague who were demanding more freedom from the Soviet Union. In the United States, it was mainly young people who held protests and supported the Civil Rights Movement. As a rule of thumb, it is young people who bring about change in society. Change, whether it is backwards-looking or progressive, is an expression of youth culture.

By nature, youngsters are more inclined, and even willing, to take risks. Some are not afraid to use violence to achieve their objectives. Young people tend not to have social and economic obligations. If things go wrong, they have little to lose in terms of social status. This makes it easier for them to stand on the barricades and fight for what they believe is right, without having to pay the consequences of losing their jobs and endangering their family's livelihood.

One of the reasons why young people are capable of changing society is that they simply have more leisure time than any other age group. In the early modern era, people in general had more recreational time than today. Unlike the regimented work schedules of today, the working day in the seventeenth century was shaped by external factors. Weather and technological conditions regularly stopped the work of laborers, who then had to wait and literally had 'free time'. Men employed at sea and in the fisheries worked on a seasonal basis and had nothing to do during the winter months. Even during working periods, ships could remain at dock for days, sometimes months, waiting for favorable winds before they could sail. In the meantime, a small army of sailors and dockworkers had little to do. Other sectors were also dependent on weather conditions. Millers, for example, were dependent on wind, and construction workers and farmers had to wait for dry weather before they could build and sow.

Unlike in modern Western society, where free time is equated with wealth and luxury, in early modern society it simply meant that many people had nothing to do for several days.

For a young person, having too much time on one's hands could be disastrous. When young people were bored, they were more likely to commit acts of violence, obsess about their appearance, drink too much alcohol, fornicate, take drugs, and play music. During every period of economic prosperity, these aspects of youth culture seem to reappear, but they often assume a different shape or form. In the Dutch Golden Age, for example, juvenile violence was rampant. Young people did not hesitate to use violence against each other or the authorities. Moreover, many young people suffered from pent-up aggression, and violence was a means of venting this. In this respect, early modern society understood this problem and turned a blind eye. Society recognized that violence in young people was temporal. Today, by contrast, politicians take violence and juvenile delinquency seriously.

In the Golden Age, violence committed by youngsters was commonplace. What is more, violence played an important role for boys who were becoming men. University students, for example, were granted a special privilege that allowed them to carry a firearm. Young men from the lower classes, who did not have that privilege, were known to be just as violent, if not more. Foreign students who came from the countryside were particularly notorious for their frequent clashes with the officers of the peace, who were responsible for maintaining law and order.

Young people in the Republic

This book will examine the great social changes that young people brought about in the Dutch Golden Age. It will unveil the contribution that young people made to seventeenth-century Dutch society, and what remains of this today. In this book, I use the term 'youth' to refer to male adolescents and young men between the ages of thirteen and thirty. In the early modern era, young unmarried men were still considered to be youths. Once they crossed the threshold of marriage, they 'graduated' and were considered adults.

A wide array of sources has been examined in order to reconstruct youth culture in the Golden Age. Primary sources such as moralistic treatises, educational books, and emblem books, where textual messages were reinforced with images, played a key prescriptive role, while the archives of the university courts reveal the wayward side of young people and their mishaps. Another source that was consulted were songbooks, which reveal the leisure activities of young people. In this study only male youths will be examined, for the simple reason that more sources reveal the behavior of boys and young men in the early modern period. In general, males were raised in the public domain and their misdoings were often recorded in public records. Sources that reveal the behavior of adolescent girls are rare, namely because they were raised by mothers or other female relatives in the private sphere of the home.

In Chapter Two, I shall look at how violence played an important role in the process of becoming a man. Parents and institutions were equally concerned about juvenile delinquency and the rampant violence that was committed by young people. Violence in the early modern period was not only a danger to others, but also their children were often the victims of violence.

Chapter Three will examine the hedonistic lifestyle of young people. Moralists accused wealthy parents of indulging their offspring with expensive clothes. The 'calculated slovenliness' of new trends in young people's clothes and fashion in the seventeenth century was considered an omen of moral and social decay.

Besides violence and hedonism, parents were concerned that their children were drinking too much alcohol. Young people in the seventeenth century were notorious for their binge drinking. In Chapter Four, we shall see how parents taught their children to drink in moderation, and how doing everything in moderation was a sign of maturity. Chapter Five, in turn, will discuss how young people dealt with their budding sexuality and learned to temper their sexual urges in a period when there was no contraception and venereal diseases such as syphilis were rampant among young people.

Much like the youth of today, the young people of the Dutch Golden Age also experimented with mind-altering stimulants. In Chapter Six, we shall see how tobacco from the New World became the new experimental drug in the early seventeenth century. The young people of the Golden Age were the first generation in history to embrace smoking and turn it into a mainstream habit and national pastime. Indeed, one of the most striking aspects of the young people of the Golden Age was how they spent their leisure time. In almost every society and era in history, young people have found ways to rebel against their parents and spend time with their friends. Chapter Seven examines how the youth of the Golden Age entertained themselves with music and song. The lyrics were often about young people and the dilemmas that they faced. As such, they were universal and equally fitting today.

This brings us back to the earlier question, of whether the generation of the early seventeenth century was revolutionary in historical terms, or whether it was just like any other generation of young people. In the Conclusion, we will return to Otto Copes and consider the consequences that the youth of the Dutch Golden Age had for the youth of today.

2.   Violence

If a distinctive sound could capture a time and place in history, then the Dutch Republic in the early seventeenth century would be represented by the clamor of breaking glass. This was the dominant noise at night. Throwing stones at windows was the most common form of vandalism by students. Regardless of whether they were locals or foreigners, young men vented their frustration by throwing stones at windows. The city council of Schiedam went so far as to forbid young people from playing *kolf,* a primitive form of golf where balls were battered around on the ground with sticks. A common sport for youngsters to play on town squares, it became a problem when the golf balls became airborne, smashing windows and damaging roof tiles on public buildings and churches.

College life

In university towns, the vandalism was of a different nature. Whereas flying golf balls accidently caused damage to property, in university towns the violence was deliberate. The academic court of the University of Leiden, which held jurisdiction over the students and protected them from civil law, offers a glimpse of what student life in the seventeenth century entailed. One of the most common crimes committed by students was throwing stones at windows. Most Dutch houses in the seventeenth century had shutters on the outside, which the inhabitants closed at night to conserve heat. One of the most common misdeeds committed by students in Leiden was to open the shutters and smash the tiny paned windows with the butts of their pistols or cobblestones from the street.

On a December night in Leiden in 1623, Lucas van Hulten and Otto Farmesom were struck by the same idea. Both young men were law students and had known each other a long time from their student days in Groningen. Six months earlier they had arrived in Leiden, where they enrolled at the university. Like many students, they went out late at night, gallivanting and throwing stones. This time, however, everything went wrong. Having thrown stones through somebody's window, the boys ran in opposite directions and 23-year-old Otto was arrested. After two days of incarceration, Otto finally confessed, claiming that he had not thrown any stones and that he was an innocent by-stander. It was his friend, Lucas, who had tossed the stones. Not long afterwards, Lucas was arrested. He eventually confessed to his crimes, having first been incarcerated in a cold prison cell and given only bread and water. Lucas had to pay 40 guilders to the tribunal and had to pay for the repair of the windows. Moreover, he had to serve another six weeks in prison. Otto, by contrast, was given a mild sentence and had only to pay a 20-guilder fine, and was put under house arrest in his landlord's house. Lucas did not give a reason for his crime in his confession. Both Lucas and Otto came from Groningen, where they had been enrolled at the university and where both had lived with their parents. Their families held important administrative and church positions in Groningen, and most likely they were kept on a short leash. Once the two boys arrived in Leiden, they escaped the leash and consequently ran wild.

The rebellious behavior of Lucas and Otto was by no means exceptional in the Golden Age. It was an important aspect of the camaraderie between young men that helped forge friendships and male bonding. The unruly behavior of students took place at night, usually after a lot of drinking. In Leiden, the academic court often made a distinction between student misdemeanors that happened under the auspices of night and those that occurred in broad daylight. The academic court was more lenient regarding the transgressions that occurred at night than those that happened during the day.

Lucas learned a valuable lesson from his incarceration. His brush with the law and brief stay in a student prison had no ramifications for his career. He finished his law studies, worked as an administrator for the magistrate of Groningen, and eventually became a member of the Council of State for the province of Groningen. If Lucas had not confessed to his crimes, however, his career would have been quite different. Students who did not admit their wrongdoings, or who even tried to flee the city, faced having their names officially removed from university registers.

This is what happened in 1624 to Jacob Velius, who was also accused of breaking windows. He was banished for three years from both the university and the province of Holland and West Friesland. Velius objected to the ruling and appealed to the Prince of Orange for help. The stadholder did not come to his rescue, however, something that was not altogether unexpected. Six years earlier in 1618, as a political and religious conflict raged between the Remonstrants and Counter-Remonstrants, Jacob's father had sided with the Arminian strongman, Johan van Oldenbarnevelt, who was a sworn enemy of the Prince of Orange. After this conflict ended, Velius' father had been ousted from the magistrate of Hoorn. The young Jacob was thus unable to count on political favors from the House of Orange. In the end, Jacob's name was removed from the University of Leiden's records, as if he had never studied there or even existed at all.

Frères d'armes

In the seventeenth century, students would sometimes band together like brothers in arms. On the night of 22 February 1626, two brothers, Jacobus and Juriaan Sevelt, together with 22-year-old Caspar von Nostitz, had their minds set on celebrating carnival. The three probably belonged to a fraternity of students from Silesia in Germany. In the early seventeenth century, Roman Catholic festivals such as Shrove Tuesday, known for their excessive consumption of food and drink, were not welcomed by the city magistrates or by staunch members of the Protestant Dutch Reformed Church. That evening, however, the boys were out to make trouble. Dressed in disguise and wearing masks, they paraded through the streets of Leiden, where they slammed open shutters, smashed windows, and ransacked houses, including the home of Isaac Doreslaer, who was a devout Protestant. Moreover, he was rector of the Latin School. At the time, Doreslaer was also enrolled as a law student at the university. The following evening, the three German boys went out again and did the same. This time, they returned to Doreslaer's house and 'scandalously' abused his servant girl. The sources are unclear as to what exactly this meant, but most likely the three boys sexually abused the innocent girl. The boys were apprehended for their crimes, and the Sevelt brothers lost their privileges as students at the university. They were banished for twelve years from the province of Holland and West Friesland. Worst of all, their names were removed from the university records as if they had never attended the university or studied there. The primary sources leave us in the dark as to what happened to Caspar von Nostitz. As he belonged to the Silesian nobility, it is most likely that behind the scenes, his parents or associates arranged for him to be exonerated. The shame would have been too great for him.

As for Isaac Doreslaer, within a year he had moved to England, where he was made a professor of history at Cambridge. Unfortunately for him, he continued to make enemies, mainly due to his outspoken political and religious views. Doreslaer was a supporter of Oliver Cromwell in England, and during the 1640s he would play an important role in a smear campaign against the English king, Charles I, who was ultimately convicted as a traitor and beheaded. The Scots were not happy with the trumped-up charges of treason against the English monarch, however. When Doreslaer visited the Republic in 1649, a Scottish royalist stabbed him in the back while he was quietly eating his dinner in a tavern.

Throwing stones through windows was not only a cheap thrill for young men. There was also a deeper underlying meaning, with social connotations that included the public disciplining of the person's whose windows had been smashed. When someone's windows were broken, they were publicly humiliated. It was a public means of expressing that someone's conduct or behavior was not appreciated. This was probably the case for Isaac Dorselaer, whose windows were demonstratively broken on the street side for all passers-by to see. The deed was a public humiliation for Dorselaer. By contrast, when the windows at the back of somebody's home were smashed, it was a different story; then it was a personal vendetta.

This distinction was evident in the numerous cases of smashed windows that were recorded in the archives of the Republic's university courts. Students preferred to break the windows of the houses of men in authority or buildings that represented power, such as university buildings and the homes of university professors or rectors. From the University of Franeker's founding in 1585 to its dissolution in 1812, most cases of windows reportedly broken by students at the university occurred between 1605 and 1650. One possible reason for this is that glass was a costly material in the early seventeenth century, and windows were expensive. In the second half of the century, the production of glass became cheaper and there were far fewer cases of vandalism involving windows.

Armed young men

During the early modern period, one of the many privileges that students were granted when they enrolled at a university was the right to carry a weapon. This was an old privilege dating from the Middle Ages, when university students were mostly from the nobility, which was the only class in Medieval society allowed to bear arms. When new universities were founded in the Dutch Republic in the late sixteenth and early seventeenth centuries, administrators followed the example of the medieval universities and granted students the right to carry a firearm or sword, or even both. In a trading nation like the Dutch Republic, such weapons were easy to come by. Metalworkers in Utrecht, for example, were known for producing the best guns in Europe.

In the course of the seventeenth century, with growing affluence in Dutch society and demand for more highly educated people, more young men from the upper and middle classes started to attend university. During this period, several universities were founded. After the outbreak of the Dutch Revolt, Willem of Orange, the stadholder of the country, granted the city of Leiden the right to found a university in 1575. In a period of less than 75 years, universities were also established in the towns of Franeker (1585), Groningen (1614), Utrecht (1636), and Harderwijk (1648).

The quality of education at the newly established academic institutions in the Republic was comparable to, if not better than, that of the older universities founded in the Middle Ages. The new universities followed the same structure and created senates and faculties, and even copied medieval rituals such as wearing special gowns and caps and granting exclusive privileges to students, including the ancient privilege that allowed them to carry a weapon. Thus the seventeenth century saw an alarming number of armed young men wandering the streets of university towns.

Towns in the Dutch Republic that had a university started to witness a large influx of young men. The combination of young men and weapons became a growing source of violence and social upheaval for urban residents. It became a burden for the municipal guards, who were responsible for maintaining law and order. The city guard frequently had confrontations at night with disorderly students who had had too much to drink and become unruly. In the early seventeenth century there was no street lighting in Dutch cities, which made the city guard's task especially difficult. Students usually went out late at night or in the early morning hours when it was still dark, often with the intention of stirring up trouble. The rapier was the most popular weapon among students in the early seventeenth century. It was a narrow, sharp sword, measuring little more than a meter long and 2.5 centimeters wide, and had a protective handle with which to hold it. With a quick stab to the heart or one of the other vital organs, the rapier was more lethal than a standard sword, which was blunt.

For the city councils of university towns, the students' recklessness in drawing their rapiers became a major headache. During the seventeenth century and even well into the eighteenth century, the ownership of weapons and violence committed by students resulted in an ongoing battle between the municipal governments and the university administrators. Several times, universities tried to restrict the right of students to bear arms. In 1637, the University of Groningen banned students who had a scholarship from carrying guns, sticks, or other weapons. However, these measures were never considered far-reaching enough by the city councils, which had to deal with city dwellers complaining about the continual noise and ensuing disruption of the peace. In the end, there was little that municipal councils could do when universities threatened to close and move to another town.

In Leiden, for example, the members of the town council were asked to be more lenient towards the students; after all, students were an important source of income, not only for the university, but also for the local economy. Grocers, landlords, booksellers, and taverns all profited considerably from the presence of the students. However, the overwhelming presence of students in Leiden came at a price. The academic court was often tolerant of student crime, which required the good citizens of Leiden to turn the other cheek. In the course of the seventeenth century, they were often the victims of student violence and the disturbance of the peace.

It is noteworthy that most mischievous acts recorded in the academic courts were committed by foreign students. In many cases, these students hailed from the upper social classes, which gave them a feeling of contempt for the local population. This was especially the case for foreign students, who were usually of aristocratic blood. In the Republic in the early seventeenth century, there were hardly any nobles left. In Leiden, the conflict between the classes was often between the lower classes who were employed in the textile industry and related industries, and aristocratic students. Leiden's working-class women were often the ones to suffer most from their arrogance and disdain.

Student armed with a rapier, in: *Tegenspoed is God een toeverlaat*, Gaspar Bouttats, F. Franciscus Lijftocht and Arnold van den Eijnden (1679) (Rijksmuseum, Amsterdam).

Leiden's women felt intimidated by the overwhelming presence of young male students in their city. They were often surrounded in the street by groups of young men, who if they had the chance would put their hands up their skirts or grope them. Sometimes their intimidating behavior did not stop at wandering hands. If a young woman was caught on the street late at night, she risked running into groups of drunken students, who might force her under threat of a knife to have sex with them. This was what happened in 1640, when a pregnant woman, walking alone late at night, ran into three students. The young men threatened her and forced her to have sex with them. While the number of rape cases reported by the academic court in the early seventeenth century was relatively small, there were plenty of incidents where students intimidated the local women of Leiden by dragging their swords over the cobblestones, making a frightening, screeching sound.

Besides harassing Leiden's working-class women, the students also antagonized the municipal guard. The guardsmen were the only men in the city, besides students, who were allowed to carry a weapon. In this respect, the municipal guard – as armed men – were the students' equals. In 1627, Anselm van der Deurverden van der Voort, a twenty-year-old student from Utrecht, opened fire and hit a municipal guardsman in the head. Anselm, who had arrived two months earlier in Leiden and had enrolled at the university as a law student, had little experience in handling a weapon. The young man was probably trigger-happy and overly anxious when he aimed at the guard's head. The academic court fined him 100 guilders and he lost his student privileges.

In Groningen, there were even cases of students aspiring to become guardsmen. In September 1629, twenty-year-old Cornelis Damman, a philosophy student, was infatuated with the guardsmen, and after only five months at the university wanted to join the civic guard. The academic senate of the University of Groningen was opposed to this, however, and prohibited students from becoming members, arguing that the university had a responsibility (to the students' parents) and had to guarantee their physical safety. Nevertheless, many students were mesmerized by the militia and wanted to join. This was probably for the simple reason that guardsmen used their weapons on a regular basis. The ordinance that forbade students from joining the municipal guard had to be renewed repeatedly in 1639, 1666 and 1667.

In Leiden during the seventeenth century, the magistrate had to reinforce the municipal guard several times in order to maintain law and order among the students. There were too many incidents such as that involving Caspar von Waldo, a 21-year-old son of a Saxon nobleman who studied in Leiden and caused a great deal of trouble. In 1638, Von Waldo was involved in a skirmish with a member of the guard after one of his servants had been in a fight with a Dutch student. What began as a simple ruckus between two men ended in tragedy after the municipal guardsman, Franco van der Burg, was killed. The academic court sentenced a 27-year-old student, Henricus van Aleveld from Holstein, and 24-year-old John Graro from

Brandenburg for the murder. Von Waldo and his household of servants (it was common for students from the nobility to travel and study at a university with their entire entourage) were accused only of being accomplices. This was not the first time that Von Waldo had stood before the academic court. Three months earlier, he had had to explain why he and his servants had challenged the municipal guard. In that incident, nobody had been injured.

Student violence

Violence of this level was nothing new for young men who wanted to show their bravado. There is little doubt that Von Waldo was quick-tempered and not inclined to eschew a good fight. With his violence, he wanted to show the other students that he was brave and not afraid of taking risks. Today we would call Von Waldo a real 'alpha male'. By putting his own life in danger, he earned respect from his fellow students. At the first sign of a student commotion in public, the municipal guard was usually quick to restore peace and order. They were eager to suppress any kind of rowdiness, especially at night, when students were most likely to disturb the peace. Everardus Bronckhorst, professor of law at the University of Leiden, remarked that Leiden's municipal guard had no reservations about using violence against students. In 1607, after the professor had spent an evening drinking with students, he saw the guard's ruthlessness with his own eyes. Because the group had made too much noise, the civil guard opened fire on the young men. Twenty-one shots were fired at one student alone. However, these incidents were more the exception than the rule. In Leiden, most of the fighting and violence was between students.

In December 1640 a Danish student named Dionysius Christianus challenged another student, Johannes Schönborner, to a duel. Schönborner, who was a Silesian, was encouraged by his friend and compatriot Jan Frederick Nimptisch to accept the challenge. The two agreed to meet in an open area outside the city gate (Haarlemmerpoort). The Dane was assisted by his friend, Caspar Hendriks Bonsdorft. The records did not cite the reason for the challenge, but it is likely that the Dane's honor had been insulted. In the early seventeenth century, the honor of one's family, one's country, or even a friend, was justification enough for a challenge or to accept a challenge. The duel proved fatal for the 26-year-old Dane. He died on the spot from a jab from his opponent's sword. According to the rules of dueling, Schönborner should have lunged at Christianus and hit him with the flat side of his sword. However, the Silesian must have struck him with the tip of his sword and punctured his side. Immediately after the duel, Schönborner knew the fate that awaited him. After all, like most men who had a sword, he was familiar with the rules of fencing. The academic court accused him of murder and sentenced him to death.

Those who received the death sentence had usually committed crimes such as repeated theft, murder, arson, and counterfeiting. Death sentences could also be carried out in different ways. A criminal from the lower classes was usually hung or strangled to death. The more severe the crime that was committed, the crueler the punishment would be. The limbs of a convict would be tied to a rack, which was designed to dislocate every joint in the person's body. The rack consisted of a wooden frame with two ropes on the bottom and other ropes tied to a handle at the top. Once the convict was tied in, the torturer would turn the handle until all the limbs were dislocated. They would continue to turn until the limbs had been completely pulled off the person's body. Only at the last moment did the torturer give the convict a final blow to the heart with a hammer. Because Schönborner was a member of the nobility, however, he would have been beheaded with a sword. Before the authorities could arrest him and sentence him to death, Schönborner fled Leiden and most likely returned to Silesia.

Nations

Schönborner and his friend Jan Frederick Nimptisch belonged to the same 'nation' or fraternity of students from Silesia. The Danish students, Christianus and Bonsdorft, were also members of the same association of students from their country. In the early modern period, these fraternities and associations were called 'nations' because they were based on geographic origin or country. In the administrative councils of the Italian universities in Bologna and Padua, which had been founded in the Middle Ages, the nations had considerable authority. They played an important role in student life and had significant influence on university policy, sometimes to the dismay of the university's senate.

In the newly established 'enlightened' universities of the Republic, the senate was not willing to yield authority to the nations, with their uncontrollable behavior and tendency towards violence. University administrators in the Dutch Republic were aware of the nations' capabilities and preferred to keep the students under strict control. In 1659, the States of Holland decided to ban nations from universities, but this did not stop students from congregating and uniting in fraternities. From the time of the official ban, the nations went underground and operated clandestinely. This means that little is known about them. Much of the information we have is from one book, which includes the names of members of the nation from the provinces of Gelderland-Overijssel in the Dutch Republic. This nation had 670 members between 1617 and 1660.

There is likewise a book with a list of students from the same nation who studied at the University of Franeker. The book also contains regulations for the holding of meetings, which usually began with a song of praise. In quasi-military fashion, early modern universities tried to shape the characters of young men. This is evident from the secretive practices of the nations, which made members swear an oath to the nation and also to the university. Nations were especially grateful to their universities for granting students the privilege of carrying a weapon. The nations even stipulated rules of etiquette on how their members should use their weapons. According to the rulebook, members of the nation were not allowed to challenge each other. Offenders were fined. If a member was caught verbally challenging someone to a duel, he was fined four guilders. If a member accepted a challenge, he was fined two guilders. And if a member was wounded, the fines were doubled. In other words, violence and challenges were strictly forbidden by the nations, but if they did take place, then they did so in secret and violence was sanctioned.

Karel Vijgh

There could be no doubt about it: everything that happened within the confines of the nations was supposed to remain a secret. Members were sworn to secrecy about the nations' initiation rites and other suspect activities. This became apparent to the outside world in 1652, when Karel Vijgh, a student in Groningen, refused to become a member of the nation from Gelderland-Overijssel. At that time, Karel was living at the home of Samuel Maresius, who was also the rector of the university senate. Karel told Maresius about the coercive practices of the nation. It is not exactly known what Karel disclosed to Maresius, but the rector and senate reprimanded the nations. By now, Karel had betrayed not only the Gelderland-Overijssel nation, but also all the nations in Groningen.

Shortly afterwards, a large group of students gathered from various nations in Groningen, armed with swords and pistols, and marched in the direction of Maresius' home. The nations had united and were about to vent their frustration on the university senate. They intended to defend the autonomy of the nations and the privileges of students. They felt that the rituals of the nation were an internal matter that was none of the university's business. During their march towards Maresius' home (where Karel lived), the nations became involved in a skirmish with the municipal guard, who were unable to stop the students. Once they arrived at the house of the rector, the students unloaded their firearms into the windows of Maresius' home. By the time the smoke had cleared, there was not a pane of glass left unbroken in Maresius' house or that of his neighbors.

On the other hand, the nations fulfilled an important role for foreign students. Members helped each other in times of need, and when a student was sick or had an accident, it was usually his fellow countrymen from the nation who cared for him. In the nations, these mutual relations often turned into lifelong friendships, which included defending each other's honor. It was precisely this latter element of the nations that posed a danger to the university and municipal authorities. They were not just groups of students; they were bands of blood. Once the honor of a member had been tarnished, the entire nation of students was affected and came to the defense of that one member. After nations were officially banned, the universities lost any influence they might have had over them and their activities were pushed underground.

There were only a few incidents that revealed to the university senate what happened behind the closed doors of the nations. One of these was an episode that occurred beyond the White Gate of Leiden in June 1624, after Johannes Vossius and Johannes Luce Bevervoorde attacked a German student named Cuno von Bodenhausen with a torrent of stones. The attackers were members of the Dutch nation, who used their guns to intimidate students from the German nation. The two also egged on spectators against the Germans. Two days later, Bodenhausen took his revenge on Johannes Vossius. Early in the morning, the 22-year-old German assaulted Vossius with a stick and stones. The academic court was aware of public displays of violence among the students, but most of the aggression took place within the world of the nations and never saw the light of day.

Each nation had its own rituals with which it initiated new members. In Leiden, freshmen students were known as *groentjes* or greens, and were bullied and teased. On the street they were booed, and in the classrooms the older students harassed them. Sometimes an older student would come to their defense and protect them. But most of the time, they demanded some kind of financial compensation in return.

These mafia-like practices, whereby some freshmen lost all their scholarship money, were child's play in comparison to the initiation rituals endured by German students in the Middle Ages. In medieval Germany, a freshman was called a *beanus*, from the French phrase *bec jaune,* meaning 'yellow beak'. It is not clear where the name originates from, but it is probably a reference to the color of the beaks of parakeets that are yellow when they are first born. As they mature, their yellow beak slowly turns blue. During the initiation ceremony, the *beani* were treated like cattle by the older students. Before the ritual started, a hood with protruding horns was placed over a freshman's head, and he had to wear teeth from a wild boar in his mouth. Throughout the ceremony the *beani* were continuously humiliated by the older students, who lectured them about how unworthy they were to become members. In the course of the ritual, parts of the initiation outfit were removed with extremely large tools in order to magnify the sense of fear.

In the Middle Ages and early modern times, humiliation fulfilled a symbolic purpose, marking the transition from boyhood to manhood. Like a phoenix, an adult man was resurrected from the ashes of childhood. The initiation symbolized the transition from boy to man, or rather from savage to civilized human being. The ceremony and its symbolism were deeply rooted in the Christian faith, with its notion of resurrection from the dead.

The same ritual was described in Crispijn de Passes' book, *Academia sive specvlvm scolasticae Vitae* [The University, or Mirror of Student Life], which was published in 1612. The book prepared pupils at the Latin school for their life as university students. One of the emblems in De Passe's book shows students wearing a cap with horns, waving axes and other frightening implements. A young man is strapped to a table, anxiously looking around while older students swing their axes. When the book was published,

Initiation of freshman students in the Dutch Golden Age, portrayed in: *Academia sive specvlvm vitae scolasticae* (1612), printed in Ilja Veldman's *Profit and Pleasure*. Print Books by Crispijn de Passe (Rotterdam: Sound and Vision Publishers, 2001).

De Passe was living in Leiden. The initiation ceremonies that he portrayed were probably based on the rituals that he had witnessed or heard about in stories. Below the illustration is the text: 'To help the freshman with his uncivilized behavior, he has to make sacrifices to the gods to become sophisticated'. The freshman has to be tortured with whips and axes. De Passe noted that the act might seem barbarous, but that it nevertheless symbolized the transition from childhood to adulthood. We do not know, however, whether the prospective young students understood the greater purpose of the rite when they experienced it.

Loco parentis

In the early modern period, the unruly behavior of university students must have been a true horror for parents. To keep an eye on their sons, parents often hired a *loco parentis* or governor. In Leiden, parents who had sons attending the university had three options from which to choose. The first was to have their son live at the home of a professor, who usually kept a sharp eye on their young son. The second was to have their son stay with relatives who lived in Leiden. It was not uncommon for young men to reside at the homes of their uncles, cousins, brothers, or other family members for the entire duration of their university schooling. The third possibility was more drastic and entailed the entire family moving to Leiden, whereupon the young student would remain under the direct supervision of his parents. In Leiden, there was no other student in the seventeenth century who caused more fanfare than the 18-year-old prince Radziwill Janis from Poland. When he became a student at the University of Leiden in 1631, he arrived with an entourage of fifteen members of his court, including his court master, chaplain, and several servants. For the inhabitants of Leiden and his fellow students, it must have been a real spectacle to witness Radziwill and his court move through the narrow streets of Leiden.

Group behavior

In the early seventeenth century, committing acts of violence was an integral part of the socialization process for young men. The group played an important role in the development of boys into men, a process in which tomfoolery played an intricate part with a pedagogical component. In public, boys had to display their boldness. They were required to show their bravery and valor, and most importantly, take risks. Today it is known that males have the highest level of testosterone between early puberty and around the age of 25. This accounts for the level of aggression often found in young men. In the early modern period, many young men in the countryside had a certain degree of autonomy, and their tendency towards tomfoolery was often channeled in the right direction. The rural community tended to tolerate their rowdiness and misbehavior as an outlet for their pent-up sexual energy. After all, adolescent boys and young men were expected to refrain from giving in to their sexual urges until their wedding day, which was often not until their late twenties. In other words, committing acts of juvenile mischief and insubordination was their way of letting off steam. Young men in the country misbehaved against conventional authority in many ways, from dressing up and masquerading on Roman Catholic holidays to parading and dancing in the streets, begging for money and candy, and making their presence known with loud noises and other cacophony. Sometimes their mischief had a playful element and included stealing chickens in the middle of the night, soiling clean laundry hanging from a washing line, and even defecating in people's vegetable gardens. Obviously, the targets of these incidents were not happy, but the behavior was condoned for the simple reason that the culprits were youngsters and their antics reflected their time of life.

Immigrant families that moved from the countryside to the cities of the Dutch Republic did not find it easy to adapt. Their adolescent children had the most difficult time adjusting to the new norms of city life. City magistrates, in particular, did not appreciate groups of young people with their own norms and conventions, operating autonomously within the city. After all, the municipal government's main task was to maintain law and order. An independent group with its own norms and values posed a threat to municipal authority. Although there are no precise statistics relating to non-native youngsters, it can be presumed that the majority were foreign-born or from the countryside, where young people were socialized in collective groups. For example, there was an old rural tradition that newly-weds were obliged to give money to the local youth group to buy drinks.

In the town of Almelo in the eastern part of the Republic, young men wanted to uphold this tradition, but the city council refused to tolerate it. In November 1630, after Steven Lucas and his bride were married, the newly-weds were ambushed by four young men, who poured beer over them. They pulled off Lucas' coat and tossed it in the mud. Afterwards, the couple reported the incident to the sheriff, and the young men were forced to pay a fine.

The old rural traditions were deeply rooted in Almelo. On the night of carnival in 1636, a group of young people gathered outside the home of the newly ordained minister, Molanus, and his wife. The youngsters demanded a gift of money or a chicken to celebrate carnival. Molanus refused. One of the boys threatened to kill some of the minister's chickens, and another called Molanus a 'stingy dog'. Eventually, the crowd left without any fracas. Molanus did not let it go, however, and complained to the city council about the boys, because he believed that papal rituals belonged to the past.

Channeling violence

By passing numerous municipal ordinances, towns and cities throughout the Republic tried to discourage young people's violence and tomfoolery. The senates of universities were also active in trying to restrain the misbehavior of students, especially because they were responsible for the physical wellbeing of their students. After the death of Dionysius Christianus in 1641, the University of Leiden banned dueling altogether. When students were caught, they were fined 100 guilders and lost their university privileges. Even in death, violators were to be shamed; if a student died during a duel, he could only be buried without a religious service and at night. No family or friends were allowed to attend, and those who did faced a fine of 60 guilders. A student who had died during a duel could not be glorified. The authorities wanted to prevent the culprit from becoming a martyr or hero in any way whatsoever.

The academic court was relentless in its determination to ban violence among students. In the same month that Christianus was killed in a duel, Leiden's academic court discovered that a German student from nobility, Baron Bernard von Khevenhüller, had challenged another student to a duel. For the verbal challenge alone (no physical duel had yet taken place), the young baron had to pay a fine of 150 guilders, but was not banished from the city. Between 1620 and 1630, German students in particular were involved in challenges to duel. This was mainly due to the fact that honor played a more important role in German culture. If one of the German students was insulted or offended, they were more likely to resort to physical violence to restore their honor. Students from other countries were more apt to seek compensation for their honor through other means, such as the legal system or financial indemnity.

In Leiden, a wine merchant named Van Cortenbosch insulted the Danish student Dirck Quitzau by calling him a *mof* (kraut) and a dick. Quitzau, a descendant of the Danish nobility, felt that his honor had been insulted and dragged Van Cortenbosch to the academic court, demanding restitution for the shame brought to his good name. Quitzau claimed that he had suffered from the wine merchant's accusations. The academic court agreed with the Dane and ordered Van Cortebosch to pay him a 400 guilder fine.

In the early modern period, attitudes toward the use of force changed. In the largely urbanized Dutch Republic, where trade and good relations had become valuable assets, there was an increasing tendency to refrain from resorting to violence and a move towards judicial compensation, where the shame that had been incurred was reimbursed with money. This was starting to become noticeable in many cities throughout the Dutch Republic in the early seventeenth century. In university towns such as Leiden, however, with their many foreign students, often from the nobility, the transition was less noticeable. Moreover, students had more leisure time on their hands than adults, and would commit acts of violence out of sheer boredom. In the early seventeenth century, the university recognized this problem. Students did not have enough educational distractions while they were not studying; they needed recreation that would release their pent-up energy.

Sports

Through sports, students and young men could vent their frustrations in a civilized manner and show their courage and manliness at the same time. This was the reason why Girard Thibault opened a fencing school in Leiden in 1622. Thibault had been a fencing master in Spain, the home of fencing. From there, the sport had been exported to all the corners of the Spanish Empire, including the Northern Netherlands before the Revolt. Fencing was a good sport for young men. It taught them discipline and courage, and they also learned good carriage and posture. In the late sixteenth and early seventeenth centuries, the sport had become popular among the elite and university students, and was considered preferable to the Italian *vendetta*, which involved fighting with knives in a manner usually more reminiscent of animals than men. After Thibault returned from Spain, he started a fencing school in Amsterdam at the Nes, a side street off Dam Square where the famous Dutch poet Bredero also learned to fence. Thibault expected to make a greater profit from teaching university students in Leiden, however, and considering that Amsterdam did not yet have a university, at the age of 40 he left for Leiden and enrolled at the university. Thibault lived in the boarding house of Richard Jean de Nerée, where many other students lived.

Thibault was an expert swordsman. In Spain he had developed new techniques and methods, whereby fencers had to maneuver within the parameters of an imaginary circle, with areas of middle lines, cords, and home lines that mathematically demarcated the boundaries of one's opponent. The circle later became known as the 'mystical circle of Thibault'. The method was new and innovative, and it was not long before it had become popular among wealthy young men. Along with dancing, fencing became an important part of the education of young men, especially for the elite, who could afford to take lessons. After all, both physical activities were good for the posture and helped create a balanced body.

Fencing according to the mystical circle of Girard Thibault, in: *Académie de l'espée, ou se demonstrent par reiglés mathématiques sur le fondement d'un cercle mystérieux la theorie et pratique des vraix et iusqu'à présent incognus secrets du maniement des armes a pied et a cheval* (c. 1630) (Courtesy of the Special Collections, University of Amsterdam).

Having an elegant carriage and good posture were considered signs of a well-educated and honorable gentleman. Parents with children who stooped and had poor posture were willing to pay what was necessary to correct their children's physical disposition. In this respect, fencing was an ideal sport for young people to improve and correct their posture and an excellent means to vent their energy. In the early seventeenth century, there was explosive growth in fencing schools in most towns and cities in the Dutch Republic.

Besides the popularity of fencing in the Dutch Republic, playing tennis also became a trend among men. In Leiden, young men did not have to wait for good weather to show off their physical strength; indoor tennis halls already existed in 1600. In 1616, the University of Groningen issued a permit to Cors Louriszoon to operate a tennis court for students. The university, which had been founded two years earlier, was concerned about the *eerlijck* or honest recreation facilities it had to offer its students. The same occurred at the University of Franeker. In 1628, Johannes Coumans, an administrator at the university, requested permission to start a tennis court for the students. According to Coumans, the tennis court would attract more domestic and foreign students to the university, and moreover he argued that it was a noble sport that was played by kings, princes, dukes, counts, and their children. Coumans stressed that the university urgently needed facilities for its young people. There was an urgent demand for a place where they could do *eerlijcke lichamelijke exercitia,* or 'respectable physical exercise', instead of wasting their leisure time drinking and engaging in other tomfoolery.

In his *Academia sive specvlvm vitae scolasticae,* Crispijn de Passe, who we mentioned earlier, also encouraged students to play tennis. It was the ideal sport, good for both body and mind. After hours of studying, it was an excellent means of refreshing the mind. Besides tennis, other sports became popular in the early seventeenth century. One of them was horseback riding, which was initially a sport of the nobility and elite, but slowly became common among university students.

In the wake of the Dutch Revolt in the late sixteenth century, unlike most countries in Europe, the Republic did not have a court culture. Horseback riding was an essential part of the upbringing of young noblemen, which is why this sport did not play an important role in the education of the sons of merchants and the urban elite in the sixteenth century. This attitude changed quickly in 1621, however, after the exiled King Frederick of Bohemia (nicknamed the Winter King, because he reigned for only one winter) and his wife Elizabeth settled and made their court at The Hague. The couple introduced their passion for riding and dressage to the court of the Dutch stadholders and other elite families of The Hague. One of first games they learned was the tilt at the ring, which required horsemen to develop special riding skills. In 1624 and 1626 there were ring tournaments that lasted several days. These games required a rider to jab his lance through a small ring that hung from a hook. Not long afterwards, these events were hosted at The Hague's prestigious Hofvijver and Lange Voorhout squares, where Queen Elizabeth congratulated the winners.

In the course of the early seventeenth century, sports such as fencing and tennis gradually became a major physical outlet for young men. Sports became an important means for young men to display their skills in public. Through sports, they were able to demonstrate that they were willing to take risks. The rowdy and hooligan-like behavior exhibited by young men in the countryside slowly began to make way for more civilized sports. The new institutions of the Dutch Republic, such as the universities and municipal councils, played a key role in this development. These institutions did so mainly in their own interests, not those of young men. Through sports, municipal councils had more control over young people. This was not enough, however; numerous factors influenced the behavior of young people. The taming of the youth of the Dutch Golden Age would require more than just fencing schools and tennis courts.

3. The Prodigal Son

In the seventeenth century, one of the most common metaphors for the immoral behavior of young men was the biblical story of the Prodigal Son. Early modern painters, engravers, and playwrights often used the topic in their works. They admonished the young men of the country for their debauchery, but also the children of foreigners, especially those from Flanders, who were known for their supposedly wayward and excessive lifestyles. The theme of the Prodigal Son was the epitome of everything that could go wrong when raising children. It symbolized the foolish behavior of young men who would simply not grow up. The story, based on the Gospel of Luke in the New Testament, is about the younger of two sons who asks his father for his inheritance before his father dies. After receiving the money, the young man travels to a distant country where he squanders his inheritance on expensive clothing, wine, women, and other vices. He is left penniless and without a home, and is forced to live with pigs. Eventually, the young man comes to his senses and returns to the family home, where his father welcomes him with open arms.

The story is one of forgiveness and redemption. In the early modern era, painters such as Rembrandt used the story to symbolize the topsy-turvy transition from childhood to adulthood. The parental and moral anxiety represented by the Prodigal Son reflected many facets of youth culture and masculinity in the early modern period. Johan van Beverwijck, a well-known physician and author of medical and moralistic books, alluded to this parental fear. Referring to the Prodigal Son, he hinted at the concerns of parents and moralists in the early modern period, and their worries about how young people spent their leisure time.

The history of youth culture in the early modern period runs parallel to the history of recreation. Most parents were concerned about what their adolescent offspring were doing when they were not at school, at work, or engaged in normal activities such as eating, drinking, and sleeping. According to moralists in the seventeenth century, the real danger for young people occurred when they were not engaged in everyday activities. The Prodigal Son was an example of everything that could seduce young men in the Golden Age. Moralists were especially concerned about young people, because they were known to be vain. They were mainly interested in expensive clothes and obsessed about their appearance.

The book *De Secreeten* [The Secrets] describes how far young people were willing to go to change the way they looked. This work, which was originally published in Italian, was translated into Dutch for the first time in the early seventeenth century. It contained a range of beauty tips on how men and women could remove hair from their armpits, bleach their teeth, and even dye their hair blond and green (!). Throughout the book, hair is a recurring theme. In the early seventeenth century, it became more fashionable for men to have long hair. Rembrandt painted a self-portrait of himself in 1629 with mid-length hair. The new fashion of long hair for men formed a stark contrast to the hairstyles of the older generation, who kept their hair short. Staunch Calvinists, in particular, ridiculed men with long hair; they considered it unmanly and believed that it defied the codes of masculinity.

The Mennonites, who shunned any display of color and luxury and only wore black, denounced the new fashion as a sinful. According to the story 'Mennonite Vryagie', or Mennonite Love Affair, which was included in Jan Jansz Starter's popular songbook *Friesche Lusthof* [Frisian Paradise] (1621), long hair is problematic for young men. The girl in the story, who comes from a Mennonite community, turns down the advances of a young man with long hair. As the story progresses, the young man becomes completely frustrated and asks himself: 'What have I done wrong? I told her that I was madly in love with her, but nothing affects her. He bemoans that she lives according to the Bible and' has Moses in her head... and; everything is wrong [with him]. The girl can only complain: she grumbles that his hair is too long, his collar and sleeves are too wide, the starch in his clothes is too blue, his pants are too baggy, his jerkin is too big, and even protests at his little bows for shoelaces. Slowly, the young man finds out that the Mennonite girl will only show an interest in him if he wears a black coat and white collar, and cuts his hair.

Starter's *Friesche Lusthof* was widely read, and mostly purchased by the children of wealthy parents who lived in the cities of the Republic. They were the 'fashionistas' of their time, following their generation's latest trends. This is probably why they enjoyed making fun of the old-fashioned clothes of the Mennonites depicted in Starter's story. The Mennonites were known for looking down on everything that was colorful, frivolous, excessive, and worldly. The Mennonites themselves were austere and wore black clothes without any decoration or pattern. Starter, who was 27 years old when he published his songbook, also dressed in the latest fashions. On the title page of his songbook, the picture of the author shows a trendy young man with a mustache, a goatee, and medium-length hair.

In the early seventeenth century, young men had long hair down to their shoulders. In the course of the 1630s and 1640s, this new fashion was not only followed by the trendy youngsters known as the *jeunesse dorée*, but also became more commonplace among the more traditional and conservative young men who worked as schoolteachers, professors, and even ministers. When the latter group of young men started growing their hair, the older generation of ministers became alarmed, fearing that these respectable young ministers were not setting the right example for the impressionable youngsters in their congregations. Godefridus Udemans (1582-1649), one of the most outspoken Dutch Reformed pastors of the early seventeenth century, believed that young ministers with long hair were offensive (as was long hair on men in general). In a 406-page discourse entitled *Absalom-Hayr* [Absalom's Hair] (1643), Udemans explained in detail why everything was wrong with men with long hair. The title alluded to the biblical story of Absalom, the third son of David. Absalom was a good-looking young man with long hair. As an adult, he led a rebellion against his father at the Battle of Ephraim Wood, and his long hair was caught on oak tree. He was then captured by his father's soldiers and killed.

The 'Hair War'

When his book was published in 1643, Udemans was already a well-known author of many moralistic treatises and essays. Given the number of young men with long hair, Udemans knew *Absalom-Hayr* would be a controversial work. For this reason, he used the pseudonym Irenaeus Poimenander. The publication touched a nerve with theologians, and sparked a wave of pamphlets about long hair that went down in history as the 'Hair War'. This was primarily a moralistic conflict, conducted by theologians from Leiden and Utrecht. Udemans' arguments were based on the Old Testament, in which short hair sometimes signified sorrow and grief, and long hair did not necessarily imply triumph and joy. He compared men with long hair in the Dutch Republic to the pagan American Indians. The comparison with barbarians should have been reason enough for young men to keep their hair short. But that was not all; heathens were 'uncouth, arrogant, and promiscuous'. Moreover, long-haired men risked disturbing the economic and social order. According to Udemans, until then, the men who had traditionally worn their hair long were the French nobility, kings, and princes. Udemans argued that it was another matter altogether for commoners to imitate their behavior. If young people from the lower classes tried to mimic the wealthy, there would no longer be a visible difference between the ranks in society. It would be entirely inappropriate for young people to copy the nobility, because today's youngsters were already pretentious enough. Udemans himself, however, had nothing to worry about; he was slightly balding and kept his hair short.

Most of Udemans' claims and allegations came too late. By the 1640s, most young men, and often older ones, had long hair. Youths, students, university scholars, the urban elite, and even members of the clergy, especially the younger ones, were all letting their hair grow long. Maybe Udemans wanted to fire his arsenal of arguments for short hair because he knew he was fighting an uphill battle. Udemans cited every conceivable motive, from vanity to conspicuous consumption. But the argument that struck a nerve was that young men with long hair were endangering their masculinity. Simply put, Udemans thought men with long hair had become *she-men*; *wijven*, or wenches. With his use of the derogatory term *wijven*, Udemans was hinting at the mundane and flamboyant fashion of the French court and the Roman Catholic king; Dutch Reformed Protestants such as Udemans considered the latter the epitome of corruption and immorality. Men who had long hair not only resembled women, they also started to behave like them. In Udeman's opinion, men with long hair were vain, squandering endless hours in front of the mirror washing, brushing, and perfuming their hair. They were just like women. Vainly caring for one's hair was a woman's activity, not a man's. But now, if they wished to look their best, men with long locks were more or less forced to engage in these grooming rituals. As a middle-aged man, Udemans recognized that young men had the good fortune to grow their hair long, but considered this a waste of time that would be better spent on more important matters.

The timing of his publication could not have been better. In August 1641, men with long hair had been discussed at the annual synod of North Holland. *Absalom-Hayr* was published two years later, just before the annual synod of the Dutch Reformed churches. It had not been Udemans' intention to offend young men with long hair, but it was a slap in the face for young chaplains who followed the latest fashion and had long locks of hair. According to Udemans, young pastors were supposed to be role models for youngsters in the congregation. They were not supposed to follow the latest trends. The delegates from

Groningen, in particular, considered young pastors who had long hair and dressed in the latest fashions to be a thorn in the side of the church. The complaint was also directed at their wives. The delegates from Zutphen were furious that schoolmasters were letting their hair grow long, and the members of the delegation from Woerden bemoaned the students who were following suit.

For the synod, the theology students were the straw that broke the camel's back; it could not get any worse. After all, according to the old ministers, they were role models for the younger members of the congregation. As role models, ministers were supposed to radiate respect and wisdom with their short haircuts. It was one of the physical characteristics of the profession.

In 1645, the Hair War reached its climax. During the annual synod, the supporters and opponents of long hair stood across from each other as if they were armed and ready to engage in battle. Naturally, Udemans was leader of the faction against long hair, but his opponent Claudius Salmasius (1588-1653) was equally passionate about the cause. Salmasius, who succeeded the French classicist Joseph Scaliger at the University of Leiden and was a professor of classical languages, turned every one of Udemans arguments on its head. In Leiden, Salmasius was known for not backing down and for engaging in lively discussion with his colleagues. As a rebuttal to Udemans' discourse, he wrote a 484-page treatise (even longer than Udemans') on why long hair was a non-issue. The work, entitled *Brief van Claudius Salmasius aen Andr. Colvium, belangende naamwoord het Langh haren der Mannen nl de lokken der Vrouwen* [Letter from Claudius Salmasius to Andr. Colvium, about long hair on men and locks on women], was originally published in Latin. One year later, it was translated into Dutch, so that it could be read by those who had not been to Latin school or university. Like a true scientist, Salmasius based his arguments on examples from history, pointing out times in the history of mankind when there had been different hairstyles. There were times when men had had short hair, or long hair, and even times when they had shaved their heads. According to Salmasius, long hair on men did not affect their masculinity in any way. It is likely that Salmasius felt personally attacked in the Hair War. The 57-year-old had a thick mane of bushy hair, which most of men of his age probably envied.

The debate about men with long hair was intense, but short. Salmasius had time (and hair) on his side. After 1645, long hair disappeared as an item of discussion at the synod. Long hair on men had become a fact, and the fashion continued to make its way through the social classes. More and more men, including theology students and young pastors, had long hair that dangled below their shoulders.

The fashion had originated at the French court. Already in the early seventeenth century, the French king and his courtiers were the prime trendsetters in Europe. The princes, elites, graduates, and students who traveled through Europe on the grand tour wanted to be seen donning the latest fashions from Paris after they returned home. The other classes also wanted to be fashionable and followed the trends of the elite. It was one of the few ways in which commoners could still belong. In addition, there was a further social element to fashion: people also followed fashion trends as a courtesy to the people around them. It would have been an insult not to wear the same style as one's superiors. In 1673, when the French King Louis XIV was 35 years old, his long locks of hair started to thin and his hairline began to recede. It obviously became difficult for the young, vain monarch to maintain the long-hair look. Louis decided to shave his head and have a wig of curly long hair made, and his subjects never knew about his balding. From that moment, the trend of wearing wigs became popular, and remained in fashion until the end of the eighteenth century and the French Revolution of 1789. After that, short hairstyles for young men back came back into style.

Youth fashion

The vanity of the young was not limited to the length of their hair; fashions in headwear were pushing the conventional boundaries of manhood as well. Young men started wearing wide-rimmed hats decorated with feathers. In the sixteenth century people started collecting feathers, which were considered a sign of masculinity and virility, just as the feathers on a rooster or a peacock symbolize pride and self-confidence. In addition, the young men of the early seventeenth century started growing a mustache, goatee or pointed-beard, which were also signs of masculinity. However, this was the only body hair that was fashionable on young men; according to the fashions of the time, young men should not have any other hair on their bodies. The aforementioned book *De Secreeten* advised men on how to remove hair from under their armpits, chest, and even groin area. This was recommended for hygienic purposes. A young man should not allow his private parts to get sweaty and start to stink. For young adolescents who had just started to sprout a beard, *De Secreeten* also included a remedy for permanently removing hair under the armpits and wherever undesirable hair might start to appear. Besides being hairless, the ideal young man was muscular, with full calves and clean feet.

There were several remedies for removing or hiding pimples and other spots on the face. Youngsters who had been scarred with smallpox as children could cover the blemishes with white powder or black dots (known as 'beauty marks'). In the early modern period, it was not uncommon to have had smallpox as a child. If someone were fortunate enough to survive smallpox, however, they were usually marked with facial scars for the rest of their life. For aesthetic reasons, early modern men wanted to hide them.

Just as with their hair, young people took a meticulous approach to their clothes. They left little to chance. The latest trend in the 1620s and 1630s was the new flat collar, which made a clean break with the older fashion of wearing a millstone collar. The new flat collar was more practical and did not require having 15 meters of folded fabric around one's neck. One of the reasons why long hair became fashionable among young men was simply so that their long hair would not get stuck in the many ruffs of the millstone collar. Long hair and a millstone collar were impractical bedfellows.

Young men started wearing a flat version of this collar that gently rested over the top of their doublet overcoat. At the end of the sixteenth century, this corset-like jacket was lined on the inside and buttoned up at the neck. In the first few decades of the seventeenth century, however, the shape of the doublet changed drastically. Instead of having a tailored shape, it became a loose-fitting garment that more or less draped over the upper body.

The sleeves, which had initially fallen at the wrist, were worn rolled up. Besides the loose doublet, the trousers also were different. Young men wore pants known as 'bombasts' that were baggy and puffy. They were fitted at the knee, where they were fastened with a garter, ribbons, or buttons. This style was in stark contrast to the tight, leotard-like pants that had been in vogue at the end of the sixteenth century; a style that most young men's fathers had worn when they were young. This new fashion originated at the French court.

In fact, everything that French king and his court wore influenced the young urban elite in the Dutch Republic; at least, if they could afford it. The new trousers were wide around the waist and tight at the knee. Unlike the fashion of the older generation, this new style, with its excessive use of fabric, seemed to drape and hide the contours of the buttocks and legs. In many ways, it defied the norms of masculinity of the older generation, who had wanted to emphasize their muscular legs and buttocks with tights that included a codpiece. The latter, a flap-like piece of cloth that covered the reproductive organs, had accentuated the size of the genitals. In the late sixteenth century, the codpiece became fashionable among young men at the court of Queen Elizabeth I of England, known as the 'Virgin Queen' because she turned down all her suitors. No doubt, the men did everything they could to attract her attention. The garment had originally become fashionable among young Italian men, as it made it easier for them to play sports, while at the same time drawing attention to their physique and private parts. The new, baggy-look fashion must have felt like a challenge to the older generation's codes of masculinity.

The new fashion for baggy pants also had its advantages. The old-style tights with their codpieces had restricted the movement of young men. With looser-fitting clothing and bombasts, young people could move more freely and even play sports.

They wore high, silk stockings that extended down to the shoe. The stockings were fastened at the knee with garters and ribbons, and the male knee became a prominent eye-catcher. Silk was a popular fabric for stockings and clothes, especially for the wealthy, who could afford the expensive material from Persia.

Bling-bling

As if all the shiny, silk clothing were not extravagant enough, young men also decorated their clothes with gold and silver accessories. By the early seventeenth century, demand for gold and glittery metals for clothing had increased dramatically. Youth fashion in the early seventeenth century was all about *bling-bling*. The shinier, the better.

Historically, it was nothing new; European history was characterized by periods such as the Italian Renaissance, when fashion was dominated by luxury and extravagance. The Italian republics of the fourteenth and fifteenth centuries in particular were affluent societies where it was fashionable to wear expensive fabrics, decorated with precious metals. In Venice, the young trendsetters of the late fifteenth century made their appearance more flamboyant by wearing gold and silver. The Senate of Venice thought that clothing and fashion had become too extravagant, and introduced measures in 1456 to fine young people who wore expensive fabrics. Taking the opportunity to improve its own financial situation, the city council forced wealthy citizens who wore ornate clothing to loan the city 1,000 lire each.

Dutch youngsters not only used expensive fabrics for their wardrobes, but they also accessorized with costly materials, such silk-spun ribbon for shoelaces. Shoes were fastened with gold and silver ribbons and knotted in the form of a rosette. This new style among the youth resembled the uniforms of the cavalry soldiers known as *cuirassiers*. These rugged men wore a breastplate as a harness, gloves, and wristbands. In the course of the seventeenth century, metal for the uniforms slowly was replaced with fabric. The harness-shaped coat was decorated with slashes in the fabric, so that one could see through to what was underneath. The outfit resembled the uniforms that Leonardo da Vinci had designed for the Swiss Guard – the same uniforms that can be seen at the Vatican today.

Adolescents and young men growing up in the early seventeenth century were spellbound by everything that had to do with the military. During that period, the Dutch state army had soldiers who fought at the front and kept the Spaniards outside Holland. In addition, the Dutch state continued to use war propaganda to keep the fight for independence from Spain alive. This propaganda served an important purpose; after all, the population had to bear the costs of the war, and the States General and local cities and towns imposed excise duties on various products. Without this income, the States General could not afford to keep the war going. The young people in Republic's cities, on the other hand, found the war exciting, especially the heroic soldiers that protected the country against the Spanish fury. Their uniforms, and the way they spent their leisure time drinking, smoking and going after women, were considered the epitome of manhood by adolescent boys and young men.

Until his death in 1625, Prince Maurits, the stadholder, was also the commander in chief and seen as the savior of the country. This was the role that his father, Willem of Orange, had assumed when the Revolt broke out in the sixteenth century, and it was a role played by all of the princes of Orange in the course of the seventeenth and eighteenth centuries. However, there was another reason why army fashions became popular among young men in the early seventeenth century. In general, the image of the military under Maurits' stadholdership had changed drastically.

The stadholder and his military advisors modernized the army and made it more organized and disciplined. Under Maurits' helm, the Dutch army became the most modern in Europe. The troops were trained in the latest fighting techniques and fitted with proper uniforms and weapons. Most importantly, they were a paid army. Before that, most armies in Europe had been paid from what they could loot. Local populations therefore had a disdain for armies and soldiers. But now, with their fancy uniforms and discipline, people started to look up to them with respect. Young men in particular, who sought male role models, idolized them and copied their clothing style.

Bright colors

The contrast between the older and younger generations in the seventeenth century was captured best by Bartholomeus van der Helst in a pair of portraits that he painted. In 1642, he was commissioned to paint Andries Bicker and his 20-year-old son. Father Bicker (1586-1652) was a wealthy merchant who traded with Russia and Scandinavia. He had also been mayor of Amsterdam several times. Van der Helst painted the slightly balding Bicker with cropped hair, dressed in a black doublet and with a snow-white millstone collar around his neck. That he wore black was no coincidence; during the first decades of the seventeenth century in particular, black was in fashion. Wearing black was also a status symbol, because it was expensive and difficult to produce. The white millstone collar around his neck likewise emphasized that Andries Bicker had money, because he could afford to have his clothes whitened. Every spring and summer, all the white garments of the country's wealthy citizens were packed up and brought to the bleaching fields outside Haarlem. The area around Haarlem was the ideal place for bleaching clothes, as there was an abundance of clean water and buttermilk, which was used to make clothing whiter. After the garments were washed and cleaned, they were laid out in the fields so that

Gerard Bicker's father, Andries, dressed in black and wearing a millstone collar, a style preferred by elderly people that had been fashionable twenty years earlier. Painting by Bartholomeus van der Helst, *Andries Bicker* (1642) (Rijksmuseum, Amsterdam).

the sun and wind could lighten them further. Andries Bicker's generation believed that the whiter one's clothes, the cleaner they were.

Van der Helst portrayed Bicker's son, Gerard Andriesz Bicker (1622-1666), quite differently. The 20-year-old wears a

The *fashionista* Gerard Bicker sporting the latest fashion for young people: a flat collar, a salmon pink-colored coat and long hair. Painting by Bartholomeus van der Helst, *Gerard Andriesz Bicker* (1642) (Rijksmuseum, Amsterdam).

pink salmon-colored velvet coat with a flat collar. In his hands, Gerard is holding yellow leather gloves. In addition, his hair is long and reaches the top of his shoulders. The most striking feature is that Bicker's son is corpulent. His large body takes up almost the entire 70.5 centimeter-width of the canvas. Gerard probably suffered from obesity, a disease that he most likely inherited from his mother, who was also heavy. In Gerard's day, there were rumors that he weighed 220 kilos, and he was called 'Fat Bicker' behind his back.

In the early seventeenth century, young people started wearing more colorful clothing. Many of the same bright colors that can be seen in the portrait of the young Bicker were also represented in the painting genre known as the 'merry company'. In this genre, fashionable young people were dressed in bright-colored clothing and represented the prosperity of the Republic. Young men were often dressed in cheery shades such as bright red, yellow, and moss green. The painter Willem Buytewech from Rotterdam specialized in this genre. His young male figures are shown dressed in pants that come to the knee and accessorized with silk ribbons. During the 1620s, Constantijn Huygens (1596-1687), secretary to stadholder Frederick Henry, sneered at the latest trend among affluent young people. He was contemptuous of the new fashion:

> pants tied at the knee with ribbons, a hanging shoulder flap,
> a doublet as stiff as a harness, shoes that are so deep that the
> vamp is barely attached to the heel, and hats that look more
> like a dish turned upside down meant to house lice, flashy
> pleated collars that could house rats, tight-fitting stockings
> in which the legs look like a sausage about to squeeze out
> of its casing, too many rosettes on the shoes, high heels,
> and an impractical outer coat which is more like a flag than
> providing coverage, and is more ballast than protection.

Calculated sloppiness

Young people's fashion in the early seventeenth century was utterly nonchalant. The older generation considered it casual and sloppy. Instead of wearing hats the traditional way, straight on the head, youngsters wore theirs tilted slightly backwards. Overcoats were worn hung loosely over the shoulders and doublets were only half-buttoned. The strings that fastened shirts were barely attached, which meant that the collar came loose. To the older generation, with their tight-fitting doublets, millstone collars, and hats placed firmly on the heads, the new fashion looked disheveled. It resembled someone who had been called out of bed in the middle of the night. Still, youth style left little to chance. Every detail of this new look was considered carefully by the fashion-conscious young men of the early seventeenth century. In the 1630s and 1640s, the English referred to this style as 'calculated slovenliness'. For the Dutch youths of the 1620s and 1630s, it was certainly calculated. They had invested a lot of time and money in creating that nonchalant look.

In the early seventeenth century, affluent youths in Dutch cities were the first in Europe to embrace this calculated, slovenly style. The *fashionistas* of the Dutch Republic probably followed the royal courts of Europe as an example for trends. The younger monarchs of Europe in particular were the trendsetters of new fashions for young people. In the early seventeenth century, it was King Louis XIII of France and King Charles I of England who determined men's fashions. For the affluent young men who finished their education with a grand tour of Europe, a visit to Paris was an absolute must. One of the first things young men did was to shed their provincial garments and shop for a new wardrobe. It was practically a ritual; the last thing a young man wanted was to be mistaken for a country bumpkin while he was visiting Paris. He had to look like a *honnête homme* or gentleman, which was more fitting to his station in early modern society.

Pimped-up clothing

Not everyone could afford the newest Parisian fashions; only young men from the wealthiest families were able to purchase the latest designs from France. For the majority of the population in the early seventeenth century, clothing was expensive. When Dirck Alewijn, a wealthy cloth manufacturer from Amsterdam, died in 1637, he left his wardrobe of expensive clothes to his sons Frederick and Abraham. Because his clothes were costly and still valuable, he left some pieces to his wife so that she could sell them afterwards.

Young men who could not afford expensive clothes and still wanted to follow the latest trends were forced to be creative. They had to rely on an *uitdraagster,* a woman who sold second-hand clothes door to door, acquired through bankruptcies and dissolved estates. Another option was to buy clothes at a second-hand clothes market. The used garments were usually mended, patched up, and decorated with accessories. By dyeing them or adding stitch-work, and filling the shoulders, old clothes could be easily updated and pimped up in the latest styles.

There were other ways to be trendy, even if one had little money. An old suit could look fashionable again if it was accessorized with new gloves, collars, ribbons, or feathers. Even with a modest income, a young man could avoid looking outdated. In Amsterdam, youngsters who had very little money usually purchased second-hand clothing at the Nieuwmarkt, Westermarkt, or Noordermarkt – where still to this day there is a second-hand clothes market every Monday morning. However, buying second-hand clothes did have its downside. Already in the sixteenth century, these markets were derogatively known as 'flea markets'. They were given that name for a reason, mainly because some of the garments sold there were teeming with fleas and other insects. Especially during outbreaks of the plague, these markets were considered places that spread pestilence.

During periods when there was no plague, however, second-hand markets were the most popular place for young people to buy clothing. Because the supply could not fulfill the demand for used clothing, as the original owners did not dispose of their clothing quickly enough, an odd situation arose. Thieves played an important role in speeding up the process. By the middle of the seventeenth century, there was a gang of juvenile thieves in Amsterdam that operated in neighborhoods with second-hand clothing markets. The boys specialized in stealing expensive clothing made of linen and silk. They were especially good at heisting garments from stores while their owners were distracted. One of the most common ways to steal clothing was from a barber's shop, where customers' overcoats were hung at the entrance. While the client went for a shave and was paying close attention to the sharp knife gliding across his neck and chin, it was an opportune moment for a young crook to sneak inside the barber's shop and nick his coat. By the time the innocent victim realized that his coat was gone, it was too late. In most cases, stolen goods were already resold and had a new owner within the hour.

Fashion and moralism

Many moralists criticized young people's new fashions as improper. In their view, fashion caused many social and moral problems, let alone the fact that poor young people were more or less forced to keep up with the latest trends. Their criticisms were sparked by a deeper underlying fear, namely that the newly affluent were spoiling their children with fancy clothes. The young people were not the problem; it was their parents who had failed to teach their offspring the virtue of moderation.

During the economic boom of the Golden Age, for many merchants, money was not an issue. Their accumulated wealth became visible in every aspect of their lives. Fortunes were lost just as quickly as they were made, however, and for the new affluent class in the Dutch Republic, who amassed their wealth in a period of ten to twenty years, losing their money was their greatest fear. In the satirical pamphlet *Den Rechten Weg nae 't Gasthuys* (1536) [The Direct Road to the Poorhouse], the nightmare of economic ruin and losing all one's worldly goods is portrayed in great detail. The story tells how a wealthy merchant family that lived beyond its means was forced to sell everything and go to the poorhouse. This fear was not unrealistic in the seventeenth century, and the author emphasized how important it was for parents to teach their children the virtue of moderation. If they did not, then the family could lose everything. They were likely to end up in the poorhouse and depend on charity.

The word 'rechten' in the title was ambiguous. On the one hand, it literally meant 'directly to the poorhouse'. One could also read a note of moral judgment in the term, as right or 'just'. In the early seventeenth century, the affluent young people of the Republic became a symbol of the country's modernity and newfound prosperity. Young people were exuberant and excessive, with their long hair, flat collars, calculated sloppiness, bright-colored clothing, golden buttons, silk ribbons and feathered hats. They reflected how abundant the material culture of the Republic had become, and how those excesses could flow into other facets of daily seventeenth-century life, such as eating food and drinking alcohol.

4.   Alcohol

In the early seventeenth century, Dutch and foreign students in the Republic had many traits in common. For one, they knew how to get drunk. In their inebriated state, students would disturb the peace and cause social mayhem. If a Dutch student was regularly arrested for drunken behavior, he risked ruining his family's reputation. On the night of Thursday 7 March 1624, Petrus Robertus, together with ten other students in Leiden, caused so much disturbance and destruction of private property that he was arrested by the municipal bailiff. The University of Leiden's academic court recommended that Robertus' father keep him at home until he learned how to behave himself. If the young man were to return to the university before that time he would be disgraced, and this would permanently tarnish the family's reputation.

Students who were enrolled at a university were well aware of the risk they were taking when they participated in violence. For the ruling families of the Dutch Republic, who all knew each other, a dent in the family's reputation could be especially detrimental for their future. A decent name and reputation were essential preconditions for maintaining an individual's economic and social position, as well as that of an entire family and the family's extended network. Ruining one's reputation meant squandering one's chances of obtaining a political office, closing commercial deals, and even finding the right marriage partner, which was of strategic importance for the entire family. Often a family's name was most at risk when a young man was under the influence of alcohol.

Students did anything and everything to maintain their good reputation and honor their family name. In 1623, Reinier van Leeuwenhuijzen, a Swedish law student in Leiden, petitioned the academic court to erase his name from the ledger of student transgressions, after he had agreed to compensate a local innkeeper for his outstanding bar tab. Although he was not necessarily concerned about his reputation in the Dutch Republic, he was worried that one of his fellow Swedish students in Leiden, also from the nobility, would tell of his wrongdoings once he returned to Sweden. For the elite of the Dutch Republic, gossip about immoral behavior spread like wildfire, and there was much at stake for a young man from a noble family.

No one knew that better than Hester della Faille. In Leiden, she and her son-in-law asked the academic court to lock up her 29-year-old son, Daniel, who had become violent and was in a state of delirium. Moreover, he was consorting with the wrong kind of people. After the death of her husband, Daniel van der Meulen Sr., Hester della Faille had become the *mater familias* of the Van der Meulens, a wealthy merchant family that fled Antwerp in 1585 and had established a good reputation in their new home country. When her husband was still alive, he was a respected merchant in Leiden with an extensive trade network throughout Europe. Daniel Jr., however, was a troubled young man who had enrolled as a student at the University of Leiden a year earlier. Although there was no mention of alcohol as the problem, his widowed mother and friends had hoped a period of confinement would shield him from the bad influence of his friends.

College life

One of the major factors that contributed to the excessive consumption of alcohol by students (and professors) in Leiden was that they could buy duty-free liquor. As a way of attracting more students to Leiden, students and staff enrolled at the university were exempt from paying excise taxes on alcohol. This special privilege, which had been established in 1577, gave students the annual right to purchase 194 liters of house wine and 10 barrels (approximately 1,500 liters) of beer tax-free. This amounted to more than half a liter of wine and four liters of beer a day. When the University of Franeker was founded in 1586, the university granted the same rights to students.

Besides universities, several illustrious schools were founded in the early seventeenth century. These were academic institutions comparable to today's community or junior colleges. They allowed students to follow the first couple of years of an academic curriculum, but were not certified to give degrees. On many levels, illustrious schools competed with universities in trying to attract students. The illustrious school of Middelburg, for example, granted its pupils the same duty-free liquor privileges as the universities. Despite the fact that students were renowned for their excessive drinking habits and causing violence, these academic institutions would not think of abolishing the privilege.

For the students and university staff, it was a lucrative system. In Leiden, some citizens even took advantage of it and had their sons enrolled as students at the university without their ever attending a single class. The miller Harmen van Rijn and his wife Neeltje were one example of a couple that wanted to take advantage of the tax break. In 1620, they enrolled their 14-year-old son Rembrandt as a student at the University of Leiden. Rembrandt probably never saw the inside of the building. Local magistrates and universities soon realized that people were taking advantage of the special privilege, and started applying stricter regulations for enrollment.

While cities tried to lure as many students as possible by offering duty-free alcohol, the university administrators also wanted to curtail binge drinking. They tried to introduce every possible measure that might prohibit students from imbibing too much. For example, students who received a scholarship were not allowed to consume alcohol where students played sports.

Students at the University of Groningen did not receive a tax-break on alcoholic beverages and had to pay the full price, just like ordinary citizens. Unfortunately, we do not know whether this had a negative effect on student enrollment. In any case, it did not prevent students from drinking too much. In 1616, the German students Johannes Fabricius from Oldenburg and Hieronymus van Lengen from East Friesland were admonished for public drunkenness and wayward behavior. Indeed, the academic court in Groningen had apprehended and reprimanded them earlier for delinquency. Van Lengen was a known prankster and troublemaker. Two years earlier, he had been caught throwing stones at the window of a fellow student, Moerling, and had injured him in the face. On another occasion, Van Lengen had hung provocative posters up all around town, and another time he had hired a street musician to play music outside the university building to disrupt a lecture. Despite Van Lengen's licentious behavior and tomfoolery, he turned out all right in the end. He later became mayor of his town.

The students in Groningen certainly knew how to binge drink. In 1618, Bertholdus Beilen was arrested by the municipal guard for wandering around in an inebriated state. According to eye-witnesses, the philosophy student was spotted entering a cafe as early as 10 o'clock in the morning. His drinking binge continued throughout the day and only ended at 11 o'clock in the evening. Beilen was a violent drunk. After he left the cafe late in the evening, he became aggressive and was arrested by the municipal guard. The academic court had him incarcerated and put on bread and water.

After numerous cases of drunkenness, the senate of the University of Groningen decided to restrict the excessive consumption of beer and wine among students. In 1619, the senate endorsed new measures that forced bar owners to regulate how much alcohol students consumed in their establishments. Students were not allowed to consume more than a *rijksdaalder* worth of alcohol in an evening, which resembles a current restriction that prohibits grocery and liquor stores from selling alcohol to minors. Thus in Groningen, bar owners, not students, became responsible for curbing excessive drinking. Moreover, in the seventeenth century a *rijksdaalder* bought a lot of alcohol, and a student could easily get drunk for that amount. Getting drunk was simply a part of being a student.

Symposia

In the early seventeenth century, the consumption of alcohol was just as important to student life as books, if not more. In the humanist tradition, the ancient Greek 'symposium' was originally a convivial meeting where the consumption of alcohol was combined with stimulating intellectual conversation. Drinking was the mainstay of intellectual life, and alcohol was consumed in abundance when professors and students had deep scholarly conversations. In the academic world, students looked up to their professors, who were often heavy drinkers. Unlike today, in the early modern period professors and students interacted and socialized with each other outside the classroom. It was not uncommon for students to rent a room at a professor's home, and professors were less likely to remain within the confines of their study. They mingled much more with their students, often at the pub. Some men chose to take up a professorship so they could pursue their academic interests and continue to be a bachelor. Among the professors at the University of Leiden, one-fifth of the academic staff was unmarried. Some professors felt that marriage and family life would interfere with their scholarly pursuits.

Daniel Heinsius (1580-1655), who was a professor of Greek and Latin at the University of Leiden, thought a wife would be an inconvenience to his career as a scholar. Because he liked to read in bed, the professor laid out his books all over his bed at home. There was literally no place for a woman in his bed, and consequently in his life. In Leiden, Heinsius was known as a drunk. On one occasion, students found a note tacked to the classroom door stating that the lecture had been canceled because Heinsius had a hangover. Heinsius' tipple of choice was wine and he made no secret of it. In his collection of poems *Nederduytsche poemata* [Dutch Poetry] (1616), which was a compilation of stories and engravings about love, he devoted an entire chapter to wine entitled *Het Lof-sanck van Bacchus* [The Song of Praise for Bacchus], which honored Bacchus, the

Roman god of wine. In the early seventeenth century, it was not uncommon for deeply religious men such as Heinsius to honor the pre-Christian gods, even pagan ones; the epitome of excessive drinking. While writing his chapter, Heinsius knew exactly who his readers would be. They were young academics and colleagues who had a humanistic education and were acquainted with the classic Greek and Roman authors.

In his story, Heinsius portrayed Bacchus as an older man who felt young again after drinking wine and hanging around with young people. Drinking wine made him feel as though the world lay at his feet. The way Heinsius told the story aroused the interest of young readers. As the story progressed, a bitter truth was revealed. The story had an educational message: wine was a magical elixir that would make the elderly feel better. According to Heinsius, wine was not meant for the young, because their temperament was warm-blooded and sanguine. Young people were better off drinking water; according to myth, Bacchus, as a motherless young child, was raised by water nymphs.

The story about Bacchus was an allegory. Young people have to drink water, just as a vineyard needs to be watered, or it will not grow. In essence, *The Praise of Bacchus* relayed the same message as other seventeenth-century publications in which Bacchus was revered. In *Satyra or Schimpdicht. Prijsende den Godt Bacchuys, of't Droncken drincken* (1632) [Satire or Farce. Honoring the God Bacchus or Intoxicated Drinking], the author H. Rulant satirically warned young and old about the dangers of drinking too much alcohol.

When Rulant's second edition *Satyra or Schimpdicht* was published in 1634, he changed the subtitle for educational reasons to *Proces Van Drie Gebroeder-Edellieden: den eenen zynde een Dronckaert, den Tweeden een Hoereerder, den Derden een speelder* [Trial of Three Noble Brothers: The First a Drunkard, the Second a Whoremonger, and the Third a Gambler]. The story was an entertaining portrayal of three brothers named Philip, Carel, and Maximilian. The brothers were from an affluent family and were aged around 16 or 17 years old. Their parents invested a lot in ensuring they had a good moral education. One might think, *so far, so good*. However, from the moment they started their academic education and enrolled at university, everything went downhill. It did not take long for Philip to become an alcoholic, for Carel to become a whore-hopper, and for Maximilian to become addicted to gambling; a nightmare for any parent.

In the course of Rulant's satire, one brother, Philip, is also given a voice, and turns to the reader to defend his 'thirst' for alcohol with the remark that 'een goed gezel zig wel dronken drinkt, maar een schelm zelden, ende een verrader nimmer-meer' [a good man drinks in company, but a scoundrel seldom, and a traitor never]. In other words, if a virtuous man becomes drunk, he has nothing to fear, an immoral one plenty. The readers could recognize in the brothers all three vices – alcohol, sex, and gambling – but they probably identified the most with Philip, because consuming alcohol was a social activity in which many people participated. Frequenting prostitutes and gambling, on the other hand, were individual acts and took place in secrecy.

One of the professors at the University of Leiden was Domini-cus Baudius (1561-1613), who was a celebrated scholar of rhetoric, law and history. But he was also known as a notoriously heavy drinker. It was no secret in Leiden that the professor had problems with money, women, and alcohol. He liked to gamble and play dice, but his greatest problem was squandering money on alcohol and women. After it became public knowledge that he had fathered an illegitimate child, the senate of the University of Leiden suspended him. His crime was not necessarily father-ing an illegitimate child from a prostitute; his wrongdoing was that he had broken his promise to marry the child's mother. The situation only became more dramatic after Baudius decided to marry another woman. In Leiden, people gossiped that she was richer than him, and he was only marrying her for her money. Unfortunately for Baudius, his life with his wealthy wife was short-lived. A few days after the wedding, he died. It was rumored that his early death was the result of his alcohol addiction.

In Leiden, Baudius was not an ideal role model for his students. Neither was Everardus Bronckhorst (1554-1627), a professor of law at Leiden. Bronckhorst liked to go out barhopping with his students. In his diary, he narrated on several occasions that he wanted to stop drinking – something he usually wrote on days when he was suffering a bad hangover. Drinking at graduations and other academic celebrations started to take its toll on his health. When it came to alcohol, Bronckhorst had little self-discipline (he also chased women, despite the fact that he was married).

In 1631, a conflict erupted in Leiden between the students and one of the professors. The newly appointed professor of ethics, Johan Bodecher Benning (1606-1642), authored a satirical pamphlet in which he portrayed Leiden's students as drunks and whore-hoppers. In the pamphlet entitled *Satyricon in corruptae iuventutis mores corruptos* [Satire on the corrupt morality of depraved youths], Bodecher Benning did not use recognizable names and places. However, due to the detailed descriptions of the taverns and brothels around Leiden, his readers knew exactly which venues the professor meant. In the story, a freshman student becomes friends with older students who seduce him into the immoral world of alcohol and tobacco. His new friends are a bad influence on him, which eventually leads to his downfall.

After Bodecher Benning's work was published, the students in Leiden felt attacked by his accusations. Leiden's students did not take his accusations sitting down, however; some of them retaliated and wrote their own satirical pamphlet about 'a certain 22-year-old professor who was still wet behind the ears'. The pamphlet, entitled *Juventus Academia ad Hermophilum Tanugriensem* [The student's Hermophilis Tanugriensis], portrayed an experienced young professor and criticized him for being an academic nobody. Although the pamphlet was anonymously authored and Bodecher Benning's name was never used, the similarities between the main character and Bodecher Benning were uncanny.

The conflict did not stop there. In another pamphlet, entitled *Sermo in Corrupti Hermophilis Tanugriensis Corruptos Mores*

[Sermon on the corrupt ways of the wicked Hermophilis Tanugriensis] (1631), another anonymous student-writer depicted Bodecher Benning as an alcoholic. With the same logic that Bodecher Benning had used in his pamphlet, the student argued that Bodecher Benning's insightfulness about alcohol consumption could only come from a man personally acquainted with drinking. In other words, professors should consider their own behavior before lashing out at students. In Leiden, where the drinking problems of professors like Heinsius and Baudius were public knowledge, the residents of the town probably sided with the students.

Before most young men enrolled at university, they already knew that going to the pub was part of being a student. Crispijn de Passe's *Academia sive specvlvm vitae scolasticae* [The University or Mirror of Student Life] (1612) prepared them for college life, which included visiting pubs and taverns. The book provided valuable insight into what every prospective student could expect in academic life. A young man was advised to spend his leisure time painting, fencing, and playing music. After all, it was a known fact that students had a lot of free time; indeed, they had too much. In the academic year of 1595, there were only 144 days with lectures for students. In the academic year of 1650, there were only 101 days when classes were taught. In reality, this meant that students had 264 days off and nothing to do. Most of them passed the time drinking in pubs and visiting inns.

De Passe knew that a large part of student life took place in the pub. In *Academia*, one of the emblems depicts a tavern scene where young men and women are playing games, drinking, eating, and kissing. Ironically, hanging on the wall behind the young people are four paintings: a landscape, a seascape with a boat, a portrait of a woman, and one of Venus and Cupid. Each painting has a moral message for the viewer. However, prospective students are not supposed to get too excited about consuming alcohol, because behind the amorous couple the engraving shows a fool (always a warning). The accompanying text spells out that 'chastity and moderate drinking agree with the Muses and Apollo, but the combination of wine, playing dice, and womanizing is apt to ruin a scholar's character'. The moral of the story is that students are better off staying at home and avoiding the pub. In reality, however, students did not stay at home. Drinking was just as important to student life as reading books and attending lectures, if not more.

Drinking games

There were several drinking games in the early seventeenth century. The best-known game was played with a *pasglas* or measuring glass; a long cylindrical glass marked like a measuring cup. The marks indicated how much a player had to consume from the glass. In seventeenth-century Dutch paintings, the *pasglas* was often depicted in the still life genre because it symbolized the transience and temporal nature of life. After a player had sipped exactly to the mark indicated on the glass, he was allowed to pass the glass on to the next player, who was required to do the same. If they missed the mark, they had to take another swig until they got it right. It did not take long for the players to get drunk, especially the younger, inexperienced ones.

Another game was played using a *molenbeker* (windmill cup). This goblet-like cup was often made from silver, and had a foot on its base in the shape of the arms of a windmill. The only way to set it down was by putting it on its top. When someone blew into a pipe, the sails turned a dial that indicated how many times the contestant would have to empty the cup. And because the goblet could not be put down, it would have to be completely emptied. The unlucky player would have to drink everything to the last drop, or risk having to take another turn. With these drinking games, young people would quickly become drunk. But as they played, they soon learned how to be cautious with alcohol and know their limits.

Like the symposia where students and professors drank together, drinking games in the seventeenth century had a social

Drinking games commonly played by young people included the 'pasglas' or measuring glass. Painting by Jan van de Velde, *Still Life with 'Pasglas'* (1647) (Rijksmuseum, Amsterdam).

function. Consuming alcohol together strengthened cohesion between all groups in society, from the poor to the rich. The many drinking bouts gave rise to life-long friendships between young men. Unconsciously, an element of trust that emerged from drinking together, which created a mutual commonality. In the early modern period, having trust in someone was considered a form of social capital. If an apprentice wanted to become a member of a guild, a round of drinks was often served with the rest of the guild members. This ensured that the older men in the guild could trust the new member. It was a ritual of being accepted as an equal. Moreover, becoming a member of the guild also implied that a young man was accepting responsibility. For a young man it was a rite of passage in which male members bonded, like a brotherhood. This was known as 'contractual drinking'. A contract was created, whereby men learned to trust each other and accept newcomers in their midst.

The Bentvueghels

Ritual drinking was also customary among young Dutch painters in Rome. After they had finished their apprenticeship with a master painter, they completed their education with an extended sojourn in Rome, during which they usually practiced and studied works from Antiquity and the Renaissance. When these artists returned to the Republic, their stay in Rome was regarded as an asset to their painting range.

During their stay in the eternal city, the young artists from the Dutch Republic, just like university students, were organized in groups according to their country of origin. The Bentveugels (Birds of a Feather) were such a group. They were founded in 1623 at a Dutch inn in Rome called *De Witte Valck* (The White Falcon). Run by a Dutch innkeeper, the inn was a popular meeting place for travelers from the Low Countries. The young founders also chose the name of the inn for another reason, namely because it was a bird known for its speed and its ability to change direction quickly, which had an allegorical meaning for the young painters. The falcon was the symbol of youth.

Most of the members of the group were between 20 and 24 years old. They often rented the same house together, and would have their studios on the upper floors where the light was good. To belong to the Bentveugels, prospective members had to go through an initiation ceremony. These usually took place in a local tavern and started with a *tableau vivant* performed with characters from ancient history. Antiquity played an important role for the Bentveugels; it was the period in history that had produced the most art. During the initiation of Joachim von Sandrart and Michel le Bon in 1628/1629, there was a performance featuring Apollo on Mount Parnassus, accompanied by Mercury reciting poetry about sculpture and painting. Of course, Bacchus the Roman god of wine was also included in the *tableau vivant*.

Bacchus was the patron of the Bentveugels. During each initiation ceremony, novices were given a comical nickname, which was part of the Bacchanalian tradition. The ceremony usually ended with a toast. The first drink and toast were contractual. However, the numerous drinks and binge drinking that followed were just as important in the initiation ceremony, known as the *doopfeest* (baptismal feast). The initiation lasted until the early hours of the next day and ended with a pilgrimage to the tomb of Bacchus located in the Santa Costanza Church, a few miles away from the city gate. For the Bentveugels, drinking together was an important social lubricant, and Bacchus played a cohesive role. In a drawing made by one of the Bentveugels in 1623, Bacchus was portrayed standing naked in the middle, surrounded by the other founding members. The message is clear. The group of young men living abroad liked to drink. Every time a novice became a member or one of them returned home, there was a reason for celebration, which usually ended in a night of excessive drinking.

Chambers of rhetoric

Members of another group, the chambers of rhetoric (*rederijk-skamers*), were known for their heavy drinking. These groups of men, which included all age groups, shared a love of writing and reciting poetry. The chambers of rhetoric originated in the Southern Netherlands during the fifteenth and sixteenth centuries, and spread to the Dutch Republic in the late sixteenth and early seventeenth centuries. Just as today, every city or town has a local Rotary Club, in the seventeenth century every town and every village had its own chapter of rhetoricians who shared poetry with each other. Young men who wished to develop their intellectual faculties were particularly drawn to the chambers of rhetoric, where they learned to write poetry, the art of rhetoric, debating, and also how to write and stage plays. They were by no means homogeneous groups. Besides being from all age groups, the members were also from various social and professional backgrounds. With such diversity, drinking functioned as an important social lubricant. After the performances, but also during them, copious amounts of alcohol were consumed. They also drank a lot during their parades and other festivities.

For the Gouda chamber of rhetoric, taking a swig of alcohol was integrated into a literary game. A filled goblet was passed around, and all the members had to take a sip and pass it to the next person. With every gulp, a member was required to recite the verse of a poem to the chairman of the meeting. The member had to address the chairman every time as 'prince'. The poem had three or more stanzas, in which the last verses were repeated at the end. This determined the theme of the poem. The members had to keep their wits about them and not get drunk, otherwise they would forget the last lines of the poem. This kind of social drinking had a ritual character. The older members taught the younger ones how to consume alcohol in moderation, or at least drink a lot and act as if they still had their wits about them, which is a talent in itself.

Foreign youths

Compared to the ritualized or 'tolerated' drinking behavior of young men from the upper and middle ranks, the drinking habits of the lower classes were quite another thing altogether. As far as we know, there were no ritualized drinking games with fancy silver goblets or verses recited before opening the *ole hatchet* and guzzling away. In the Dutch Republic during the seventeenth century, young people with a foreign background were notorious for their excessive drinking. They often came from rural areas of Germany, Norway, Sweden, or Denmark. Many of them came from the Southern Netherlands, and these young people were renowned for their wayward lifestyle. In 1629, Gillis Quintijn,

Young people in the early morning after a night of partying, portrayed in: G. Quintijn, *De Hollandsche-Lijs met de Brabandsche Belij* (1629) (Courtesy of the Special Collections, University of Amsterdam).

a merchant from Haarlem, revealed how immoral this group of young people could be. In his book, *De Hollandsche-Lijs met de Brabandsche -Belij* [Holland's Tortoise with Brabant's Greenhorn], he portrayed these young foreigners as vulgar sots and lambasted them for not conforming to Dutch customs and morals.

Just like today, in the seventeenth century foreigners in the Dutch Republic preferred to reside in the same neighborhoods. The Flemish, whom the Dutch called 'garlic eaters', all lived in the same neighborhood, where they continued to follow their own customs and raise their youngsters in the way they would have done at home. According to Quintijn, the most offensive aspect of the Flemish was how they allowed their young people to drink excessive amounts of alcohol. During the neighborhood parties in the Flemish district, young people drank exorbitant amounts of booze. The youngsters then lost all control, usually by first dancing provocatively with each other. Their parties went on into the small hours. Afterwards they would descend onto the streets, where they made noise and disturbed the peace as they headed towards the beach. Along the way, they defaced doors, destroyed window boxes with flowers, molested cats, and vomited on people's doorsteps. However, the orgy of misconduct was not over yet. When they arrived at the beach, their tomfoolery became more serious. The young men splashed the blouses and dresses of the young women, and eventually their breasts and buttocks became visible. According to Quintijn, this was foreplay, and it did not take long before the young men were coupling with the girls, who were coerced into having sex with them in the dunes. Quintijn exaggerated these incidents, and even accused Haarlem's promiscuous young people of murder. Two corpses of babies had been found floating in Haarlem's Spaarne River, and Quintijn insinuated that the babies had been conceived out of wedlock during one of those youthful orgies at the beach.

From bad to worse

According Quintijn, excessive drinking formed a slippery slope for Haarlem's immigrant youngsters. One carnal vice led to another. In the pedagogical treatise *Practijcke* [Practice] (1632), young readers were told in detail how they could avoid all the cardinal vices. Godefridus Udemans, the author of the treatise, was a Protestant Reformed pastor from Zierikzee, who was mentioned above in the account of the 'Hair War'. He was obsessed with the immoral behavior of young people, especially their excessive drinking habits. He tried to safeguard young people from playing dice and frequenting pubs by scaring them with stories about God's wrath. One of his examples was based on an old story of how in 1546 a bolt of lightning had struck a tavern in the town of Mechlin in the Southern Netherlands, where 800 barrels of gunpowder had been stored. One of the victims was an innkeeper named Kroes, whose corpse was found with cards in his hands. 'Kroes' is also a Dutch word for 'goblet', a pun that the young reader would have picked up on, and according to Udemans this was no coincidence. God had punished him.

In the seventeenth century, the calls for moderation in the consumption of alcohol were quite different from those of the temperance movement two centuries later. In the nineteenth century, advocates fought for complete abstinence. In the seventeenth century, that was almost impossible. Consuming alcoholic beverages such as beer, wine, and brandy was safer than drinking water from canals and other waterways; especially in the cities, where there was no safe drinking water available. Before coffee and tea became affordable for the general public in the 1670s and 1680s, beer was the most widely consumed and safest beverage.

That is why seventeenth-century moralists like Udemans emphasized 'moderation' when it came to drinking, and not complete abstinence. In *De Christelycke Zee-vaert* [The Seafaring Christian] (1611) and *Geestelick Compas* [Spiritual Compass] (1617), Udemans offered young sailors moral advice for the nine-month voyage to Batavia. These devotional booklets were especially helpful for inexperienced boys and young men who were at sea for the first time and had to go ashore at ports such as the Cape of Good Hope, where veteran sailors sought rest and relaxation at inns and brothels. Udemans urged young seaman to be chaste, but in order to stay chaste, they first needed to remain sober. In a poem, Udemans described what could go wrong for a sailor once he went ashore:

> *drincken en schrinken,*
> *brassen en suypen,*
> *dansen ende springen,*
> *ende soo worden sy dickwils hoere-vast*
> *eer sy het weten.*

> (Drinking and being served,
> bingeing and guzzling,
> dancing and jumping,
> then comes the whore,
> before you know it.)

In other words, being drunk was in itself not so bad; it was what happened when young men were in an inebriated state that caused most concern. In the early modern era, parents and moralists knew exactly what was hidden in the dark when young men were drunk, namely promiscuity; and that was the gravest of all vices.

Daniel Souterius

Drinking was the ultimate sin for Daniel Souterius, a pastor in Haarlem. In his treatise *Nuchteren Loth* [Sober Lot] (1623), he used the biblical story of Lot as an example of how the excessive drinking of alcohol could unleash a chain of events that led to disgrace and dishonor. According to Souterius, Lot had initially been a pious man, but he was seduced by alcohol to commit incest with one of his daughters. Souterius re-interpreted the story of Lot for the modern context of the Dutch Republic in the early seventeenth century, which, in his view, had lost its moral compass to prosperity and material excess. He considered alcoholism to be a grave sin and a sign of barbaric behavior. Souterius argued that the alcoholic ruined his mind and his body. After all, he stammered and acted like an animal, and Souterius emphasized that the mind is what distinguishes man from animals.

According Souterius, alcoholism opened a Pandora's box. It could lead to idolatry, blasphemy, defying the Sabbath, the breaking of laws, murder, adultery, theft, dishonesty, and greed. Souterius believed that pubs, wine taverns, and *suypkotten* (drinking holes) were the root of all evil in the Dutch Republic. He called for city governments to take harsh measures to crack down on drinking establishments. Souterius urged municipal councils to follow the example of the English town of Sandwich, where individuals had to pay a penalty if they were caught drinking in taverns on Sunday. For those who were drinking and playing cards, their fines were doubled.

Dirck Pietersz Pers

The most effective means of keeping young men from drinking too much was through moral education. Moralists were more successful when they presented their message to young people as a form of self-control, instead of one that came from an external authority such as a parent, minister, or civil ordinance. Today, the most successful anti-smoking campaigns are those that emphasize the health dangers of smoking and passive inhalation. In the seventeenth century, the publisher Dirck Pieterszn Pers used the same tactic to influence young people. Many of the books he published were geared towards young audiences, and Pers was quite notorious among the young people of Amsterdam. He knew how to convince them that it was better to drink in moderation than to drink until they were completely intoxicated. In his book *Bacchus. Wonder Wercken* [Bacchus Working Miracles] (1628), Pers sketched how alcoholism could lead to an immoral man's downfall and demise. It was a realistic depiction of someone with an alcohol problem. Pedagogically, it was quite effective. The young reader quickly realized that the alcoholic was far from being a role model. The message was clear. Pers did not have to bore his readers with pedantic warnings; he knew his young readers and was aware of the best way to present a message. His book *Bellerophon tot Wysheyd of Lust* (1614) was aimed at the affluent young readers of Amsterdam. Pers recognized that the youth of Amsterdam's elite and middle classes were potential buyers of his books. He also knew the problems that adolescents faced and the trials that parents experienced with adolescent children.

Pers was a professional when it came to selling books. He had a sixth sense for what the consumer wanted and knew exactly what young people were not interested in buying. By choosing the title *Bacchus. Wonder Wercken*, Pers knew that he would attract young readers. The title referred to the ancient Bacchanalian culture that honored Bacchus, the Roman god of wine. Pers knew that young people were interested in alcohol, but what they did not know when they bought the book was that it was a satire with an educational message.

As Souterius had done, Pers referred to the biblical story of Lot, a man who lost his wisdom through his love for the bottle. In the preface, Pers urged his readers to drink in moderation, and stressed that it was better for young people to lead a sober life. For the older generation, Pers had less hope; they were already ruined. Pers had used the same technique to market other books, but with *Bacchus, Wonder-werken* he also tried something new. When buyers bought the book, they were given the booklet *Suyp-stad of Dronckaerts-Leven* [Guzzle-City or Life of a Drunk] as a supplement. This was an extra perk that made the book more appealing for youngsters. Similar to other stories in which the world was presented upside-down, *Suyp-stad* was a story where being drunk was the norm. Many of the rogue scenes in *Suyp-stad* resembled those in the 'merry company' painting genre. The life of a drunk was praised. It did not take long to realize that the story was a satire, but first the young reader had to witness the main character's bout of alcohol abuse. The message was subtle, but also crystal clear: young people were better off staying away from alcohol or only drinking in moderation. The young public that Pers targeted were the affluent, gilded youth with long hair, dressed in bright and colorful outfits. They were the same youngsters that Willem Buytewech and Pieter Codde had portrayed in merry companies, playing cards and throwing dice.

Yet the portrayal of merry companies was no moral admonishment to the young. These depictions were meant as a joke, and were intended to make the viewer laugh. The early twentieth-century series *Dogs Playing Poker* by the painter C.M. Coolidge had the same effect. For seventeenth-century viewers, paintings of frolicking and boozing young people were just as absurd as Coolidge's cigar-smoking and card-playing dogs. They made people laugh. The primary intention of painters of merry companies was not to reprimand young people for their behavior. However, viewers did need to understand the prevailing mores if they wanted to get the humor. In the early seventeenth century, humor was one of the most effective ways to communicate a message. The biggest problem experienced by moralists was that excessive drinking was deeply rooted in Dutch culture. For an adolescent, consuming large quantities of alcohol was an important rite of passage in becoming a man. For moralists, curbing young people's thirst for alcohol was truly an uphill battle.

Father Cats

Jacob Cats, the bestselling author of didactic books in the seventeenth century, understood the nature of young men like no other. In his popular *Spiegel vande Oude en Nieuwe Tijdt* [Mirror of the Old and New Times] (1632), he argued that parents needed to give leeway to their adolescent children so they could find their own boundaries. In his proverb *Men moet een paer narre-schoenen verslijten, eer men recht wijs wort* (one has to wear out a pair of fool's shoes before one can be wise), Father Cats, as he was known in the Golden Age, understood that youth was a psychologically turbulent and confusing phase. Cats emphasized that it was a difficult period for parents, who tried to teach their adolescent children moderation, but he also recognized that youngsters had to make mistakes before they could get on the right path. That was part of becoming an adult, and parents understood his logic. Cats' advice consoled parents; he comforted them with the idea that there was light at the end of the tunnel. The proverb was illustrated with an emblem of a slightly inebriated young man who is dancing and wearing a jester's shoes, while on the ground lie a tennis racket, a stack of cards, and other attributes associated with youth. For a seventeenth-century audience, the message was clear. Only a fool would wear shoes like that, and his behavior was foolish and should not be taken seriously.

Yet the young man's foolish behavior was risky. In the late Middle Ages and the early modern period, young men had been repeatedly warned about the dangers that came with adolescence. According to the humoral theory of the Roman physician Galen (131-201/216 A.D.), which was still being used in the seventeenth century, the human body had four bodily fluids or humors: phlegm, blood, yellow, and black bile. The doctrine was based on the theories of Hippocrates, who believed that each bodily fluid represented a certain temperament. Galen linked the fluids in the body to four basic qualities, namely hot, cold, moist and dry, which were associated with phases in a human life. For example, youth was represented by warmth and humidity, and had a sanguine temperament. Due to their temperament, young people had a strong desire for alcohol. In art, Venus and Bacchus were commonly used to represent young people. They symbolized unrestrained youth, unable to control body or mind. Johan van Beverwijck, a physician from Dordrecht, argued that when young people drank alcohol, their bodies became unbalanced. In his *Schat der Ongesontheyd* [Treasury of Ill-Health] (1644), he warned that drunkenness was a 'disease of the mind', a *razernye sonder Coortsche* (frenzy without fever), because alcohol disturbed the mind's reasoning. Alcohol and the hot-blooded nature of the youngsters were a bad combination. This argument was a recurring theme of many educational and moralistic treatises in the seventeenth century.

This fear was not unfounded. In the early seventeenth century, children who were unable to control their urges were a common topic in Dutch society. During a period of unprecedented wealth and material riches, pedagogues and moralists were especially concerned about the children of upper and middle-classes parents who had come into money in a short period of time and who spoiled their children. It was also a period when many consumer goods came onto the market for the first time, and parents bought everything for their children. Children with wealthy parents had become accustomed to getting everything their hearts desired and had trouble controlling their urges. Consequently, temperance was not a strong character trait of this generation of pampered young people, and this would have detrimental consequences.

5. Sex

If young people in the seventeenth century were unable to drink alcohol in moderation, then there was another evil lurking around the corner that was far worse for their well-being: namely, promiscuity. In the early modern period, getting drunk and having sex went hand in hand. According to the story that Gillis Quintijn told about the young people of Haarlem, foreigners were a bad influence on the Dutch, and Quintijn did not mince his words when it came to expounding the consequence of excessive drinking. Groups of single men such as students, sailors, and apprentices were the most likely to engage in licentious behavior. For them, going to brothels and picking up prostitutes was a way of life.

Whore-hopping

In his satire *Satyricon in corruptae iuventutis mores corruptos* (1631), which depicted the corruption of the students of Leiden, professor Jan Bodecher Benning described how a young student lost his virginity after visiting a brothel. As we saw in the previous chapter, in the same book Bodecher Benning had already castigated students for their excessive drinking. One thing led to another. Bodecher Benning had left too many clues in his descriptions, however, and the students picked up on them. The keen student recognized many details of the local brothels in Bodecher Benning's depiction, and figured out that the young professor must have visited them himself, and not only for field research. One student scathingly commented that the ethics professor should have consulted Kaspar Barthius' Latin translation of *La Celestina* (1624). The original was published in Latin (*Pornoboscodidascalus* [Teacher of the Brothel Master], 1499). The student viciously pointed out that if Bodecher Benning had read *La Celestina Benning*, it would have helped him with his jargon.

What Bodecher Benning failed to understand was that womanizing was an important part of academic life. It was just as relevant as attending classes. In the popular academic albums where students recorded their poems and witty expressions, a student named R. Schatton scribbled down a verse for another student about how arousing he found girls' bottoms. The thought alone helped the young man get out of bed, more than the ringing of 25 church bells:

> *Laat de lide seggen wat sie willen*
> *Ick seg dat twie wackere Juffren billen,*
> *Meer jonggesellen komen locken*
> *Als vijfentwintich kosters mit haer locken.*

> (Let people say what they want,
> I say that a nice woman's bottom,
> Awakens more young men
> Than the ringing of twenty-five church bells.)

The student who is seduced by a licentious woman was a popular theme in the seventeenth century. In *Academia* (1612), a handbook on academic life, Crispijn de Passe the Elder warned students about excessive drinking and vice. His son, Crispijn de Passe the Younger, was more explicit and went one step further. In his book *Spiegel der Alder-schoonste Cortisanen des Tijdts* [The Looking Glass of the Fairest Courtiers of These Times] (1631), he cautioned young men about the dangers of visiting brothels. The engraving on the title page depicts two young men in a house of ill repute. One sits in front of a fireplace with a pipe in his right hand. The other scans the portraits of beautiful girls that hang on the wall, as though he were ordering from a menu at a restaurant or swiping through profiles online. There are also two women present: one is a prostitute and the other is the madam of the brothel. The fireplace in the scene is a metaphor for the young men's burning desire, and the extra-long pipe held by the seated man symbolizes his sexual excitement.

Young men visiting a brothel, in: Crispijn de Passe, *Spieghel der alder-schoonste Cortisanen des tijdts* (1631) (Courtesy of the Special Collections, University of Amsterdam).

De Passe the Younger's book starts with a series of dialogues and illustrations of pretty young girls from France, Italy, England, Germany, Bohemia, and East Prussia. In an emblem, De Passe shows his young readers the naked bosom of 'La belle Zavonnare Courtisan'. In the early seventeenth century, it was highly unusual to display nudity, as the first books with titillating and erotic illustrations were published only after 1680. However, it was no coincidence that most of the women depicted were from abroad, for young men who went on a grand tour of Europe after graduating from the university were likely to visit these countries.

Students did not need to go abroad if they wanted sex, however; in early modern cities, temptation lurked around the corner of every street, literally and figuratively. In an industrial city such as Leiden in particular, many young women who worked in the linen industry supplemented their meager income with prostitution. Susanne Jans, for example, earned a living as a seamstress by day and as a prostitute by night. When she was arrested in

July 1626, she explained to the bailiff that she could not survive on the low wages that she earned in the textile industry. Near the buildings of the university in Leiden, certain neighborhoods that were notorious for street prostitution had earned suggestive names such as 'Joy Empire' and 'The Promised Land'. At a walking distance from their lecture halls, these addresses were well known to students, who could pursue their carnal urges there. Despite the fact that students in Leiden could easily indulge their sexual appetites, discretion was required. It was an unwritten rule that young men were obliged to be vigilant and not boast about their sexual conquests. What happened during the night was supposed to remain there.

The grand tour was considered the last stage of education for the young men of the urban elite. It was the last stop before adulthood, the phase of life when they would have to behave responsibly. Many young people were aware of this, and saw the grand tour as their last chance to pull out all the stops and sew their wild oats. The young men from the Dutch Republic considered Roman Catholic countries in the 'South', such as France and Italy, to be particularly sexually exciting. The women of these countries were known for their loose morals. It was no secret that young men on the grand tour pursued such forbidden fruit.

Once they violated the 'male code' and bragged about their sexual escapades, however, they not only risked harming their own reputation, but also the good name and honor of their family. Matthijs van Merwede failed to follow this golden rule of manhood. In 1647 the 22-year-old Van Merwede, who was the son of the Lord of Clootwyck, visited Rome. His parents hoped that he would gain inspiration and wisdom from admiring the beautiful paintings and sculptures in Italy. What his parents did not anticipate was that their son was also a womanizer. After his return from Rome, he published two volumes of poetry, *Uyt-heemsen oorlog ofte Roomse min-triumfen* [Foreign War, or Roman Love Conquests] (1651), and *Geestelyke minnevlamme* [Spiritual Love Affairs] (1653), in which he blabbed in detail about his sexual escapades.

In juicy detail, he revealed how he had bedded many young Italian women. In the introduction he stated that it had never been his intention to marry a foreign woman, merely use them 'recreationally'. His poetry, which referred to *verwaende pop* (prostitutes) and *heeten kerkgang* (syphilis), left little for the imagination. Van Merwede, who was known for his blue eyes and blond hair, was without a doubt a popular young man among the dark-haired Italian women. The parents of his last romantic conquest had had to send their daughter to a convent, because her reputation had been ruined by Van Merwede's sexual relations with her. She would never be able to find a marriage partner after her fling with the Dutchman.

Van Merwede turned seducing young girls into a true art form. His preference for 'the younger the better' was probably in line with the advice that he received from his physician, who may well have told him to sleep with virgins because that would reduce his chance of getting syphilis – which is probably why he was later accused of deflowering a 12-year-old girl. When his first book was published, it provoked a wave of criticism. Critics thought that Van Merwede had gone to too far and overstepped the boundaries of morality. In no time, Van Merwede became a *persona non-grata*. He had to flee his home in The Hague, and booksellers were fined 25 guilders if they had a copy of his book in stock. Even Jacob Cats, the country's most moderate moralist, condemned the book because of its scandalous content, and stated that Van Merwede had flaunted his promiscuous behavior. In other words, Van Merwede had clearly broken the 'gentlemen's agreement' whereby young men were supposed to be discrete and modest about their sexual escapades.

Public courting

The most popular meeting place for young men and women was at the annual *kermis* or fair. This was the yearly event where young people from all walks of life gathered and socialized.

Originally, the kermis had been an annual mass to celebrate the church. Each village and town hosted its own kermis, and specific social groups would attend the kermis on specific days. On Thursdays for example, the kermis at The Hague was attended by the middle classes, the elite, and members of the stadholder's court. The upper classes avoided visiting the kermis on Tuesdays and Wednesdays, when the horse and cheese markets were held. On those days, famers and peasants flocked to the kermis. The kermis was a combination of annual market and entertainment. There was a potpourri of stalls selling cheese and other foods. There were also exotic caged animals, humans with deformities, and entertainers ranging from musicians, tightrope walkers, acrobats and magicians to charlatans who sold special remedies for every imaginable human ailment.

For local youngsters, the annual kermis was nothing short of a meat market where young men and women would strut and compete for the attention of the opposite sex. The young ladies' attempts to gain the affections of popular young men sometimes degenerated into scratching and hair-pulling. Besides the cat-fights, there was a lot of drinking, which heightened the sexual tension. According to one eyewitness, one kermis in Zeeland was transformed into a veritable Sodom and Gomorrah, with prostitution and other immoral behavior. For the impoverished laborers working in Leiden's textile industry, the kermis was the only form of recreation in their dreary lives, and often the only place where unmarried workers could meet and pick up sexual partners.

In the countryside there was another sexual outlet for young people, known as 'night-walking'. On the island of Texel, where the tradition was known as *kweesten*, a young woman would leave her bedroom window open at night. This was not only for fresh air, but also to draw the attention of her lover, so that during the night he could climb in and spend the night with her. Rural parents were not as open-minded and liberal as this might suggest, however. The young man was supposed sleep on top of the blankets, and not next to the girl underneath. The young couple were allowed to lie side by side in bed, fondle and kiss each other. Although we have no records of what took place, most likely their activities included everything from heavy petting to mutual masturbation, but absolutely no coital penetration. There were cases when a young man wanted to go all the way and risked the honor of the girl. Then she would alarm her parents and neighborhood by banging on a kettle that was next to her bed. By doing so, she protected her honor, which was especially important if she hoped to have any other prospective husband. If she was deflowered or became pregnant, her reputation would be permanently damaged. When a young man proved reliable after a few years of *kweesten*, he was considered a suitable marriage partner.

Puberty in the Golden Age

In 1642, when Mary Stuart of England married the Dutch Prince Willem II, she was only ten and a half years old. Her marriage to the son of the Dutch stadholder, Frederik Hendrik, was considered a good match from a political and economic standpoint. Both families benefited from the prearranged union. The House of Orange became aligned with the English monarchy and the Stuarts married into the family that held the highest office in the richest country in Europe at that time. It was a win-win situation for both families. However, Mary and her 16-year-old prince were not permitted or expected to have intercourse yet. For Mary it was physically impossible, in any case. At the stadholder's court in The Hague, she was referred to as Willem's 'child-bride'. It is unlikely that Willem was ready for intercourse, either, and the couple had to wait a few years. In 1646, when Mary was 15 years old and Willem was 20, they finally consummated their marriage.

In the Dutch Golden Age, parents and moralists became concerned about their children's sexuality at a much later stage than parents nowadays. Today, boys start growing facial and pubic hair around the age of twelve, and girls have their first menstruation as young ten or eleven years old. Every decade, the age at which puberty starts is getting earlier. In 1860, girls had their first menstruation, on average, when they were 16.6 years old. Since then, this age has gradually become younger. In 1920 it was 14.6 years old, in 1950 13.1 years old, and in 1980 the first menstruation came at 12.5 years, on average. There has been a similar development for boys, and they have their first ejaculation and become sexually mature at a younger age.

Rembrandt, the late bloomer

One of the best-known characters of the early seventeenth century is a miller's son from Leiden named Rembrandt van Rijn. In an early self-portrait from 1629, the painter depicted himself with a messy mop of hair, and without a trace of a beard or five o'clock shadow on his chin. The 23-year-old painter had a baby face as smooth as milk. In the same year, Rembrandt met Constantijn Huygens. The statesman mentioned in his diary that the young painter *still* had no beard growth. This comment alluded to a previous encounter with Rembrandt. Two years earlier, Huygens had met Rembrandt and the 20-year-old Jan Lievens, with whom he shared a studio. He described them both as being beardless. In their physical appearance and their features, Huygens considered them boys rather than men.

Later, in 1629, Rembrandt painted another self-portrait of himself. This time he had a downy mustache and some whiskers on his chin, but he still did not have the beard of a grown man. It was not unlikely that Rembrandt wanted to portray himself on canvas looking more mature and 'manlike'. Two years later, when he was 25 years old, the painter looked more mature. By then, he had a full mustache with a curl in it, although he still did not have the full beard of a grown man. In the seventeenth century, facial hair was important for young men. It was the only physical feature that showed others that they had matured into a man. Growing a beard also signified that they could reproduce.

There are no sources from the early modern period that tell us when boys first became sexually mature. However, one can assume that it was at an older age than in today's affluent society. According to physiologists, the early sexual development of young people in recent decades has mainly been due to the increase of fat in the body. The age of sexual maturation can be delayed by external factors such as hunger, poverty, war, and political and social unrest. A lifestyle with a balanced diet and minimal stress accelerates the age of sexual maturity. The economic welfare and prosperity of the twentieth century thus played a decisive role. In the seventeenth century, conditions were not always stable. Early modern society was plagued by frequent crop failures, famine, pestilence, war, and political and social unrest. At this time, the wealthy Dutch Republic was an exception in northern Europe. The country escaped the recurrent famines and epidemics. However, its population was affected by the social unrest and conflict caused by the Reformation and the Eighty Years' War, and diseases such as the plague and syphilis posed a threat to public health. Many residents came from areas in Europe where they had experienced war, disease, stress, and trauma, which according to some modern biologists can be imprinted in human DNA and passed down to future generations.

There was also a difference in the age of sexual maturity between the economic and social classes. Youngsters from the upper classes did not suffer from hunger and famine, and were more likely to mature sexually earlier than their peers from poorer classes, who did not always have a balanced and stable diet. Differences in physical growth between the classes remained until the early twentieth century, and can be seen in school photos of pupils who were all the same age, but some were amazingly tall while others were significantly shorter. Today, the age of sexual maturity in the Netherlands and most Western countries is more or less the same for all children regardless of their social and economic background. Young men in the seventeenth century probably had their first ejaculation around their sixteenth or seventeenth year. It is also unlikely that there were many teen fathers in the seventeenth century. Although little can be gleaned from letters and diaries, baptism, marriage and burial records do reveal that unmarried young men were sexually active. There were many 'shot-gun weddings', where couples were forced to marry because the woman had become pregnant. Yet this group was still small compared to the number of women who gave birth to their first children nine or more months after they married. Nevertheless, young people sought channels for their sexual urges.

Masturbation

The easiest way for young people to satisfy their sexual urges was masturbation. Seventeenth-century primary sources leave us in the dark on this subject, largely due to the division between the public and private spheres. What happened in public received attention and was recorded. Masturbation in general, was an activity that took place behind closed doors. Sometimes it did not: in 1613, Harmen Jansz from Delft dropped his trousers and exposed himself in front of the church building in broad daylight. The women who were leaving the church at that moment were given a front row seat of him fondling his genitals. This act of exhibitionism was not tolerated and was considered a felony. But functional nudity such as swimming in the buff was accepted by seventeenth-century society. In the cities of the Dutch Republic, men easily stripped naked and jumped in the water without any sense of shame or prudishness.

In the Dutch Republic during the seventeenth century, pedagogues and moralists never wrote a word about masturbation in their treatises. Neither was it mentioned in the diary of Constantijn Huygens, who blabbed about the sexual intrigues of the nobility at the English court and that of the stadholder in The Hague – despite being surrounded by a wide range of sexual deviations ranging from whore-hopping, homosexuality and lesbianism to cross-dressing. Almost every taste on the sexual palette was noted, with the exception of masturbation.

The only intimate glimpse we have into the sex life of an adult male in the seventeenth-century Dutch Republic is from the diary of the Frisian stadholder Willem Frederik. He proudly noted how he was able to control his lust every time he saw a beautiful woman. Instead of following his 'John Thomas', he would masturbate at night thinking of her. For him, there was no shame involved. The Frisian stadholder thought jerking off was a healthier solution than getting the clap. This was a common attitude until the eighteenth century, when 'shame' became associated with masturbation. In the seventeenth century, autoeroticism was still considered one of the most natural bodily urges, as long as it was done privately. It was neither condemned nor considered an immoral act. Moreover, it was considered a practical solution to a man's natural urges.

By the eighteenth century, the age of innocence had officially ended. In the Dutch Republic, masturbation as a sexual outlet became morally laden with guilt and shame after 1730, following the translation into Dutch of the English book *Onania; or the Heinous Sin of Self-Pollution, and All Its Frightful Consequences* (1730). The anonymous author and translator admonished young people of both sexes for participating in masturbation, claiming it caused a wide variety of medical conditions, ranging from back problems to early blindness. The reader was maliciously led to believe that their autoeroticism, which was a widespread practice, was in fact 'self-pollution' and a profanity that would unleash a long list of medical ailments. *Onania* would not have had such a sustained impact on eighteenth-century Western society if it had not been published in an era with a booming trade in books and quackery medicine.

The book had a long-term impact on the mentality of the eighteenth-century. Within a few years of the publishing of the first edition, it became a huge success. The publisher used advertisements in newspapers to promote sales of the book.

In newspapers throughout the country, ads were placed and the work was discussed in other books. Within a short period, masturbation became a social issue and topic of public debate. It was one of Europe's first media hypes. Affordable books had become a new mass media and *Onania* became a commercial bestseller, with the result that masturbation became a popular topic.

The reason why *Onania* became a bestseller was simple. The publisher's marketing techniques were similar to those used in TV commercials that advertise pharmaceutical products, by asking leading questions such as 'Do you ever feel tired?' The author of the *Onania* described how a masturbator suffered from fatigue, back pain, and other ailments. In the eighteenth century, it was no wonder that readers should suffer from such symptoms. In the early years of the Industrial Revolution, the average man worked long hours and did hard physical labor. People slept on poor mattresses, and exhaustion and back pain were commonplace.

As with many media hypes, there were numerous victims. In the eighteenth and nineteenth centuries, people became ashamed of self-arousal. Initially, masturbation became associated with guilt in the public psyche. According to a study on prostitution in the early modern period, before 1750, arrested prostitutes' accounts of the tricks they performed on their clients never made mention of masturbation. By the late eighteenth century, Amsterdam's bailiff was frequently using the term 'vergaande vuyligheden' or extreme vulgarities, to refer to this practice. In 1771, after a prostitute was arrested in the woods outside The Hague, she confessed that a man had asked her to jerk him off, which at first she had refused to do because she thought it 'unnatural'.

Masturbation also became associated with sin because of the story of Genesis in the Old Testament. According to the story, Onan was obliged to marry Tamar, the widow of his elder brother, which was known as levirate marriage. Onan had to procreate in his deceased brother's name, but not beget offspring in his own.

However, Onan failed to produce children because 'he spilled his seed on the ground' and the Lord struck him dead. It is unclear whether Onan masturbated or practiced *coitus interruptus*, as onanism later became known in Roman Catholic moral theology.

Not only did *Onania* associate masturbation with guilt, shame, and self-pollution, more importantly, it became associated with sodomy. Masturbation was a private vice committed in secrecy, as was erotic male friendship. It is probably no coincidence that *Onania* was translated into Dutch and published in 1730 at the height of the first wave of sodomite persecutions in the Dutch Republic (1730-1732), when homosexual men were arrested, interrogated, and executed.

Sodomy

Sodomy was a far graver matter than masturbation for young men. According to early modern usage, the term sodomy referred to a wide range of sexual deviations, from having sex with animals (bestiality), having oral and anal sex, and fornicating with Jews, to buggering other men. The latter became the eventual meaning of the term. German reformers accused the pope and the cardinals in Rome of being sodomites. Many of the reigning popes in the sixteenth century were suspected of having sexual relations with the younger men at their court. The pope and 'his sodomitical court' became a stock phrase in Protestant treatises, but many authors' use of the word was vague, and sodomy remained more or less a term of sexual innuendo.

During the Renaissance in Italy, sodomy as we understand it today was regularly practiced. In Florence, it was almost a normal phenomenon for young men to have sexual relations with older men before they married. This usage resembled the Ancient Greek pattern of an active mature man engaging in relations with a passive youth. Italian women usually married when they were teenagers, but young men sometimes had to wait until they were 30 years old. A man had to hold off for ten to fifteen years before he could satisfy his sexual urges. Sex with an older man was a practical solution, a sexual outlet during the long wait for the conjugal bed. Once young men married, their same-sex encounters ended. In the northern Italian republics, homosexual relations between unmarried men were common.

But the practice was different in the rest of Europe, especially in the northwestern countries of the Continent. According to judicial sources, there is little evidence that sodomy and homosexual relationships occurred in the Republic on the same scale as in northern Italy. There were a few reported cases of sexual acts between a younger and an older man. Three of the six reported cases of sodomy in Middleburg between 1545 and 1655 involved adult men who were forty and older and young men who were still minors. In the early modern period, it was common practice for people to share a bed with more than one person, usually of the same sex. In some cases, it was considered a social honor for an apprentice to sleep in the same bed as his master or pedagogue.

On the downside, there were also older men who took advantage of the situation. In 1596, there were rumors in the town of Arnhem that a teacher had sexually abused his students, and in 1633 it was suggested that a master had sexually abused his apprentice. In 1620, the boatman Jan Symons Bossuyt of Leiden was burned at the stake in Delft after he was found guilty of raping several *jonggezellen* or youths. Most cases of sodomy were brought to light after a young man turned down the sexual advances of an older man. The young men in question were not prosecuted because they were minors, but the older men were sentenced. In other all-male environments, such as universities and aboard ships, sexual relations between men took place in secret. Once these acts were discovered, however, the men involved were convicted. While on board a VOC ship sailing to the Far East, two adolescent boys (one was 11 years old and other 16) were caught masturbating together with a soldier. The three were tied together, thrown overboard, and left to drown in the open sea. There was an enormous taboo around same-sex relations.

We have to assume that most homosexual acts in the early seventeenth century went undetected. Homosexuality only became a problem when one of the boys or men did not consent. Fooling around and mutual masturbation took place in various forms and guises. Men could easily find willing sex partners in green and wooded areas. At night, these were ideal cruising spots for men not only to pick up prostitutes, but also to have sexual encounters with other men in the bushes and woods. Regardless of their sexual orientation, handsome young men knew they could attract the attention of older men. At the beginning of the eighteenth century, for example, one 33-year-old man described how easy it had been to earn a lot of money when he was 16 by selling sexual favors, and how difficult it had become once he grew older.

Sex education

We do not know for certain how young people in the seventeenth century learned about sex. Personal documents such as letters and diaries from this period reveal little about how young people were introduced to the birds and the bees. Not a word is uttered about sex in educational and moralistic books, simply because moralists were afraid they would induce immoral thoughts in young people (even if they were giving them a warning). Youngsters probably found out what happened on the wedding night from older brothers, parents, uncles, other family members, or even friends and neighbors. The topic was certainly not considered inappropriate. People talked a lot about sex. It was a popular topic of discussion in the streets, in taverns, and in the cafes frequented by young people. Most likely innuendos about sex were relayed to children and young people through language, humor, and even gestures. One common gesture was to hold the thumb between the index and middle fingers. This was the precursor to holding up the middle finger, and meant the same as: 'fuck you'.

In the early modern period, youngsters did not need to know any details in addition to the sexual act itself; at least, not how conception worked. From an early age, children and adolescents most have known how babies were made. Some teenagers felt comfortable and at ease with their naked bodies, and frequented bathhouses and were not embarrassed by nudity. They slept naked, often with several people in the same bed, and sometimes even with the opposite sex. In addition, people in the early seventeenth century were used to physical contact. They stroked, caressed, hugged, and kissed each other more easily than people in the West do today. In this regard, the Dutch of the seventeenth century resembled southern Europeans. In the course of the seventeenth and eighteenth century, this open attitude towards sexuality underwent a drastic change, as society became more concerned with controlling carnal urges. People had to learn to control and hide their physical and sexual desires.

At the beginning of the seventeenth century, however, there was still an open attitude towards sex. Despite their carnal urges, young men between the ages of 14 and 21 were advised to wait before having sex. In *Schat der Gezondheyt* [Treasury of Health] (1636) the physician Johan van Beverwijck argued that the act would only weaken the young body. If young men had sex before they were ready, their bodies would become cold, dry, and numb. This would upset the balance of their young bodies and have an effect on them for the rest of their lives.

Beverwijck's old friend Jacob Cats approached the topic of sex for young people from a different perspective. In his book *Spiegel vande Oude en Nieuwe Tijdt* [Mirror of the Old and New Times] (1632), Cats devoted in an entire chapter to the issue of sex. It was the first book in the seventeenth century to address the sexuality of young people. When it was first published in 1632, Cats was already a celebrated author. Previously, he had been the national advocate or prime minister of the Dutch Republic – the most important office in the country. After he retired, he started writing moralistic books and earned much fame as a writer, just like a retired prime minister or president of a country does after retiring from office today. However, Cats' books were especially known for their moralistic bent. He earned the nickname 'Father Cats' because his advice crossed all social, economic, and religious boundaries, and was not aimed at one specific group. Because his advice was non-denominational, his books were popular throughout Dutch society.

In *Spiegel*, Cats revealed how much he understood of human psychology and the sexual frustrations and problems experienced by young men. In the first chapter, *'Eerlijcke Vrijage'* [Earnest Courtship], he explained how important it was for a young man to find a suitable marriage partner. Cats made a clear distinction between 'fooling around' with women and seriously looking for the right woman and life partner. Cats empathized with his young readers and advised them to have patience, stressing that he knew how difficult that was. In retrospect, Cats understood all too well what it felt like to lose patience and submit to one's carnal urges. When he was a student, Cats feared that his housemaid was pregnant with his child. It turned out to be a false alarm and that someone else was the father. Nevertheless, Cats had the scare of his life.

In another part of *Spiegel*, Cats explains what happens to a young man who is not patient and cannot curb his sexual desires. Under the title 'Hoeren, ende ongemacken van de selve herkomende' [Whores and the Discomforts that Originate from Them], Cats lists the diseases that young men can catch when they go to prostitutes. This message was reinforced by an illustration titled *Een rupse op een kool, een hoer in huys* [A Caterpillar on a Cabbage is like a Whore in a House]. The illustration depicts an elderly man walking next to a young man in a vegetable garden. He is pointing to a head of cabbage that has been half-eaten by caterpillars. The scene is a metaphor: the cabbage swarming with caterpillars is like a young man who longs to have sex with women. Once a young man gets started, he will not be able to control his urges and will want more.

However, there was an even more important message. The cabbage was also a metaphor for the dangers that faced young men,

A word of advice from 'Father Cats' about visiting prostitutes: *Een rupse op een kool, en een hoer in het huis* [A caterpillar on a head of cabbage is like a whore in a house]. In: Jacob Cats, *Spiegel van de Oude ende Nieuwe Tijdt* (1632) (Courtesy of the Special Collections, University of Amsterdam).

namely becoming contaminated with syphilis. The half-eaten cabbage symbolized the pockmarked face of a young man who suffered from this disease. Besides having blemished genitals, it was common knowledge that victims of syphilis could easily be recognized in public from their scarred faces, perforated noses, baldness, missing teeth, and paralyzed legs. Not only could the physical appearance be horrifying in its advanced stages, but also having the disease or being related to someone who did would ruin the reputation of a young person. The social stigma and social implications of syphilis in the early modern period were similar to those ascribed to HIV-AIDS in the 1980s.

In another example, Cats did not resort to a metaphor to express the dangers to a young man's health if he visited prostitutes. In the chapter 'Hoeren en Slimme Streken van de selve' [Whores and Clever Tricks of the Same], an illustration portrays an attractive woman offering a young man a pan of burning coals. The burning coals symbolize the young man's inflamed sexual desire. In the text, Cats explains that although a woman might be offering a *geschenk* (gift), the young man might end up with something he does not want: *'U kool doet als haer vrouw, sy brand, of sy besmet'* [Your coal is just like a woman, she burns or she infects]. In other words, by giving in to his carnal desires, the young man is likely to become burned or infected.

Cats purposely warned young men about the dangers of syphilis. In the early modern period, it was single young men (pupils, students, sailors, and soldiers) who suffered the most from syphilis. Venereal diseases were the most dreaded diseases of the era, and cut down young people in the prime of life. They were a vital group in society. In addition, they were the group that traveled the most and could easily spread the disease.

Venereal diseases

In the early modern period, syphilis was a common disease for soldiers. Although we do not have any statistics on how rampant venereal disease was in the early modern period, in the eighteenth century the French philosopher Voltaire estimated that approximately two-thirds of soldiers were infected with syphilis. Based on this, soldiers in the Eighty-Years War were more likely to be a victim of syphilis than to suffer from a gunshot or cannon wound.

One way of being cured of the dreaded disease was to be admitted to a hospital where a *pokmeester*, or pox healer, administered a laxative, followed by daily steam baths and drinking an extract made from Guajak wood, a tree native to South America. In the Dutch Republic, people infected with syphilis were often removed from densely populated city centers and relocated to facilities on the outskirts of cities and towns, known as *pesthui-zen* or 'pestilent homes', where syphilis patients were treated together with the victims of smallpox. As the sufferers of both diseases were treated together in the same facilities, it is difficult to determine how widespread syphilis was in the Republic.

Cats repeatedly warned how addictive visiting prostitutes could be for young men. His emblem, *De katte die veel snoepen wilt, wort licht eens op de neus geknilt* [The cats that eats (=wom-anizes) too much, will be caught by the nose], was a direct warning to young men about the risk of contracting syphilis when they had sex with prostitutes. The word 'nose' reminded young men about the perforated nose that syphilis victims had when the disease was at an advanced stage. In the text, Cats tells an anecdote about a young man who returns from a voyage at sea. Upon arrival, nobody can recognize him. He had lost his hair, his nose is flat, his lips have no color, his eyes are full of tears, his teeth have fallen out, and he has bad breath. Moreover, his hands are covered with blue pockmarks and he cannot move his legs. The young man contemplates the fact that his youth has vanished and that he is to blame for his sickness (syphilis).

In another example, Cats warns young men how tempting it is to fall for an easy woman, and in yet another, he shows an image of an attractive woman strolling around late at night, holding a lantern. She is walking in a remote area outside the city where young men often seek easy women. In the accompanying text, Cats explains to his male readers how easy it is to fall for the beauty of a young woman. She has a pretty face with pink cheeks and beautiful hair; she is sociable and fun. But Cats quickly points out that she is not the right woman for this young man to marry. She is not a woman who commits to one man. She is a woman with no shame; she is a whore, and her beauty is tarnished. The message of both the text and the image was clear to seventeenth-century readers. The woman that a young man encounters at night will be a woman of poor virtue. Good girls were already at home, sleeping.

Cats had what we would nowadays call 'emotional intelligence'. He could easily empathize with young readers and understood how they felt. This was also evident in another illustrated warning, where a woman is shown sitting in a young man's lap, caressing his face. The young man's body language betrays his lust for the young woman. The message of the scene is reinforced by the presence of the roaring flames in the fireplace. The accompanying text reads:

Ick was eens gestreelt, gekust
en ick swom in volle lust,
Want men boodt my hooger gunst...
Alsser oyt een echte man
Van sijn wijf geworden kan

(I was once caressed and kissed
And I was burning with lust,
Because I was offered ... greater favors,
than any man could
ever get from his own woman.)

Cats' message is that sexual desire is fleeting. After a young man has been to bed with a whore, the fun is over. Once he is out of money, he will be tossed out on the street and replaced by the next paying customer. Cats emphasized that the worst thing was how young men would feel afterwards:

Vrienden, wat ick bidden magh
Wort toch wijs uyt mijn beklagh,
Let niet op de geyle lust,
Want haer vyer (vuur) is haest geblust,
Maer denck om het ongeval
Dat vry langer dueren sal.

(Friends, how I do pray
Please listen to my complaint
Don't yield to your horniness
It will only be quenching
Think of the mishap
and how its effects will last longer than your lust.)

In this poem, Cats is again referring to syphilis. After reading Cats, many a young man must have been less eager to go to prostitutes and, moreover, petrified of syphilis. Cats hoped that his young readers would curb their sexual urges and opt for self-restraint. After all, in the early modern period self-restraint was the safest way of staying physically and morally healthy until marriage. In theory, the conjugal bed, was a safe haven where a young man could go wild and have as much sex as possible, without the risk of contracting venereal diseases. Cats advised young men to take finding a marriage partner seriously. In his earlier mentioned work *Houwelijck* [Marriage] (1625), Cats had already warned young men with his adage *Niemand koopt edelstenen bij nacht, zoek dus geen meisje bij kaarslicht* (Nobody buys jewels at night, so don't go looking for a girl by candlelight). The message was both clear and practical.

With this adage, Cats was revealing a change in attitudes to sex and courting in the seventeenth century. The young men of the early seventeenth century were used to looking for marriage partners in the evening and at night; this had been the custom of young people from the countryside, who had moved to the cities. However, a new trend was underway: the modern youth was one who learned to control his desire. That was Cats' underlying message.

Cats also had advice for young unmarried women. He recognized the dangers to which they were exposed if they went to bed with a man before they were married. If she became pregnant, the young woman would be stuck with the child, while the young man in question had no obligations. In *Spiegel* [Mirror], Cats relayed this message to young women with an illustration depicting a young woman walking next to a pig wearing a golden earring in its nose. In the accompanying text, Cats and the young woman are engaged in dialogue. Cats points out to the young woman that the golden earring belongs in the ear of a young virgin bride, instead of in the nose of the pig. During their dialogue, a prostitute interrupts, adding that young women should not throw the gold of their youth in the muck; in other words, a young woman should not squander her virginity before she is married.

Unmarried women who had sex with men were taking great risks. There were no reliable methods of birth control, and terminating an unwanted pregnancy was dangerous, to say the least. Women secretly shared all kinds of recipes for ending a pregnancy, ranging from various herbs to oral remedies. Wearing tight clothes or even self-injury were also known means to induce a miscarriage. Herbs were the most widely used method, but the ultimate means of birth control was simply not to go to bed with a man.

That was the theory. In reality, it was a different story. For the young men from the elite class who had to wait until they were in their late twenties or early thirties before they could marry and have sexual intercourse, abstaining from sex was almost impossible. The period between becoming sexually mature and the age for marriage could last ten years, sometimes even longer. Not all young men could remain chaste and wait until marriage.

For students in the early seventeenth century, society often turned a blind eye to their sexual horsing around. That was certainly the case for students who came from another village or town. In a university town, there were few or no social controls on young men. In Leiden, for instance, there were many romantic relationships between students and lower-class women. According to the academic court, students made numerous promises of marriage to girls from Leiden. It was not uncommon for a woman to have sex with a young man if he promised to marry her. However, a student's parents would never have allowed him to marry a girl from the working class. Too often, these young men never married such girls.

In April 1625, Neeltje Jorisdochter filed a complaint with Leiden's academic court against Jacob Porret, a 29-year-old medical student. Jorisdochter demanded that Porret marry her daughter Marijtje. If he did not, Porret would have to pay 1,100 guilders for violating her daughter's honor. This amount also included the cost of the midwife and the food for her daughter's baby.

In her complaint, Jorisdochter emphasized that the child bore Porret's name. However, Porret had no intention of ever marrying Marijtje, and the academic court refused her claim. Moreover, the academic court also considered the requested amount to be too high, and made Porret pay only 200 guilders for 'deflowering' the woman. Porret did have to pay for the midwife, however, and 60 guilders a year in child support.

A similar case was brought to the academic court in Groningen. Johannes Goldbach had promised to marry Anneken Babelers. On 22 December 1632, the couple filed a license to marry, which meant that they were required to marry within four to six weeks. In the meantime, however, Goldbach got cold feet and fled Groningen. The student was still young, only 20 years old, and far from home. His father was a well-respected Lutheran preacher in Ratingen, in the Duchy of Berg in Germany. Goldbach's future bride, on the other hand, had been previously married and was a widow. The pressure to get married probably came from Anneken, who was eager to find a husband. Another factor that probably played a role was the fact that Anneken had agreed to sleep with Johannes only under the condition that he would marry her. It was a condition that Johannes had all too willingly accepted.

For Anneken Babelers, the public shame must have been great. In March 1633 she filed a complaint with the academic senate of the University of Groningen. Babelers argued that the couple had had sexual relations and she demanded that Goldbach return to Groningen. He had to justify himself for breaching his promise of marriage. In the meantime, Babelers requested the senate treat her as a widow, and that she would henceforth only dress in black, the color of mourning. In the next two and half months, letters were exchanged between the university senate and Johannes' father. The entire situation must have been a disgrace for the Goldbach family; the incident threatened to drag the good reputation of Reverend Goldbach through the mud. It would only be a matter of time before the news of Anneken Babelers and the Reverend's son reached the Duchy of Berg. To prevent the affair from turning into a public scandal, Reverend Goldbach must have convinced (or threatened) his son to marry the widow. Shortly thereafter, Anneken Babelers traveled to Ratingen, where she was married to the minister's son.

It ended well. But if the incident had escalated, Johannes Goldbach would not have been the only one to pay the price. It could have become a scandal that engulfed the entire Goldbach family. Anneken Babelers' reputation would have also been ruined, and she would not have been able to find a suitable marriage partner. The University of Groningen's senate would also have found itself in an awkward position. The academic body was supposed to protect the interests of its students. An incident such as this one reflected badly on the university, and would have cost the university students in future. The senate was aware of what had happened and shortly thereafter took action to prevent further incidents. The university introduced a new regulation stating that all student requests for marriage had to be first approved by the university.

Thus besides internal control of one's sexuality, as advocated by Cats, now there was also an external regulator, namely the university. These two control mechanisms were intended to discipline the sexuality of young people in the early seventeenth century and put youngsters on the right track. This did not imply, however, that parents no longer needed to worry about their young adult offspring. On the contrary, the youngsters of the early seventeenth century had too much leisure time on their hands, and that posed an even greater threat.

6.   Drugs

In August 1622, the young guests that attended the wedding party of Manuel Colyn and Catharina Cloppenburgh would have been smokers; or at the least, they would have known the lyrics to the song 'Lof van de toback' [In Praise of Tobacco], written by Jan Jansz Starter. The lyrics describe how wonderful it is to take a puff of tobacco. In another poem in his bestselling songbook *Friesche Lust-Hof* [Frisian Paradise] (1621), which he published a year earlier, Starter included a snappy verse about how Jupiter encouraged the other gods to start smoking tobacco. In the poem, Jupiter enjoys sipping a beer and smoking from his pipe. These were two bad habits that went hand in hand. At weddings and garden parties, young people amused themselves by reciting poems and singing songs. In the early seventeenth century, Starter's was one of the most popular songbooks of the period. His lyrics were certainly not moralistic and they had a salacious undertone. When *Friesche Lust-hof* was first published, Starter was only 27 years old, not much older than the young people for whom he wrote. His poems and lyrics were the ultimate form of entertainment. The topics that he wrote about were popular; and in the 1620s, smoking tobacco was the latest fad among the young.

A new trend

The new fashion among the young also became a new subject and attribute for artists. In his painting *The Merry Company* (circa 1620-1622), Willem Buytewech portrayed three young men and a woman sitting around a table with a tobacco pipe lying in the middle. The 'merry company' genre was very popular in the early seventeenth century. Such paintings often portrayed wealthy young men dressed in the latest fashions, playing cards, drinking wine, and flirting with pretty girls. As a new symbol of all the vanities of life, painters in the early seventeenth century added a tobacco pipe to the scene. Buytewech's *Merry Company* was the epitome of *la dolce vita* of modern young people.

The characters portrayed were the rich children of foreign-born merchants who had become wealthy in the Dutch Republic and spoiled their offspring with worldly goods. The youngsters were happy-go-lucky and carefree, and had far too much leisure time on their hands. Although the genre of the merry company was already established and was similar to the theme of the Prodigal Son, contemporaries of Buytewech, including Dirck Hals (the brother of Frans Hals) and Pieter Codde, were fascinated by the topic. It was also popular among art-lovers and those who purchased paintings. The painters modernized the theme of the Prodigal Son by adding the latest vice to the portrait, namely smoking. Pieter Codde's portrait of a young student at his desk, for example, depicts him with a pipe in his hand.

Adriaen Brouwer

The Flemish painter Adriaen Brouwer (1606-1638) was also fascinated by the new trend. Brouwer, who worked in Amsterdam and Haarlem, enjoyed painting rowdy peasant scenes, usually in taverns. Most of the time his subjects were peasants and social outcasts who were playing cards, drinking, and smoking tobacco. Brouwer was a bohemian long before the term was invented, and rebelled against the norms and conventions of his time.

In his group portrait *The Smokers* (1636), Brouwer placed himself in the middle. If the painting had been a photo, Brouwer would be looking right into the lens of the camera. Brouwer has mischievous eyes and puckered lips, and is exhaling rings of smoke. The men next to him are his friends and fellow painters, Jan Davidsz de Heem and Jan Koessiers. Like Brouwer, they are also enjoying their tobacco. However, when we take a closer look, we notice their gaze is not at the camera, like Brouwer's. They seem to be staring at the ceiling, as if in a deep trance. Upon closer examination, Brouwer's smokers do not seem to be puffing on their pipes, but rather sucking on them. Most likely, pipes did not only contain tobacco. According to Brouwer's biographer, the painter and his friends were probably smoking cannabis or hemp.

It is difficult to say how widespread smoking hemp was in the early seventeenth century. This herbaceous fiber was an important crop in the Republic. It was mainly cultivated in the region between Gouda, Utrecht, and Dordrecht, which was the largest supplier of hemp. The plant was used by the VOC to make cables and ropes. Together with tar, it was used as a sealer to waterproof the underside of boats. In the early seventeenth century, it was already known that cannabis had an effect on humans. However, not everyone experienced it as a positive one. After begging was outlawed in Amsterdam in 1613, offenders were punished and forced to work in the house of corrections, where they processed hemp. It was generally known that inmates became sedated after working many hours with the cannabis.

In the Republic, everything that was mixed with alcohol or tobacco and had a hallucinogenic effect was called *belladonna,* meaning 'beautiful woman' in Italian. The term had its origins in the Po Valley of Italy, where hemp was grown. The Italians who worked in the fields or in the factories where the hemp was manufactured into other products knew that the plant had a narcotic effect. During the Renaissance, women placed a few drops of the hemp juice in their eyes. It made their pupils larger, making their eyes appear darker and shinier. Although these women could not see very well, this was a price they were willing to pay to be beautiful.

Belladonna

After people started using tobacco in the early seventeenth century, many medicinal herbs such as *atropa belladonna* and *datura stramonium* were added to tobacco and beer. They were also called 'belladonna', because they had the same mind-altering effects as cannabis. These mixtures were strictly forbidden by the Church and were probably only consumed in special clandestine pubs. In the seventeenth century, tobacco had a heavier quality than the tobacco that is found in cigarettes today. It resembled the loose tobacco that can be purchased for rolling one's own cigarettes and was smoked in special pipes made of clay. According to a description by the sixteenth-century physician and botanist Rembert Dodoens, tobacco had a calming effect on people.

In a seventeenth-century reprint of his *Cruydt-Boeck* [Book of Herbs] (1554), Dodoens explained to readers that smoking tobacco 'relieved the body of its pain and grief'. In this aspect, it resembled cannabis. But then he added, tobacco 'also alleviated hunger and thirst,' which is not the effect of hemp. After all, one of the main side-effects of smoking cannabis is that it increases the appetite and makes people hungry. Dodoens declared that tobacco makes smokers happy, as if they had drunk wine, and ultimately makes them tired, 'as if they have taken opium'.

The strong and penetrating odor of tobacco made some people unwell. In the beginning, tobacco was only smoked in special smoking rooms or parlors that were known as 'tobacco houses'. They must have resembled today's smokers' clubs, where members are allowed to smoke a cigarette with the purchase of their beverage. In the beginning smoking was a social habit, similar to the consumption of alcohol. Smokers lit up a pipe with other smokers, and they probably had their own rituals. And there are several reasons why young men and students from the upper classes were the first in Dutch society to take up smoking tobacco.

Young people and novelty

In general, students (then and now) had more freedom to experiment. For one thing, they often did not live at home and were not supervised by parents, professors, and other people in authority.

And second, these young men were in an academic environment where they were exposed to new thoughts and ideas. They came into contact with students and professors from other cultures with different customs. Students embraced smoking because they were more open to new ideas and wanted to experiment with novelties.

The first group to have taken up smoking tobacco was that of Spanish sailors who had been to South America and the Caribbean, where they had witnessed native Indians rolling up leaves of tobacco and smoking them in a pipe. They discovered how tobacco stilled their appetite and thirst. Moreover, they noticed how it gave them energy while at the same time calming their minds and giving them a high. It did not take long for sailors and soldiers to take up smoking.

In principle, burning leaves and hoping for an intoxicating effect was nothing new. Since antiquity, young people had been experimenting with inhaling the vapors of all kinds of plants that were known for their narcotic effects. The only real novelty of tobacco was that it was inhaled into the lungs. This could only be done with the help of a special pipe, something that Columbus had encountered when he met the Indians in 1492. It took more than a century for this new practice to come in fashion. Students from the upper and middle classes in the Dutch Republic copied the habit from sailors and soldiers, whom the urban elite and middle classes regarded as low-class and uncivilized.

In the 1620s and 1630s, smoking lost its connotations with the low life and peasantry after students started consuming tobacco. This change partly occurred because tobacco became an object of research at universities. Otto Sperling, an 18-year-old student from Hamburg, first tried smoking shortly after he arrived in Leiden. In 1620, the young man was suffering from pleurisy and constipation. Sperling had tried all the known remedies to relieve himself, but nothing worked. A good friend advised him to smoke a pipe of tobacco and see if that would help. Sperling thought he had nothing to lose. He smoked tobacco and his problems disappeared shortly afterwards. He wrote euphorically that it

Wealthy young people addicted to tobacco, symbolized by a tobacco pipe on the table. Painting by Willem Buytewech, *Merry Company* (c. 1620-1622) (Museum Boijmans van Beuningen, Rotterdam).

felt as though he had been reborn. Sperling considered tobacco to be a miracle healer. Later in life, after Sperling had become the personal physician to the Danish King Frederick III, he noted that smoking had cured his constipation when he was a student but he had become a lifelong addict of tobacco. He died at the age of 79.

It was no coincidence that Sperling, like his fellow students, had started smoking tobacco. Sperling studied medicine in Leiden and was therefore acquainted with the experimental plants that were grown in the university's *Hortus Botanicus*, a botanical garden that collected specimens from all over the world, and especially the Dutch East Indies and other Dutch colonies. The botanical garden was part of the medical department of the university, but it was also used by apprentices who were training to become pharmacists. In the early modern period, pharmacists did not have an academic education, but learned about their field by studying plants and their medicinal properties.

Willem Willemsz. van der Meer was also enrolled in the medical department at the University of Leiden. In 1592 he was a student in Leiden when the botanical garden first opened. Van der Meer experimented with tobacco, not because he was suffering from constipation, but because he thought it was interesting. He was encouraged by a couple of English and French students, who also smoked. Van der Meer, who became a physician in Delft, recalled later in life what his first puff of tobacco had been like. He immediately had problems with his stomach. Most of the students who tried tobacco, however, were immediately hooked, and not only students who studied medicine. After 1620, smoking tobacco became a rage among all the students. From the university towns, smoking spread throughout the entire country and infiltrated every layer of Dutch society. By 1650, smoking tobacco had been completely integrated into the Dutch way of life. As one traveler to the country remarked: 'the Dutch Republic stank of tobacco'.

Doom and gloom

Moralists watched with dismay as this new vice, which had been introduced by the country's young people, became a mainstream habit. Some moralists proclaimed that young people were going too far in pursuing their hedonistic desire for amusement and entertainment. With their vain leisure activities, they were neglecting to read the Bible and other religious books. Besides their flamboyant clothing, excessive drinking, and tendency to chase women, now there was the vice of smoking.

Samuel Ampzing, a pastor from Haarlem, saw doom and gloom on the horizon. Just as some people today resent the obsessive use of smartphones, in the seventeenth century, Ampzing was annoyed by the way in which young people squandered their time in tobacco houses smoking tobacco. In his book *Spigel ofte Toneel der IJdelheyd ende Ongebondenheyd onser Eeuw* [Mirror of the Vanity and Uncontrollable Spirit of Our Age] (1633), Ampzing remarked that society should expect little from the younger generation. The caption under the engraving 'A young man holding a pipe and tankard' reads:

Smoke is my passion and beer my life,
yet, I would give up the pipe for a tankard.
I am a stinking rotter, I am a drunken sot.
I like smoke too much, and the precious malt more.

Five years earlier, in 1628, Dirck Pietersz Pers had given the same warning. In *Bacchus. Wonder Wercken*, in which he poked fun at binge drinkers, Pers also lashed out at those who smoked too much. Pers stressed that too much tobacco was just as bad as too much liquor. The text is accompanied by an emblem featuring a monkey that is sucking on a pipe of tobacco on the foreground. The animal is surrounded by young children who are also smoking. Pers could not hide how ridiculous he thought smoking was:

Tobacco is the banquet that is consumed in company everywhere,
supposedly it was first used by monkeys
now it is imitated by other monkeys.

The emblem and text transmitted a clear message about parenting in the seventeenth century. Pers uses the word 'monkey', which gives us a clue as to how parents regarded their children in the seventeenth century. The Dutch word *aap*, or 'monkey' in English, was a common nickname that parents gave to their children when they did foolish things such as break objects or imitate silly adult behavior. The verb 'to ape' or imitate stems from this, and was the seventeenth-century version of 'monkey see, monkey do'. The illustration warned young people not to imitate their parents or other adults.

Parents were again being reminded that they had to be good examples for their offspring. Moralists encouraged parents to live piously when raising children. This was not only for their own salvation, but also because they were role models for their children. Whereas young girls looked up to their mothers at home, boys looked up not only to their fathers, but also to other men outside the home. Unlike girls, young men grew up outside of the house in the public sphere, and had to find good examples to copy in the public domain. This was an important factor for moralists, as they had to warn against bad behavior that took place in public, where they had little or limited control.

Smoking: a burning issue

In the emblem book *Sinnenpoppen* [Dolls for the Spirit] (1614), the well-known poet Roemer Visscher recognized the human fascination with novelty, but conservatively dismissed it as 'no good'. He argued that new hypes were seldom good: *Veeltijdts wat nieuws, selden wat goets* (New things are frequent, but are seldom good). The 67-year-old saw little promise in the latest fad. In general, the youth of the seventeenth century had a fascination with novelty and new things. Young people wanted to express themselves differently from the older generation. They had to have their own hairstyles and clothing, and needed to experiment. Today, that is still the hallmark of the younger generation.

Smoking became a controversial issue. Moralists and physicians discussed whether tobacco was good or bad for the body and the mind. The greatest opposition to tobacco came from a conservative movement within the Reformed Church. This group, known as the Further Reformation, believed that the Reformed Church had become too lenient. The supporters of this movement hoped that after the Roman Catholic Church had been ousted from the country, the population of the Dutch Republic would become pious and live devout lives. Although the country had become materially wealthy in the meantime, the Further Reformation complained that people had become spiritually impoverished. The supporters shared many of their ideas with English Puritans, including William Perkins.

In the Republic, the best known leader of the movement was a man named Gisbertius Voetius. In 1634, when Voetius was appointed as a professor at the Illustrious School in Utrecht, he complained that the students smoked like chimneys. Voetius saw evil and vice in everything. He also had a sense of drama, which led his admonishments to become even more exaggerated. According Voetius, the students smoked so much that they resembled 'the burning flames of Sodom and Gomorrah'.

The moralist Jacob Cats, however, regarded the adolescent phase as a turbulent period in a human being's life. He integrated this insight into his writings about smoking. In the preface to *Proteus ofte Minne-Beelden verandert in Sinne-Beelden* (1627), an entertaining moralistic treatise, Cats addressed his readers as foolish youngsters who surrendered to the *mallicheden der jonckheydt* (silliness of youth). Cats considered the latest fashion among the younger generation to be a foolish addiction. In the illustration that accompanies the text, Cupid, the god of love, is depicted holding three pipes, while across from him at a table, a young man sits furiously puffing on his pipe. The emblem entitled *Fumos Vendit Amor* means that love can be just as fleeting as tobacco smoke. According to the riddle in the accompanying text, it can be concluded that the young man is addicted to smoking: 'Smoke comes from his nose, it comes from his mouth, smoke swarms around his eyes so that they start to water. Nevertheless, he still likes it. Smoking is everything to him'. Cats was arguing that the youth had become addicted. He had failed to master the art of moderation, which meant he did not belong to the world of men; not yet, in any case. Cats understood adolescent behavior all too well, and how young people sought immediate gratification instead of thinking about the long-term consequences of their actions.

Today, neuroscientists know that the desire for quick gratification is caused by the *nucleus accumbens*, the part of the brain known as the pleasure center. It is strongly influenced by emotions and is sensitive to reward, gratification, and laughter, all of which play a role in addictive behavior. When tobacco is inhaled, this area of the brain releases a chemical called dopamine, which gives a feeling of pleasure. According to modern neurological research, during adolescence the collaboration between the emotional and rational parts of the brain is not yet optimal. During puberty, the rational frontal cortex is dominated by the emotional part, overruling rational behavior and moderation. As we saw in the chapter on sex, Cats understood that young people had a tendency towards addictive behavior. However, he thought that smoking was a passing fad, just as fleeting as the phase of youth. The moralist was right about one thing and wrong about another. Youth was a passing phase in life, but smoking did not turn out to be a fleeting whim.

Because the urge to smoke was too strong, external restrictions were placed on smokers. For example, university administrators tried to curb students from smoking and even banned smoking in some areas. In Leiden, theology students who received a scholarship risked losing it if they were caught smoking. In Groningen, scholarship students were forbidden to smoke in their homes. Universities were generally in a precarious position when it came to placing restrictions on student behavior. After all, early modern universities were commercial enterprises.

Local and national governments, on the other hand, did not have a problem imposing excise taxes on tobacco. In 1621, after the Twelve-Year Truce ended, the States General desperately needed to find new sources of revenue to finance the costly war against Spain. Consequently, it was decided in 1623 to impose a tariff on tobacco. Unlike the universities, municipal governments made no effort to restrict people from smoking. Oddly enough, not in one criminal case in the seventeenth century did a young man confess and report that he had been under the influence of tobacco when he committed his mishap. Early modern urban magistrates were well aware of how important it was to reduce hunger and limit unrest in the streets. The fact that excessive smoking, unlike excessive drinking, was not considered a crime suggests that magistrates profited from having 'sedated' young people who remained calm and quiet. It made their task of maintaining law and order much easier.

Medical discourse

The medical discourse on smoking was much more substantial than the moralistic one. In 1622, a 26-year-old student named Johann Neander became fascinated with the new tobacco plant from South America. Neander, who was from Bremen and enrolled as a student of medicine at the University of Leiden, undoubtedly knew Otto Sperling, the German student from Hamburg who had experimented with tobacco two years earlier. Neander researched the medical properties of tobacco and published his findings in a scientific work, *Tabacologia: Hoc est tabaci seu nicotianae* [Treatise on tobacco and nicotine. Tobacco as a medicine] (1622). The work praised tobacco as a miracle drug. Neander argued that the plant had healing properties and that tobacco could cure diseases such as syphilis. To support his findings, Neander used various testimonies from doctors who had also experienced the same healing effects. This marketing ploy was similar to that used in American commercials for cigarettes in the 1950s, which quoted doctors' recommendations that cigarettes were good for the health. This practice is still used today to promote products, in the form of labels stating 'scientifically proven' and 'recommended by doctors'.

The role played by Leiden's *Hortus Botanicus* in initiating the use of tobacco among students in the late sixteenth and early seventeenth centuries should not be underestimated. When the first tobacco plants were cultivated in the botanical garden, there were two types: *Nicotiana rustica* (Tabacum minus) and *Nicotiana tabacum* (Tabacum majus). It is a matter of 'chicken and egg' as to which happened first. Did the scientific cultivation of tobacco in the gardens cause students to experiment with smoking, or was smoking the reason for scientific interest? Nevertheless, the lion's share of medical discourse about the use of the plant in the early seventeenth century was researched by students and graduates from the University of Leiden.

In *Schat der Gesontheyt* [Treasury of Health] (1636), Johan van Beverwijck, the renowned doctor and alumnus of the University of Leiden to whom we referred earlier, recommended smoking for its medicinal properties. Before he visited the homes of plague victims, Van Beverwijck first smoked tobacco. For him, smoking was a preventative. Just the same, the good doctor considered it a filthy habit and thought that it smelled awful. Van Beverwijck advised young men to keep their hair cut short so that it would not stink of tobacco. IJsbrand van Diemerbroeck, a physician and professor at the University of Utrecht, believed tobacco to be a reliable form of prevention against smallpox.

Van Diemerbroeck, who studied medicine in Leiden shortly after Neander, smoked tobacco as a prophylactic against pestilence. During the 1630s the plague swept through the country, and in Leiden the outbreak of 1635-1636 claimed more than 20,000 victims. Van Diemerbroeck, who had visited more than 120 pestilence patients and corpses in Nijmegen, advised readers to take 'a short puff ... and then exhale'. According to him, this was the best preventative. The smoke counteracted the effects of inhaling the foul miasmic air. According to Van Beverwijck, this prevented the disease from spreading.

Some doctors advised pregnant women to smoke just before delivery, as the nicotine high was believed to ease the pain during contractions. The scholar Petrus Scriverius (1576-1660) also praised tobacco. He applauded the medical effects of tobacco, but condemned those who used it recreationally. In *Saturnalia. Ofte poëtisch Vasten – Avond Spel. Vervatende het gebruyk ende misbruyke van den Taback* [Saturnalia, or the Poetical Shrove Tuesday Game. Concerning the Use and Misuse of Tobacco] (1630), he argued that the weak (women and children) should be forbidden to use tobacco for any other reason than medical purposes. However, Scriverius felt that the fine line between the medical and recreational use of tobacco had been crossed. He recommended that young people stay away tobacco because they consumed it much more than they needed and it made them act as though they were crazy. By calling his treatise *Saturnalia,* Scriverius was associating the use of tobacco with the Roman festival to honor Saturn. This winter festival was known for immoral and orgiastic behavior.

There were not only admonitions against the excessive consumption of food and drink, but also against smoking. In most moralistic works, it was called 'drinking a pipe of tobacco'. The narcotic state it induced in people was not new in the seventeenth century. Many Europeans in the early modern period lived in a sedated or drugged state on a daily basis. Sometimes this was accidental, such as induced by famine, or by eating moldy bread and stale food. Sometimes it happened deliberately, as when people consumed fermented beverages, mushrooms, poppy seeds or other distillations, or sniffed lotions, or rubbed oils and other essences on their bodies. Throughout history, man – and young people in particular – has always looked for new ways to reach ecstasy. In the late Middle Ages, brewers spiked beers with herbs such as black henbane seeds, thorn apples, and belladonna, perfectly knowing this would give consumers a hallucinogenic kick. In the late seventeenth century, young men visited coffee houses to drink the new beverage of coffee and experience the effects of caffeine. In the late sixteenth and early seventeenth centuries, smoking tobacco was a habit of the same caliber; in fact, only the 'smoking' part of it was new. In the late sixteenth century, the Dutch historian Emanuel van Meteren described smoking: 'you put a bit of dried powder in a small bowl the size of a hazelnut, light it with a candle or glowing coal, and inhale the smoke through a pipe-stem, then blow it out through your nostrils'.

In a relatively short period of time, from 1590 to 1650, the Dutch Republic had gone from being a country of non-smokers to being the *tobaccophile* of Europe. During the early seventeenth century, smoking had become so widespread in Dutch society that it was not uncommon for an executioner to allow a convicted criminal a pipe of tobacco as a last request. The craving for nicotine had become addictive, and commerce tried to profit from this as well. To satisfy the growing demand, the WIC started a lucrative trade with the English Colony of Jamestown in North America. This trade was later extended to the WIC colony of New Netherland in the same country. Numerous people who had settled in New

Netherland grew tobacco as a cash crop to supplement their incomes. Even the pastor of New Amsterdam, the famous Evert Willemsz Bogardus, grew tobacco in order to supplement his salary.

As the supply outstripped the demand, farmers in the Dutch Republic started to cultivate tobacco. In the 1620s, farmers in Zeeland and around Amersfoort began growing the plant. In the following decades, Amsterdam emerged as one of the major tobacco centers in Europe. It became the depot for the tobacco harvest, which was distributed throughout Europe. Tobacco could not be smoked without a pipe. In Gouda, clay pipes were produced on a large scale. Clay pipes were fragile objects that broke easily, and users often threw them away and bought a new one. According to archaeological excavations, Amsterdam's canals were filled with them. The clay pipes of Gouda were the first mass-produced disposable products of the seventeenth century. Today, clay pipes from Gouda can be found in former Dutch settlements including those in New York and Indonesia.

In the early seventeenth century, young people's appetite for novelty turned smoking into a mainstream habit in Dutch culture, and eventually in Western society. Four centuries later, the craving for nicotine is still part of Dutch culture, although it is slowly disappearing now that government policy and social norms are changing. Whether smoking will remain part of Dutch culture in the next 400 years remains to be seen. According to a recent survey, smoking is on the rise among young Dutch people, while the older generations are quitting. In hindsight, we know that the moralists of the Golden Age, with their warnings of doom and gloom, were not far off the mark. Smoking's harmful effects on health have been scientifically proven. In view of their tobacco and alcohol consumption, it would appear that the youth of the Golden Age were a self-destructive crowd. Yet there was more: this generation of young people had other distractions that were also time-consuming and addictive. There was even more for Dutch parents in the early seventeenth century to be alarmed about.

7.   Rock 'n' Roll

Besides smoking, the young people of the Golden Age had another habit that they indulged to excess: namely, their own form of rock 'n' roll. Obviously the seventeenth-century version was very unlike that of the 1950s, but it was equally entertaining and addictive. The young people of the age were musically inclined and loved to sing, preferably from specially compiled songbooks. In the Dutch Republic, singing was a popular pastime for young and old alike. The Dutch were known for their love of singing, and singing was the rock 'n' roll of the youngsters of the Golden Age.

They sang from songbooks that were usually compiled by one songwriter. The music consisted of familiar old tunes that had been modernized with new lyrics. These seventeenth-century songwriters were similar to today's DJs, who remix old songs and add a techno-beat. Some songwriters became celebrities, such as Gerbrand Adriaensz Bredero (1585-1618). His songs were included in many songbooks. By the time he released his own songbook, Bredero enjoyed an idol-like status, especially in his hometown of Amsterdam. He proudly named his first songbook *Bredero, Amsterdam* (1617). The lyrics of the songs praised everything that was Dutch and made fun of foreign habits. Bredero had a talent for such things. He satirized peasants and low-class foreigners, portraying them as boorish while at the same time glorifying the Dutch and their cities.

Bredero

Bredero was a well-known figure in Amsterdam, especially among young people. His lyrical style and topics touched the hearts of youngsters; Bredero could easily relate to them. His songs were primarily about love, and no doubt the 32-year-old poet and bachelor based his lyrics on his own amorous adventures and heartbreaks. Bredero had a reputation for falling in love with beautiful women who eventually turned him down and broke his heart. His songs and poems refer to at least eight different women.

The most famous heartbreak was caused by Maria Tesselschade, the daughter of Roemer Visscher, who was also a well-known poet and writer. Maria's father had named her after one of his grain ships that had been wrecked off the island of Texel. Hence the name *Tessel* (the name of the island) and the Dutch word *schade* (meaning loss). Later in her life, this curious name suited her personality. Tesselschade was an eccentric woman, acclaimed for her charm, beauty, and intellect. Tesselschade also painted, made music, and could even engrave glass. She drove men crazy and was pursued openly and covertly by numerous men. They included Constantijn Huygens, who was secretary to the stadholders in the seventeenth century, and Caspar Barlaeus, the poet and professor of philosophy and rhetoric at the illustrious school of Amsterdam.

Bredero's last great love (and heartbreaker) was 19-year-old Magdalena Stockmans. With her blonde hair and brown eyes, Magdalena was the ideal of beauty in the early modern period. Stockmans was flattered by Bredero's interest, but instead chose to marry Isaac van der Voort, a silk merchant from Antwerp who was 22 years older than her. After they were married in June 1618, Van der Voort and Stockmans embarked for Naples, Italy, where they planned to live. Bredero was devastated by Magdalena's decision. He wrote a poem for her entitled 'Things Can Happen', with high hopes that she would change her mind and return:

Oogenblik vol Majesty
Vol grootse heerlyckheden
Hoe comt, dat ghy nu scheyt
Van U eerwaerdicheyt
En soete aerdigheyt
Laes wat lichtvaerdigheyt
Aanneemdy sonder reden

(Eyes full of majesty,
Full of great delightfulness,
How can it be that you leave
From you grace
And sweet charm
Leave some frivolity
Do you take for granted, without reason)

By the time Magdalena received Bredero's poem in Naples, the lyricist had already died. It was unclear what caused his death at the age of 33. It may have been a neglected case of pneumonia, exhaustion, syphilis, or even a broken heart. Within hours of his death, other poets honored Bredero with a laurel wreath, the highest honor that could be bestowed on a poet. More than twenty fellow poets commemorated him in a collection of poems that also included one of Bredero's plays. The anthology contained an illustration of Bredero wearing a laurel wreath on his head.

The tragic love life and early death of Bredero dealt a hard blow to Amsterdam's young people. The poet had been a welcome personality in the city's cafes and theaters. During his life, Bredero's farces and plays were extremely popular, and with his early death, his notoriety only grew. That was reason enough for Lodewijcksz Cornelis van der Plasse, who ran a publishing house, to request exclusive rights from the States General to publish the rest of Bredero's work. When the poet died, he had left a pile of unpublished songs and poems. Three years later, Van der Plasse published Bredero's *Geestigh Liedt-boecxken* [Comical Songbooks]. This publisher was an expert in marketing; he knew exactly how to sell Bredero's book to young consumers. Van der Plasse was sure young people would buy the book if it had a good illustration of Bredero on the title page. With his mustache and goatee, Bredero looked hip and trendy. Above his head were printed the words' *'t Kan Verkeeren'* [Things Can Happen], the title of Bredero's love poem for Magdalena Stockmans.

The compilation became an instant bestseller, and had to be reprinted three times within that year. A year later, Van der

't kan verkeeren' [Things can happen], the title of a poem by the jilted Dutch poet, Bredero, after Magdalena Stockmans rejected him and married somebody else. Title page of posthumous volume of poems dedicated to Garbrandt Adriaansz Bredero after his untimely death: G.A. Bredero, *Geestigh liedt-boecxken* (Amsterdam: Cornelis Lodowijcksz Van der Plasse, 1621) (Courtesy of the Special Collections, University of Amsterdam).

Plasse published an extensive and more luxurious edition. He commissioned six well-known artists for the illustrations, and sold it for 1.70 guilders. Taking into account that the average laborer earned only a guilder a day, the book was not for everybody; it was intended for Amsterdam's wealthy young people, whose parents had acquired their fortunes in the early days of the Dutch Golden Age. With the posthumous publication of Bredero's works, the poet became even more famous in death than he had been in life. Bredero's turbulent lifestyle was truly a seventeenth-century version of *live fast, die young.*

Jan Jansz Starter

One of the greatest admirers of Bredero was a 23-year-old man named Jan Jansz Starter. Like Bredero, he was also a poet and playwright, and member of one of the chambers of rhetoric, a group of amateur poets and writers. As mentioned above, Starter was well known in the 1620s for his compilation of songs *Friesche Lust-hof* [Frisian Paradise] (1621), which included a special tribute to Bredero. The work was a compilation of verses, wedding poems, and drinking songs that was illustrated with emblems, and later became the best-selling songbook of the decade. It should come as no surprise that it was a great success. The lyrics were about everything that could go wrong when dating and the trials of finding a suitable marriage partner. *Friesche Lust-hof* addressed matters of the heart, such as the rejection suffered by a young person before they found the right partner. Opposite the title page, there was a portrait of Cupid, the son of the goddess of love, who was pictured at the helm of a boat that was pulled by two swans. Underneath Cupid, there was an illustration of the good-looking writer himself, wearing the latest fashion. In the picture, Starter has medium-length hair and is sporting a mustache and goatee.

In the seventeenth century, book covers were made of leather and therefore did not feature illustrations. The first picture was on the title page of the work. From a quick glance at the title page, it is clear that *Friesche Lust-hof* was meant for young people. The illustration depicts a group of young people who are singing, dancing, and playing music. They are located on the main square in Leeuwarden, the capital of the province of Friesland. Starter dedicated the book to the women of Friesland and added a few sentences in the Frisian language. Despite the reference to Friesland, the book was certainly not just for young people from that northern province. It was sold across the country and was a bestseller, being reprinted 31 times between 1621 and 1634.

Like Bredero's songbook, more luxurious editions of Starter's book were also published that featured high-quality illustrations and fancy leather covers. These were primarily for the wealthy young people who could easily afford the price of two guilders. For young people with less money, there were also cheaper editions that only cost three *stuivers* (15 cents). Just like Van der Plasse's editions of Bredero's *Groot Liedt-Boeck,* the marketing of *Friesche Lust-hof* was canny. Starter used his social network and friends in the publishing industry to help him sell the book. It is likely that Catharina Cloppenburgh and Manuel Colyn, for whom he wrote and recited a poem at their wedding in 1622, helped him to promote his book.

What is more, Starter had already been a famous writer before *Friesche Lust-hof* was published. He had previously authored a satirical play called *Jan Soetekauw* that had been so successful that it had been reprinted 19 times. We can draw many parallels between Starter's popularity among youth audiences during the 1620s and 1630s and that of Bredero. By seventeenth-century standards, Starter lived an adventurous and somewhat bohemian-style life. His personal life was chaotic and his finances were a disaster. Starter had his fair share of failed business ventures, was involved in a number of lawsuits, and even had to file for bankruptcy.

Not everyone was charmed by Starter. His plays, which often glorified romance and excessive drinking, were banned several times by ministers who protested at their corrupt content and considered them unsuitable for young people. In 1625, at the height of his success, Starter died on the battlefield in Bosnia, where he was fighting in the Thirty Years War. Starter was only 32 years old, just a year younger than his role model Bredero when he died. It is unclear why Starter had joined the army. We can only speculate that it was for financial reasons, or perhaps motivated by idealism. Starter was employed as reporter by Count von Mansvelt, a famous war hero who fought for the Protestant cause. In the Republic, he was considered a distinguished and successful military commander and a living legend. When he dined in a tavern, people would gather from far and wide to catch a glimpse of him. Like Bredero, Von Mansvelt must have been a hero and role model for Starter. In the appendix to the *Friesche Lust-hof,* Starter devoted a drinking song to the German Count and honored him for fighting the Spaniards and the emperor.

Songbooks such as those written by Bredero and Starter formed an integral part of the song culture of the early seventeenth century. They were first marketed in 1610 and sold as emblem books. In subsequent decades, many more songbooks followed. Some of them were written and published especially for a young audience. Songbooks had a profound impact on Dutch culture, because singing in the early modern period was also a means of transmitting information. In the first decades of the seventeenth century, a transition took place and books gradually filtered through to the less wealthy classes. Due to technological advancements, the printing press could produce books more cheaply, and they became affordable for the middle and poorer classes. The very poorest people could not afford them, and as they did not have any education, nor could they read them.

In the early modern period, singing tended to be a group activity. Singing was a social event, and songs were usually sung after a dinner or on special occasions such as weddings and other parties. In order to compose songs, one first had to master the art of poetry. Because books and paper were expensive, rhyming was an important facet of early modern education. Students were graded by their teachers for their ability to memorize long texts and rhymes. In an educational sense, learning was facilitated by the use of rhyme.

Educationalists believed that younger pupils in particular would learn more easily if the words sounded sweet and pleasant in the ear. This was the didactic approach that was taught to boys at the Latin school, and a device that they continued to use after they had joined literary societies such as chambers of rhetoric, as Bredero and Starter had done. At the weekly meetings, their poetic skills were fine-tuned during the opening ritual, when each member was required to address the chairman, called 'the Prince'. The last word of each phrase had to rhyme with the word 'prince'.

Rhyming, playing with words, and composing poetry were not only pastimes for the educated. All strata of Dutch society expressed themselves through poetry, from rich to poor. Sellers at the market tried to peddle their wares and attract the attention of customers with catchy slogans. Acclaimed and professional poets such as Vondel and Bredero earned a living composing eloquent poetry for the country's rich and famous. No wedding celebration or party was complete without a poem tailor-made for the occasion. Reciting verse was *the* Dutch national pastime. The current practice of writing a poem for the feast of St Nicolas is a remnant of that tradition.

Besides writing poetry, young people also enjoyed writing lyrics to music based on existing melodies. In the early seventeenth century, this became an integral part of Dutch culture, as the Dutch regarded singing as second nature. People would sing at every opportunity that presented itself – especially weddings, which were the favorite. Many of the songs collected in songbooks from the late sixteenth and early seventeenth centuries had already withstood the test of time, because they had been used over and over again with different lyrics.

In the early seventeenth century, there were two predominant types of songbook, namely the religious and the secular genre, which regularly overlapped in content. Some of them were clearly religious, such as Cornelis Pietersz Biens' *Handt-boecxken of Christelijcke Gedichten* [Handbook of Christian Poems] (1627). This songbook was intended for youngsters from a devout background and included several religious songs that praised God for his great miracles.

The songbook *Den Amsterdamschen Geestelijcke Lust-hof* [The Comical Paradise of Amsterdam] (1637), written by I. Teerincx, took this religious message a step further. Young readers were supposed to dedicate every part of the day by singing a pious song to God. There was a song for before morning prayers, a song before eating, a song for after eating, a song of gratitude for good health, and so on. The compilation also included a special song that had to be sung during periods of plague. Teerincx aimed to cultivate piety in young people by giving them songs that would protect them from their worldly desires. There were numerous other songbooks with lyrics that aimed to protect the hearts and souls of young people and urged them to become pious Christians.

Secular songbooks

Between the spiritual and secular songbooks, there existed a large gray zone of songbooks that contained a moral message, but were neither entirely devotional nor purely for amusement. These were often marketed as entertainment books. Many writers and compilers of spiritual and secular songbooks knew young readership all too well, and were aware of how they needed to present or market their message; or rather how *not* to. Nobody sold moralistic books better than Father 'Jacob' Cats. He understood that youngsters would never purchase a book with a pious title; he knew for a fact that they would not even look at it, let alone pick it up. If it had a catchy title and featured an appealing illustration with Cupid on the title page, however, then it was another story.

Cats had previously applied this same method in many of his moralistic books. He wrapped his moral message in amusing and witty poems, packaged with entertaining illustrations that required little explanation. With this sugar-coated approach, Cats managed to convey practical advice to youngsters, so that they could understand and swallow it better. Cats had copied this method from physicians who prescribed the herb *worm cruyt,* or tansy, often used to cure digestive problems. Because the herb tasted horribly bitter and was almost impossible for young children to swallow, physicians such as Johan van Beverwijck recommended mixing it with something sweet. Cats used the same method to relay bitter moral truths to his young readers.

Niet anders dan gelijck men
de kinders, tot haer eygen voordeel
Somtijts bedriegt, wanneer men
Desselve het bitter, doch gesond
Worm-kruyt met suycker.

(Nothing's different than what parents do
they give their children, for their own benefit
despite being deceptive
the same bitter pill, for their health
and sugar-coat it so they can swallow it.)

In other words, sometimes parents had to disguise the truth to children for their own well-being, and give them tansy with sugar for the sake of their health.

Many compilers of songbooks used Cats' method and disguised their hard-to-swallow moral message with a catchy title and an enticing illustration on the title page. During the 1620s and 1630s, a new subgenre of songbooks became quite popular. They were known as Arcadian songbooks, characterized by idyllic texts and illustrations of pastoral settings. 'Arcadian' as a general theme had become fashionable in the early seventeenth century. A school of artists and painters, mainly from Amsterdam, Utrecht and Haarlem, specialized in portraying Arcadian surroundings, which had become increasingly popular among the art-buying public. Members of the Republic's elite were particularly fond of paintings that depicted pastoral settings and rough foreign landscapes, especially Greek ones. The Arcadian landscape radiated something exotic to a Dutch audience.

Around 1650, an estimated 30-40% of all paintings were landscapes. The Arcadian was the complete opposite of the flat meadows and marshlands with which the Dutch were familiar. Since the Middle Ages, nature had been cultivated in the Dutch Republic. With the exception of the sandy dunes around Haarlem, the province of Holland was largely urbanized and intensively farmed. Moreover, remote areas such as forests and wild landscapes were considered dangerous, because criminals and other social outcasts had traditionally sought refuge there. These uncultivated and untouched landscapes had a magical effect on audiences and were romanticized in literature.

The few wooded areas and pastoral surroundings in Holland were crowded locations, especially on Sunday afternoons, when urban dwellers sought leisure and relaxation outside the city. In Amsterdam, which had been a huge construction site 1612 due to the building of the city's three major canals (Herengracht, Keizersgracht, and Prinsengracht), the city's residents sought peace and quiet in the countryside. In the balmy summer months, the constant noise of construction, traffic, and the stench of polluted water must have been unbearable. The inhabitants of Haarlem took refuge in the nearby dunes and wooded area known as the Haarlemmerhout. Local writers from Haarlem praised the natural beauty of the environs of the city. The painter and writer Karel van Mander was especially fond of the white dunes near his hometown, which were known as the *Wittebrink* (White Crest). He lyrically compared them to the mythological Helicon, the Greek mountain of poetry where the muses lived in ancient times. At a height of 30 meters, the Wittebrink towered above the surrounding flat, monotonous landscape of the countryside like a mountain. For Dutch poets, the Wittebrink became an inspiration for the new Arcadian trend in poetry.

The lyrics and illustrations in songbooks glorified the beauty of the uncultivated countryside, and promoted it as the place to be for young people. When we consider that young people had to spend more than three quarters of the year inside due to the weather conditions, we can see that summer and the beauty of nature were glorified in these books in a way not unlike that used by travel brochures nowadays to illustrate pristine beaches and stunning scenery. (Today in the Netherlands, most summer vacations in southern destinations are booked in February, the middle of winter.) The illustrations in songbooks depicted fashionably dressed young people on warm summer days in idyllic locations. Although the lyrics praised summer and warm weather, in practice, young people sang from songbooks throughout the year. Weddings and other special occasions, such as picnics, were the most common occasions for a song. In the Zaan Region, known for its green wooden houses and located only a few kilometers from the northwest of Amsterdam, a young woman would carry her songbook in a special wooden *mopsjestrommel,* or box. This wooden box had an ornately decorated handle and lid, and was a precursor to the lady's handbag.

In the early seventeenth century, the countryside symbolized freedom for young people. That was especially the case for youngsters who lived in cities, and whose lives had become more regimented. Municipal ordinances and regulations tried to restrict young people from gathering in public squares, on bridges, and in the streets, whereas in the countryside youngsters were free to do what they pleased. This sense of freedom was expressed in the lyrics of many songs.

In songbooks about Amsterdam, the lyrics idealized the tranquility and Arcadian beauty of the city's rural surroundings. The lyrics often described how young people would stroll through the countryside and take boat trips on the Amstel, Amsterdam's main river. For a country with an abundance of canals, rivers, and lakes, sailing was by far the most popular way for young people to enjoy Holland's nature.

On the title page of the songbook *Schoonhoofs Lust-Prieelken* [Schoonhoven's Summer Joy] (1624), the authors, J.C. Weydstraet and A. E. Drost, dedicated the book 'to the happy maidens and youngsters of Schoonhoven'. The engraver depicted a sailboat full of young people who were fishing, singing, and having fun. Most songbooks for young people included a 'Mei-liedt' [May Song], a song dedicated to the month when life returned and flowers started to bloom again. In *Schoonhoofs Lust-Prieelken,* the lyrics to the May song were accompanied by an illustration featuring Cupid, depicted as the captain of a boat filled with young people. The engraver wanted to stress that love and matters of the heart dominate the month of May and the phase of life known as youth.

De Speeljacht van Venus d' Godinne
'k Sagh daer docht mijn ontmoet d' jeught verselt
Daer Cupido d' regentes der minne
Als meester was aen 't roer ghestelt

(In the pleasure yacht of the Goddess Venus
I saw myself in the same boat with the youth
Where Cupid, and the regent of love,
Is made the skipper at the rudder)

For the young people of Dordrecht, a city located on the Merwede River south of Rotterdam, Abraham Aertsz Plater wrote *Dordrechts Lijstertje* [Dordrecht's Lark] (1624). The songs were mainly satires, and young people could easily identify with the descriptions of well-known locations outside the city, and references to eating duck and salmon and drinking Rhine wine, the city's main culinary specialties. Since the Middle Ages, Dordrecht had had exclusive rights as a staple market for Rhine wine. The illustration on the title page depicted young couples strolling in the countryside on the outskirts of the city, with Dordrecht's church tower looming in the background.

Besides boat trips, the youngsters of the seventeenth century also enjoyed taking rides in the countryside in an open carriage. This cart was known as a *speelwagen* or 'recreational wagon', because it was purely for recreation and leisure. The vehicle held two to three couples and a driver, and was made for taking trips through the countryside. During the trips, the couples passed the time singing. In a song from *Minne-kunst, minne-baet* [Art of Love, Profit of Love] (1626), Johan van Heemskerk romanticized the fresh country air and joy of taking rides in the wild. In the illustrations in songbooks, the recreational wagon was often decorated with branches and had moss growing on the sides. In the seventeenth century, it was the ultimate symbol of youth.

The clearest evidence that the recreational wagon was associated with youth comes from Jacob Cats, who described in one of his many dialogues how an elderly man suddenly became nostalgic for his own youth when he heard the galloping of horses, cracking of whips, and roar of laughter after a recreational wagon filled with young people passed by. The elderly poet P.C. Hooft cheerfully recollected how much fun he had had as a young man, sitting in the back of a recreational wagon. He added, 'It was the best place to cuddle and kiss, without being seen by others'.

In *Eerlycke Tytkorting* [Honest Recreation] (1634), Jan Harmensz Krul described how aroused a young man became during a country ride. He sat next to a girl, whom he wanted to kiss. She only ignored him, however, and he became more frustrated. The young man in the story feared he would suffer the same fate as Acis, the lover of the Greek nymph Galatea. The latter had turned Acis into a river after having to listen to his whining. In *Haerlemsche Duyn-Vreucht* [The Pleasure of Haarlem's Dunes] (1636), the songs also described the sexual tension between young men and their girlfriends as they took country rides in the recreational wagon. The author, Wesbusch, described how Haarlem's young people would take a trip to the beach at Zandvoort, and how excited the young men became while sitting next to their girlfriends and kissing them. After they arrived at the beach, the young men needed to take a swim to 'cool off' from their aroused state.

In *Batavische Arcadia* [Batavian Arcadia] (1637), Van Heemskerk also idolized the fun that was had by young people while journeying in a recreational wagon. The backdrop of the Dutch countryside was presented as idyllic. Van Heemskerk had written the story a decade earlier, and it was probably based on his own experiences as a young man. During their trip, the young people stop at an inn, where they sing songs. Afterwards, they continue to

Carrying young women into the sea, an old Dutch ritual practiced by young people. Adolf van der Laan, *Ritual of dragging young girls from Katwijk into the sea* (c. 1750) (Rijksmuseum, Amsterdam).

the beach at Zandvoort. According to Van Heemskerk, it was not uncommon for young men to carry the girls – especially those who talked too much – into the sea and dunk them in the cold water.

The Dutch called this type of horseplay *in zee dragen* (carrying into the sea), and it was another form of innocent physical contact between the sexes and part of the courting ritual. The girls, usually dressed in their best outfits, did not go voluntarily, and would yell and scream at the top of their voices. For the young men, it was a way of showing off and proving to the ladies that they were in charge. On the other hand, the whole charade of carrying the girls into the sea tempered the passions of the young men and women after all the kissing and petting in the recreational wagon. Having dunked the ladies in the sea, the young men carried them back to the beach, where they helped them dry off in the sand. For some couples, this was a perfect moment to kiss and make up before seeking an isolated place in the nearby dunes and woods.

The woods symbolized danger in the Middle Ages, but they also had an ambiance of sexual excitement, especially after dark. Having sex outdoors is something people have done throughout the ages. According to a recent survey in the Netherlands, 39% of respondents find having sex in the woods very arousing, 30% prefer the beach, and 13% find the sea exciting. People also made love in the great outdoors in the seventeenth century, but then it was often out of necessity. Nature provided a 'private' place where young people could have sex without being disturbed. The forests around The Hague and Haarlemmerhout in Haarlem were popular rendezvous for young lovers. At night, these green and wooded areas were the places where men tended to look for sexual encounters. In the seventeenth century, every town and city in the Dutch Republic had its green space where people would walk and exercise in the daytime, and that would turn into the ideal place to look for sex at night.

The texts and images from the songbooks reveal that Dutch parents in the seventeenth century were more indulgent when it came to their offspring than English parents, who would have had their unmarried daughters chaperoned on such trips. Dutch young men and women knew the consequences of premarital relations all too well – especially children from the upper and middle classes, where a forced marriage due to a pregnancy reflected badly on the entire family, not just the individual. The children of the urban elite usually had arranged marriages that strategically maintained or improved the economic and political standing of the family. However, that does not mean that no physical contact was permitted between unmarried young people. In the ritual of courting, young people flirted, caressed, kissed, and innocently horsed around.

One of the best-known examples of tolerated horseplay between young men and women is captured in Gerard ter Borch's sketchbook from around 1620. In one of his drawings, Ter Borch portrayed a young man lying on the ground while five girls pick grass and throw it over him. The scene is in Dutch called *te grazen nemen,* literally to be taken to grass, and meaning to be thoroughly taken for a ride. This harmless activity reveals the playfulness with which Dutch young people could interact with each other. Romping between the sexes was not only something for the upper classes; the children of the lower classes did the same. In his satire *Moortje*, a play about the life of commoners, Bredero referred to the custom of rolling around in the grass with a woman named *Trijntje*.

Hoe plech ick onse Trijn
In't lange gras te graeslen.

(How can I get our Trijn
to go for a romp in the tall grass)

The caption below states:

Ick bin int soeet gewellt
En leg nu onverbaest/
Neer in het groene vellt
Alwaer ick werd gegraest.

(I am pleasantly rolled up,
and now lie unsurprised/
down in the green field
where I am being taken for a ride.)

Making music

The most common innocent physical activity in which young people engaged was to make music together. In *Ultrajectina Tempe ofte S. Jans Kerck- of-versch wandel-groen* (1640), the songwriter Regnerus Opperveldt described how the young people of Utrecht would dally in the courtyard of the medieval church of St John. During the evening hours, they would go there to listen to singers and lute players. In the seventeenth century, the lute was a popular instrument among young men, similar to how teenagers regard the guitar today. A young man with a lute in his hand was a common attribute of emblem books and paintings. The ideal combination was a young man playing the lute and a young woman accompanying him singing. Between 1590 and 1630, the painting genre of the 'musical company' became popular. The depiction of a man playing and woman singing symbolized harmony, and consequently, if a young man and woman could play and sing well together, it promised to be a good match.

A couple's harmony and ability to collaborate were also tested in the games that young unmarried adults played with each other. Playing games was a popular pastime, especially during the long winter evenings. The winters of the 1620s and 1630s were extremely cold and long; in meteorological history, this era is known as the 'Little Ice Age', because of the extremely cold winters when the canals and waterways remained frozen for months on end. During the long winter months, the young people of the country were confined to indoors. To relieve the boredom, the young people played games and sang songs from their songbooks. Jan Jansz. Starter's *Steeck-boecxken* [Pin Book] (1624) was exactly what young people needed during the long winter nights. With its subtitle *Ofte 't Vermaak der Jeugdelijker herten* [Or the Pleasure of Youthful Hearts], audiences knew that it was a game for groups of young couples to play. The book was a better alternative to playing cards, checkers, or game-of-goose, which parents considered a waste of time. *Steeck-boecxken* was, as the title implies, a book that one poked at random with large knitting needle or pin in order to select a page. The page that was pricked described a character trait of a young man or woman. The opposite page was decorated with a heart, and other attributes associated with the depicted character. The other players had to say whether the character sketch described the couple correctly. The game was played by around six couples, usually at parties, weddings, and picnics.

The art of love

The pin book was by no means unusual; it was typical of the genre of emblem books known as *ars amatoria,* or the art of love, which had become popular in the early seventeenth century and was re-invented in other forms. If the description on the page did not fit the couple, there was usually a roar of laughter from the other players. But if it did match, then it was even funnier. The accompanying illustrations were often salacious and full of sexual innuendo. For example, on page 102, the word 'birding' actually refers to copulating, and if the book were opened at page 133, the young couple would see an image of a tennis racket, tennis balls, and a tennis court. The associated text reads as follows:

> *Hoe wel 't een vreugd is in de baen*
> *Te kaetzen en de bal te slaen.*
> *Zo is 't nogtans veel meer plezier*
> *Te kaetzen met een Venus-dier.*
> *Ja zulken baen, daar koord nog, Net*
> *Dan doen is/maer het zagte bed.*

> (Even though it is a pleasure to be on the court
> To chase after and hit the ball.
> It is even more delightful
> To chase after a woman
> Yes, such a court would be a catch
> Then to do it, in a soft bed.)

It is clear tennis has its charm, but life gets really fun when the tennis court is swopped for a soft bed: the texts of *Steeck-boecxken* were risqué, to say the least. But after all, that is what young people wanted. Their parents would doubtless have disapproved of such provocative texts, but only if they had read beyond the book's preface. In this, Starter encouraged his readers to be virtuous, and to 'keep the savior Jesus Christ faithfully in their hearts'. Unfortunately there are no surviving copies of *Steeck-Boexcken* from the seventeenth century. However, according to an edition from 1725, we know that the book was only 10 cm x 8 cm in size, which suggests that it could have been hidden under a skirt or placed in a pocket to conceal it from disapproving eyes. It was probably not the intention that parents should know its true contents.

The writers and compilers of songbooks, such as Bredero and Starter, knew exactly what their young readers wanted. They gave voice to young people's experiences in their quest to find the ideal marriage partner. Bredero and Starter often drew on their own experiences, which struck a chord with young people. In the major cities such as Amsterdam and Haarlem, songbook writers were well known personalities in the streets and taverns and honored guests at wedding celebrations. Their seventeenth-century contemporaries revered them as celebrities.

After 1640, that all changed. A new generation arose, with its own notions of fashion and recreation. The number of *new* songbooks that were published each year declined drastically. The same songbooks were either reprinted, or more religiously themed songbooks were produced for young people. By the 1650s, the pastoral and Arcadian themes had gone out of fashion, and were replaced by themes such as the *kermis* and binge-drinking. In the late seventeenth century a new genre of books for young men came onto the market, namely pornographic novels such as *De Haagsche Lichtmis* [The Courtesan of The Hague] (1679) and *D' Openhertige Juffrouw* (1680), which was a translation of *The London Jilt.* In many respects, these autobiographical novels containing tell-all sex stories left little to the imagination of young men. As such, they often resembled a seventeenth-century version of Xaviera Hollander's *Happy Hooker.*

8. Conclusion

While finishing this book, I was struck by the desire to return to Heidelberg. Since I first visited with my eldest brother, I had never been back. Once I was there, I realized that it had been nearly 30 years since I had seen the university's *Studentenkarzer* (student prisons) for the first time. Standing there, admiring the walls with their early modern graffiti, I also realized that my fascination with the history of education and adolescence had been sparked by those walls. In a flood of memories, I reflected on everything that had happened in my own life in the last three decades, and had an overwhelming sense that things had come full circle. I also wondered whether those long-haired, gun-carrying, binge-drinking young men of the Dutch Golden Age had also reflected on their own youth, once they became older?

Otto Copes, 1650

Let us return to Otto Copes, and fast-forward his life 21 years to the year 1650. By that time, the world had changed dramatically and the Dutch Republic was a different country. In 1648, the Dutch Republic had negotiated peace with Spain, the first period of peace for 80 years. But the following decades did not bring the same level of economic prosperity that the country had experienced in the early seventeenth century. Peace in Europe brought hard times for the Republic, which had profited from the lucrative arms trade. The economy went into decline, growth stagnated, and upward social mobility stalled. The Dutch Reformed Church realized that it would never become a state church, like the Roman Catholic Church had been before the Revolt. Population growth slowed down and fewer foreigners came to the Republic. And the young men who had caused so much trouble in the early seventeenth century by breaking windows, fighting, dueling, and drinking excessively, had become adults.

By 1650, they had become fathers and middle-aged men. Moreover, this generation had now become the Dutch establishment, and the non-natives had integrated and were longer foreigners. This was a new generation, which helped to shape a new identity for the country.

A new generation

In the two decades after 1650, the Dutch Republic endured a series of setbacks. In 1651, parts of Amsterdam were flooded during a storm. Between 1652 and 1654, the country became entangled in a series of trade wars with England, causing it to slide into further economic decline. The WIC lost its territories in Brazil to the Portuguese. In 1664, the British conquered the North American colony of New Netherland and the Dutch Republic lost the prized port city of New Amsterdam (later New York) in the New World. In the late seventeenth century, moralists considered this series of setbacks to be a sign of God's wrath. In their view, God was punishing the Republic for the economic prosperity of the Golden Age, which had spoiled the country with an excess of wealth. Once again, moralists were quick to put the blame on young people. A new generation of youngsters had come of age by the middle of the century, and they, too, were guilty of excessive drinking and of wasting their leisure time reading lewd books.

By 1650, Otto Copes, the drunken young man who was arrested in 1629 for opening fire on Groningen's municipal guardsmen, had become an upstanding citizen of the community. He was married and was the father of five children. Four months after he was arrested in 1629, he left Groningen and enrolled at the University of Leiden to study law. In the following years, he completed his law degree, became a member of the municipal council for the city of Den Bosch, and represented the province of Brabant in the States General. He established a good social and political network, and was on good terms with the stadholder and his advisors. Moreover, he became an elder of the Walloon

Church and, ironically enough, officer of Den Bosch's municipal guard.

Founding fathers

With the benefit of hindsight, we can say that Otto Copes landed on his feet. His unruly behavior as a youth was not unusual for someone of his rank and generation in early modern Dutch society. In comparison to other young men from the same background, Otto's behavior and life course was quite normal for that period. Despite the temptation posed by sex, drugs, and rock 'n' roll, the influence of institutions such as universities and city regulations were decisive in steering youngsters such as Otto onto the right path. In the years after Otto had been arrested, Dutch society had witnessed many changes. From this perspective, Otto and his cohorts were the founding fathers of the new Dutch Republic.

Juvenile violence had declined considerably and those youngsters who still engaged in violent behavior were considered barbaric and uncivilized. The academic court gave us a glimpse of how this change took place during the early seventeenth century. This important source reveals how young people began to refrain from using physical violence when their honor had been violated, and instead resorted to the legal system. The government also discouraged young people from using violence. Municipal councils became less tolerant of violence and tried to curb juvenile troublemaking with legislation, banning uncivilized behavior. Even to this day, physical violence is relatively rare in the Netherlands. The Netherlands has one of the lowest levels of private gun ownership in Europe, and there are fewer deaths from shootings than in other European countries.

Municipal governments and universities offered young people alternative means of letting off their pent-up energy and frustration. In the Golden Age, sports such as tennis and fencing were popular among students and young people. In general, young people in the early seventeenth century started to pass their time doing sports and civilized activities, such as playing music and singing from songbooks. To this day, this aspect of Dutch culture is still visible and strongly embedded in Dutch identity. Not a wedding or birthday party goes by without family and friends composing (and performing!) a special song. The same is true of the celebration of St Nicolas on 5 December, when poems are composed for every family member and read out loud.

Moderation

In the Golden Age, moderation was an important virtue that was promoted in the upbringing of Dutch youngsters. The prosperity that went with the economic boom enabled young people to become more interested in their personal appearance. They demanded expensive clothing made from costly fabrics, accessorized with precious metals. Young people rebelled against the older generations with their 'calculated slovenliness' or sloppy, disheveled look and long hair, causing their parents and moralists to admonish them for their excessive behavior. Moralists were all too quick to draw a parallel with the biblical story of the Prodigal Son. They blamed the younger generation for squandering their parents' hard-earned money on alcohol and sex.

Like every generation of youngsters, Otto and his peers had to master the art of moderation. That was especially true when it came to consuming alcohol. Dutch youths of the Golden Age were most challenged, however, when it came to learning to temper their sexual urges. Even though sexual morals were not stricter than those in other ages, sexually transmitted diseases such as syphilis were life-threatening. In the seventeenth century, young men were the most common victims of this disease. Syphilis was accompanied by a social stigma similar to that associated with HIV-AIDS in the 1980s. What was new for this generation was that they were the first to be warned about the disease through educational books. Father Cats advised them not to have sex until marriage, because this was the surest way of avoiding infection. The echoes of this tradition of educating children about sexuality are still visible in today's approach to raising teenagers. Today, the Netherlands has the second lowest teen pregnancy rate in the world. Only 14 births in every 1,000 are to 15-19 year-olds. Other developed countries, including the UK (England and Wales) with 47 per 1,000, and the USA with 57 per 1,000, are still battling with how to reduce the number of teen pregnancies.

In the Golden Age, Dutch parents were worried about their children smoking tobacco. Having children who experimented with smoking was a new phenomenon for parents in the Golden Age. This generation of young people was the first in history to make smoking tobacco a national pastime and popular habit. They were also the first to manifest a distinctive youth culture, which was portrayed in the lyrics and themes of their songbooks. It was a youth culture produced *by* young people *for* young people. Entertaining books such as emblem and songbooks also became a new means for moralists to instruct and provide young people with moral guidance. The youngsters of the early seventeenth century were the first generation in Dutch history to be raised and informed with these new printed media. These books also show us how young people spent their leisure time, taking boat trips, riding in recreational wagons, and enjoying horseplay on the beach.

Contemporary youth culture and child-rearing practices have their roots in the Dutch Golden Age, when educational institutions and city officials were influenced by humanism. After the outbreak of the Dutch Revolt against Spain, they tried to create a new Republic, one in which Church and State were separated. It was a new country, dominated on the one hand by liberal mercantilism, and on the other by a multi-confessional society, in which many religions co-existed without one dominating the rest. University administrators, city officials, and parents all played an important role in creating a new Dutch mentality in the Golden Age. Today, the belief that Church and State should be separate and that the market should be free remain keystones of Dutch culture, as typically Dutch as windmills and wooden shoes.

Education and the Dutch mentality

In the early seventeenth century, the Dutch Republic was a state in the making. Like an adolescent, it was a country that was maturing and growing, its gangly body taking on an adult physique. Young people played a major role in the maturation of the Dutch state. And like a teenager, it was a country that was preoccupied with its identity. This is clear from the number of pamphlets that addressed the question of what it was to be Dutch.

Johan van Beverwijck, a physician and historian, stressed how important it was for the young republic to have a common identity. In order for the country to remain united, it needed a sense of cohesion. He argued that the solution to the problem was a 'Dutch' upbringing. A republic that valued respectable citizens should focus on the education of its children. In the seventeenth century, nowhere in the world were there more paintings of children with attributes that symbolized the importance of a good education. In addition, there were numerous books on how to raise children, emphasizing the importance of education for the betterment of society. Raising good citizens would help to make the Republic a strong secular state. Young people not only looked up to religious men, such as clergymen, as role models, but they also looked beyond the church. In the secular realm, military men were key role models. As the Dutch military became a professional army in the early seventeenth century, young people looked up to these men for their discipline and training.

Moreover, the soldiers of the early seventeenth century were national heroes. They defended the country against Spain. Adolescents admired them and began to imitate their dress and behavior. On the other hand, the soldier was also notorious for his wayward lifestyle. The paintings of the *Kortegaard* (*corps de garde*) formed a popular genre in the Golden Age. These minute paintings often depicted the licentious side of a soldier's life. Young soldiers often squandered their copious leisure time drinking, chasing womanizing, and smoking.

In 1650, Otto Copes commissioned a painting of his wife Josina Schade van Westrum, together with the couple's five children. In the painting, his wife is shown pointing her finger up to the sky. At the lower left-hand corner of the portrait, we see the vices that Copes family hoped their children would eschew: alcohol and sex, symbolized by a depiction of Venus, Cupid, and Bacchus. The painting is an allegory; Copes and his wife were concerned about the moral upbringing of their children. They seem to have wanted to say that sex, drugs and rock 'n' roll are associated with youth, but a good education will always prevail. Otto was living proof of that.

Acknowledgements

When I was in high school, my favorite teacher, Mrs. Doris Cothron, was a great admirer of John Donne. She introduced me to his poem, 'No man is an island, entire of itself'. The words never resonated more than during the four months in the winter of 2014 that I spent in solitude re-writing this manuscript in Dutch. In the winters of 2016 and 2017 I again chose to isolate myself on the same Greek island of Paros, where I wrote the sequels *More Sex, Drugs,* and *Rock 'n' Roll: Fatherhood in the Dutch Golden Age* and *Beyond Sex, Drugs, and Rock 'n' Roll: Old Age in the Dutch Golden Age* (both forthcoming). For my writing, solitude has become a trusted friend, but my friends have become even dearer and more appreciated (in general, I highly recommend solitude as a way to appreciate the people in our lives).

I am greatly indebted to my friends Jacques Dane and Jan Willem Dammer, who advised and commented on the manuscript. The process of writing would have been unimaginable without the constructive advice of my publisher, Marjolein Voogel at AUP, for the Dutch edition, as well as Chantal Nicolaes from AUP. For the English version, I am incredibly thankful to my publisher Inge van der Bijl of AUP, who pursued the translation of the book. I also owe much to my assistant publisher Lotte Heldoorn, who helped me profoundly in preparing the manuscript for publication as well as Vivien Collingwood for her superb editing skills. As a source of inspiration, I have always looked to Willem Frijhoff, emeritus professor at VU University Amsterdam, for wandering onto new paths in the scientific world and opening up new frontiers in historical research. From the beginning, he encouraged and advised me while conducting my research. During the writing and translation of this book I was supported and aided in numerous ways by Maarten Eddes, Dimitroula Kyres, Katerina Latsi, Stratos Latsis, Rena Nasta, Nicole Schneider, Vlado Skovrlj,

Paula Swenson and – as sentimental as it might sound, but it's true – my faithful Golden Retriever, Aeas. Indeed, *no man is an island, entire of itself.*

Paroikia, March 2017

Index

Tales
of Ancient
India

Tales of Ancient India

Translated from the Sanskrit by

J. A. B. Van Buitenen

The University of Chicago Press
Chicago & London

Library of Congress Catalog Card Number: 59-10430

The University of Chicago Press, Chicago 60637
The University of Chicago Press, Ltd., London W.C. 1

Preface

Although I have attempted to give these Indian stories a modern tone, they are presented as translations only. I have neither embroidered nor re-created, for I assumed that the style and fantasy of the original would be of greater interest to the reader than any embellishment or "updating" of my own. A note on the sources will be found at the end of the book.

The book grew out of a small collection of translations that I made for a college course in Indian Civilization at the University of Chicago. I could never have gone ahead with the book except for the encouragement of George V. Bobrinskoy and Milton B. Singer, to whom I owe a debt of gratitude of which I have more ambition than hope ever to acquit myself. I thank Milton and Helen Singer, as well as Edwin Gerow, for their criticisms concerning language and style.

J. A. B. Van Buitenen

Contents

Map of Classical India

TO CHINA

TO ANTIOCH

Kashmir

TAKSASILA

R. VITASTA

Kurus

R. YAMUNA

R. INDUS

MATHURA

Avanti

Malava

UJJAYINI

BHARUKACCHA

VINDHYA RANGE

PRATISTHANA

R.

TO BERENICE

AND ALEXANDRIA

R. KAVER

MUZIRIS

MADUR

Pandyas

Classical India

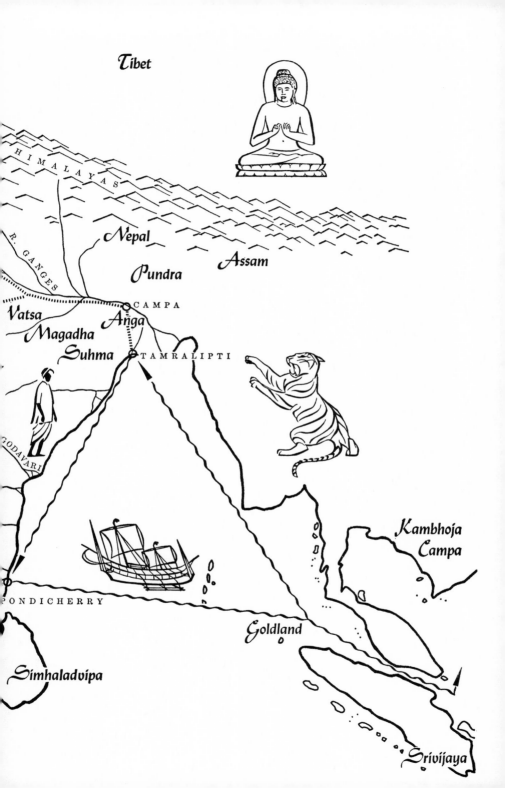

Introduction

The majority of the stories brought together here have been taken from two Sanskrit works—one very famous, the other virtually unknown—which themselves are translations and adaptations of a lost original. The more famous collection, which is also the larger one, is the *Bṛhatkathāsaritsāgara*, "Ocean of the Rivers of the Great Romance." It was composed in the twelfth century A.D. by a Kashmirian brahmin, Somadeva. He dedicated his work prudently to Queen Sūryavatī of Kashmir, "who has adorned Kashmir with holy monasteries, like so many Trees of Wishes, which dispel the sorrow of those who approach them with hope." He was inspired by the wish "to divert Her Majesty for a while when her mind has become tired of her unceasing study of the sciences." There is no doubt that he succeeded.

Somadeva notes that he has followed his original with the utmost fidelity but has abbreviated its prolixity. "I want to state," he continues, "that I have preserved both appropriateness of language and continuity of subject matter and have also retained the manner in which separate parts of the poem are joined together, but without disturbing the characteristic mood of the narrative." However, his Sanskrit rendering, which is a delightful one otherwise, is rather handicapped by this fidelity, for the main narrative has almost irretrievably got lost in the maze of stories that are added to it. At the slightest provocation a speaker recalls a tale in which a speaker recalls another tale; and the banquet consists of nothing but hors d'œuvres.

Somadeva's version was, except for a negligible condensation by a contemporary, all we had left of the celebrated Great Romance until the French scholar Félix Lacôte found, edited, and translated a wholly new version that had been preserved in Nepal. This Nepalese version, which obviously represents an earlier and less overgrown stage in the transmission of the original, is simply called *Bṛhatkathāślokasaṃgraha*, "Abbreviation in Verse of the Great Romance." It was composed around the eighth century by an otherwise unknown author called Budhasvāmin and is, unfortunately, incomplete. Nevertheless, it complements the "Ocean" in the most felicitous fashion. It gives the main story in full detail and only incidentally adds a relevant tale. In style and spirit the "Abbreviation" is superior to the "Ocean." Budhasvāmin is lively, observant, irreverent, and colloquial, while Somadeva is a little pedestrian at times and very loyal to the brahmin way of life. Together they make an excellent team.

The "Great Romance"—the *Bṛhatkathā* from which both versions borrow their titles—was written in a language that the fastidious Sanskrit grammarians called "troll's tongue." Its author was Guṇāḍhya, whose name, appropriate but not very authentic-sounding, means "Rich in Virtue." His biography is even less authentic but at least more imaginative. Guṇāḍhya, according to legend, started on his literary career with no less than seven Great Romances, all about Aerial Spirits, and he had to write them down in the forest for fear that the Spirits would steal their chronicles before they could be used to edify man. And he wrote down all seven hundred thousand couplets in his own blood, because he had no ink.

This mighty literary labor was a penance imposed by a goddess who had turned him into a troll. According to her curse, his sin would be expiated and he would return to his own form only when his work had become current in the world of men. Therefore he had two pupils of his take his poem to the King of Pratiṣṭhāna, who, it turned out, was disgusted with both the language and the blood. Guṇāḍhya was mortified and cremated his magnum opus ceremonially on a hill, reading page after page to the birds and beasts of the forest before committing them to the sacred fire. He saved just one story, the Romance of the Aerial Spirit Naravāhanadatta, the "Great Romance."

Rarely, however, do romances begin on earth, and this one too began in heaven. Once upon a time, the story goes, God Śiva sat on Mount Kailāsa in the Himalayas with his wife the Daughter of the Mountain. And in a sudden burst of affection "the moon-crested God, alert to her praises and flattered, put her on his lap and asked, 'What can I do to please you?'" The Goddess asked for a story, but it displeased her; and to restore her good temper Śiva promised another tale. Thereupon the Goddess ordered Śiva's bull, which watches his gates, to allow nobody in, and the God proceeded to tell the Seven Romances of the Aerial Spirits. Meanwhile a familiar of Śiva, his favorite Blossom-Tooth, wanted to get in to his master and was barred by the bull; whereupon he made himself invisible, entered, and heard all. Delighted, he told the stories to his wife. "For who," wonders Somadeva, "can keep money or a secret from his wife?" The woman told the story in the presence of the Goddess: "Why would women hold their tongues?" Blossom-Tooth was cursed to the earth, where his tale eventually reached a fellow victim, Guṇāḍhya.

Guṇāḍhya's "Great Romance" remained a much-used source for later novelists and playwrights, but—this much we can still sense through its later adaptations—it had a character and a tone peculiarly its own. The language in which he wrote appears to have been a Northwest Indian vernacular. It is characteristic that he did not write in Sanskrit; for he aimed not at the brahmins but at the merchants. His hero Naravāhanadatta is a prince, but a prince with the name of a merchant, "Gift of the God of Riches." The prince is a conqueror, but not in the epical manner by martial prowess; in fact, Budhasvāmin's version still shows that

Guṇāḍhya had little sympathy with the warriors of the epic. Naravāhanadatta's weapons are his charm and his songs, and he conquers by marrying. Likewise the ideals displayed in Guṇāḍhya's romance are not the hermit's serenity or the warrior's triumph; they are, frankly and in a civilized way, the ideals of success and acquisition.

The age in which he wrote was indeed the most acquisitive and the most successful in the history of India. It truly possessed the splendor to which later Sanskrit poetry nostalgically responds in magnificent language that too rarely evokes the lustre that inspired it. In northern India, with which these tales are mostly concerned, this age extended from the first until the seventh century A.D., reaching its zenith in the fourth and fifth centuries under the Gupta dynasty. It witnessed the meteoric rise of great trade cities, where Alexandrian brokers bargained with Chinese silk merchants and where the Romans kept factors. It was also the age when Indian merchants set sail to the east to seek gold and in passing sparked a splendid culture to which Angkor Vat and Barabudur are the perennial monuments.

A dozen great cities, many of them on the banks of the Ganges and its tributaries, gave shape to the golden age. The ancient citadel Paṭaliputra, residence of the Maurya dynasty, was past its prime and was soon overshadowed by Ujjayinī in the west and Tāmraliptī in the east. Between them up and down the Ganges and northward toward Central Asia flowed the commerce that opened India for a brief period of glory to the outside world. Ujjayinī was on one of the routes by which silk came from China, and it was the depot of the westward trade. The region long formed part of a Scythian satrapy which kept the city open to Hellenistic influences. Here brahmins might study Greek texts and ascribe in certain matters (astronomy, for instance) as great authority to the barbarians as to the seers of the eternal Veda.

As Ujjayinī was open to the northern frontiers and the western seas, so Tāmraliptī opened on the eastern ocean. Sanskrit literature is rather reticent about this city far out east. The place must have been a cosmopolitan port where Chinese pilgrims came to study Sanskrit, where Indonesian Buddhists disembarked for the monasteries inland, and where everybody enjoyed a scandalous reputation for wit and practical jokes. The great merchant houses of the city had agents in south India and Indonesia, and more than one story suggests that overseas relations were often sealed by marriage.

What remains of these two once splendid cities is a sleepy provincial town, Ujjain, and a village called Tamluk, which is now far from the river and the bay that once carried its merchantmen. It seems as though the urban culture quietly went to sleep for a thousand years. After the Huns had broken up the Indian empire and the lucrative western trade had declined with the fall of the Roman empire, the yawns of village India finally drowned out the cries of the city barkers. Hardly a memory remains, only the wistful nostalgia of epigonic literature. One has to travel to Southeast Asia to see the culture which the merchants sparked, for in all of India not a picture of the ships that carried it abroad survives.

If Ujjayinī and Tāmraliptī have dwindled to insignificance, Madura in the south still stands where it stood in the days when it prospered on the spice trade and transport business that depleted the Roman empire of much gold and more silver. On the threshold of Central Asia far to the north, Takṣaśilā, the Taxila of the ancients, lies in ruins on the bank of Horace's fabled Hydaspes.

Along the sides of the irregular figure formed by Tāmraliptī, Madura, Ujjayinī, and Takṣaśilā moved Indian commerce, and with commerce romance. And both moved in search for Profit. This word, *artha* in Sanskrit, has a revealing completeness of meaning; it can mean "profit," "wealth," "success," and "goal." An entire literature grew around it, both a severely scientific one and a more popular commentary in the form of stories of those who made good. A large portion of Indian narrative literature is made up of success stories. Kauṭilya, the author of a celebrated *Manual of Artha*, maintains in his textbook that of the three principal goals of life—the pursuit of virtue, the pursuit of profit, and the pursuit of love—the second ranks highest. And his opinion is echoed in the present stories. The popular tales that carried his message succeeded immensely. One Sanskrit storybook, which was designed to illustrate how to make good and get ahead in the world, is probably the most widely distributed work of literature in the world. It is the *Pañcatantra*, translated since the sixth century into all major languages of the

Middle East, Europe, and South Asia. It is encouraging to know that at least on one level of human values there are no cultural barriers.

Kauṭilya, who could hardly qualify as a moral arbiter himself, describes the merchants whose spirit pervades the narrative literature as "thieves except for the name." It is not just profitable dishonesty that the Indian success story advocates, however, but a very effective sort of oneupmanship. This happy attitude supposes a good many virtues, among which the Indians prized presence of mind highest and practical knowledge second. Words for "witty," "clever," "worldly," and "crooked" are often the same, and this combination characterizes many heroes of the success stories.

Curiously, despite his firm belief in male supremacy, the Indian loved to find the qualities of success in the women of his stories. Proverbially, woman is an utterly fickle creature, forever waiting her chance to cuckold her husband and almost invariably able to do so with impunity. The prospect of a world in which no woman could be trusted was too bleak even for the Indian, however, and he centered his suspicion around the figure of the courtesan. The most frequently discussed characteristics of the courtesan are not her amorous propensities and aptitudes but her faithlessness and rapacity.

A certain ambivalence was perhaps inevitable where sharp dealing was admired; for the person who could outwit all the others was the very one who could humiliate them most. It is not unusual for harlotry to be associated with infidelity, but there is in many Indian stories an emphasis that seems distinctive. And it is the more intriguing because the appetites to which the courtesan catered were not merely the obvious ones; the cultured man about town depended on her for more.

The Indian woman, if sufficiently highborn, was kept at home until she could be married off at the earliest opportunity. Her education was slight, her interests entirely domestic. For cultural companionship the Indian gentleman had to look to the courtesan, who played in cultured society an artistic role comparable to that of the hetaera of Pericles' Athens or the geisha in Japan. She was an accomplished musician, dancer, actress, and singer, and she probably contributed more to the special grace and elegance of civilization in the age of the Guptas than she will ever be credited for.

Another attitude complicates the image of the courtesan even further. In spite of the ill repute in which she was held (and which often may simply have reflected the rustic's distrust of the demimondaine), the Indian was very sensitive to the peculiar tragedy of the born courtesan. It seems likely that hereditary harlotry originated with the temple girl who, supposedly married to a god, developed into a dancer and an actress in a culture that had many roots in religious pageantry. Yet despite her considerable talents and accomplishments she could never pass for highborn and, in a suitable marriage, have the children that to an Indian justified womanhood. There is always a special fascination about a courtesan in love, but the Indian has added a redeeming element of compassion. In the "First Prince's Story" the ambiguity of the courtesan is beautifully brought out by the two sisters: Kāmamañjarī, example of ruthless rapacity and faithlessness, and Rāgamañjarī, the loving actress and mistress. Gaṅgā, the harlot in "The Travels of Sānudāsa the Merchant," represents both greed and decency. In "The Man Who Impersonated God Viṣṇu," the compassionate storyteller happily marries off the loving courtesan.

With important feminine functions delegated precariously to the harlot, the romance of love, at least as presented in the stories, is the romance of love before and outside marriage. This is partly of course because it makes better listening, but it may also be a realistic appraisal of marriage. When alliances are arranged by families for convenience and the bride soon reduced to mother and drudge and foreman of her servants, the wife commands at best courtesy. Quite characteristic is the reaction of Sānudāsa in "The Travels of Sānudāsa the Merchant," who is deeply embarrassed by his wife's shame when a local courtesan goes through his fortune. He fails less as a husband, he feels, than as a good provider: he has fallen short of the mother of his son. When the same merchant eventually marries a second wife, who happens to arrive at his home before he does, the embarrassment reduces itself to a mild concern about a point of etiquette. In the same tale it is noteworthy how present the hero's widowed mother is.

Interestingly enough, moreover, in the Indian stories it is not the quest for love which acquires deeper romantic significance but the quest for gold. Our age seems to have lost most of its sense of the curious mystique of commercial ex-

Introduction

ventured into the unknown, often staking his life as well as his wealth, he did it for profit no doubt; but soon his journey became a search for paradise. Typically, Western man has recognized this mystique of the exploration of the farthest reaches of one's limitations more readily in the conqueror than in the merchant, and for him commerce was the natural harbinger of conquest. The Indian merchant, who left his marks all over Southeast Asia, never confused the one with the other.

Thus the romance of the sea in India was a peculiar one. The sea was the "mine of all treasures," but the Indians were either poor sailors or poor shipbuilders; for their own story-teller never misses a chance to wreck them. The mythology of the long voyage made the sea into a kind of purgatory for man. In "The City of Gold" and "The Travels of Sānudāsa the Merchant" we find the favorite pattern of a first voyage that fails dismally and a second voyage that succeeds gloriously. At a later period in Indian history, anyone who ventured to sea was considered to court suicide and therefore had to undergo a rite of purification when he returned.

Travel, which in Burton's Arabic phrase is travail, becomes in these stories a pilgrimage, and in the end man is able to transcend his human condition and find the Gold. Man can and should, according to this tradition, become superman. This concept came late to, and is already discredited in, the Western tradition, though it still continues to inspire the typical voyage literature of science fiction. But to the Hindu it has always had a much more profound philosophical content than his Western fellow man could lend to it out of the Judaic and Christian tradition of the paternal God. The word used for this "superman" in the stories is *Vidyādhara,* which has been translated as Aerial Spirit. It means literally "possessor of the redeeming knowledge" and is undoubtedly a popular reflection of that high mystical ambition which has motivated almost all Indian thinking: the ambition to transcend the sorry limitations of being a man and to be released to a higher state. This ideal is reflected in a great variety of ways in the Indian culture, and one of its reflections is the voyage as pilgrim's progress and self-discovery.

The merchant's part in the culture which these tales embroider has been emphasized here because he is the forgotten man of India. But he is not the only hero. You will find a parade of hermits, harlots, and kings carrying a goodly number of corpses and skulls about. Besides the main sources, two other collections have been drawn upon: the *Vampire's Tales,* in Somadeva's version, and the *Tales of Ten Princes.* The number of religious stories and morality tales has been deliberately reduced, for there is a surfeit of holiness in the currently available translations of Indian literature. Among the few included are two short stories from the vast Buddhist collections, which were written in Pāli. The large repertory of animal tales is not represented, because good translations are already accessible.

A number of stories will be familiar to readers from other sources. "The Transposed Heads," for example, inspired Thomas Mann to write a delightful novella, *Die Vertauschten Köpfe,* on which was based the libretto of an American opera performed in 1957 with indifferent success. The story of the third fastidious brahmin (in "The Three Fastidious Brahmins") found its way through Central Asia to Siberia and Lapland and from there to Jutland, where Hans Christian Andersen wrote his "Princess and the Pea." And it is hardly necessary to name the counterpart of "Mahosadha's Judgment."

In spite of the limitations, I believe this anthology does justice to Indian narrative literature. If I have toned down the "spiritual," it is because sometimes one wishes to protest against the image of Indian spirituality—here as well as in India. The classical civilization was not overly spiritual. Even its skull-bearing hermits and vagrant saints had the zest to find humor in a funeral pyre. The homely Buddha of history becomes a towering pantheon of tier upon tier of beings teeming with a restless splendor that owes little to resignation. For a brief span even free will could be an issue. There was a spirit abroad that fleetingly allowed itself to be captured in a living form before it lost itself in formless spirituality. It is hard to believe that so much life would die even in a thousand years.

The King
and the Corpse

On the bank of the river Godāvarī lies the kingdom of Pratiṣ-ṭhāna; and in that kingdom long ago there was a famous king named Trivikramasena, the son of Vikramasena and Indra's equal in might.[1] Every day when the king held court in the audience hall, a wandering mendicant by the name of Kṣānti-śīla came to pay his respects and to give the king some fruit. And every day the king accepted the fruit and handed it to his treasurer who stood by his side.

So ten years went by, until one day when the mendicant had given the fruit to the king and left the audience hall, the king threw the fruit to a little house-monkey that had slipped away from its keepers. When the monkey began to eat, a price-less jewel fell out of the fruit. The king saw it and picked the gem up. Then he demanded of his treasurer, "Where have you kept the fruits which that mendicant has been giving to me and which I have handed over to you?"

[1] Indra was the chief god of the ancient pantheon.

"I have thrown them in the storeroom, through the window, without opening the door," said the frightened treasurer. "If you so command, Sire, I shall open the storeroom and look for them."

The king nodded, and the treasurer left the court. Soon he rejoined the king and reported, "I could not find the fruits in the storeroom; they must have rotted away. But I did find a glittering pile of precious stones."

When the king heard this, he was pleased with the honesty of his treasurer and gave him the stones.

The next day when the mendicant came as usual, the king interrogated him. "Sir, why do you come every day to pay your respects in such an expensive fashion? I shall not accept your fruit today if you fail to explain."

The mendicant took the king aside and said, "Sire, I want to perform a certain magic spell for which I need the assistance of a brave man. I implore you, most courageous of heroes, to lend me your help!"

"I will," promised the king, and the pleased mendicant continued, "Then come to the great burning ground on the fourteenth day of the coming dark moon and meet me at nightfall inside the burning ground. I shall be awaiting you under the vaṭa tree.

"I shall certainly come," repeated the king, and the wandering mendicant went joyfully back to his home.

When the fourteenth day of the dark moon came, the faithful king remembered the promise he had made to the mendicant, and as night fell, he left the royal residence unobserved, wrapped in a dark blue cloak and wearing on his face the marks that ward off evil spirits; he kept his sword ready in his hand. He entered the burning ground, which was enveloped by ghastly fog and smoke-filled darkness. The frightening flames of funeral pyres leered like ghostly eyes about him, and frenzied Ghosts and Vampires horrifyingly closed in around him as he stepped over the piles of bones, skulls, and skeletons of the innumerable dead. Yet this utterly frightful burning ground, resounding with piercing screams of ghoulish malice, like an apparition of the Dread God himself, could not perturb the king, and he traversed it swiftly. He looked about him and found the mendicant at the foot of the vaṭa tree where he was drawing a magic circle.

The king drew nearer and said, "I have come, Reverend Sir. Tell me what I can do for you."

The mendicant looked gratefully up to the king and replied, "Sire, since you have shown me your favor, pray go some distance to the south until you come upon a solitary sissoo tree. In that tree hangs the corpse of a man. Bring me that corpse: be gracious, bold king, and help me!"

"I will," said the king, who was always true to his word; and he turned south and departed. He walked in darkness, but his path was illumined by the flames of burning and smoldering pyres, and at length he found the sissoo tree. The dead body of a man hung down the trunk of the tree which, tanned by the smoke of the crematories and reeking of burnt flesh, seemed like a Stalker of the Night. The king climbed the tree, cut the rope, and dropped the body to the ground; the corpse struck the ground and screamed as if it had hurt itself. The king climbed down and touched the body gently, for he feared it was still alive. At his compassionate touch the corpse shook with ghastly laughter. The king now knew that the body was possessed by a Vampire.[2]

"Why are you laughing?" he asked, unafraid. "Come on, let us go." But the instant he spoke, he found the body gone; it was hanging again from the tree. The king again climbed the tree and lowered the corpse—a brave man's heart is more adamant than diamond. Silently he lifted the body on his shoulder and started back to the mendicant.

And while he was going, the Vampire spoke in the body on his shoulder. "Your Majesty, I shall tell you a story to enliven the walk. Listen!"

The Faithful Suitors

On the bank of the Kalindī is a brahmin freehold called Brahmasthala; and there lived once a brahmin by the name of Agnisvāmin who was a great scholar of the Veda. His wife

[2] The Vampire is a Vetāla, a chthonic godling who takes possession of corpses.

bore him a girl so very beautiful that when the Creator had brought forth her fresh and precious loveliness he must have scorned his earlier creations of celestial maidens.

When this girl, who had been named Mandāravatī, had reached the marriageable age, three young brahmins arrived from Kanyakubja, all of the same virtuous character. Each of them proposed to her father for the hand of Mandāravatī, and each grudged her to the others to such an extent that he threatened to kill himself if she were to wed another. So, lest he cause the death of at least two brahmins, Agnisvāmin did not marry her off at all; and the girl remained a virgin. Meanwhile the three suitors settled down there and gazed day and night upon her moonlike radiant face with the devotion of cakora birds.[3]

Then suddenly Mandāravatī, still unmarried, was carried off by the hot fever which struck without warning. Consumed by grief the three brahmins conducted the funeral rites, carried her to the burning ground, and cremated her.[4] One of them erected a little hovel on the spot and bedded down on her ashes, living on the food he begged. The second gathered her bones and went to the Ganges. The third became a wandering mendicant and departed to roam in other lands.

This mendicant came in the course of his wanderings to a village called Vakrolaka and was invited into the house of a brahmin to be his guest. When he sat down to his meal after the honors had been done, one of the children in the house started to cry. The mother tried to calm the child, but when it would not stop screaming, she lifted it angrily by the arms and threw it in the blazing fire; and no sooner did the infant fall into the fire than its tender body was burned to ashes.

At this hair-raising spectacle, their guest cried: "Oh, horror! I have entered the house of a brahmin Ogre! I refuse to take any of this food, which is sin itself!"

But the father said, "Now behold the power of my spell, which as soon as it is spoken can resurrect the dead!"

He took a small manuscript which contained the spell, recited the charm over some dust, and threw the dust over the

---

[3] Cakora birds are supposed to feed on moonbeams.

[4] The dead were, and are, almost invariably cremated; the bodies were taken to a field outside the populated area, cremated on pyres, and left behind.

ashes. And the little boy rose up alive with his former body. Relieved, the mendicant returned to his meal. His host hung the book on a peg in the wall, had his meal and at nightfall shared his bed with his guest.

As soon as the household was asleep, the mendicant got up stealthily and took down the book. Immediately he departed thence and walking day and night came at last at the burning ground where Mandāravatī had been cremated. There he saw the second of the brahmins, who had returned simultaneously from the Ganges where he had gone to commit her bones to the sacred waters. Together they joined the third brahmin, who had stayed in the burning ground, building himself a hut and sleeping on the girl's ashes.

The mendicant said, "We must tear down this hut so that I can resurrect my beloved from the ashes with the charm of a spell."

He insisted until he had put the others to work, and when the hut was torn down, he opened the little book and recited the spell over some dust; then he threw the charmed dust on the ashes. And instantly Mandāravatī stood up alive; and the body she bore now had gained in splendor, surpassing even its unmatched beauty of yore now that it had been purified in the fire—it was as though it had been fashioned out of gold.

At the first sight of the girl who was reborn so beautiful, the three brahmins were smitten with love and, longing to take her, began to quarrel over her.

One said, "She is my wife, for I have won her through the power of my spell."

"She is reborn through the power of the holy Ganges," said the second, "and therefore she is mine!"

"No, she is mine, for I have guarded her ashes and revived her through my mortifications!" said the third.

"Now tell me, Sire," resumed the Vetāla, "how should their quarrel be decided: to whom does the girl properly belong as wife? Your head will burst asunder if you know it and fail to speak!"

And the king replied: "The one who brought her to life with his magic spell after considerable efforts is her father rather than her husband, for the part he took was a father's part. The one who committed her bones to the Ganges may pass as her son. But the third one who mortified himself on the burning ground out of his love for her and slept on her ashes—he, I say, is truly her husband."

When the Vetāla had heard King Trivikramasena's reply, he vanished from the king's shoulder and returned to his own haunt. And the king, who kept only the mendicant's end in view, decided to catch him once again. For a man of great character refuses to break his promise, even at the peril of his life.

Thus King Trivikramasena returned to the sissoo tree, again took the Vampire out of the tree, lifted him on his shoulder, and started back in silence. And while the king hurried on, the Vampire spoke.

"Sire, you are a wise and mettlesome man, which pleases me. Therefore I shall tell you a diverting story. Listen to this riddle."

The Transposed Heads

Long ago there was a king on earth who was known as Yaśaḥketu, Banner-of-Fame. His royal residence was the city of Śobhāvatī. In this city stood a beautiful temple dedicated to the White Goddess. South of the temple site was the temple pond, which was known simply as the Goddess' Pond. Every year, on the fourteenth day of the light moon in the month Āṣāḍha, a large procession of pilgrims came to this pond from all parts of the country to take a purifying bath.[5]

One year on that day a young washerman, Dhavala, came on a pilgrimage from his village Brahmasthala to take the holy bath, and at the pond he saw a young girl who had likewise come to bathe, Madanasundarī, the daughter of a washerman called Śuddhapaṭa. His heart was stolen by the girl, who robbed the moon of its splendor, and after he had found out

[5] The year was traditionally divided into 12 months of 30 days each, and every month was divided into 2 wings or fortnights of 15 days each. The "bright" fortnight corresponded to the waxing moon, the "dark" fortnight to the waning moon. The date in the story therefore is Full Moon's Eve falling somewhere in the Western months of June or July.

what her name was and her caste, he went home, passionately
in love.

At home he suffered from separation; he behaved abnor-
mally, did not touch his food, and so on. Anxiously his mother
questioned him, and he told her that he was in love. She went
at once to tell her husband Vimala, who, when he joined them
and saw the condition of his son, said: "Why are you so down-
cast, my son, when it is not at all difficult to get what you
want? If I ask Śuddhapaṭa, he will certainly give you the
hand of his daughter. We are not inferior to him, in caste or
income or profession. I know him, and he knows me; so it
will be quite easy for me to arrange it."

After these reassurances he pressed his son to eat his meals,
and the next day father Vimala went with Dhavala to Śuddhapaṭa's house in the city of Śobhāvatī. He asked Śuddhapaṭa to give his daughter in marriage to his son Dhavala,
and Śuddhapaṭa agreed with all proper formalities. An auspicious hour was fixed for the next day, and Śuddhapaṭa
gave Dhavala the hand of Madanasundarī, who was of the
same caste. When the wedding was over, Dhavala returned
contentedly with his bride, who had fallen in love with him
at first sight, to his father's house in Brahmasthala.

After they were living happily together, it so happened
that a son of Dhavala's father-in-law, brother to Madanasundarī, come one day to visit them. He was hospitably received, and everybody embraced him in welcome. He inquired
how his relatives were doing, and, after he had rested, he
said: "I have been sent by father to invite Madanasundarī
and her husband over, for we are going to have a special
celebration for the Goddess." [6] They gladly accepted the invitation, and the rest of the day his sister and all the other
members of the household served him with choice food and
drink.

The next morning Dhavala departed with Madanasundarī
and his brother-in-law to their father's place. Arriving in
Śobhāvatī the third of the company, Dhavala happened to
pass the great temple of the White Goddess. When he saw
the temple, he was moved with piety, and he said to his sister

---

[6] The Great Goddess, also known as the White, Dread, or Fierce
Goddess, Kālī, and Durgā, represented creation, as well as destruction,
and she was considered to be the spouse of Śiva.

and her brother, "Come, let us visit Our Lady the Great Goddess here!"

But his brother-in-law tried to stop him, saying, "We cannot all of us visit the Goddess empty-handed."

"Then I go alone. Wait for me here."

So Dhavala went off to visit the Goddess. He entered the temple, prostrated himself before her image, and meditated upon the Goddess—how she had crushed the insolent demon Ruru with her eighteen arms, and how she had trampled the demon Mahiṣa under her lotus-like feet. At the prompting of fate a thought occurred to him.

"People bring all kinds of bloody sacrifices to the worship of Our Lady. Could I not please her then in order to gain the highest end by sacrificing myself?" And he took from the inner sanctum, which was deserted, a sword that had been left by some pilgrims as a votive offering to the Goddess. He tied his head by the hair to the bell rope and then cut his head off with the sword. His dead body dropped to the floor.[7]

When Dhavala had been gone a long time and still did not return, his brother-in-law stepped into the temple of the Goddess to look for him. And when he saw his sister's husband with his head cut off, he was so upset that he cut off his own head with the same sword.

When her brother, too, failed to return, Madanasundarī became very anxious, and she likewise entered the temple. As she came in, she saw her husband and her brother, both without heads. Wailing "Oh, what is this? I am lost!" she collapsed on the floor. After awhile she rose, and, mourning her two loved ones who had so suddenly come to their end, she thought, "What use is it now if I live?" And resolving to do away with herself, she prayed to the Goddess: "O Goddess, supreme Queen of all gods, you who dispense happiness and a virtuous life, you who share your body with your Consort the Foe of Love, O refuge of all your devotees, dispelling all their miseries, why have you taken my husband and my brother? I did not deserve it, for I have always been devoted to you. I throw myself on your mercy; hear my dismal prayer. I shall give up this ill-fated body, but grant, O Goddess, that in whatever kind of life I shall be born again, my husband

[7] The weight of his head would sound the bell as it was sounded when an offering was made.

and brother will again be my husband and my brother!" And
when she had finished her praises and prayers, she bowed
before the Goddess. Then she fashioned a creepervine on an
aśoka tree into a noose. But when she tightened the noose
around her neck, a Voice sounded from heaven above.

"Do no violence to yourself, my daughter, for I am pleased
to find such great virtue in one so young as you. Remove the
noose. Join the heads of your husband and your brother each
to its trunk, and I bestow this boon on you that both will rise
and live."

When Madanasundarī heard the Goddess' command, she
let go of the noose and ran happily toward the temple. But
the very young woman was so confused by all the violent
things that had been happening to her that she did not look
closely, and, as luck would have it, she joined her husband's
head to her brother's trunk and her brother's head to her
husband's body. And both were raised from the dead and
stood up alive and unharmed with the wrong bodies, because
their heads had been changed. The men and the woman
prostrated themselves before the Goddess and, joyously talking over their experiences, they went their way. But when
they had gone for some distance, Madanasundarī discovered
that she had changed their heads; and she was perplexed and
did not know what she was to do.

*"Tell me therefore, Your Majesty," resumed the Vampire,
"which of those two mixed-up men was really Madanasundarī's
husband? If you know the answer and keep silent, your head
shall burst in a hundred pieces!"*

*King Trivikramasena had listened to the Vampire tell the
story and the riddle, and he replied: "The body that carries
her husband's head is her husband; for the head is the most
important part of the body, and the rest of the body is identified by the head."*

*When the king had spoken, the Vampire again mysteriously
disappeared from his shoulder, and the king retraced his steps
to catch the wizard once more. He found the Vampire again
in the sissoo tree, took him on his shoulder, and started anew.
And while the king walked on, the Vampire spoke from his
shoulder.*

"Listen to another of my riddles and forget your labors!"

The Three Fastidious Brahmins

In the country of the Angas there is a large settlement of
brahmins which is called Vṛkṣaghaṭa. At that place lived
once a wealthy brahmin by the name of Viṣṇusvāmin who
performed regularly the great sacrifices of scripture. He had
a brahmin wife, and three sons were born to them in succession; and all three were preternaturally perceptive and exceedingly fastidious.

One day their father sent them off to catch a tortoise, which
was needed for a sacrifice that he had undertaken. The three
brothers went to the seashore.

When they had found a tortoise, the eldest brother said to
the others, "One of you must carry this tortoise for father's
sacrifice. I cannot bear to touch the filthy slippery thing."

But the other two brothers said, "If you don't like to touch
it, neither do we!"

"But you must pick up the tortoise," said the eldest one.
"Else it is your fault if anything goes wrong with father's
sacrifice, and you will be sure to go to Hell, both of you!"

The others laughed. "You know our duties, but you don't
seem to know your own, which is precisely the same."

"But you know how fastidious I am about food, don't you?"
complained the eldest brother. "I am so fastidious that I
cannot possibly touch anything I loathe."

Thereupon the second brother said, "Then I am even more
fastidious, for I am extremely particular about women."

"Well," said the eldest, "let the youngest pick up the
tortoise."

But the latter frowned angrily and replied: "What fools!
I am more particular about beds than either of you about
anything!"

So the three brothers began to quarrel, and in order to
force a decision they left the tortoise and, totally engrossed
in their pride, hurried off to the king of a nearby district, one
Prasenajit, in the city of Vitaṅkapura. They were announced

by the chamberlain, and when they had been admitted, they told the king their story.

"Remain here for the while," said the king, "until I have examined each of you in turn." They agreed and stayed.

When dinnertime came, the king seated the brahmins at the place of honor and ordered a regal dish to be served of sweet rice flavored with all six flavors. When all were eating heartily, one of the brahmin youths, the one who was so particular about his food, refused to eat and pinched his nose disgustedly.

"Why don't you eat, brahmin?" asked the king softly. "The dish is quite tasty and well flavored."

The brahmin whispered back, "Your Majesty, there is a definite smell of burnt corpses about the cooked rice, and tasty though the dish may be, I can't possibly eat it."

The king ordered everyone to smell the food, but they all said that the rice, which was of a special kind, was perfect and smelled delicious. Nevertheless, the fastidious youth kept his nose covered and refused to eat. Having thought about it, the king made investigations, and he discovered from the cooks that the dish had been prepared with rice that had been grown on an acre near the burning ground of a village.

Most surprised and pleased, the king said to the youth: "You are indeed sensitive about your food! You must eat something else."

After dinner, when the three brahmins had gone off to their rooms inside the palace, the king had a most beautiful concubine from his own seraglio brought in to him and sent the perfectly shaped and gorgeously adorned woman at nightfall to the second brahmin who was so fastidious about his women. Accompanied by the king's flunkeys she came to his bedchamber, and, with her face as radiant as moonbeams, she seemed to be the very torchbearer of the God of Love. But when she entered the room, which she brightened with her splendor, the fastidious youth, pressing his left hand to his nose and nearly fainting, groaned.

"Drag her out. I shall die if she stays! She smells like a goat!"

The flunkeys took the exasperated courtesan along, brought her to the king, and told him what had happened. The king summoned the fastidious brahmin and said: "This courtesan moves in clouds of the pleasantest perfumes, she has scented herself with the best musk and camphor and aloe, and yet you declare that she smells like a goat!" But in spite of the king's assurances the fastidious youth did not give in, and the king began to have his doubts. He inquired and coaxed the courtesan herself into revealing that, when she was a child, she had had neither mother nor wet nurse and had been brought up on goat's milk. The king was amazed and praised the fastidiousness of the fastidious brahmin.

Then the king ordered his servants to gratify the tastes of the third brahmin who was so particular about beds—to make him at once a bed with seven layers of mattresses piled on top of the couch. The sensitive brahmin slept on the magnificent bed for one and a half hours. In the middle of the night he got up, crying in pain and holding his side with his hand. The attendant flunkeys saw on his side a curved red mark that was deeply imprinted in the flesh like a seal in clay. They went to the king and reported, and the king ordered them to inspect the tops of the mattresses and to see if there was anything lying on them. They examined the mattresses one after the other, and finally, under all seven mattresses, on top of the couch itself, they found a hair. They brought the hair to the king and showed it to him, and when the king saw the same mark on the side of the sensitive youth, who had been brought in, he was astounded.

"How can a hair leave a mark on his body through seven mattresses?" the king wondered, and he spent the rest of the night marveling.

The next morning he passed judgment that all three of them were miraculously perceptive and sensitive and rewarded the three fastidious youths each with a purse of a hundred thousand gold pieces. Forgetting the tortoise, they stayed happily in that country and incurred great sin by bringing their father's sacrifice to an untimely end.

When he had finished this wonderful story, the Vampire, unruffled, again questioned King Trivikramasena: "Your Majesty, remember my curse, which stands as before, and tell me which of these three youths who were so fastidious about food, women, and beds was really the most sensitive?"

And the wise king replied: "I consider the last one, who

was so particular about his bed, the most fastidious of the three, because he could not have cheated. On his body, for all to see, was the imprint of the hair which tallied exactly. The other two might have obtained their information from someone else."

The Vampire disappeared as before from the shoulder of the king because he had spoken; and, unfailing in endurance, the king went back after him. Once again King Trivikramasena took the Vampire from the sissoo tree and strode onward.

The Vampire said to the king from his shoulder, "Sire, I will tell you a curious story. Listen!"

The Three Sensitive Queens

In the city of Ujjayinī there was once a king by the name of Dharmadhvaja. He had three wives, all of royal blood, whom he loved to excess. One was called Moonstreak, the second Starburst, the third Doeskin; and the beauty of them all was matchless. The king had defeated all his foes and, his duties fulfilled, lived happily, dallying with his three queens.

Once when the day of the Springtime Festival had come, the king went with his queens to the park to play. He gazed upon the vines which bent under the burden of blossoms, like the bows of Love readied by Spring with beestrings for bowstrings, and harkened to the songs of koil birds in the treetops as though they were the commandments of the Mind-born God whose only mood is the mood of love; and as he gazed and harkened, the king and his queens drank deep of the intoxication which is the life of the living God. And as he drank, he rejoiced in the lees of the mead which his mistresses had left fragrant with their sighs and reddened by their cherry lips.

While they were dallying, the king playfully ruffled Moonstreak's hair, and the lotus over her ear fell whirling on her lap. The flower dropped on her thigh and made a wound; and the highbred, delicate queen cried out and swooned. The king and his retinue were overcome with anxiety when they saw the accident and gently comforted the queen with fans that were dipped in cool water. Thereupon he conducted her to the palace, and when the wound had been bandaged, he administered to her the unguents that his physicians had prepared.

Night fell, and seeing that Moonstreak was doing well, the king went up to the moon pavilion on the roof of his palace with his second queen Starburst. While she slept in the king's arms, the cool beams of the moon strayed through the trellis and fell on her nude body. She woke up exclaiming, "Oh, I am burned!" and she jumped from her bed to feel her limbs. The king awoke and anxiously asked what had happened; and he got up and saw blisters all over her body. He questioned Queen Starburst, who said, crying, "I was nude, and the beams of the moon fell on me." Anguished, the king summoned her maids who came running in panic and confusion. He ordered them to make her a bed with moist waterlily petals and to apply damp ointments of sandal to her burns.

The third queen Doeskin learned of the accident and decided to join her consort. She stepped out of the seraglio, and as she stood in the open, she heard in the hushed night the clear sound of a mortar grinding rice somewhere far away in a dwelling. No sooner did she hear the sound than she cried, "Oh, I am dying," and stretching out her arms the doe-eyed queen sank in pain on the road. Her maids, just returning, took her to the seraglio and the groaning young woman fell on her couch. They examined her and, bursting in tears, found her hands covered with calluses like lotus flowers dotted with bees. They went to the king and told him; and Dharma-dhvaja came and questioned his beloved queen concerning her accident. She showed him her hands and said, "When I heard the sound of a mortar, my hands became callused." He had ointments of sandal and other remedies such as soothe the pain of burns applied to her hands; and he was full of wonder and despair.

"One was wounded by a falling lotus, the second was burned by the moon, and the third, oh horror! had her hands callused by the mere sound of a mortar. . . . Aho! All at once fate has turned the exquisite delicacy of my highbred queens from virtue into vice!"

Harboring such gloomy thoughts, the king wandered about the seraglio and waited through the three watches of the night as though they were a hundred. The next morning the physician and his chirurgeons took measures so that the king to his joy soon saw his queens well.

When the Vampire had related this most wonderful tale, he asked King Trivikramasena from his shoulder: "King, tell me, which queen was the most sensitive of them all? The old curse will strike you if you know but fail to speak."

The king replied: "Surely the most delicate was she who was callused by the mere sound of the mortar, without even being touched. The other two were actually touched by the lotus and the moonbeams which wounded and burned them. Therefore they cannot compare with the other."

Once more the Vampire, leaving the king's shoulder when he had broken his silence, returned to his haunt; but still the king persisted in his firm resolution and went in pursuit. When King Trivikramasena had again fetched the Vampire from the sissoo tree, he started once more on his way back to the mendicant. And while the king was making haste, the Vampire on his shoulder spoke.

"Your Majesty, I have another story. Listen."

The Man Who Changed Sexes

In the land of Nepāl was a city named Sivapura; and there, once upon a time, ruled a king who was justly called Yaśaḥketu, Pennant-of-Honor. This king had placed the burdens of government on the shoulders of his councillor Prajñāsāgara, Ocean-of-Wisdom, and with his queen Candraprabhā indulged in the pleasures of love. In the course of time the queen bore him a daughter who received the name Śaśiprabhā, Moon-Lustre; and indeed she displayed to the eyes of the world the incarnate beauty of the moon.

In due time the girl became a woman.

Once the princess came out in the palace garden to watch

with her companions the celebrations of the festival of spring. And as she was gathering flowers, one hand hidden in a splendid new-cut bouquet and her other delicate arm stretched out in such a way as to reveal one charming breast, she was seen by the son of a rich brahmin, Manaḥsvāmin, who had likewise come to the spring festival. The instant he set eyes on her, his mind was stolen from him, and in spite of his name "Mind's Master," the young man, bewildered with love, was no longer master of his mind at all.

"Is she the Goddess of Lust who is gathering the flowers bestowed by Spring for the arrows of her master the God of Love? Or is she a sylph that has come from the woods to worship Kṛṣṇa?" While he stood wondering, the princess saw him too; and as soon as she had seen the youth, who might have been the God of Love embodied, she was so overcome with longing that she forgot her flowers, her body, and her soul.

While they stood loving each other with sudden love, there arose a loud clamor of anguished cries, and they raised their heads to see what had happened. Bearing down on them, up-rooting the trees along the road, came a rutting elephant which, his heat aroused by the smell of other elephants, had thrown off his mahout and, bursting loose from his chains, was running wild with the hook dangling from his ear. The companions of the princess took flight in terror, and the princess was left alone. Instantly Manaḥsvāmin ran toward her, lifted her up in his arms with passionate excitement, and carried the girl, who experienced fear, love, and shame at the same time, a safe distance out of the elephant's path. Then the princess was again surrounded by her attendants, who, praising the brahmin's courage, took her back to her own quarters, while she kept turning around to look back at her beloved. At home the princess could not stop thinking of the love of her life and suffered pangs of passion; night and day she burned with the raging fire of love.

Manaḥsvāmin himself had followed the princess and watched her disappear into her chambers. And he thought: "I cannot hope to survive without her. My only refuge is my teacher, Master Mūladeva, the cunning magician."

Somehow he wore through the day, and the next morning he went off to visit Master Mūladeva, whom he found in the

company of his inseparable friend Moon; like the vault of the
sky his mysterious turns were miracles of magic. Manaḥsvāmin bowed to the master crook and told him his desire; and
with a smile Mūladeva promised to satisfy it. The master
crook took a magic pill, put it in his own mouth, and changed
himself into an ancient brahmin; then he gave Manaḥsvāmin
another pill to put in his mouth and changed him thereby into
a beautiful girl. Thereupon the crafty Mūladeva went with
the transformed Manaḥsvāmin to the father of the boy's beloved, the king himself, and, attending on the king in the
audience hall, made to him the following request.

"Your Majesty, I have one son, and for him I have asked
this girl in marriage and brought her here from afar. But
now my son has left for some place, and I shall have to find
him. While I am away, pray keep this girl in your protection
until I have fetched my son. For you are the protector of all."

Fearing that he would be cursed if he refused, King
Yaśaḥketu promised to do as he was asked and had his
daughter Śaśiprabhā brought in to him. He said to her:
"Daughter, keep this girl in your own chambers and let her
eat and sleep at your side!"

So the princess promised, and she conducted the transformed Manaḥsvāmin to her own chambers. And while Mūladeva, himself changed into an ancient brahmin, went his way,
Manaḥsvāmin remained near his beloved in the shape of a
girl.

After a few days the princess had come to trust her companion's friendship and affection; and one night Manaḥsvāmin whispered softly from the next bed and questioned the
girl, who was suffering so badly under the separation that she
had grown thin and at night lay tossing on her bed.

"Why are you so unhappy, my dear? Every day you grow
paler, and you look colorless and thin as though you were
separated from a lover. Tell me, what is the matter with you?
Is there any reason why you should not trust your loving and
innocent friend? If you don't tell me what is wrong, I shall
refuse my meals!"

The princess sighed and whispered back: "But why should
I not trust you? I will tell you, my friend. Listen. One day I
went out to watch the flower festival of spring, and there I saw
a handsome brahmin youth. He was as cool as snow or pearls

or moonlight—he was like Spring who, with a glance, had raised his friend Love from the dead and was now making nature splendid for his eyes to rejoice in. But while my eyes feasted on the elixir of the beauty of his moonlike face and lovingly sought to fly out to him like two cakora birds, there was sudden thunder as though Doomsday had burst loose upon us out of time, and a monstrous bull elephant which had broken his chains came down on us with his rutting sweat flowing. My attendants panicked and fled, and I was terrified. But that young brahmin boy took me in his arms and carried me out of the way. When I touched his body, it was as if I were rubbed with musk or sprinkled with nectar, and I felt . . . I don't know what. Almost at once my companions rejoined me and took me home. I was helpless. It was as though I had been cast down to the earth from paradise!

"Ever since that day, even when I am wide awake, I see the lord of my life beside me, having found his way to me by various tricks. And at night in my dreams I see him do clever things to me and force me with his kisses and embraces to abandon all modesty. . . . But I know nothing about him, neither his name nor his family—nothing—and I have no way of reaching him. And so the pains of separation from the lord of my soul burn me with fire."

Her words filled his ear like nectar, and the boy with the body of a girl blissfully saw his end attained. Judging that this was the right time to reveal himself, he took the pill from his mouth and showed himself as he really was.

"Darling with the shining eyes," he said, "I am the one whom you have bought with your glances in that garden and led into undisguised servitude! When my meeting with you was cut short immediately, I came to such grief that in the end I was changed into a girl. Therefore bring the miseries of separation which I have endured to a happy end, for my love, darling, can bear it no longer."

When the princess saw the lord of her soul appear so suddenly, awe, amazement, and love engulfed her that very instant. They married each other in the manner of Gandharvas,[8] as their longing dictated, and there was such a feast of love as their passions commanded. And henceforth Ma-

[8] The Gandharvas were the musicians of the gods, and they were associated with informal marriage based on mutual consent.

nahsvāmin contentedly lived in two different forms, by day with the pill a maiden, by night without the pill a man.

Several days passed. Then King Yaśahketu's brother-in-law Mṛgāṅkadatta gave his daughter Mṛgāṅkavatī with a very large dowry in marriage to Councillor Prajñāsāgara's son, a brahmin. Princess Śaśiprabhā was invited to the wedding of her cousin, and she went to her uncle's residence. The brahmin youth Manahsvāmin, still disguised as a beautiful virgin, accompanied her in her retinue of maids-in-waiting.

Now, listen to this! When the Councillor's son saw the would-be girl, he was utterly smitten with passionate love; and, robbed of his senses by that deceptive maiden, he went with his new bride to a home which now seemed empty. And there, totally immersed in abysmal concentration on the beauty of the supposed girl's face, he passed suddenly into a stupor, bitten as he was by the poisonous snake of severe passion. Wondering anxiously what could be the matter with him, his family deserted the wedding festivities, and his father Prajñāsāgara came too as soon as he heard of the crisis. Comforted by his father, he roused from his stupor, and raving deliriously he spat out his yearning. His father was terribly upset and thought that his son had lost his senses; and the king himself, being notified, appeared at the house. When the king had seen the boy whom the suffocating embrace of love had instantly carried to the seventh stage of sickness, he consulted his ministers.

"The girl has been entrusted to me by a brahmin," he said. "How can I marry her off to him? But without her he will certainly reach the last and fatal stage. When he has perished, his father, my Councillor, will die too, and at the Councillor's death the kingdom will collapse! Tell me, what can we do about it?"

The ministers replied: "The duty of the king, so has it been ordained, is to protect the virtue of his subjects. The foundation of this protection is the prudence vested in the councillors. When the Councillor dies, the foundation succumbs and the collapse of virtue inevitably follows. Evil would result from the murder of the Councillor, who is a brahmin in the bargain, and his son. This immediate threat to virtue ought therefore to be averted first. The maiden whom the brahmin has left in Your Majesty's custody must be married off to

breach of trust, but that matter can be dealt with later, when
it arises."

The king agreed with the advice of his ministers and
promised to give the supposed girl to the Councillor's son.
When an auspicious hour for the wedding had been set,
Manaḥsvāmin was fetched from the princess' chambers. He
said to the king: "Your Majesty, if you marry me to one man
while I have been brought here by someone else to marry another, that is naturally your responsibility. It is yours now,
whatever merit or sin will come of it. I consent to the marriage, but on this condition: I shall not be forced to sleep with
my husband until he has returned from a pilgrimage of six
months to the holy places. If this condition is not granted,
you may be sure that I shall kill myself by biting off my
tongue!"

The king conveyed Manaḥsvāmin's condition to the Councillor's son, who was overjoyed. He accepted the condition,
and as soon as the wedding was over, he lodged his first bride
Mṛgāṅkavatī and his mock bride Manaḥsvāmin in a well-
guarded apartment and stupidly departed on a pilgrimage to
please his beloved bride. Manaḥsvāmin, the man who was a
woman, lived in one house with Mṛgāṅkavatī and shared her
seat and bed.

So life went on until once upon a night, when their servants
were asleep outside, Mṛgāṅkavatī whispered to Manaḥsvāmin
in their common bedroom: "Tell me a story, my dear, for I
cannot sleep."

The young man, still changed into a woman, told her the
story of King Īla—how he, scion of the Solar Dynasty,
had been cursed by the White Goddess and became a woman
who bewitched all the world, and how he and King Budha
met, fell in love, and united in the courtyard of a temple, and
how the hero Purūravas was born from their union. When he
had finished his story, he continued cunningly: "So it may
happen once in a while, either at divine command or by the
power of magical drugs, that a man becomes a woman and
a woman a man. And in their new state even the Great Ones
had carnal experiences that sprang from their passion."

When the young and innocent Mṛgāṅkavatī, whose bridegroom had gone on his travels as soon as they were married,

heard this, she admitted with the confidence she had gained from the close intimacy of their lives: "While I was listening to your story, my body began titillating and my heart missed beating. What could that mean? Tell me, my friend!"

"Those are the signs of love, my dear!" said the brahmin. "Is this the first time you feel them? I won't conceal from you that I too felt the same."

Softly Mṛgāṅkavatī said: "Darling, I love you as I love my life. What I am asking you is improper, but could a man somehow be smuggled into our rooms?"

Manaḥsvāmin saw his hopes come true, and, true pupil of the master of crooks, he replied: "If that is what you want, I shall tell you something. God Viṣṇu has granted me a special favor by which I can change myself at will into a man by night. And for your sake I shall now become a man." He took the pill from his mouth and showed himself a handsome and violently virile young man. And with all inhibitions dispelled and intimacy already established, a feast of love was celebrated with a zest that suited the hour.

So from then on, the brahmin lived with the bride of the Councillor's son, by day a woman and a man at night. When he knew that the Councillor's son was due to return in a few days, he took the girl and eloped with her secretly at night.

At this point Manaḥsvāmin's teacher Mūladeva, who knew all that had happened, once again assumed the form of an ancient brahmin. Accompanied by his friend Moon, who had been changed into a young brahmin, he betook himself to King Yaśaḥketu.

"Your Majesty," he said, "I have brought my son. Give me my daughter-in-law now."

The king, fearing that the brahmin would curse him, took counsel and replied: "Brahmin, I do not know where your daughter-in-law has gone. Forgive me, please! To compensate for my breach of trust I shall give you my own daughter for your son."

Mūladeva, prince of crooks, feigned anger and spoke harshly; but finally he allowed himself to be persuaded, and the king bestowed his daughter Saśiprabhā ceremoniously on Mūladeva's friend, Śaśin, who passed as his son. Thereupon Mūladeva took the couple, who were now bride and groom and, rejecting the riches which the king offered him, went back to his own home. There they met Manaḥsvāmin, and a violent dispute arose between him and Śaśin while Mūladeva looked on.

Manaḥsvāmin declared: "Śaśiprabhā should be turned over to me, for I have already married her as a virgin with the consent of Mūladeva."

Śaśin said: "What has she to do with you, fool? She is my wife, for her own father has married her off to me in the presence of the sacred fire!"

And they clamored over the princess they had won through the power of magic without reaching a solution.

"Tell me therefore, Your Majesty," resumed the Vampire, "to whom did the princess belong as his wife? Solve the problem! The old condition of the curse is still in force."

The king, on hearing the riddle from the Vampire on his shoulder, replied: "In my opinion she is legally the wife of Śaśin, for to Śaśin the king had married his daughter regularly and publicly. Manaḥsvāmin had taken her by stealth and married her without ceremony. It has never been the law that a thief is the owner of property he has stolen."

When the Vampire had heard the king's answer, he suddenly disappeared from the king's shoulder and again returned to his haunt. Trivikramasena went after him.

The brave king returned to the sissoo tree, seized the Vampire, and resumed his journey. And from his shoulder the Vampire spoke.

"Sire, listen. I will tell you a story to make you forget your toils."

The King and the Spiteful Seductress

On the bank of the Ganges there was once a city named Kanakapura where the boundaries of the law were inviolate and discord was barred. It was ruled by a monarch called Yaśodhana, Rich-in-Fame, who bore his title with honor. Like the mountains of the coast, he protected the land from the tides of disaster. So glorious shone the fire of his majesty to the joy of the world, and so immaculate did he maintain the orb of his realm, that in him fate seemed to have fashioned Sun and Moon at once. Foolishness was found only in the slander of his foes, not in his explication of the lawbooks; poor he might be in vices, not in treasure or armed might. Fearful he was—lest he sin; and greedy—for honor; and a eunuch—to other men's wives. And his people sang his praises as the epitome of bravery, generosity, and love.

In this king's city there was a rich merchant who had a daughter. Her name was Unmādinī, She-Who-Maddens, and whatsoever man set eyes on her was maddened by the perfection of her beauty, which had the Love God's very potency of fascination.

When Unmādinī had grown into a woman, her merchant father, shrewd in the ways of the world, petitioned the king. "Sire," he said, "I have a daughter to marry who is the jewel of the three worlds. I dare not wed her to another without offering her first to Your Majesty; for the king is the lord of all the jewels of all the world. Therefore, Your Majesty, deign to accept her or to release her."

When the king had heard the merchant's address, he sent his brahmins to see whether she bore the omens of good luck. They went, looked upon the girl who was the sole beauty of the universe, and were shocked out of mind. When they regained their equilibrium, they pondered. "If the king weds her, the kingdom will fall. Would he look after his royal duties if his mind were maddened by his wife? Therefore we must not tell the king that she is well favored."

Having taken counsel togther, they repaired to the king's presence. "Sire," they lied, "the girl is ill-favored." The king refused the merchant's daughter. Thereupon her father the merchant at the king's behest gave his daughter Unmādinī to Baladhara, commander of the army. She lived happily with her husband in his house; yet she harbored resentment at the king's scorn: "I have been spurned by the king because he found me ill-favored."

Time went by. Came the season when the elephant of winter, which with his tusks of blossoming jasmine vines had churned the lotus ponds, was set upon by the lion of spring, which, shaking a mane of blossom clusters and stretching claws of mango sprouts, came to disport in the woods. About this time

the great festival of spring was celebrated in the city and
King Yaśodhana mounted an elephant and rode out to watch
the celebrations. Drummers had preceded him with the proclamation that all the womenfolk of the patricians be kept away
because the sight of the king's beauty was likely to spell
disaster to their conduct.

When Unmādinī heard the proclamation, she spitefully
showed herself to the king from the roof pavilion of her
mansion. And the king gazed upon the woman, who was the
very flame of the fire of Love kindled and fanned with sandal-
scented southerly breezes by his companion Spring, and the
shock overwhelmed him. The instant he set eyes on her beauty,
which had become Love's victorious javelin to pierce the depth
of his heart, he fell in a swoon.

As soon as his followers had brought the king to consciousness, he returned to his palace. He interrogated his men and
heard that she was the woman who had once been offered to
him and rejected. Thereupon he banished from his realm the
brahmins who had lied that she was ill-favored.

Night upon night the yearning king was lost in dreams.
"Aho! Senseless and shameless is the moon that it dares rise
perpetually while her spotless face is there for the eyes of
the world to rejoice in! No solid golden water pitchers nor
the hard forehead knobs of elephants will bear comparison
with her full high-crested breasts. And where is the man whom
her buttocks like the head of Love's elephant, girt with a girdle
like the galaxy, would not smite with desire?"

So the king dreamed in his heart. And boiling on the fire
of desire he wasted away from day to day. He tried to conceal
out of shame what ailed him; but the outward marks betokened
his plight, and at length he gave in to the questions of his
trusted servants and told what caused his grief.

"Then cease suffering!" they said. "The woman is your
subject; why should you not take her?" But the king, who
was just in the law, refused.

Baladhara, his army commander, learned of it; and he came
to the king and with true devotion bowed to his master's feet
and beseeched him: "The woman of your slave is your handmaiden, my Lord, not another man's wife! I offer her to you

myself; accept my wife for your own! Else I shall surrender her to the temple,[9] my Lord, so that you may avoid the sin of taking a hearth-bound woman."

At his commander's insistent entreaties the king, with rage in his heart, replied: "I am a king. Should I commit such lawlessness? If I trespass on the boundaries of the law, who will remain on his true path? You are devoted to me; then how can you prompt me to sin which brings a moment's joy and then becomes the source of great suffering in the afterworld? Nor shall I condone that you abandon your lawful wife. Would a man of my mettle suffer such violence to the law? Better to die." Thus the king restrained him; for those of lofty spirit may give up their lives, never the path of justice.

The townsmen and country people assembled and implored the king that he take the woman; but the king stood firm by his resolution and refused them. At long last the fierce fire of love-fever consumed his body, and nothing remained of the king but his fame. The commander could not bear his lord's death, and he mounted the king's blazing funeral pyre; for the conduct of devoted followers is beyond reproach.

Having narrated this wondrous tale, the Vampire who sat on King Trivikramasena's shoulder asked, "Who was truer, the commander or the king? Answer, my Lord; you are still bound by the curse."

The king broke his silence. "The king was truer," he said.

The Vampire said scornfully, "Why! Was the commander not truer than the king? Speak, king. In his trow to the king he even offered his beautiful wife, though he had long tasted the joy of her embraces. And he burned himself on the pyre when the king had died. The king himself had never known her embrace and could lightly give her up."

Trivikramasena smiled. "That may be true; yet where is the wonder? Is it amazing that the commander, born a patrician, acted as he did in his devotion to his master? Servants are beholden to protect their lord even at the peril of their lives. But kings, swollen with the drunkenness of power, shatter, like berserk elephants, the chains of law and crane their necks for pleasure. Their wits are conceited, and as the holy

[9] Make her a temple prostitute.

water at their Consecration flows away, so flows away their judgment as though it were carried off in the crowd. They raise their waving yak-tail plumes, but with gnats and flies the dust of the learning they acquired from the ancients is also brushed away. Their regal umbrella shelters them from sun-glare and truth. Their vision is obfuscated by the dust storm of their puissance, and they no longer see their way. They all come to grief when their minds are bewitched by love, even Nahuṣa and the other kings who conquered the world.

"But this king, though his umbrella was supreme on earth, was not bewitched by Unmādinī fickle as Fortune. In the end he gave his life, but never did he step on the road of injustice. Therefore to me this wise king was the greater man."

When the Vampire had heard the answer, he suddenly withdrew from the king's shoulder and, by his magic power, returned to the limb. The king quickly gave chase to fetch him back as before. Will great men desist in the middle of their course, however toilsome it may be?

Finding his way through that jungle of the dead, which was infested with carnivorous funeral pyres like ghosts with darting tongues of fire, Trivikramasena undauntedly went back to the sissoo tree in the dead of night. When he came to the tree, he saw to his amazement a multitude of identical corpses hanging from the tree; they had been conjured up by the Vampire's wizardry.

"Aho!" thought the king, "what is the meaning of this? Why is that crafty Vampire so bent on wasting my time? If the night is going to pass before I have finished my task, I I shall kill myself on a funeral pyre! I will not bear ridicule."

The Vampire read his thoughts; and he was pleased with the king's constancy and withdrew his magic. The king now saw only one Vampire in one body, and he climbed up the tree, took the body on his shoulder, and started back again. And while the king strode on, the Vampire addressed him.

"Sire, you are wonderfully mettlesome! Let me tell you a story. Listen."

The Son of Three Fathers

There is a city named Vakrolaka which is like the City of the Gods. Over it ruled a king called Sūryaprabha, Indra's match, who, blessed with a handsome figure as the reward of his virtue in former lives, maintained his land like another Viṣṇu. In his kingdom tears only fell when smoke touched the eyes; death was heard of only in the protestations of lovers; clubs were found only in the hands of doorkeepers. Life for the king, who was rich in all perfections, would have been perfect bliss except for his one complaint that, with all his many concubines, he had never begotten a son.

At this point in the story we turn to the great port of Tāmraliptī where a certain merchant lived, Dhanapāla, richest of the wealthy. This merchant had only one child, a daughter whose name was Dhanavatī; to judge by her beauty she was a spirit of the air who had fallen because of a curse. Just when his daughter reached marriageable age, the merchant returned to the five elements, and, since the king failed to intervene, his wealth was appropriated by his kinsmen. The merchant's wife Hiraṇyavatī thereupon uncovered a hoard of jewels which had been hidden, and, in fear of her husband's heirs, sneaked with her daughter out of her own house in the dead of night. Blinded outside by the darkness of night and inside by the darkness of grief, she finally managed, while leaning on her daughter's arm, to stumble out of the city, but with much trouble. When they had come out of the town, it so happened that in the total darkness her shoulder hit the body of an unseen robber who was impaled on the top of a stake. He was still alive, and the added pain where the woman's shoulder had hit him made him cry out.

"Ah! Who throws salt on my wound?"

"Who are you?" asked the merchant's wife.

"I am a robber whom they have impaled on a stake," answered the thief. "But even on the stake my spirits refuse to leave me—criminal that I am! Tell me, my lady, who are you? Where are you going?"

The merchant's wife told her story, and as she spoke the face of the eastern sky was brightened by the moon. Light spread over the sky, and the robber saw the merchant's unmarried daughter Dhanavatī. He said to her mother: "Listen to one prayer! I shall give you a thousand pieces of gold if you will give me your unmarried daughter!"

"What use would she be to you?" questioned the woman and laughed.

But the robber said: "I shall leave no son when I die, and without a son I cannot share the worlds to come. But if she, at my command, shall give birth to a son, he shall be my legal issue-of-the-womb. This is my prayer; do what I ask you!"

Greed made the woman agree to his proposal. She brought water from somewhere and poured it over the hands of the robber while she said: "Hereby do I bestow on you my virginal daughter."

Thereupon the robber instructed his wife to bear a child for him by another man. Then he told her mother: "Go and dig under that fig tree and take the gold which I have buried there. When I am dead, have my body properly cremated, throw the unburned bones in a holy river, and then go with your daughter to the city of Vakrolaka. There, among the people who rejoice in the virtuous reign of King Sūryaprabha, you will have no fear of misfortune and you will live a happy life."

Thirstily he drank the water she had brought him; then the torment of impalement brought on the robber's death. The merchant's wife took the gold from the foot of the fig tree and sped cautiously with her daughter to the house of a friend of her husband's. She stayed there until she had seen to it, by various means, that the robber's body was cremated, his bones carried to a holy place, and the other ceremonies of the dead properly performed.

The next morning she left with her daughter, carrying her treasure concealed on her person, and journeyed in stages to the city of Vakrolaka. There she bought a house from an eminent merchant called Vasudatta, and she lived there with her daughter Dhanavatī.

At that time there lived in the city a certain teacher Viṣ-

ṇusvāmin who had a very handsome pupil, a young brahmin
called Manaḥsvāmin. This brahmin, though of high caste and
great learning, was the slave of his youth and yearned for
a certain prostitute Haṃsāvalī. But the woman demanded a
fee of five hundred golden dinars; he did not have the money
and grew more miserable every day.

One day the merchant's daughter Dhanavatī happened to
see this handsome but wasted brahmin youth from the roof-
terrace of her house. Her heart went out to him, and, with the
solemn injunction of her husband the robber in mind, she
said cunningly to her mother: "Mother, look how handsome
and vigorous that young brahmin there is! Is he not like nectar
for the eyes of the world to feast on?"

The mother sensed that her daughter had fallen in love,
and she said to herself: "My daughter has to choose someone
to beget a son on her as her husband commanded. . . . Why
should we not try to get him?" So she told one of her maids,
whom she could trust with a secret, what she wanted and sent
her to fetch the brahmin. The maid took him aside and delivered
her message.

Slave of his passion, the youth replied, "I shall come for
one night if I am paid five hundred dinars which I need for
Haṃsāvalī."

The maid carried his answer back to the merchant's wife.
The latter handed the money to the maid, and when Manaḥsvāmin had received the sum, he came back with the maid and
went to the bedroom of the lovesick Dhanavatī. And the girl,
brilliant ornament of the world, gazed longingly at the handsome youth, as a cakora bird gazes at the moon, and rejoiced.
He spent the night with her, playing the games of love, and
in the morning stole away and went as he had come.

Dhanavatī became pregnant accordingly and at the appointed time gave birth to a son whose physical marks presaged
an excellent future. Both mother and grandmother were very
happy that the child was a son.

One night God Śiva appeared in a dream to both of them
and said: "Bring the child in his basket with a thousand gold
pieces to the palace of King Sūryaprabha at dawn and leave
it at the gate. So there shall be safety!"

When the merchant's daughter and her mother woke up,
they told each other their dream; and they took the child

and, putting their trust in the Lord, left the basket with the child and the gold at the Royal Gates of King Sūryaprabha.

At the same time the Bull-bannered God appeared in a dream to King Sūryaprabha, who was ill with desire for a son, and ordered him: "Rise up, O King. A beautiful boy has been left at your gate with some gold. It lies in a basket. Take it!"

When the king awoke in the morning, his doorkeepers brought him the same news, and the king went in person to look. And when he saw the child with a pile of gold waiting at his gate—a boy most auspiciously marked on his hands and feet with the signs of a streak, umbrella, banner, and other signs presaging royalty—he exclaimed, "Śiva himself has brought me a fitting son!" and carried the basket into the palace with his own hands. And he held celebrations at which he gave away so much gold that the very word *poor* lost all meaning. The festivities of song, dance, and music lasted for ten days, and at the end of these ten days King Sūryaprabha gave his son the name Candraprabha.

Prince Candraprabha grew up as time passed, becoming ever more handsome as well as more virtuous, bestowing happiness on all who sought his mercy; and gradually the young man, who was adored by his people, became fitted by his courage, generosity, and wisdom to carry the burdens of government. When his father Sūryaprabha saw this, he anointed him king of his realm and, being an old man now, went to Benares, his duties done. And while his son ruled the earth with statesmanship, the king performed there severe austerities and abandoned his body.

When King Candraprabha learned that his father had passed away, he mourned him and performed the ceremonies for the dead. Then the religious ruler called his councillors and said: "How can I ever acquit myself of the debt which I owe to my father? Yet there is one obligation which I can discharge personally. I shall carry his bones to the Ganges and commit them to the sacred river with the proper rites. Then I shall go to Gayā and bring the offerings of the dead to all my deceased ancestors. On the same occasion I shall make a pilgrimage as far as the eastern shores."

The councillors, however, objected to the king's announcement. "Your Majesty, this is not at all a fitting thing for a king to do! For a kingdom is always threatened and should not be left unguarded a single moment. Let the offerings to the ancestors be done by another's hand. And what pilgrimage is more meritorious then doing your own royal duty? What comparison is there between the many perils that beset the traveler and the perpetual protection which guards a king?"

"The matter is closed," said the king. "I have decided to go for my father's sake. And I must visit the holy places as long as my age permits it. Who can know what may later befall himself in this ephemeral body? In the meantime guard the kingdom and await my return." The councillors fell silent when the king had spoken.

Thereupon the king had all necessaries for his journey prepared, and on an auspicious day he bathed, sacrificed in the fire, honored the brahmins, and departed on his chariot, clad in a pilgrim's new white clothes. All the gentry and the commoners and the peasants accompanied him as far as the borders of his kingdom, unwilling to turn back. So King Candraprabha, having entrusted the care of his country to his councillors, set out on his travels with his house-priest and in the company of brahmins who followed in coaches. He saw many different countries and was amused to note their picturesque dress, their different speech, and what not; and at last he arrived at the Ganges. And he saw the sacred river which with its row upon row of waves seems to build a stairway that leads man step by step to heaven—Gaṅgā the Goddess who, springing from the Mountains of Snow, imitates Ambikā's amorous gestures and playfully ruffles God Śiva's hair. The king descended from his chariot and after taking a bath in the river committed his father's bones ceremoniously to its waters.

After he had distributed alms and performed the funerary rites, the king again mounted his chariot and journeyed in stages to Prayāga, whose holiness is sung by the sages. There where the streams of the Ganges and the Jumna colorfully meet—one yellow and one blue, like butter and smoke that join in the sacrificial fire—to build a road for man to bliss, he fasted. Then, after a bath, donations to temples and priests, and funerary rites, he proceeded to Benares, which with the banners of its many temples astir in the wind seems to beckon from afar: "Come and find the way to release!"

The king fasted for three days and worshipped the Bull-bannered God with many offerings worthy of His greatness; [10] then he departed again for Gayā. He traveled through jungles and forests where with every step fruitladen trees, sounding the sweet songs of birds, bowed to him and sang his praises, while the breeze honored him with wild flowers strewn in his path. Finally he came to auspicious Gayāśiras, and there he performed the complete funerary ritual according to the scriptures and gave rich stipends to the officiating priests. Then he betook himself to the Sacred Grove.

"He made the piṇḍa offering to the dead in the Gayā Spring, but at the moment of his offering three human hands reached up from the depths of the well. The king was perplexed. "In which hand should I place the piṇḍa?" he asked his Brahmins.

"One of these hands is certainly the hand of a robber," said the priests. "Your Majesty may inspect the iron pin which is nailed through it. The second hand, which holds a few stalks of sacred grass, must belong to a brahmin. The third hand, with the marks of royalty and wearing the royal ring, is the hand of a king. But we do not know in which hand the piṇḍa should be put. What could be the meaning of this?"

The words of the brahmins did not help the king to decide.

Thus the Vampire on King Trivikramasena's shoulder ended his curious tale. Then he continued: "Tell me, in which hand should the piṇḍa be placed? The old condition still stands."

Trivikramasena knew the law, and he broke his silence to reply.

"In the robber's hand, for King Candraprabha was legally, as issue-of-the-womb, the robber's son and not the son of the brahmin or the king. The brahmin, though his natural begetter, cannot be considered his legal father, since he had sold himself for money during the night he begat him. He would be King Sūryaprabha's son, by virtue of the sacraments which he performed for the child, the gifts he gave him, and the education he imparted to him, were it not for the fact that the boy's own money, the gold that was put in the basket, was used to meet the costs of his upbringing and education. Therefore, the king can only be the son of that robber whose issue-of-the-womb he was: the robber had

[10] Śiva, to whom Benares is dedicated.

married his mother with the pouring of water over his hand, he had instructed his wife to bear him the child, he had given all the money. So the piṇḍa ought to be put in his hand alone; that is my opinion."

When the king had spoken, the Vampire again vanished from his shoulder to his own haunt; and King Trivikramasena followed him as before. He fetched the Vampire from the sissoo tree, hefted him on his shoulder, and departed quickly. While he silently sped on, the Vampire spoke from his shoulder.

"Your Majesty, why are you so persistent? Go back and enjoy the pleasures of the night. You should not bring me in the power of that miscreant monk! But, if you will persevere, listen to another tale."

The Boy Who Sacrificed Himself

There is a city which bears the name Citrakūṭa, Brilliant Peak, and does justice to its name. In that city, where the demarcations of caste were never trespassed upon, once ruled King Candrāvaloka, crown-jewel of monarchs, who rained showers of nectar in the eyes of his adoring subjects. The learned glorified him as the pen that could hold the elephant of bravery, as the seedbed of generosity, as the abode of manly beauty. But although the king possessed all that man can desire, he had one supreme concern on his mind—that he had not yet found a suitable bride.

One day, to divert his burdened mind, the king rode out with an escort of horsemen to hunt in a vast forest. Resplendent in a blue cloak, he cut through herds of boars with an incessant rain of arrows, as the sun, splendidly cloaked in the sky, cuts with its rays through the darkness. Exceeding Arjuna in power, he laid fierce lions, who shook their blond manes ferociously, on beds of arrows and, matching Indra's might, hurled down with his cruelly striking reeds rhinoceroses as huge as the mountains which Indra sheared of their wings. In the excitement of the hunt the king desired to penetrate alone into the heart of the forest; and with a sharp kick of his heel he urged his hunter on. The horse, sparked by the smarting whiplashes and kicks, galloped forward regardless of the terrain and, swifter than the wind, instantly carried the king, who had lost all sense of direction, ten leagues into the recesses of the forest.

The king reined in his horse and, completely at a loss, wandered about wearily. Then he saw a broad pond in the distance, which, with its finger-like lotuses rising and bowing in the breeze, seemed to gesture to him. "Come. Come hither!" The king rode to the pond, took off the saddle, let the horse roll on the ground, washed it and let it drink at the pond; then he tied it up in the shade of the trees and fetched some dry grass for it to eat. Thereupon he himself bathed, drank from the water of the pond, and rested awhile, allowing his gaze to wander over the idyllic surroundings. Then somewhere at the foot of an aśoka tree he discerned a maiden decked with wild flowers and charmingly clothed in a patched bark skirt— a hermit's daughter accompanied by a friend. Her hair was enchantingly tied into the tuft which is worn by ascetics, and she was strikingly pretty.

The king, who had strayed within the range of the flowered arrows of the God of Love, thought to himself: "Who can she be? Is that Sāvitrī who has come here to bathe? [11] Or is she the White Goddess who, rejected by Śiva, now tries to win him again with her penance? Or is it the splendor of the moon which after its setting by day withdraws here to observe its vows? But I had better approach and find out."

When the girl saw the king approach, her hand dropped from the garland of flowers which she had begun to fashion. Looking wide-eyed at his handsome figure, she said to herself: "Such a man in the forest! Who could he be? An angel? A spirit of the air? Surely his appearance is enough to content the eyes of all the world!" But even as she was thinking, her modesty compelled her to rise, and, stealing shy glances at the king, she started to walk away. Her legs, though, moved awkwardly and might have been wooden.

The king overtook her and addressed her with urbane courtesy: "Dispense with the welcome for a casual visitor from afar who is fully rewarded by his vision of you, my pretty girl. But is it the custom of hermits to flee from him?"

[11] The heroine of a famous epic story.

At the king's question, the girl's companion, quick to catch his meaning, sat down and honored the king with the formali- ties due a guest. Then the king, who had fallen in love, tact- fully questioned the companion.

"Good young lady, which fortunate lineage is adorned by your friend? What are the syllables of her name, drops of nectar in man's ear? And why does she maltreat a beauty as delicate as a blossom's with the privations of a hermit's life in a forlorn place?"

The companion replied: "She is the unmarried daughter of the, great saint Kāṇva and the celestial nymph Menakā, and she has been brought up here in the saint's hermitage. Her name is Indīvaraprabhā, Lotus Splendor. Just now she has come to this pond with her father's leave to take a bath. Her farther's hermitage is not very far from here."

Joyfully the king mounted his steed and rode to saintly Kāṇva's hermitage in order to ask the hand of his daughter. Leaving his horse punctiliously outside the compound, he entered the hermitage, which was peopled by bark-clad trees and bark-clad ascetics. Like the moon encircled by the planets, the saintly Kāṇva brightened with his power the anchorites who surrounded him.

The king drew near and saluted the sage's feet; and as soon as he had been offered the guest-gifts and had rested, the saint addressed him.

"My son Candrāvaloka," he said, "listen to what I must tell you for your own good. You know in how great a fear of death all creatures live in this cycle of transmigration. Then why do you hunt and kill without any cause these unfortunate animals? The creator has fashioned the sword for the warrior to protect those who are threatened. Observe the law and employ your arms to protect your subjects by uprooting the thorns that irk your realm. Endeavor to win the capricious favors of Fortune by the proper employment of elephants, horsemen, archers, and footmen. Enjoy the pleasures of royalty, give generously, spread your fame—abandon the vicious, murderous hunt which is the frolic of death! Why bring misfortune upon you in pursuits where hunter and hunted are equally neglectful of higher purposes? Do you not know what befell to Pāṇḍu?" [12]

[12] This epic hero died while hunting.

King Candrāvaloka welcomed the saint's admonitions gratefully, and, knowing his gain, he replied: "I stand corrected,
Reverend Sir! You have done me a very great favor. Henceforth I shall abstain from hunting lest my fellow creatures
should live in fear of death!"

"I am pleased with your magnanimous offer of security to
your fellow beings," the saint said. "Choose a boon!"

Knowing that this was an opportune moment, the king asked
at once: "If you are pleased, give me your daughter Indīvaraprabhā!"

So when his daughter returned from her bath, the hermit
bestowed her on the pleading king. The marriage took place
immediately, and the king took his bride, who had been dressed
and adorned by the wives of the anchorites, away with him.
Tearful ascetics accompanied them as far as the limits of
the hermitage. There the king mounted his horse and departed
in haste.

Tired from watching the king's long and eventful day, the
sun sat down on Sunset Peak; and one saw the night draw
slowly near, like a lovesick mistress with darting eyes, who,
wrapped in a dark-blue cloak, steals to a place of assigna-
tion. When the sun had set, the king encountered in his path
an aśvattha tree, which stood on the bank of a pond with
water as clear as a good man's heart. At the foot of the tree
he saw a dark lawn entirely enclosed by foliage, and he decided to spend the night there. He leaped from his horse, gave
it hay and water, and rested awhile with the hermit's daughter
on the sandy beach of the pond, enjoying the breeze that
came from the water, Then he made a bed of flower petals at
the foot of the tree and entered with his bride the intimate
enclosure. That very moment the moon lifted the cloak of
darkness and kissed the adoring face of the east; and all
the regions of the sky were embraced by the groping rays of
light and, robbed of any excuse for coyness, brightened delightedly. And at the same time as the moonbeams stole through
the interlaced creepers and leaves to shed a flickering light,
as of jeweled oil-lamps, on the lawn below the tree, the king
embraced Indīvaraprabhā and tasted a banquet of love, flavored
with longing and spiced with new passions. Carefully he removed with her veil her embarrassment, bit with his teeth both
her lip and her innocence, and wrought with his nails a new

string of starlike rubies on her breasts which were like the firm forehead bumps of the elephant of youth. Over and over again he kissed her lips, her cheeks, her eyes—drinking at all points from the rapids of beauty's elixir. The king spent a night of voluptuous joy with his bride; and the night seemed an instant.

At dawn the king rose from his bed; and as soon as he had performed the twilight ritual, he started out with his bride to rejoin his escort of horsemen. It was the moment when, ablaze with red fury, the sun sent out its first arrows of light to kill the Lord of the Night who had spoiled the comely cheeks of sun's beloved day-blooming lotuses and now, un-nerved, lurked fearfully in the crevices of Sunrise Mountain. And at that very instant there loomed suddenly over the king and his bride, like the roaring cloud of Doomsday, a Demon of brahmin caste, black with soot and lightning bristling in his hair. He was garlanded with entrails, and the brahmin's thread he wore was spun from human hair.[13] He was gulping down bites of human flesh with sips of blood from a human skull. The apparition gave forth a horrifying burst of demoniac laughter and, belching blood from a cavernous mouth spiky with tusks, roared at the king.

"Miscreant! I am Spitflame, a Demon of brahmin caste! This tree is my dwelling, and even the gods dare not violate it; but you have trespassed and wallowed in it with a woman. I came back in time from my nightly wanderings, and you shall reap the fruits of your misconduct. I shall tear your heart out, criminal, lovesick fool, and I shall drink your blood!"

When the king heard these terrible threats, he trembled, for he saw that the Demon was invincible, and when he spoke it was with great courtesy. "Forgive the crime which I have innocently committed! Treat me as a guest who has found refuge in your hermitage. I shall do whatever you may desire and bring you a human victim who is entirely to your satisfaction. Have mercy on me; appease your wrath!"

Pacified by the king's expostulations, the Demon said to himself: "Why not? There is no harm!" Aloud he said: "I shall forgive your crime, but only on these conditions: on the

---

[13] This thread, worn from left shoulder to right hip, was ceremoniously bestowed on highborn males at an initiation.

seventh day from today you shall sacrifice, with your own sword, a seven-year-old boy, the son of a brahmin, who has offered himself voluntarily to take your place. He must be magnanimous of character and discriminating in judgment. And at the time of the killing he shall be held to the ground by his own mother and father, who will hold him by his hands and feet. If these conditions are not fulfilled, I shall destroy you instantly with all that is yours."

Terrified, the king agreed to these conditions, and the Demon vanished. Thereupon King Candrāvaloka mounted his horse with his bride and departed, miserably, to find his escort.

"Aho!" he thought, "like a fool I was possessed by my passion for hunting, and I have suddenly brought disaster upon myself, like Pāṇḍu. . . . How can I ever find such a human victim for the Demon? But I must first return to my city, and I shall see what the future brings."

Thus the king thought as he looked for his escort until he found them; and in the company of his horsemen he repaired with his wife to his city Citrakūṭa. When he arrived in his kingdom, there were festivities to celebrate the king's honorable marriage, and, hiding his sorrow, the king wore through the day.

The next day he told his councillors in a secret meeting all that had befallen him; and one councillor among them, who was very quick-witted, said: "Your Majesty, do not despair! I shall find the right victim and bring him to you; for the earth is full of wonders!"

When he had thus reassured the king, the councillor ordered at once a golden statue to be made of a seven-year-old boy. He adorned the ears with jeweled ornaments and then ordered the statue to be mounted on a chariot and driven around through the city and villages and hamlets. And he passed instructions that a continuous proclamation with beat of drum should precede the statue: "If there is a seven-year-old boy who is prepared to lay down his life for the common weal and surrender it to a Demon, and if his father and mother not only approve the action of their magnanimous son but also will themselves hold his hands and feet when he is slaughtered, then the king will give them this golden and gem-studded statue with one hundred villages to compensate them for their loss!"

Now in a certain brahmin colony one seven-year-old boy, who was very profound and wondrously handsome, heard the king's proclamation. The habits of his former lives had inspired in him, young as he was, an ardent zeal for the good of his fellow beings, and he was the fruition of man's good karman incarnate.

This boy went to the criers and said: "I shall sacrifice myself for your good! I shall come with you as soon as I have told my parents."

The criers rejoiced and allowed him to go home. The boy folded his hands in a gesture of supplication and said to his parents: "I want to surrender this perishable body for the good of mankind. Give me your leave and permit your misfortune to end: for I shall bring you my likeness in gold and precious stones which the king has offered, as well as the command of one hundred villages. So I shall accomplish two ends: acquit myself of my obligations to you and serve the common good. And when your poverty has ended, you shall have many more sons."

But his parents replied with some violence: "Have you taken leave of your senses, son? What are you saying? Are you possessed by the wind or a demon? How else can you talk like that? Who would allow his son to be killed for money? And what child would offer himself?"

The boy answered: "I am not raving in madness! Listen to my meaningful words. This body, loathsome from the moment of birth, filled with unspeakable impurities, hoard of miseries, will surely perish soon. Yet the merit which one may acquire through his body is called by the wise the essence of existence. And what greater merit can be found than serving the well-being of the world? But when one has no love for his parents, what good will come from his body?"

With such words the boy, who was firmly resolved, succeeded in forcing his sorrowing parents to agree to his desire. He went back to the king's men, took the golden statue from them and brought it to his parents, to whom he also surrendered the command over one hundred villages. Ordering the king's men to lead the way, he thereupon went with his parents to the king in Citrakūṭa; and when Candrāvaloka saw that a boy of unshakeable purpose had been found like an amulet, he rejoiced. He made him mount his elephant and conducted the boy, who was auspiciously garlanded and anointed, with his parents to the Demon's haunt.

There the king's house-priest traced a magic circle beside the aśvattha tree, performed the necessary ceremonies, and offered an oblation in the fire. And with a roaring laugh, Spitflame the Demon of brahmin caste appeared, reciting the Veda. Drunk with the thick red spirits of blood, he yawned and belched continually, rolling his bloodshot eyes, and his horrifying shape cast a darkening shadow over them. King Candrāvaloka bowed deep when the Demon appeared.

"Reverend Sir," he said, "I have brought a human victim to your sacrifice. Today is the seventh day, as you specified. Have mercy and accept this sacrifice with proper ceremony."

The Demon looked over the brahmin boy and licked a drop of blood from his lips. And the saintly boy rejoiced to himself.

"May the merit which I acquire with this sacrifice of my body not lead me to heaven or release, where help to others is unknown, but may I in birth upon birth return to a body for the good of my fellow-beings!" And as he expressed this intention, the sky became instantly filled with the celestial chariots of thronging gods who showered a rain of flowers upon him.

Then the boy was fetched before the Demon, and the mother took hold of his hands and the father gripped his feet. And as the king drew his sword to slaughter him, the boy began to laugh. And all who were there, even the Demon, in amazement stopped what they were doing, folded their hands, and, staring at his face, prostrated themselves before him.

When the Vampire had finished this entertaining and edifying story, he addressed King Trivikramasena again: "Tell me now, O king, for what reason did that boy laugh under those circumstances, at the very moment of death? The question intrigues me, and if you do not reply though you know the answer, your head shall burst in a hundred pieces!"

The king replied: "Listen, I shall tell you the boy's meaning when he laughed. A weak creature, as soon as he is threatened by danger, begins to cry for his father and mother. When the parents have died, it is the king who takes their place as the guardian of the oppressed. And if there is no king, any available deity is implored. The boy had all of these at hand, but in a rather different fashion. His father and mother held him by hands and feet because they were greedy for money. The king was about to slaughter him in order to save himself. The deity was the Demon of brahmin caste who was about to devour him. What mockery of people befooled by a body which is transitory, intrinsically unessential, and tortured by pain and sorrow! Where even Brahmā, Indra, Viṣṇu, and Śiva and all the lesser gods must die irrevocably, there they exhibited such an illusion of the permanence of their bodies! And witnessing their incredible self-deception and knowing his own ends secure, the brahmin boy laughed from amazement and joy."

When the king had ceased to speak, the Vampire once again disappeared suddenly from his shoulder and, invisible through magic, returned to his own haunt. Without hesitation the king went quickly after him again. Indeed, the heart of the great is as imperturbable as the deeps of the ocean! Trivikramasena fetched the Vampire from the treetop and lifted him onto his shoulder; and as the king started on his way back, the Vampire spoke.

"Your Majesty, you are a good man, a great man! Listen therefore to this unusual story!"

Four Who Made a Lion

Long ago there was a king in the land by the name of Dharaṇīvarāha who held sway in the City of Flowers. His kingdom abounded in brahmins, and in one brahmin colony, Brahmasthala, there lived a brahmin named Viṣṇusvāmin. This brahmin had a wife who agreed as perfectly with her husband as the invocation *svāhā!* agrees with the fire of sacrifice.[14]

---

[14] One of the invocations that accompanied oblations at the large sacrifices which were the prerogative of brahmins.

The couple had four sons in succession; and when these sons had studied the Veda and grown to manhood, their father Viṣṇusvāmin went to heaven and his wife followed him. Left without a guardian, the four brothers were in a predicament; and their kinsmen stole their inheritance.

They took counsel together. "We have no future in this country," they decided. "Let us go to the village of Yajña-sthala where our mother's father lives. Why not?"

So they set out on the journey, begging their food on the way, and after many days they arrived at their maternal grandfather's house. Their grandfather had died, and the brothers were received by their cousins. It was in their cousins' house that henceforth they had their meals and pursued their studies. After some time, however, the cousins began to show contempt for their poor relations when they portioned out their food, clothes, and quarters. Their cousins' contempt and humiliating treatment worried the four brothers, and they met secretly to discuss matters.

The eldest brother said, "Brothers, what can a man do? It is fate that does everything, and man is powerless in anything, anywhere, any time! For example, today I was wandering around miserably when I happened on a burning ground. There I saw a corpse laid out on the ground, in an advanced state of decomposition, and when I saw it, I thought to myself: 'Lucky fellow. He has thrown off his burden of sorrows and can now take rest.'

"I decided there and then to do away with myself; I tied a noose to a tree and hanged myself. When I had lost consciousness, but before my spirits had finally departed, my noose was cut and I fell to the ground. When I came to, I found myself in the company of a man who waved his clothes about me to give me air and relief.

" 'Tell me, friend,' said the man, 'you are a man of learning, yet you despair. Why? Good luck comes from good karman, bad luck from bad karman, and that is all. If you are wretchedly unhappy, well, just do good! Do you really want the sufferings of hell, which are your share if you kill yourself?'

"When with his help I had recovered, the man went on. So I gave up all hopes of suicide and came back home. If fate is against it, a man cannot even die! Now I intend to go to a sacred place and burn my body away with penance and austerities; this will at least appease the pains of poverty."

"But how is it possible that you suffer under your poverty as long as you are intelligent?" exclaimed his brothers. "Don't you know that wealth is as transitory as autumn clouds? Fortune is like a disaffected wife, a false friend, or a harlot: you may win and keep them for a while, but they will never remain faithful to you. An intelligent man tries to master some specialty which will help him win back his money and his mistress with his own brains, as often as necessary."

At these words of his brothers the eldest immediately regained his composure. "What specialty should one master?" he asked.

They all began to think about this. Then they said to one another, "Let us search the earth and learn a special science."

So they decided, and after they had agreed on a place where they would meet again, the four brothers started off, each in a different direction.

Time went by, and the brothers met again at the appointed meeting place; and they asked one another what they had learned.

"I have mastered a science," said the first, "which makes it possible for me, if I have nothing but a piece of bone of some creature, to create straightaway the flesh that goes with it."

"I," said the second, "know how to grow that creature's skin and hair if there is flesh on its bones."

The third said, "I am able to create its limbs if I have the flesh, the skin, and the hair."

"And I," concluded the fourth, "know how to give life to that creature if its form is complete with limbs."

Thereupon the four brothers went into the jungle to find a piece of bone so that they could demonstrate their specialties. As fate would have it, the bone they found was a lion's, but they did not know and picked up the bone. One added flesh to the bone, the second grew hide and hair, the third completed it with matching limbs, and the fourth gave the lion life. Shaking its heavy mane the ferocious beast arose with its menacing mouth, sharp teeth, and merciless claws and jumped on his creators. He killed them all and vanished contentedly into the jungle.

Thus the four brahmins perished because of their unfortunate creation of a lion. For who can stay happy if he raises something evil? In this manner it may happen that a specialty which one has been at pains to acquire may not at all work out to his profit, if fate is hostile, but to his doom. Only if its roots are firm and watered with intelligence and encircled with trenches of worldly wisdom will the tree of human effort bear fruit.

After telling this tale on the path, the Vampire again asked King Trivikramasena from his shoulder, "Sire, which one of the four brothers carries the blame of creating the lion that killed them? The old condition still stands."

The king thought, "The Vampire will disappear again as soon as I have broken my silence. Well, let him go; I shall bring him back again."

Then he said to the Vampire, "The only one to blame is the one who gave life to the lion. The others are innocent because they were ignorant; they could not know what kind of creature it would prove to be when each practiced his skill and fashioned its flesh, skin, hair, and limbs. But the last one saw the finished form of a lion, and he gave it life only to show off his science. He stands guilty of four brahmin murders."

When the worthy Vampire had heard the king's answer, he left the king's shoulder again by magic and went back to his tree. And the king followed him back again.

Once again did Trivikramasena, noblest of kings, fetch the Vetāla from the sissoo tree, take him on his shoulder, and, defying the many apparitions which the wizard conjured, set out in silence. And the Vetāla said, "Sire, your tenacity at this impossible task is undefeatable! Let me therefore tell you a story to divert you. Listen."

The Rejuvenated Hermit

In the land of Kaliṅga was once a city named Śobhāvatī which, like Indra's city in heaven, was the abode solely of the pure and the meritorious. This city was swayed by the rule of

Pradyumna, a king of mighty sovereignty who matched the fame of Pradyumna of old with the greatness of his power and potency. In his realm it was only by love that fortunes were taxed, only in bows that the straight became crooked, only in wit that sharpness was felt, only in the expression "Age of Kali" that Kali, God of Discord, was heard of.

Somewhere near his city the king had granted a freehold of land, Yajñasthala, which was thickly settled with brahmins. And there lived Yajñasoma, a brahmin learned in the Veda and a sacrificer of great wealth who entertained gods as his guests. To this brahmin, after the prime of his life and after a hundred wishes, a son had been borne by his brahmin wife. The boy, whose marks augured well for the future—the priests ceremonially named him Devasoma—grew up in his father's house until he was sixteen years old and excelled over all in learning and in manners and in all accomplishments. Then he was suddenly carried off by the fever. And so dearly did his father Yajñasoma and his mother love their son that for a long time they refused to surrender the body to be cremated but held it tightly embraced.

"Brahmin, you who know the higher and the lower wisdom, do you not know how volatile this mirage is that we call life? How frail like a waterbubble its existence? Even the kings of men who filled the earth with their armies, who, surrounded by lovely concubines, inclined their musk-scented fragrant bodies on jeweled couches in enchanting roof-pavillions to the music of melodious tunes and disported themselves as though they were gods on earth—yea! even they have one by one come to rest on the funeral pyres of burning grounds that resounded with the wailing of their followers. And if they were not devoured by the carnivorous flames, they were maimed by the jackals and withered by time. Yet, even they are not worth our grief—how should we mourn over others? Tell us, O wise one, what profit is there in embracing a corpse?"

In this fashion the ancient brahmins who had gathered at his house admonished Yajñasoma. Reluctantly he surrendered his son's body, performed the rites of the dead, and rested it on a bier. Whereupon the kinsmen, followed by a large crowd of tearful people who had collected, carried the body to the burning ground, which was filled by their lamentations.

Meanwhile there lived on that same burning ground an aged recluse, a yogin of the Pāśupata sect,[15] who dwelt in a little cell. The body he wore was so sorely emaciated by the weight of his years and his austerities that it seemed as if only its veins kept it together for fear it would fall apart. His name was Vāmaśiva; and with the tiny hairs that covered his body all whitened with ashes, and with the matted crown of hair yellow like the lightning, he was an apparition of the Great Śiva himself. This hermit had a disciple who lived with him under a vow to subsist solely on alms—a fool and a knave to boot, an arrogant lad who had become inflated with his yogic imaginings and what not and was wearied of the admonitions he constantly received.

Presently the hermit perceived outside his cell in the distance the wailing of the funeral procession; and he told his pupil, "Get up. Go outside and find out where that unprecedented deafening noise on the burning ground comes from, and return here at once!"

"I am not going," retorted the pupil. "Go yourself! It is getting past my begging time!"

"Fie upon thee, fool, belly-worshipper! It is only half a strike of the morning; is this the hour of your begging?"

"Phooey yourself, pile of old bones! I am not your pupil, and you are not my master. I am going away. You can carry the pitcher yourself!"

With this he got up, leaving his staff and bowl behind.

Smiling, the hermit stepped out of his cell and went over to the place where they were bringing the brahmin boy to be cremated. When the yogin saw the body over which the people were mourning, a body at the very beginning of adolescence, he made up his mind to enter it, being tired of his old age. Quickly he went to a solitary spot, cried his heart out, and then started to dance with all the required postures and steps. Thereupon by the magic power of his yoga the hermit who yearned for youth abandoned his body and, at the same instant, entered into the brahmin boy's body. And that very moment the boy was revived and rose suddenly up from the ready pyre and yawned.

When his relatives and all the people witnessed his resur-

---

[15] Also called Mahāpāśupata, followers of Śiva.

rection, loud jubilation arose: "Oh, blessing, he lives! he lives!" But that prince of yogins refused to break his vow even now that he had entered the boy's body, and he lied to all those present.

"I have just been to the other world, and Śiva has restored my life with his personal command that I take the vow of the Mahāpāśupatas. I shall begin my observances immediately and retire to solitude. Otherwise my life will be lost again. Therefore leave; so shall I leave."

Having thus enlightened all those who were gathered, the avowed ascetic resolutely sent them home with mixed feelings of sorrow and joy. Thereupon the rejuvenated great yogin stole away, threw his old body in a ravine, and departed for another region to observe his vows.

When the Vetāla had finished telling this story on the path in the night, he questioned King Trivikramasena again. "Tell me, Sire, why did that prince of yogins first cry and then dance when he was about to enter the boy's body? I am very curious about that."

For fear of the Vampire's curse, the king broke his silence again and, wise among the wise, answered the question. "Listen. That hermit had this thought in mind: 'Now I am giving up the body with which I have matured for so long, the body that was cherished by my parents when I was a child, the body that made me succeed in my yoga,' and in his grief he began to weep. For the love of one's body is hard to relinquish. But then he danced for joy. 'I shall enter a new body and achieve even greater yoga!' Who does not long for youth?"

When the Vetāla heard the king's answer, he disappeared again from his shoulder and, in the dead man's body, returned to the sissoo tree. And the king hastened after him, prepared for greater effort in order to win him back. Even at the end of time the constancy of the steadfast will outlast the continental mountain ranges and remain unshakable.

Heroically the king braved the dreadful Demoness of the night in her black skin of darkness who leered at him with the fiery eyes of funeral pyres, and he strode to the sissoo tree through the ghastly burning field. He seized the Vampire from the tree, hove him on his shoulder, and started again.

And as the king hastened back, the Vampire said to him,
"King, you are not tired of this coming and going, but I am.
Therefore listen to me while I tell you the one great riddle."

58

The King
and the
Corpse

The Insoluble Riddle

There was once a satrap in the South, the very first among
righteous rulers, who had too many relatives. His name was
Dharma, and he had a wife who hailed from Mālava. She
was the diadem of beautiful ladies and very well connected.
The queen, whose name was Candravatī, bore the king only
one child, a daughter; she was given the name Lāvaṇyavatī,
the Beauteous, and did honor to her name.

When this girl had reached marriageable age, King Dharma
was dethroned by conspiring kinsmen who divided his satrapy
between themselves. The king escaped with wife and daughter
at night from his country, with a treasure in jewels which he
had contrived to save. He set out on a journey to Mālava
where his father-in-law was living, and during the night he
reached the jungle ranges of the Vindhya Mountains.

Night, his faithful companion, remained behind as the king
entered the forests, and she wept with the howling cries that
now began to be heard. The sun mounted Sunrise Peak and
stretching its hands warningly gestured to the king not to go
into that forest of robbers. Yet the king, whose soles were raw
from the thistles and the sharp blades of kuśa grass, penetrated farther on foot with his family, until he came upon a
stronghold of the Bhil tribes. The stronghold teemed with
creatures who robbed their fellow men of life and goods, like
a veritable fortress of Death whose approaches were held
by Death's familiars.

As soon as they had spied the king in the distance with
his regal robes and ornaments, a gang of tribesmen dashed
out with all kinds of weapons to rob him. When King Dharma
saw them come, he said to his wife and daughter, "Get into
the bush before these barbarians lay hands on you!" At the
king's orders Queen Candravatī fled with her daughter

Lāvaṇyavatī in terror and disappeared in the thicket; and the king, armed with sword and shield, met alone the onrushing tribesmen. The warrior laid many of them low with a shower of arrows; thereupon their chieftain alerted the entire fortress, and at last the king staggered, his shield crushed by the blows it had warded off; and the chieftain cut him down. When the hordes of blacks had gone with the king's jewels, Queen Candravatī, safe in the underbrush, saw from the distance that her husband was dead; and panic-stricken she fled with her daughter and penetrated into another remote forest.

At noon when the shade, scorched by the midday sun, withdrew with the travelers to the cooler feet of the trees, the queen sat down with her daughter under an aśoka tree somewhere on the bank of a lotus pond and wept with sorrow. About this time a certain nobleman, Caṇḍasiṃha, who lived in the vicinity, came with his son Siṃhaparākrama on horseback to hunt in that same forest.

When he discovered two rows of footsteps in the sand, he said to his son, "Let us follow these neat and promising footprints; and if we find the women, you must take the one that pleases you best."

"That one with the tiny feet looks best to me," said his son. "I am sure she will be young and make me a suitable wife. The one with the big feet must be older, and she would be a good match for you!"

"What nonsense is this!" said Caṇḍasiṃha. "Your mother is hardly in heaven! Should I want another woman when I have just lost such a good wife?"

"Don't say that, father. A family man's house is empty without a wife. Haven't you heard Mūladeva's little epigram: 'A house where no pretty woman (with firm breasts and buttocks) stands waiting and looking down the road is a jail without chains, and only fools will enter.' May I be cursed to death if you don't take the other woman as your wife, father!"

Caṇḍasiṃha agreed, and slowly they followed the footsteps. They came at last to the tree at the pond, and there Caṇḍasiṃha saw Queen Candravatī and her daughter. The queen was dark of complexion and with her many strings of pearls she was like the midnight sky brightened by the pure moonlight of her daughter. Curiously father and son drew nearer; but when the lady saw them, she thought that they were brigands, and she rose trembling.

"Don't be afraid, good Lady. We are not robbers! Your ladyships must have come here to hunt, to judge by your beautiful robes and elegant adornment?"

The two women still hesitated. Caṇḍasiṃha jumped from his horse and continued.

"Why are you so nervous? We have come to meet you with the best intentions! Rest yourselves and forget your suspicions. Tell me, who are you? Are you Lust and Joy who have come to this forest to mourn the death of Love when he was burned by the fire of Śiva's third eye? [16] Why indeed have you penetrated into this desolate jungle? Your elegance is worthy of ornate boudoirs in stately mansions! And why must your feet, which are fit to be pampered by beautiful damsels, now tread this thorny ground? It worries our thoughts. Oh, miracle, the dust that is swept up by the wind and descends on your face cannot mar your complexion. And the fierce sun which scorches us jealously playfully caresses your bodies that are as delicate as flowers! Tell us your tale, for our hearts are upset. We cannot imagine why you should be here in a forest infested with beasts of prey."

At this urbane speech of Caṇḍasiṃha the queen sighed; and softly, distracted by sorrow and shame, she told her story. When the nobleman learned that she and her daughter were left unprotected, he reassured them and won them over with kindly words. He took the two women under his care and made them mount his horse and his son's, on which he conducted them to his wealthy manse in Vittapapurī. To the queen it seemed as if she had passed on to a new existence, and helpless she clung to him. What else can a woman do who has lost her protector and has fallen on bad times in a foreign land?

The small feet proved to be Queen Candravatī's and so the son took her as wife, while his father married Princess Lāvaṇyavatī because of the girl's big feet. For that was what father and son had promised when they inspected the two

[16] When Śiva, who has a third eye, was shot by the God of Love with an arrow during his mortifications on Mount Kailāsa, he burned Love with a ray of fire from this eye.

tracks of big and tiny footsteps in the woods; and who would
violate his promise?

So, because they had been mistaken about the footprints,
father and son married daughter and mother, so that the
mother became her daughter's daughter-in-law and the daughter her mother's mother-in-law. In the course of time both
women bore sons and daughters, and these eventually had
children themselves. Thus Caṇḍasiṃha and Siṃhaparākrama
found Lāvaṇyavatī and Candravatī and lived with them at
Vittapapurī.

*When the Vampire had finished this tale on the path, he
questioned King Trivikramasena again.*

*"Tell me, king, if you know the answer: precisely how were
the children who were born on both sides from mother and
daughter by son and father related to one another? The old
curse shall strike you if you know the answer and refuse to
speak."*

*The king thought much upon it, but he could not find the
answer, and he walked on in silence. The Vampire who sat
in the dead man's body on the king's shoulder grinned to
himself and thought, "The king cannot answer this great
riddle, and he hurries happily on with quick strides! I cannot deceive this noble-hearted man any longer—but that
scheming monk will certainly not stop to play with us just
because of this. . . . I shall devise a trick with which I can
deceive the wicked mendicant and at the same time transfer
his achievements to this king who is both worthy and pure."*

*Thereupon the Vampire said to the king: "Your Majesty,
even though you must be exhausted from wandering back and
forth on this burning ground which is terrifying in the blackness
of this dark night, you look at peace and you do not waver at
all! I am pleased with your extraordinary composure. You
may now carry the corpse to its destination; I shall depart
from it. But listen and do what I shall tell you for your own
good. The monk for whom you are carrying this corpse will
soon conjure me up and worship me. Then the scoundrel will
try to sacrifice you, and he will ask you: 'Prostrate yourself
so that all eight limbs touch the ground.' You must answer:
'Show me first so that I can do it like you.' When he throws
himself on the ground to demonstrate the position, you must*

cut off his head with your sword. So you yourself will accomplish the end which he sought to achieve, the sovereignty over the Spirits of the Air. Sacrifice him and you shall rule the earth! If not, the monk will sacrifice you. That is the reason why I have pestered you all this time. May you succeed! Go now." And with this warning the Vampire departed from the corpse on the king's shoulder.

At this the king thought about the mendicant Kṣāntiśīla who now appeared to be an evil monk; and greatly relieved he wended his way toward the vaṭa tree where the monk was waiting.

Carrying the corpse, Trivikramasena at last came to the tree where he found the mendicant waiting for him, looking down the path on the burning place, which was frighteningly dark on that new-moon night. On the ground, which was soaked with blood, the sorcerer had traced a magic circle with the white powder of ground bone and placed pitchers with blood on the cardinal points. The circle was brightly illumined by lamps that burned on human fat, and beside it blazed a fire in which an oblation had been poured. All the necessary gifts for the ritual worship of a special deity were assembled.

The king approached. When the mendicant saw that he had brought the body with him, he rose in great joy and spoke in praise.

"Mahārāja! You have done me a favor which was well-nigh impossible. What has a mighty prince like you in common with these doings here, this hour of night, this grisly place? Indeed, they call you the greatest of emperors because of the unalterable trustworthiness of your given word—and justly so, for you have accomplished a fellow man's purpose with utter disregard for yourself! This is what the sages have called the true greatness of the great: not to waver once a promise is made, even when life itself is at stake."

While he was talking, the monk, who now thought his ends achieved, lowered the corpse from the king's shoulder. He washed the body, anointed it with unguents, and garlanded it with flowers; then he placed it within the circle. For a brief while he stood there, his body smeared with white ashes, wearing a brahmin's thread of human hair, cloaked in the dead man's shroud, and sunk in deep concentration. And by the power of his wizardry he conjured up the good Vampire and forced it to enter the corpse. *Thereupon he began his worship: first he proffered the guest-gifts, which were contained in a skull with immaculate teeth, then a flower and fragrant ointment, two human eyes for incense, and an oblation of human flesh. When the sorcerer had concluded his worship, he turned to the king beside him.*

"Your Majesty," he demanded, "throw yourself on the ground and perform a formal prostration with eight limbs before the sovereign sorcerer who is present here. He shall grant you a boon of whatever you may wish to achieve."

Remembering the Vampire's warning, the king replied: "I do not know how to perform it. Show it to me first, and I shall do it in the same fashion, Reverend Sir." And when the mendicant knelt on the ground to show how it was done, the king struck out with his sword and cut off his head with one blow. He tore the broken heart-lotus from his chest and offered heart and head to the Vampire.

While invisible crowds of Ghosts cheered excitedly, the Vampire spoke graciously from the dead man's body: "King, the sovereignty of the Aerial Spirits which the monk coveted shall now be yours at the end of your imperial reign on the earth. I have tormented you; therefore choose a boon!"

The king replied: "What wish is unfulfilled when you are pleased? But, lest your words be meaningless, I shall ask one wish from you: may your twenty-four ravishing, wonderful tales and this last concluding tale forever be famous on earth and forever be cherished!"

"So shall it be!" said the Vampire, "and listen, O king, I shall add a special provision. The first twenty-four tales and this last concluding tale shall be famous on earth as the Vampire's Tales and be cherished. And they shall bestow merit: whosoever shall read attentively even one of their lines and whosoever shall listen may instantly be relieved of any curse. And wheresoever these Tales are held in honor, no Kobolds, Vampires, Ogres, Witches, or Demons shall ever prevail!"

After the Vampire had spoken, he departed magically from the corpse and went wherever he wanted to go. Then the Great Lord himself appeared with the gods, and graciously He spoke to the king.

"Well done, my son! Well done your killing of this pre-

tended monk who sought to seize with force the empire of the Spirits of the Air. In the beginning I created you from a part of Myself as King Vikramāditya,[17] to defeat the Demons who were incarnated in the Barbarians. In this existence I have created you Warrior King Trivikramasena. When you shall have established your reign over the entire earth with islands and nether-worlds, you shall soon become sovereign king of the Aerial Spirits. For a long time you will delight in celestial joys but then become loth and voluntarily turn away from them. And in the end you shall be united with Myself. Receive this sword Invincible by whose favor you shall obtain all that you desire." The Auspicious God then gave the king the miraculous sword and, honored with flowers of speech, withdrew.

When King Trivikramasena saw that all had been done, while the night went by, he returned to his city Pratiṣṭhāna. There he was feasted by his subjects, who had learned about his nocturnal exploits, with long-lasting celebrations and festivities; and the king passed the day with bathing, alms-giving, worshipping the Daughter of the Mountain, and with dance, song, and music. In very few years the king, aided by Śiva's sword as well as by his own courage, ruled undisputed the entire earth with islands and nether-worlds. And after he had, at Śiva's command, for a long time enjoyed the supreme sovereignty of the Spirits of the Air, he at last united himself with the Lord, his fate fulfilled.

[17] Probably a reference to Candragupta II (*ca.* 400), who was styled Vikramāditya, "Sun of Bravery," and once defeated the invading Huns. He has become the prototype of the ideal king, and his reign is regarded as the epitome of Indian culture.

The Tale
of Two Bawds

There is in this country a great, wealthy city which is called
Citraketu. In that place once lived a merchant, Ratnavarman,
who possessed great riches. He was blessed with a son through
the favor of Lord Śiva, and hence he gave the boy the name
Īśvaravarman.[1]

When the eminent merchant, who had only this one son,
saw that Īśvara had finished his studies and was approaching manhood, he thought: "The Creator has made one creature
which is immorality incarnate—in order to rob rich young
men who are blinded by their virility—and harlot is its name.
I shall entrust my son to a bawd so that he can learn the
tricks of harlots and will never be taken in by them."

Having made up his mind, he went with his son Īśvara to
the house of a procuress called Yamajihvā, Tongue-of-Death.
He found the heavy-jowled, long-toothed, pug-nosed bawd
engaged in teaching her daughter.

[1] Īśvara is one of Śiva's names.

"Everybody has his price, daughter, and a prostitute more so. But no price is paid when she falls in love; therefore a harlot must guard against love. Passion is like the dusk: just as the twilight announces the fall of night, so passion is the harbinger of a courtesan's downfall. Like a well-trained actress a harlot must put up a false show. First she must seduce her man, then milk him of his money, and finally, when his money is gone, desert him. But when he has found new money, she receives him back. A true harlot is like a saintly hermit: whether youth, child, or old man, whether handsome or ugly, all are the same to her as to the hermit, and thus both obtain the greatest good."

Ratnavarman approached the bawd while she was instructing her daughter and, when he had been received with due honor, sat down with her.

"You must teach my son the arts of the harlot," he said, "until he is an expert. I shall give you a fee of one thousand pieces of silver." She agreed eagerly, and they struck the bargain. Ratnavarman paid out the silver, committed his son to her care, and went home.

Īśvara pursued his studies in Yamajihvā's house for one year, after which he returned to his father's house. He was sixteen years old.

"Money," he declared, "brings merit and love. Money brings honor. Money brings fame."

"So it does indeed," agreed his father and gave him a fortune of fifty million. The merchant's son took his fortune, and on an auspicious day he joined a caravan and departed for Sumatra to trade. He journeyed by land and eventually reached a city called Goldtown. The young man set up quarters in a grove just outside the city, where he had a bath, massaged his skin, and took his meal. Thereupon he entered the city and went to a temple to see a play. At the performance he saw a courtesan, Sundarī, who gave a dance—she was a wave of the ocean of beauty swept up by the wind of elegance. As soon as he set eyes on her, his mind was so full of her that the procuress' lessons were piqued and withdrew.

He sent a friend to her after the dance to make a proposition. She agreed with a bow: "I am favored!" Īśvara posted reliable watchmen in his quarters to guard his treasures and himself went to stay at Sundarī's house. There the girl's mother, Makarakaṭi, welcomed him with all the amenities of the house which were proper at that hour.

When evening fell, Sundarī took him to her own room, where a bed was made up on a couch overhung by a canopy aglitter with precious stones; and there he enjoyed the favors of the willing Sundarī, who was as adept at the various postures of love as at those of the dance. The next day when the young man saw that she did not part from his side and showed herself passionately in love, he was unable to tear himself away. For these two days the merchant's son wanted to give Sundarī two and a half million in gold, jewelry, and so forth; but she protested: "I have plenty of money, but I have never had a man like you. As long as I am with you, what do I care for gold?"

While Sundarī remonstrated—with false pretenses—and refused to accept his gold, her mother Makarakaṭi, whose only daughter she was, said, "All that we have is now his. What does it matter, then, if you take it and hold it in common?" Sundarī finally allowed herself to be persuaded by her mother and accepted; and the naïve Īśvara thought that she was genuinely in love with him. And so, seduced by her beauty, her songs and dances, the merchant spent two months with Sundarī, meanwhile lavishing twenty million on her in gifts.

Then a friend of his, Arthadatta, came and spoke to him in private: "Is it possible, friend, that the lessons of the procuress, which you have done so much to master, have proved useless just when they mattered most, like a coward's swordsmanship? For you believe that that harlot's love is real! Is a mirage in the desert real? Let us go before all your money goes. Your father won't forgive you when he learns of this!"

"You are right," said Īśvara. "Harlots are not to be trusted, but Sundarī is different. Why, Arthadatta, when she does not see me for a moment, she is ready to kill herself! If we really have to go, you must tell her yourself."

With Īśvara looking on, Arthadatta said to Sundarī and her mother Makarakaṭi: "Your love for Īśvara is certainly unparalleled, but now he must continue on his journey to Sumatra to do his trading. He will make a fortune so that he can come back and live with you happily for the rest of his life. Let him go, my dear."

Sundarī gazed at Īśvara's face with tears in her eyes. "You

know best," she said in a desperate voice. "Who am I to speak? Who dares trust another before he sees the end? But let it be enough what fate has disposed for me. . . ."

Her mother said reassuringly: "Don't be unhappy, my child. Control yourself. Your friend will surely come back; he won't desert you when his fortune is made." The daughter took hold of herself, and the two bawds plotted together. Then the mother secretly had a net fastened inside a certain well. Īśvara's heart was swinging in doubt, and Sundarī in her sorrow took very little food and drink. But she did not restrain her love in her songs, lute playing, and dances; and Īśvara consoled her with all manner of affectionate gestures.

On the day set by his friend, Īśvara left Sundarī's house while the procuress spoke benedictions. With her mother, Sundarī followed him in tears outside the city, as far as the well where the net had been fastened. And when he told Sundarī to turn back and continued on his journey, she threw herself into the well, on top of the net. Her mother and the servants cried out piercingly, "O my daughter! O mistress!" The merchant's son immediately turned about-face, with his friend, and he was numbed when he learned that his love had thrown herself in the well. Makarakaṭi, weeping plaintively over her daughter, had her trusted servants, who knew of the plot, descend into the well. As they climbed down the ropes, they shouted, "O blessing, she lives, she lives!" and they lifted Sundarī out of the well. The rescued girl feigned death, but when she was told that her lover had come back, she cried out faintly. Īśvara, completely reassured, took his beloved mistress and returned with his friend to her house. Certain in his mind that Sundarī's love was genuine, he thought that having her was the greatest boon life could offer, and he gave up all plans for travel.

When he had settled down once more, his friend Arthadatta spoke again: "Have you taken leave of your senses? Don't trust Sundarī's love just because she jumped in a well. The tricks of a bawd are as inscrutable as the machinations of fate. What are you going to tell your father when you have lost your entire fortune? Where else can you go now? Get out of here today, if you are still sound in mind!"

The merchant's son took a month in considering his friend's advice. By that time he had spent the remaining thirty million, and, when he was broke, Makarakaṭi gave him the crescent and threw him out.[2]

Arthadatta and the other friends hurried back to Citraketu and reported to Īśvara's father all that had happened. When Ratnavarman heard that, he was shocked, and the merchant prince went to Yamajihvā.

"You have taken such a large fee, but you have failed to teach my son properly if Makarakaṭi could plunder him so easily!" and he described his son's misadventures.

"Bring your son here," said the old bawd. "I shall see to it that he robs Makarakaṭi of everything she possesses."

At the procuress' promise Ratnavarman sent his son's friend Arthadatta with a message and traveling funds to bring Īśvara back. Arthadatta journeyed to Goldtown and gave Īśvara his father's entire message. "My dear fellow," he continued, "you did not follow my advice, and now you see with your own eyes the dishonesty of the harlot. You gave fifty million and got the crescent in return. What man, if he is wise, expects oil in the sands and love in a whore? Or have you forgotten the nature of things? A man is clever, serene, and meritorious as long as he avoids falling into the snares of wanton women. Therefore you must now return to your father and cure the anger that consumes him!"

Arthadatta started out at once with Īśvara to return him to his city, and, relieved, son returned to father. Ratnavarman loved his son so much that he treated him kindly. Forthwith he took him to Yamajihvā the procuress; the woman interrogated him, and he relayed through Arthadatta all that had befallen him, the loss of his money, and Sundarī's leap into the well.

"I am to blame," said Yamajihvā. "I forgot to teach him that trick. Makarakaṭi had fastened a net inside the well, and Sundarī threw herself on the net so that she did not drown. But there is something that can be done." The procuress ordered her servant girls to bring her monkey in, a pet monkey called Āla.

While they were all looking on, she gave the monkey one thousand gold pieces; then she commanded, "Swallow!" and the trained animal swallowed the gold.

[2] The universal grip of bouncers: index finger and thumb are stretched to form a crescent, firmly planted on the victim's neck and followed through with a competent push.

"Give him twenty pieces, son," she ordered, "give him sixty pieces, a hundred!" and every time the monkey produced the exact amount from the gold pieces which Yamajihvā had told him to swallow.

Having demonstrated the monkey trick, Yamajihvā said: "Take this little monkey, Īśvaravarman, and return to Sundarī's house as before. Feed the monkey every day in secret as much money as you will need for your expenses and then ask him for it in public. When Sundarī sees that, she will think Āla is the stone of wishes, and, if you insist, she will barter all she has to get her hands on that monkey. Take her money, give the monkey two days' expenses to swallow, and don't lose time getting away."

The procuress gave Īśvara the monkey, and his father added twenty million. He set out again for Goldtown with the monkey and the money, and when he reached it, he sent a messenger to Sundarī to announce his arrival and entered her house. With passionate embraces, Sundarī welcomed the young man like tenacity itself—whose entire substance is the means to succeed—and also his friend Arthadatta. Īśvara assured her of his good fortune and at her house and in her presence told Arthadatta, "Go and fetch Āla." "Certainly!" said his friend and brought the monkey in. Īśvara commanded the animal, which had already swallowed a thousand pieces of gold: "Āla, my boy, give me three hundred dinars for food and drink and another hundred for betel and dessert. And give mother Makarakaṭi one hundred, and another hundred to the priests, and give the change of one thousand to Sundarī."

At his master's command the monkey spat out the precise amount for these expenditures.

After Īśvara, with this trick, had made Āla produce as much money as he needed for his expenses, Sundarī took counsel with her mother. "Surely, this must be the stone of wishes which has been conjured in a monkey's body, if it can produce one thousand dinars every day," she said. "If he were to give us the monkey, we would have succeeded in all our designs!"

When the two women had secretly plotted together, Sundarī begged Īśvara as he was taking a rest after his meal, "If you really love me, you must give me Āla!"

Īśvara laughed. "He is my father's entire fortune. It would not be right to give it away."

"I will give you fifty million for the monkey."

'If you offered me your entire fortune," said Īśvara decisively, "and the whole city to boot, it still would not be right for me to give him to you. So what are a few millions?"

"I will give you all I own, but let me have that monkey! My mother will be furious with me," and she threw herself at his feet.

Arthadatta and the other friends said, "Give her the monkey and let it go." At last Īśvara consented to sell him to her, and he spent the rest of the day with an overjoyed Sundarī. The next morning, after he had made the monkey swallow two thousand pieces in secret, he turned him over to the prayerful harlot and received her entire fortune and her house in exchange. He left instantly and departed on business to Sumatra.

For two days the monkey Āla provided Sundarī to her great joy with all the money she asked, one thousand gold pieces a day. The third day she asked again and again, but the monkey failed to produce any money, no matter how she coaxed him, and she struck Āla with her fist. The monkey jumped on her in a rage and rent her face and her mother's with his paws and teeth while they tried to beat the furious beast off. With the blood streaming down her face the mother clubbed the monkey furiously until he was dead. When the two women saw that the monkey was dead and that all their fortune was lost, they were near to killing themselves.

The story went around, and the people jeered:

Makarakaṭi stole one merchant's money with a net,
But he made a monkey of her with a monkey pet!

Now that they had lost their money and their faces, Sundarī and her mother could barely be prevented by their relatives from killing themselves. Shortly afterward Īśvara returned from Sumatra, the Island of Gold, to his father's house in Citraketu with another fortune added to his own. And when Ratnavarman saw his son return with immense wealth, he honored the procuress Yamajihvā with gifts and held a very large feast. Īśvaravarman, having learned the matchless tricks of harlots, was forever cured of any affection for them; and he took a wife and stayed at home.

The Man Who
Impersonated
God Viṣṇu

There is a city called Mathurā, the birthplace of Kṛṣṇa, and
in that city lived a famous courtesan by the name of Lovely.
Her mother was an old procuress called Crocodile—a blot of
poison in the eyes of the young gentlemen who were attracted
by her daughter's talents.

One day, at the hour of worship, Lovely went to a temple
to make her devotions, and she saw in the distance a man. As
soon as she had seen him, the man, who was very handsome,
entered her heart so completely that her mother's lessons flew
out. She told her maid, "Take a message from me to that man
there: he must come to my house at once."

"Yes, ma'am," said the maid, and she took the message. The
man considered it for a while.

"I am a brahmin," he said, "and my name is Lohajaṅgha.
I have no money, so who am I to enter Lovely's house, which
is open only to the rich?"

"My mistress will not demand money from you," said the maid, and Lohajaṅgha gave his word: "I shall come."

When Lovely had heard the maid's report, she went home full of longing and stayed indoors, her eyes fixed on the street by which he would come. After a brief while Lohajaṅgha came up to the house, and Crocodile the procuress saw him. "Where is he from?" she thought.

Lovely saw him too, and with great courtesy she rose to welcome him herself; and, embracing him tightly, she conducted him excitedly to her room. She was so fascinated with Lohajaṅgha's charm that she thought she had won the reward of her life. Henceforth the young man lived with her at her house as he pleased, and the girl lost all interest in other men.

When her mother saw what had happened—she who had taught all the girls in the district—she was very upset. "What is the meaning of this?" she cried when they were alone. "How can you carry on with a penniless fellow? A decent harlot would rather bed with a dead man than a poor man! What has love to do with a harlot? Have you forgotten the first rule? A harlot in love is like twilight: neither will last very long. A good courtesan must be like an actress: she exhibits love for money. Let that penniless wretch go; don't ruin yourself!"

Lovely replied angrily, "Don't talk like that—I love him more than my life! I have money enough myself. Why should I want more? Don't ever talk to me like that again, mother!" Furious, Crocodile brooded on a way to eject Lohajaṅgha.

Sometime later she saw a Rājpūt on the road,[1] obviously broke, with a gang of swordsmen. She ran to him, led him off to a secluded place, and told him: "Our house is besieged by a penniless lover. If you come to our house and see to it, by any means whatever, that he gets out, you can have a turn with my daughter."

The Rājpūt agreed to the bargain and entered the house. It so happened that both Lovely and Lohajaṅgha were out at that hour; Lovely was at a temple, and he had gone off somewhere. Shortly thereafter he returned unsuspecting; and the moment he entered he was set upon by the Rājpūt's gang,

[1] Rājpūt, literally "prince," was the name given warrior castes and tribes who roamed the country as soldiers of fortune or plain marauders.

who hit and beat and kicked his body black and blue and finally threw him in a pit of rubbish. Somehow Lohajaṅgha managed to escape. Meanwhile Lovely came back, and when she heard what had happened she was wretchedly unhappy, and the Rājpūt, after one look at her, went as he had come.

Lohajaṅgha, after the outrageous abuse he had received from the procuress, suffered so badly from the separation that he decided to give up his life, and he started out on a pilgrimage. While he was journeying through the wilderness, burned in his heart by rage at the procuress and on his skin by the heat of summer, he yearned for shade. There were no trees, but he did find the carcass of an elephant that had been eaten empty by the jackals which entered it from the rear. Only the skin was left. Lohajaṅgha crawled into the skin, which was kept cool by the wind that blew through its holes, and fell asleep, exhausted.

Then, all of a sudden, clouds came up from every quarter, and almost at once a torrential rain swept down. The rain shrank the skin so that all the holes were sealed, and soon the road was flooded by a torrent which washed the elephant skin down and swept it into the Ganges. The river carried it downstream and washed it into the sea. A giant bird of Garuḍa's race saw it floating in the ocean and thinking that it was meat swooped down, picked it up, and carried it to the other shore of the ocean.[2] There the bird ripped the skin open with its beak, saw a man inside, and fled.

The violence of the bird had awakened Lohajaṅgha, and he stepped out of the skin through the hole that the bird had pecked with its beak. He was amazed to find himself on the far shore of the ocean, and he thought that he was dreaming. But then he saw to his terror two gruesome Ogres. But the Ogres, as frightened as he was, only stared at him from a distance: for they remembered their defeat at Rāma's hands, and when they saw another human come over the ocean, they were terrified.[3] They deliberated, and one of them went to

---

[2] Garuḍa, the mount of Viṣṇu, is a gigantic bird the size of a pterodactyl.

[3] In the *Rāmāyaṇa* epic, Rāma, later to be elevated to the rank of god as an incarnation of Viṣṇu, warred on a race of Ogres whose King Rāvaṇa had abducted Rāma's wife. Vibhīṣaṇa, an Ogre, made common cause with the enemy and thereafter was known as a devotee of Viṣṇu.

report to Vibhīṣaṇa, the king, on what he had seen. King
Vibhīṣaṇa, who had witnessed Rāma's might, was upset at the
arrival of a man, and he told the Ogre: "Go, fellow, and ask
that human in a friendly way to do me the honor of coming
to my house."

"Yes, Sire," answered the Ogre, and he returned. Trembling with fear, he conveyed his master's message to Lohajaṅgha.

The brahmin accepted with relief, and the Ogre conducted
him to Laṅkā.[4] Astounded by the multitudes of golden palaces
he saw in the city, Lohajaṅgha entered the royal residence
and met Vibhīṣaṇa.

The king did the honors of hospitality, spoke a benediction,
and asked, "Brahmin, how have you been able to reach this
land?"

The shrewd man answered, "I am a brahmin from Mathurā,
and my name is Lohajaṅgha. I was a poor man, and because
I suffered under my poverty, I went to a temple and before
Viṣṇu's face fasted and mortified myself. Then the blessed
God appeared to me in a dream. 'Go to Vibhīṣaṇa,' he said,
'for he is devoted to Me, and he shall make you rich.'

" 'But I am here, and Vibhīṣaṇa is far,' I said.

" 'Go,' repeated the God, 'and this very day you will meet
him!' I woke up at once and found myself here at the seashore. That is all I know."

Listening to Lohajaṅgha's words Vibhīṣaṇa considered how
inaccessible Laṅkā was and decided that the man was truly
endowed with divine powers. "Stay here," he said. "I shall
give you riches."

Thereupon he committed the brahmin to the man-killing
Ogres as a sacred trust and dispatched other Ogres to the
mountain Svarṇamūla to fetch a young giant-bird of Garuḍa's
nest. He gave the bird to Lohajaṅgha, to break it in as his
mount before starting back for Mathurā. The brahmin
mounted the bird and rode around Laṅkā for some time, resting and well taken care of by Vibhīṣaṇa.

When Lohajaṅgha wanted to return to Mathurā, the king
gave him a great many priceless jewels and entrusted to him
a lotus, a mace, a conchshell, and a disk wrought of pure gold,
which were to be the king's devotional offerings to God Viṣṇu

---

[4] The kingdom of Laṅkā is sometimes identified with Ceylon.

who resides at Mathurā.[5] With all this Lohajaṅgha mounted the bird, the king's parting gift, which was able to fly one hundred thousand leagues. Then he took off from Laṅkā and, crossing the ocean through the sky, reached Mathurā without incident. He landed in a deserted monastery outside the city, put his treasure away, and tied his bird. Then he went to the marketplace, where he sold one of the gems and bought clothes, oils, and food for the price of it. He took his meal in the cloister, fed his bird, and dressed and adorned himself with oils and flowers.

At nightfall he mounted the bird again and, carrying the disk, mace, and conchshell, flew to Lovely's house. He circled over the house in the air and, taking advantage of his opportunity, made a low sound to alert his mistress if she were alone. The courtesan heard it and came out on the roof; and she beheld the shape of Viṣṇu, aglitter with jewels, riding in the sky.

"I am Viṣṇu," he intoned, "and I have come for you!"

She prostrated herself and cried, "Mercy, O Lord, mercy!"

Lohajaṅgha dismounted, tied his bird, and went with his mistress into her apartment. When he had enjoyed the pleasures of love, he came out again, mounted the bird, and departed through the air.

The next morning Lovely refused to speak to anyone. "I am Viṣṇu's spouse," she thought, "and I shall not speak with mere mortals."

Her mother Crocodile asked, "Why do you behave in this way, daughter? Tell me!" Since she would not stop asking, Lovely had a curtain put up between herself and her mother and then proceeded to tell her about the nocturnal adventures which had brought about her divine taciturnity.

The procuress had her doubts about the story, but the same evening she had a moment's glimpse of Lohajaṅgha on his bird. The next morning Crocodile the procuress bowed deep before her daughter behind the curtain and prayed to her humbly.

"By the grace of God you have even on earth become a goddess, my daughter. But on earth I am your mother; therefore reward me as a daughter should. Please pray the God that he

[5] These are the emblems carried by the four-armed icons of Viṣṇu.

let me, an old woman, enter heaven with this same old body. Be merciful to me!"

"So I shall," said Lovely, and indeed she transmitted her mother's request to Lohajaṅgha when he came again that night disguised as Viṣṇu.

Playing his role, Lohajaṅgha replied to his mistress: "Your mother is an evil woman, and she is surely unfit to be brought to heaven. However, on the Eleventh, in the early morning, the gates of heaven are opened to admit, first of all, the hosts of Śiva's familiars. Your mother could be taken into heaven if she were properly disguised. You must therefore shave her head (save for five locks), hang a garland of human skulls around her neck, paint one side of her black with soot and the other red with vermilion, and strip her of all clothing. If she is so disguised as a familiar of Śiva, I can easily take her into heaven."

After he had given these instructions, Lohajaṅgha stayed for a while and then departed. When morning came, Lovely had her mother disguised in the manner described, and so the bawd waited, looking forward to heavenly bliss. At nightfall Lohajaṅgha reappeared, and Lovely committed her mother to his care. He mounted the bird with the naked and transfigured procuress and flew quickly off into the sky. While he was flying about, he noticed in front of the temple a very tall stone pillar which was crowned by a disk. He put the woman on top of that pillar, with the disk as her sole support, and there she huddled like the banner of his vengeance for the abuse she had heaped on him.

"Stay here for a moment," he said, "while I return to the earth and favor the world with My proximity," and he vanished from her sight.

Before the temple he saw a crowd of worshippers who had come to spend the eve of the great Procession in a vigil, and he spoke to them from the sky: "Hark, ye people! Today shall fall upon you from above the all-pernicious Demoness of Plague. Take refuge in Viṣṇu!"

When they heard this voice from heaven, all the people of Mathurā who were assembled there took fright and sought refuge in the God, imploring him in prayers for salvation. Meanwhile Lohajaṅgha descended from heaven, discarded his disguise, mixed with the crowd unrecognized, and exhorted them to devotion.

On top of the pillar the procuress thought to herself, "The God is not coming back today, and I won't go to heaven now!" She was not able to hang on much longer to the pillar, and she cried out in terror, "Haa, haa! I am going to fall!" When they heard her screams, the people below were alarmed, fearing that the plague goddess would swoop down upon them, and they implored her, "No! Don't fall, O Goddess!"

The people of Mathurā who were assembled there, young and old alike, passed the night with difficulty, dreading the fall of the goddess. But when morning broke, all the townspeople and the king as well recognized the procuress on the pillar in her ludicrous state, and now that they were past their fright they all burst out laughing. Lovely, as soon as she heard what was going on, came to the temple, and when she saw that it was her own mother, she was ashamed; and with the help of the people who were there she lowered her from the top of the pillar.

Everybody was curious and demanded that the procuress tell the whole story, and so she did. And all the people, the king, and the brahmins and merchants, thinking that this wonderful joke had been worked by a wizard or some such person, proclaimed: "Let the man who has fooled this woman who has deceived countless lovers reveal himself, and he shall receive on the spot a turban of honor!"

Thereupon Lohajaṅgha showed himself and on their demand told the entire story from the beginning. To the God he presented King Vibhīṣaṇa's votive offering of conchshell, mace, lotus, and disk, which created great wonder among all. Then the townsmen of Mathurā, delighted at his feat, wrapped him in a turban of honor and, at the king's command, made Lovely his wife.[6] And having wreaked vengeance on the procuress for his abuse and having filled his coffers with the precious jewels he had won, Lohajaṅgha lived happily with his beloved wife ever after.

---

[6] The king as the arbiter of caste relations here legalizes the brahmin Lohajaṅgha's marriage with a prostitute.

The City
of Gold

In the city of Vardhamāna, which is the jewel of the earth,
there was once a king named Paropakārin, benefactor of his
neighbors, tormentor of his enemies. Even as the thundercloud holds the lightning, so the exalted monarch had a queen,
but she was without the lightning's inconstancy. In the course
of time this queen, whose name was Kanakaprabhā, Golden
Lustre, bore her husband a daughter so lovely that it was as
though the Creator had fashioned her to humble the pride of
the Goddess of Beauty herself. The king called her Kanakarekhā, Streak-of-Gold, after her mother, and with the
passing of time the princess grew up as a little moon in the
eyes of her people.

The girl became a woman, and one day her father said to
his queen when they were by themselves: "My lady, our
Kanakarekhā has grown, and so has my concern to find her a
suitable match. My heart is burdened, for a highborn virgin
who fails to find her proper place is like a song that is out of

tune; the mere sound hurts even a stranger's ears. But a girl who is foolishly given away to an unworthy man is like sacred lore imparted to an unfit pupil; she will bring neither honor nor merit, but infinite regret. So, my dear, my heart grows heavier: to what king shall I marry my daughter? Who could be equal to her?"

The queen smiled. "You say this, while the girl herself refuses to marry!" she remarked. "Kanakarekhā made a doll today, and I said jokingly, 'When is your wedding going to be?' She reproached me. 'Don't talk like that, mother,' she said. 'I am not to be married to anyone at all! Fate forbids that I be separated from you; even as a virgin I shall bring you happiness. If I am forced to marry, I shall surely die. There is a reason.' I was disturbed by her words and came to you, my Lord. Why should we think about a husband if she refuses to marry?"

When the king heard this story from the queen's own lips, he was greatly upset and hurried to the princess' chambers.

"Can it be true that you refuse to accept a husband, my child? Even goddesses and nymphs go to great trouble to find one!"

Kanakarekhā lowered her eyes. "Father," she said, "I don't want to marry, not just now. Why does it concern you so? Why do you insist?"

Paropakārin, who was a very wise king, replied, "How can a man ever atone for his sins if he does not marry off his daughter? A girl depends on her family; she cannot afford to be independent. A daughter is in effect born for a husband, and her parents safeguard her only for a time. Except in her childhood, how can her father's house ever be a home to a woman without a husband? If a daughter remains a virgin when she is able to bear children, her kinsmen are ruined. The girl loses caste, and the man who marries her in the end is the husband of an outcaste."

When her father had spoken, the princess at last revealed what she had had in mind all the while. "If it must be so, father, then I must be married to a brahmin or a nobleman who has truly visited the City of Gold. This man, and no one else, shall be my husband. It is useless to force me into marrying another."

The king thought, "At least we are fortunate that she has agreed to marry at all on those conditions. She must be a goddess who, by some cause, was cast to the earth to be born in my house. How else could she know so much? She is only a child." The king agreed to his daughter's condition, and he rose and applied himself to his daily duties.

The following day when the king held court, he asked those present: "Is there anyone among you who knows of a city named the City of Gold? If there is a brahmin or nobleman who has visited that city, I shall give him my daughter and the title to my kingdom!"

They looked at one another in surprise, and all replied, "No, Sire, we have never even heard of such a city, much less seen it."

The king summoned his chamberlain and commanded, "Go and see to it that a proclamation is made throughout the city with the beat of drums and ascertain if any person has seen that city."

The chamberlain departed at once with the king's orders and passed instructions to the king's men. Drummers were sent around to arouse people's curiosity, and all over town the drum was struck and the proclamation made: "If there is a brahmin or a noble youth who has visited the City of Gold, let him speak! The king will bestow his daughter on him and the title of crown prince."

When the citizens heard this proclamation, they were astonished. "What is this City of Gold in the proclamation?" they asked one another. "Even the oldest among us have never seen a city of that name, and we have never even heard of it." And no one declared that he knew the city.

Now there lived in Vardhamāna a certain Śaktideva, a brahmin, the son of Baladeva, and he, too, heard the proclamation. He was still a young man and a slave of his vices; he had gambled away his entire fortune at a game of dice. When Śaktideva heard that the king promised to marry off his daughter, he pricked up his ears and thought, "Now that I have lost all my money gambling, I am no longer welcome in my father's house nor in a brothel. I have nowhere to go. The best thing I can do is to pretend to the criers that I know the city. Who is going to find out that I don't? Nobody has ever seen the place. Perhaps I can even win the princess this way!"

Having made up his mind, Śaktideva went to the king's men and lied. "I know the City of Gold!"

"Bless you," they said. "Come along with us to the chamberlain." He went with them straightaway. Before the chamberlain Śaktideva repeated his lie, and with great courtesy the dignitary conducted him to the royal presence. Even when he faced the king, he did not hesitate to tell the same lie; what is impossible to a gambler who has been ruined by the dice?

The king in turn sent the brahmin to his daughter Kanakarekhā to hear her decision. Śaktideva was announced by the chamberlain.

"Is it true," the princess asked, "that you know the City of Gold?"

"It is true," he replied. "I visited the city once when I was a student and traveled about the country in search of knowledge."

"What road did you take to the City," she inquired, "and what is the City like?"

"I traveled from here to a town called Harapura, from which I journeyed in stages to Benares. After I had spent a few days there, I left Benares for the city of Pauṇḍravardhana, and from there I traveled to the town that is called the City of Gold. Yes, I have seen the City. It is a paradise of pleasure for those who have earned great merit—and magnificent like Indra's heaven whose splendor can only be seen by the unblinking eyes of the gods.

"That was the route by which I traveled, and that is what the City looks like."

When the crooked brahmin had told this fictitious story, the princess laughed in his face.

"Aho!" she cried. "Yes, great brahmin, you certainly know the City. Please, please, tell me again what road you took!"

Again Śaktideva tried to brazen it out, but the princess told her maids to lead him away. When he had been thrown out, she went to her father.

"Did that brahmin tell the truth?" the king asked.

"Father," said the princess, "you may be a king, but you do act thoughtlessly! Don't you know that there are crooks and that they try to deceive honest people? That brahmin tried to cheat me; the liar had never seen the City! Don't be too hasty now in marrying me off. I will remain unmarried; we shall see what the future has in store."

"My daughter," insisted the king, "it is not right for a woman to remain too long a virgin. Wicked people who are envious of virtue will slander an unmarried woman. And people like best to smear the best. Let me tell you the story of Harasvāmin. Listen.

"On the bank of the Ganges lies a town named City of Flowers, and once a certain hermit dwelt there, seeking blessings in the sacred river. The hermit, whose name was Harasvāmin, lived on alms in a hut of leaves on the riverbank, and his extraordinary austerities had won him great devotion from the people.

"But one day when the hermit went out to beg his food, a vicious fellow in the crowd that watched the hermit from a distance remarked, 'Do you know what a hypocrite that hermit is? He eats all the little children in town.'

"Another one, equally wicked, added, 'Yes, I have heard people tell the same thing for truth.'

" 'Yes, indeed,' confirmed a third.

"The agreement of the wicked is a chain that ties censure to the righteous. The rumor gradually spread from ear to ear and grew bigger all over town, until all the citizens kept their children inside by force, because, as they said, Harasvāmin kidnapped all the children and devoured them.

"At last the brahmins, who were particularly worried lest their lineage be broken, assembled and deliberated and decided to banish the hermit from the town. No one among them dared to go to the hermit for fear that he would devour him in his fury, and they sent messengers. The messengers went and delivered their message from a safe distance: 'The brahmins order you to leave town!'

" 'Why?' asked the hermit in surprise.

" 'You eat our little children,' they said.

"At this the hermit decided to find out for himself, and while the crowd shrank away in terror, he made his way to the brahmins. The brahmins fled and climbed on the roof of their monastery; a man who has been fooled by a rumor is rarely capable of sense. Harasvāmin called the brahmins one by one by their names and, standing below, shouted to those who were hiding above.

" 'What is this foolishness now, brahmins! Ask among yourselves which children I have eaten and how many.'

"The brahmins asked one another, and they found that each of them had all his children alive and well. Thereupon the hermit instructed the other citizens to do the same, and they also found their children accounted for. And all of them, brahmins and merchants alike, exclaimed, 'Aho! In our folly we have made false accusations against a holy man. All our children are alive; who has eaten them then?'

"His innocence proved, Harasvāmin proceeded to leave the town. What pleasure can a man find in a bad country of indiscriminate people whose loveless minds turn against him at the slander of unscrupulous crooks? But the brahmins and the merchants all prostrated themselves at the hermit's feet and implored him to stay; and not without difficulty they prevailed on him to consent.

"This shows," concluded the king, "that for vicious people to see a person live righteously is to hate and slander him; and often they will bring false accusations against the just. If they find any opportunity, even the slightest, you will see that they kindle a fire and pour buckets of melted butter upon it. Therefore, if you want to pull this thorn from my flesh, you must try, now that your womanhood has come to flower, not to foster the easy slander of the wicked by remaining at your own choice and for a long time unmarried."

But when her father repeated his admonitions, Princess Kanakarekhā, who stood firm by her decision, again replied, "Then find me quickly a brahmin or a nobleman who has visited the City of Gold and give me to him; for that is what I have said."

The king thought that his daughter, who was so firm in her resolutions, must have memories from a former life; and seeing no other way to find her the husband she wanted, the king ordered that every day thereafter the same proclamation be heralded with the beating of drums to tell the newcomers in town that "the brahmin or nobleman who has truly visited the City of Gold must speak up, for the king will bestow on him his own daughter and the title to the throne." The proclamation continued to be made, but nobody was found who knew the City of Gold.

Meanwhile Śaktideva, who had been ignominously thrown out by the princess, thought glumly, "The only thing I have gained by my lies is contempt, and no princess. But now I will conquer her, and I shall travel on the face of the earth until I have found that city or lost my life. What use is my life now, unless I find the city and can return to claim the princess as the stake in this gamble?"

With this solemn vow the brahmin departed from Vardhamāna and, turning southward, set out on his journey. After he had traveled for some distance, the wayfarer reached the great jungle ranges of the Vindhya Mountains, abysmal and vast like his own ambitions, and he penetrated into the wastelands. The forest fanned him, when he was hot under the pounding sun, with the tender blossoms of its trees that swayed in the breeze. It was as though the land, which resounded with the tortured cries of deer that were slaughtered by lions and beasts of prey, cried out in grief over the violence of its teeming robbers. Above the vast untamed desert tracts the air quivered so glaringly that the jungle seemed bent on outshining the fierce fires of the sun.

For days he traveled the road through the jungle in a region where no trace of water could be found and danger lurked everywhere; and the country, though endlessly traversed, kept stretching to the horizon. Then he discovered in a secluded spot a large pond with cool, clear water, a king among ponds which bore a regal umbrella of lotus flowers and yak-tail plumes of dancing swans. He bathed in the pond and washed himself. Thereupon he discerned on the northern shore, amidst shady fruit-laden trees, a hermitage. He approached, and he found there a very ancient hermit, Sūryatapas by name, who was sitting at the foot of an aśvattha tree. He was surrounded by a circle of anchorites. A string of beads, which bead by bead seemed to count the centuries of the hermit's life, adorned an ear grizzled and whitened by extreme old age.

Śaktideva bowed and drew near and was graciously welcomed by the hermit, who offered him hospitality. The traveler ate some fruits, roots, and other forest fare, and when he had finished eating, the hermit questioned him.

"Whence do you come and whither are you bound, my son?"

"I have come from the city of Vardhamāna, Reverend Sir,"

Śaktideva answered with a deep bow, "and I am bound by a vow to journey to the City of Gold. But I do not know where that city is. If you know, Sir, tell me!"

"My son, for eight centuries now have I lived in this hermitage, but never have I even heard a city of that name mentioned."

At the hermit's reply Śaktideva gave up hope.

"Then nothing remains but to wander over the earth until I die."

Bit by bit the saint found out the whole truth of the matter, and he said, "If you are so determined, then do what I tell you. Three hundred leagues from here is the country of Kāmpilya. There is a mountain named Mount Uttara, and on this mountain is a hermitage; there lives my eldest brother Dīrghatapas. Go to him. He is old and may know about that city."

Śaktideva immediately agreed, and having passed the night with the saint, he started out with new hope the next morning and made good speed. After a long journey which took him through rough and perilous jungle ranges, he reached, exhausted, the country of Kāmpilya and began the ascent of Mount Uttara. He found the hermit Dīrghatapas in his hermitage on the mountain and bowed a greeting. The saint offered him hospitality which he gladly accepted.

"Reverend Sir," he said at last, "I am bound for the City of Gold, the name of which was made known to me by the princess of my country. I have sworn an irrevocable vow that I would find the city, and the sage Sūryatapas has sent me to you that I may find it."

"In all my long life this is the first time that I have heard of this city," answered the hermit. "None of the wayfarers from distant countries who have visited me here have acquainted me with its name. This place has never been mentioned within my hearing, much less have I myself ever set eyes on it. But I know that it must be somewhere in a very remote country, perhaps as far as the Archipelago, and I can tell you the way there.

"In the middle of the ocean lies an island named Utsthala. On this island lives Satyavrata, who is the chieftain of the fisher-tribes and a rich man. He travels back and forth between all the islands of the Archipelago, and he may have

seen or at least heard of your city.[1] You must first go to
Vitankapura, which is a port on the ocean, and sail with a
merchant on his ship to the island of Utsthala where the
fisher-tribes live, if you want to reach your goal."
Śaktideva at once accepted the saint's advice, took his
leave, and departed from the hermitage. He journeyed many
leagues through different lands and at last reached the port
Vitankapura, which lies as a beauty mark on the brow of the
seashore. There he sought out a merchant, by the name of
Samudradatta, with whom he made friends. The friendship
was sealed with a present of victuals, and the brahmin embarked with the merchant on his ship and set sail on the ocean.

When they were but a short distance from their destination,
a thundering black giant of a stormcloud suddenly reared its
head, licking its lips with tongues of lightning, and a terrible
tempest began to rage which lifted the light and lowered the
heavy like fate itself. Huge waves rose from the ocean under
the force of the hurricane like winged mountains of the sea
outraged by the violation of their realm.[2] One moment the craft
was hurled down, only to rise up again after an instant, as if
to illustrate the rise and decline of the wealthy. Then the ship
jumped up in the air and the next moment, filled with the
agonized cries of the merchants aboard and collapsing under
the burden, burst asunder. Samudradatta, the ship's owner,
was thrown free when the ship foundered and managed to
swim over to a drifting plank from which he was later
rescued by another ship.

Śaktideva sank into the yawning mouth and throat of a
large fish and was swallowed down whole. The fish played
around for a while in the ocean and, as fate would have it,
drifted toward the island of Utsthala. By a whim of destiny
the servants of fisher-king Satyavrata were seining thereabouts for śapharas and caught the fish. They were amazed at
the size of their catch and carried the fish to their king.
Satyavrata, on seeing the monster, was curious and ordered
his servants to slice it open; and Śaktideva stepped out of its
belly, alive and well, reborn after a second and remarkable
gestation.

[1] The Archipelago is Indonesia.
[2] Originally, the mountains flew about upsetting the earth's equilibrium until Indra cut their wings.

When the king saw the young man come out blessing his
savior, he asked in astonishment, "Who are you? How did you
happen to be in the belly of that monster? Where do you come
from, brahmin, and what wonderful adventures did you have?"

"I am a brahmin," he answered. "My name is Śaktideva, and
I hail from the city of Vardhamāna. I have vowed to visit a
city which is called the City of Gold, but not knowing where
to seek it I have roamed the farthest corners of the earth.
From a hermit whose name is Dīrghatapas I learned that the
city must be on an island. So I sailed out for the island of
Utsthala so that I might learn from Satyavrata the fisher-king
where that city is. Our ship was wrecked in a storm. I sank
to the deeps of the ocean and was swallowed by this fish, and
now I am here."

"I am Satyavrata!" said the king. "This is the island for
which you were bound. I have seen many islands, but the
island you want I have never seen myself, although I have
heard about such a place at the fringes of the Archipelago."
Then, seeing how disappointed Śaktideva was, he added,
"Don't lose heart, brahmin. Stay here for the night, and tomorrow morning I shall find a way to lead you to your goal."

With these reassuring words the fisher-king sent the brahmin to a brahmin cloister where he found ready hospitality.
One of the brahmins who lived there, a certain Viṣṇudatta,
served him his meal and engaged him in conversation. While
they were talking, Viṣṇudatta asked him detailed questions
about his country, his family, and all his circumstances, and
Śaktideva told him everything.

And as soon as Viṣṇudatta had heard all, he clasped
Śaktideva in a close embrace and exclaimed in a voice that
was muffled with tears of joy: "Oh, blessing, you are my
cousin on my mother's side; we are fellow countrymen! I came
here from your own country, long ago when I was a child.
You must stay here, and before long you will find out what
you wish from the reports that are passed on from steersmen
and merchants who come here from the Archipelago."

Having established their kinship, Viṣṇudatta waited on his
cousin with all the proper amenities, and Śaktideva forgot the
trials of the journey and was happy; for finding a kinsman in
a foreign land is like nectar in a desert. And he thought that

the success of his venture was imminent, for luck on the way spells luck at the end.

When the morning dawned on the island of Utsthala, the fisher-king Satyavrata met Śaktideva at the monastery and, true to the promise he had made the day before, said to him: "Brahmin, I have thought of a way that will lead you to your goal. In the middle of the ocean is a beautiful island called Ratnakūṭa, Jewel Peak. On that island is a temple of Viṣṇu which was founded by the Ocean. Every year on the twelfth day of the bright fortnight in the month Āṣāḍha a festival is celebrated in the temple, and from all corners of the Archipelago zealous people come on a pilgrimage. Somewhere among them there must be someone who knows the City of Gold. Come with me and let us go there together, for the day of the festival is near." Śaktideva agreed and joyfully packed the provisions which his cousin Viṣṇudatta had prepared for him.

They embarked on a little craft that Satyavrata had procured, and with the king at the helm they set sail immediately on the highway of the ocean. And while they sailed over that treasure house of wonders, infested by whales like floating islands, Śaktideva asked Satyavrata at the helm: "What is that beautiful object that is just visible in the sea far away on the horizon? It looks like a lofty winged mountain that can emerge from the deeps at will!"

"That is the divine banyan tree," answered Satyavrata. "They say that just below it there is a broad maelstrom which tapers down to the submarine fires. We must steer clear of it, for once a ship is caught in it, there is no escape."

But even while Satyavrata was speaking, a gust of wind carried the craft in that very direction. When the skipper realized it, he cried: "Brahmin, the end has come for us now, no doubt about it. Look, the ship has suddenly started drifting toward the maelstrom, and I cannot steer away from it anymore. We shall be hurled into the bottomless whirlpool as into the mouth of Death and swept off by the sea as by the karman that governs our life. I do not care for myself; for whose body is eternal? But it does grieve me that despite all your efforts your goal will be lost forever. So I shall hold the ship for as long as I can, and you must try to get a hold on a branch of the tree, quick now! With your robust build you stand a chance to save your life. Who can fathom the vagaries of fate and the waves of the ocean?"

Even as the magnanimous Satyavrata was speaking, the craft drifted toward the tree, and at the same instant Śaktideva jumped up with the strength of terror and grasped one thick branch of the ocean tree. But Satyavrata, sacrificing his body and his ship for the other, was dragged into the submarine fires.

Śaktideva, clinging in safety to a branch of the tree which rose out into heaven, thought in despair: "Still I have not seen the City of Gold, and now, after causing the fisher-king's death, I shall perish in desolation. But fate has branded its mark on the forehead of all mortals; who can defy his destiny?" Thinking such thoughts, which indeed suited the occasion, the young man passed the day on the shoulder of the tree. Then, at nightfall, he saw a multitude of giant birds arrive from all directions. Filling the skies with their chatter, they alighted on the tree and were instantly welcomed as old friends by the ocean waves which rose and rolled under the wind of their broad wings. And hidden behind a heavy cover of leaves, Śaktideva heard the roosting birds converse with one another in human language. They told one another where they had flown to spend the day—one to an island, the other to a mountain, a third to another region of the sky.

One among them, an ancient bird, said, "I went today to the City of Gold to spend my time leisurely, and tomorrow I shall go there again, for I can no longer bear the fatigue of long flights."

At the bird's words, which were like a sudden shower of nectar, Śaktideva's despair was extinguished. "I am saved!" he thought. "The City really exists, and now I have a way to reach it—if I use this monstrous bird as my mount."

He crept slowly nearer and, when the bird had dozed off, installed himself on its back between the wings.

The next morning, after the other birds had flown in different directions, Śaktideva's bird rose too like destiny with a wondrous force of wing, carrying Śaktideva unseen on his back. After a while the bird reached the City of Gold, and when it alighted in a park to disport itself, Śaktideva lowered himself stealthily from its back and made off.

While he sauntered around the park, he encountered two women who were gathering flowers, and cautiously he drew near. The women started in surprise when they saw him.

"What country is this?" he asked. "And who are you, good ladies?"

"This is the City of Gold, realm of the aerial spirits. A fairy queen lives here whose name is Candraprabhā, and we, friend, are her gardeners in this park. We are gathering these flowers for her."

"Be kind enough to conduct me to your mistress," he said.

Thereupon the women conducted the young man to a regal mansion, which, like a meeting place where all joys held tryst, was splendid with golden walls and gem-studded columns. When the servants saw him approach, they all hastened to tell Candraprabhā of the miraculous arrival of a mortal man. At once she ordered her lady chamberlain to conduct the brahmin into the palace without any delay; and he entered and feasted his eyes on her beauty, at which the Creator had toiled to the limits of his divine powers. Long before he was near, she arose courteously from her splendidly jeweled couch and, entranced at the sight of him, gave him a most courteous welcome.

When she was seated, she asked him in great wonder: "Handsome mortal, who may you be? How did you reach this country which is forbidden to human beings?"

Śaktideva told her his country, his caste, and his name and narrated how he had staked his life on finding the City of Gold in order to conquer the princess and how he had found it. When he had finished his account, she sat for a moment enwrapped in her thoughts. Then she heaved a deep sigh and addressed him in an intimate tone.

"Listen, I shall tell you a little now, my love. In this country reigns Śaśikhaṇḍa, Sliver-of-Moon, who rules the aerial spirits. He has four daughters, of whom I Candraprabhā, Radiant Moon, am the oldest. The second is Candrarekhā, Streak-of-Moon; the third Śaśirekhā, Touch-of-Moon; and the fourth Śaśiprabhā, Shining Moon. We grew up one after the other, and one day my three sisters went out together to the Ganges to bathe while I stayed home to pray for a husband. There was a hermit in the Ganges, Agryatapas, who did penance in the water; and while my sisters played in the river with the high spirits of young women, they splashed water over him. They went too far, and the hermit grew angry and cursed them: 'Wicked girls, all of you shall be reborn in the world of mortal men!' When my father heard about this, he went to the hermit and prevailed on his mercy, so that he told under which circumstances the curse of each of them would end. The great saint granted that even in their mortal state all of them would have the power to remember their old life and that this power would be supported by their celestial knowledge. Thereupon they left their bodies and descended to the mortal realm; and grieving over his bereavement my father gave me his city and went to live in the forest.

"Since then I have lived here. One day the great Mother Goddess appeared to me in a dream and said: 'Daughter, thou shalt have a mortal husband.' And ever since I have rejected the many aerial spirits who wooed me, and, to my father's distress, I have remained a virgin until this very day. But now I am conquered by your miraculous arrival and wonderful beauty, and I give myself up to you. On the coming fourteenth day of the moon I shall go to the peak of Mount Ṛṣabha to tell my father. For on that day every year all the eminent spirits of the air foregather there from all regions of the sky to worship God Śiva. I shall come back at once, and then you must marry me. Now rise!" And Candraprabhā thereupon served Śaktideva with the choicest delights that are reserved for the spirits of the air.

Śaktideva agreed to her proposal, and, happy as a man scorched by a brush fire who plunges into a lake of nectar, he lived with her. But when the fourteenth day of the moon came, Candraprabhā said to him: "I shall go to my father today to tell him about you. All my servants will accompany me, but you must not be unhappy if you have to remain by yourself here for a few days. However, while you are staying here alone in the palace, you must under no circumstances go up and enter the middle storey!"

Candraprabhā departed, leaving her heart in trust with the young man whose thoughts accompanied her on her journey. And alone in the palace Śakitideva diverted his mind by wandering from chamber to luxurious chamber. Then he began to wonder why the daughter of the fairy king had forbidden him to ascend the roof-terrace, and he became curious and went up to the middle storey of the palace: for man's mind will always turn to forbidden sensations. And when he had gone up the stairs, he saw three private pavilions. Two of them were closed, but the door of the third stood ajar, and he entered. And as he entered he saw the shape of a woman wrapped in a sheet of cloth; she was reposing like a beauty mark on a gem-encrusted couch. He lifted a corner of the sheet and stared at the beautiful face of Princess Kanakarekhā from Vardhamāna; and she was dead.

"What is this wonderful miracle?" he thought as he looked. "Does she sleep the sleep of no awakening, or am I bedeviled by my imagination? Here she lies dead, the woman for whom I went a-journeying, and at home she was alive! But her beauty has not faded. . . . It must be a snare of illusion in which fate saw fit to enmesh me!"

He left that pavilion and entered the other two on the same storey, and in each pavilion he found a girl lying on a couch, dead. Wonderstruck, he walked out on the terrace. Below he saw an enchanting little lake, and on its bank stood a horse with a jewel-studded saddle. He descended the stairs and walked curiously up to the horse. Seeing that there was nobody to ride it, he wanted to mount it; but the horse kicked at him with its hoof and pushed him into the lake. Śaktideva went under; and when he emerged from the water, struggling, he came up in his own city of Vardhamāna. And there he suddenly found himself to his consternation in the middle of the garden pond of his home town.

Bereft of his Radiant Moon, his face faded like a night-blooming lotus, and he exclaimed, "Vardhamāna! Vardhamāna after the City of the Spirits! Aho, what is the meaning of this bewitching show of jugglery and magic? I must have been fooled, ill-fated wretch that I am! But is there anybody who knows the workings of fate?"

Brooding, Śaktideva waded out of the pond and went wonderingly to his father's house. There he pretended that after he had been ruined by his gambling he had wandered abroad as a drummer. His father and family rejoiced at his homecoming and welcomed him with a feast.

The next day he left his father's house and went out into the city. And again he heard the old proclamation that was heralded about with the beating of drums: "If there is any-

one, brahmin or nobleman, who has truly seen the City of
Gold, let him speak! The king will bestow his daughter upon
him and his throne."

Śaktideva went to the drummer—for now he had succeeded
—and he said: "I have seen the city!" They conducted him
to the king, but the king recognized him and assumed that
he was lying, as before.

"I now stake my life that I am not lying and that I have
visited the City of Gold! Let the princess question me at
once."

The king went and ordered his lackeys to fetch his daughter.
When she recognized the brahmin, she said to the king:
"Father, the fellow will lie again."

"I am telling the truth!" Śaktideva said, "or, if I lie, then
explain to me one curious fact, Your Highness. How is it
possible that I saw you lying dead on a couch in the City
of Gold and now find you here in good health?"

When Śaktideva had proved himself with this question,
Princess Kanakarekhā immediately turned to her father and
said: "Father, this noble man has really visited the City of
Gold, and soon he shall be my husband when I have returned
there. He will also marry my three sisters and reign in the
city as the sovereign of the aerial spirits. Now I shall have
to return to the City and to my real body, for I was cursed
by a hermit to be reborn in your house. But he set an end to
the curse: as soon as a mortal man looked on my body in the
City of Gold and revealed the truth to me in the realm of
mortals, my curse was to end, and the man would become my
husband. I knew all this, for even in my mortal estate I remembered my former life.

"I shall return now to the realm of the spirits for the fulfilment of my destiny." Thereupon the princess departed
from her body and disappeared; and there was consternation
in the royal palace and loud lament.

Śaktideva now had lost both his women—ultimately defeated even though his unequaled efforts had been victorious.
Yearning for the two women he loved, he blamed himself for
his suffering and the frustration of his desires. But as he
wandered out of the palace, a thought occurred to him.

"Kanakarekhā said that my ambitions are destined to suc-

ceed in the end. Then why should I despair? Success depends
on character. I shall return again to the City of Gold by the
same route, and fate will have to see me through!"

So Śaktideva once again set out from Vardhamāna; for
resolute men who have made great efforts will not desist
before they have achieved their ends. After a long journey
he reached the port of Vitaṅkapura on the dunes of the ocean.
And there he happened to meet the same merchant with whom
he had sailed before and whose ship had foundered.

"That must be Samudradatta!" he thought. "How could he
have been saved after he was thrown into the sea? But small
wonder—I myself am another example!"

When he accosted the merchant, the latter recognized him
and embraced him delightedly. He took Śaktideva to his home
and, when the amenities had been complied with, asked him,
"How were you saved from the sea after the shipwreck?"

Śaktideva told what had happened to him, how he had
been swallowed by the fish and reached the island of Utsthala.
Then he put the same question to the excellent merchant:
"And how did you cross the ocean in safety? Tell me all!"

"I fell into the sea, and for three days I floated around
clinging to a piece of driftwood. Suddenly a ship appeared
and sailed my way. I shouted, and the sailors saw me and
pulled me on board. When I climbed aboard, I saw my own
father who had just returned from a long expedition to the
Archipelago. He recognized and embraced me and crying for
joy asked what had befallen me. I told him: 'Father, when
you did not return for a long time after you had sailed away,
I thought it my duty to carry on the business. On a voyage
to the Archipelago my ship was wrecked, and I myself was
thrown into the sea, to be found and rescued by yourself!'

"My father said reproachfully: 'Why did you venture your
life on such perilous enterprises? I am rich, son, and I am
getting richer still! Look at the ship I have brought, chockful
of gold!' Comforting words indeed! So father took me back
on his ship to our home in Vitaṅkapura."

That night Śaktideva rested with the merchant. The following morning he said, "Merchant prince, I have to leave
again for the island of Utsthala. But tell me how I am to
go there."

"Agents of mine are about to sail for Utsthala on business," he said. "You may embark on their ship and travel with them."

So the brahmin took passage with the merchant's agents to the island of Usthala. On his arrival the sons of the fisher-king Satyavrata saw him in the distance and, as fate would have it, recognized him. And they said to him: "Brahmin, you went with our father to search for the City of Gold. How is it that you now return alone?"

"Your father fell into the sea when heavy waves shattered the ship near the submarine fires."

But the sons of the fisherman were enraged, and they issued orders to their servants: "Fetter this criminal. He has murdered our father! How else is it possible that of two persons on the same ship one falls in the submarine fires and the other escapes? Tomorrow morning we shall sacrifice the murderer before the image of the Fierce Goddess."

So the sons of the fisherman had their servants fetter the brahmin and lock him in the dreadful sanctuary of the Fierce Goddess, in whose swollen belly innumerable lives had been sacrificed—a veritable mouth of death with bones, licked bare of flesh, like protruding tusks. There Śaktideva spent the night in chains, despairing of his life; and in his despair he prayed to the Fierce Goddess.

"O Goddess, with your body red like the sun at dawn— as if still bloody with the gore from the throat of Ruru the Demon which you drank when you slew him—you once saved this world. So, O granter of boons, deign to save me, your constant devotee, now that, coming from afar in quest of love, I have fallen in the hands of those who hate me without cause!"

Having prayed to the goddess he at last fell asleep. And in his dream he beheld a divine woman who appeared from the inner sanctum of the temple, and she drew near and spoke with compassion.

"My son Śaktideva, do not fear, for nothing untoward will befall you. The sons of the fisher-king have a sister, Bindumatī, and tomorrow she will see you and desire you for her husband. You must agree to marriage, and she shall bring about your release. She is not a fisher-maid but a celestial nymph who has fallen because of a curse."

When he awoke the next morning, the fisher-girl, shower
of nectar for his thirsty eyes, came to the temple of the
goddess and approached him. She made herself known and
said to him lovingly, "I shall have you released from this
prison if you do what I wish. I have refused all suitors whom
my brothers approved, but the instant I saw you, I fell in
love with you. Take me!"

Remembering his dream, Śaktideva gladly agreed to
Bindumatī's proposal. She had him released from his prison,
and he married the comely girl with the consent of her
brothers who, warned in a dream by the Mother Goddess,
had done their sister's bidding. And he lived with the celestial
woman who had assumed a mortal form as with the perfect
bliss which is the reward solely of virtue.

One day he stood with her on the roof-terrace of their
house and saw below him on the road an outcaste who carried
a load of beef. He said to his beloved, "Look, my slender-
waisted bride! How is it possible that this evildoer dares eat
the flesh of cows, which are honored throughout the three
worlds?"

"Indeed, it is an incredible crime," answered Bindumatī.
"What can one say? Through the power of the cows I myself have been reborn in a fisher-tribe, though my sin was
very small. How will he ever atone for it?"

"How curious!" Śaktideva said. "Tell me, darling, who
are you? And why have you become a fisher-girl?"

When he insisted, she finally said, "I shall tell you—though
the secret must be kept—on condition that you shall do what
I am going to ask."

"I promise I shall do it," he said and swore an oath on it.
Thereupon she first told him what she wanted him to do:
"You will shortly take another wife on this island, and she
will soon become pregnant. In the eighth month you must cut
open her belly and tear the fruit from it, ruthlessly!"

"What is that?" he asked with surprise and pity.

But his wife continued: "There is a reason why you should
do as I tell you. But, listen, I shall tell you why I have become a fisher-girl. In a former life I was the daughter of
the spirits of the air, while now I am cursed to a sojourn in
the realm of mortals. But once when I was still a spirit, I
used my teeth to bite off a piece of sinew to make a string on

my lute. That caused my birth in a dwelling of fishers! Just because my mouth touched the dry sinew of a cow I have fallen so low now. What fate is there in store for one who eats the flesh of cows?"

Even as she was telling this, one of her brothers came running toward their house in great consternation and cried to Śaktideva, "Come out at once! A monstrous boar has suddenly come out and is heading this way. He has killed many people already in his fury!"

Immediately Śaktideva came down from the roof, mounted a horse, and with a spear in his fist stormed at the boar. He hit the boar with his spear, and the wounded beast, seeing a hero attack, took to flight and disappeared into a cave. Śaktideva followed it into the cave to hunt it down. As he passed through the cavern, he saw a large wooded park with a house; and he entered the park and found there a girl of wondrous beauty who nervously ran toward him like a sylph of the woods sped by love.

"Who are you, beautiful girl?" he asked. "Why are you so excited?"

"I am Bindurekhā, daughter of King Caṇḍavikrama, protector of the Deccan, my good sir, and I am a virgin. But today suddenly a malignant demon with fiery eyes abducted me treacherously from my father's house and carried me here. Then, yearning for meat, he assumed the shape of a boar and went out; and now, before his hunger was stilled, he was struck by a hero with a spear. I escaped into the open, a virgin still."

"Then why should you be upset?" said Śaktideva. "I am the one who hit the boar with my spear, princess."

"Tell me who you are!"

"I am a brahmin, Śaktideva."

"Then you must become my husband!" she said.

"So be it," agreed Śaktideva and conducted her out of the park through the cave to his house. At home he told his wife Bindumatī what had happened and with her consent married the virgin Bindurekhā.

While Śaktideva was living with his two wives, one of them, Bindurekhā, became pregnant. In the eighth month of her pregnancy his first wife Bindumatī came to him privily and said: "My hero, remember what you have promised to me. This is the eighth month that Bindurekhā is with child. Go to her, rip open her belly, and take the child. You cannot belie your own oath!"

Śaktideva, overcome with love and compassion but bound by his oath, remained speechless for a while. Then, torn by grief, he went out to where Bindurekhā was; and when she saw how dejected he looked, she spoke to him anxiously.

"Why are you so downhearted today, my husband? Tell me, is it because Bindumatī has instructed you to tear out my child? But that has to be done, for something is to come of it. And there is no cruelty in it at all; so you must not pity me."

Still Śaktideva hesitated, and a Voice was heard from heaven: "My son Śaktideva, take the child from the woman's womb and fear not. Hold it by the neck and clench your fist, and it shall become a sword in your hand."

At this divine command the brahmin quickly parted her womb and tore out the child. He grasped it by the neck, and —behold!—when he gripped it like the tress of Luck in a firm grasp, it changed in his hand to a sword. And in the same instant the brahmin was transformed into an aerial spirit, and that very moment Bindurekhā vanished.

When he saw that the woman had disappeared, he went in his new form to his first wife, the fisher-king's daughter, and told what had happened.

"My husband," she said, "once we were three sisters, daughters of the king of the spirits, and we were cast from the City of Gold because of a hermit's curse. One of us was born a princess in the city of Vardhamāna, under the name of Kanakarekhā, and you have seen yourself how her curse ended and she returned to her own city. Just now you have witnessed the wondrous ending of Bindurekhā's curse which was ordained by fate. I am the third sister, and now the end of my curse has come too. I must go back to my city, my love. There are the bodies which we have as aerial spirits. Our eldest sister, Candraprabhā, is waiting for us there. Come with me at once, by the power of your magic sword. Our father who now lives in the forest as a hermit will bestow all four of us on you. Even more, he shall enthrone you in his city."

When Bindumatī had at last given this true account of

herself, she flew with Śaktideva along the pathways of the
sky to the City of Gold. There he saw again the divine bodies
which he had found lying on couches in the pavilions of the
middle storey; then they were dead, but now they were brought
back to life again by Kanakarekhā and her sisters. And he
rejoined his three beloved women, who prostrated themselves
before him, and also their eldest sister Candraprabhā, who
ceremoniously bade him welcome and feasted her eyes on his
presence after the longings of separation. As he entered the
inner palace, his coming was hailed by the servants and companions who each of them were engaged at their own tasks.

Candraprabhā said, "Good sir, this is my sister Candrarekhā,
Streak-of-Moon, whom you knew in Vardhamāna as Princess
Kanakarekhā. This is her younger sister Śaśirekhā, Touch-of-
Moon, whom you have already married in the island of
Utsthala as Bindumatī, daughter of the fisher-king. This is
the youngest of us, Śaśiprabhā, Shining Moon, who became
your wife as Princess Bindurekhā after she had been abducted
by the demon. Now come with us to meet our father, and
when he has given us to you in marriage, do not delay the
wedding!"

When Candraprabhā had thus voiced Love's command with
urgency and boldness, Śaktideva departed in their company
to the outskirts of the forest where their father lived. Prostrate
at his feet, his daughters told him in unison their desire, and,
admonished by a Voice from heaven, the king of spirits joyfully bestowed all the girls at once on Śaktideva. And after
that he imparted to him the rich domains in the city as well
as all the divine sciences which he possessed.

Then he gave Śaktideva, who had now achieved his end,
a new name to bear among the spirits of the air whom he had
now joined. His name was Śaktivega, and to Śaktivega the
king said: "No one shall ever defeat you. Yet, from the mighty
and powerful dynasty of Vatsa an emperor shall arise with
the name of Naravāhanadatta who shall be your sovereign
and to whom you shall bow."

After the old and mighty king Śaśikhaṇḍa had honored
his son-in-law, he gave him leave to depart from the forest
where the king performed his austerities and to return with
his beloved consorts to their royal residence. And as the
sovereign now, Śaktivega entered with his wives the City of

Gold which is the pennant of the Realm of the Spirits. And he lived in his city, which blazed with the golden splendor of its mansions like a magnificent shower of concentrated sunlight from the sky to which it reached, in the constant company of his four loving queens. And dallying with his bright-eyed loves in the gorgeous parks where stairs paved with precious stones led down to charming lakes, he tasted the perfection of happiness.

The

Red Lotus

of Chastity

In this world is a famous port, Tāmraliptī, and there lived
a rich merchant whose name was Dhanadatta. He had no
sons, so he assembled many brahmins, prostrated himself
before them, and requested: "See to it that I get a son!"

"That is not at all difficult," said the priests, "for the
brahmins can bring about everything on earth by means of
the scriptural sacrifices.

"For example," they continued, "long ago there was a
king who had no sons, though he had one hundred and five
women in his seraglio. He caused a special sacrifice for a
son to be performed, and a son was born to him. The boy's
name was Jantu, and in the eyes of all the king's wives he
was the rising new moon. Once when he was crawling about
on all fours, an ant bit him on the thigh, and the frightened
child cried out. The incident caused a terrific disturbance in
the seraglio, and the king himself lamented—'My son! O
my son!'—like a commoner. After a while, when the ant had

been removed and the child comforted, the king blamed his own anxiety on the fact that he had only one son.

" 'There must be a way to have more sons,' he thought, and in his grief he consulted the brahmins. They replied: 'Indeed, Your Majesty, there is one way by which you can have more sons. Kill the son you have and sacrifice all his flesh in the sacred fire. When the royal wives smell the burning flesh, they will all bear sons.' The king had everything done as they said and got as many sons as he had wives.

"Thus with the help of a sacrifice," concluded the brahmins, "we can bring you, too, a son."

So at the advice of the brahmins, merchant Dhanadatta settled on a stipend for their sacerdotal services, and the priests performed the sacrifice for him. Subsequently a son was born to the merchant. The boy, who was given the name Guhasena, grew up in due time, and his father Dhanadatta was seeking a wife for him. And the merchant voyaged with his son to the Archipelago to find a bride, though he pretended that it was just a business expedition. In the Archipelago he asked the daughter of a prominent merchant, Dharmagupta, a girl named Devasmitā, On-Whom-the-Gods-Have-Smiled, in marriage for his son Guhasena. Dharmagupta, however, did not favor the alliance, for he loved his daughter very much and thought that Tāmraliptī was too far away. But Devasmitā herself, as soon as she had set eyes on Guhasena, was so carried away by his qualities that she decided to desert her parents. Through a companion of hers she arranged a meeting with the man she loved and sailed off from the island at night with him and his father. On their arrival in Tāmraliptī they were married; and the hearts of husband and wife were caught in the noose of love.

Then father Dhanadatta died, and, urged by his relatives to continue his father's business, Guhasena made plans for a voyage to the island of Cathay. Devasmitā, however, did not approve of his going, for she was a jealous wife and naturally suspected that he would love another woman. So with his relatives urging him on and his wife opposing, Guhasena was caught in the middle and could not get on with his business.

Thereupon he went to a temple and took a vow of fasting. "Let God in this temple show me a way out," he thought. Devasmitā came along, and she took the same vow. God Śiva appeared to both of them in a dream. He gave them two red lotuses and spoke: "Each of you must keep this lotus in his hand. If one of you commits adultery while the other is far away, the lotus in the other's hand will wither away. So be it!" The couple woke up, and each saw in the other's hand the red lotus which was an image of the lover's heart.

So, carrying his lotus, Guhasena departed, and Devasmitā stayed home watching hers. Presently Guhasena reached Cathay and went about his business, trading in precious stones. But the lotus he carried around in his hands aroused the curiosity of four merchant's sons who noticed that the flower never seemed to fade. They tricked him into accompanying them home and gave him quantities of mead to drink; when he was drunk, they asked him about the lotus, and he told them. Calculating that the merchant's trade in precious stones would take a long time to be completed, the mischievous merchant's sons plotted together, and, their curiosity aroused, all four set sail at once for Tāmraliptī, without telling anybody, to see if they could not undo the chastity of Guhasena's wife. Reconnoitering in Tāmraliptī, they sought out a wandering nun, Yogakaraṇḍikā, who lived in a Buddhist monastery. They ingratiated themselves with her and proposed, "Reverend Madam, if you can bring about what we wish, we shall reward you richly."

"Of course, you boys want some girl in town," said the nun. "Tell me. I shall see to it. I have no desire for money, because I have a clever pupil named Siddhikarī, and thanks to her I have amassed a great fortune."

"How is that? You have acquired great wealth through the favor of your pupil?" the merchant's sons asked.

"If you are curious to hear the story, my sons," said the nun, "I shall tell you. Listen.

"Some time ago a merchant came to town from the North. While he was staying here, my pupil, in disguise, contrived to get herself employed in his house as a maid of all work; and as soon as the merchant had come to trust her, she stole all the gold he had in his house and sneaked away at dawn. A drummer saw her leave town and, his suspicions aroused by her fast pace, started with his drum in his hand to pursue and rob her in turn. Siddhikarī had reached the foot of a banyan tree when she saw the drummer approach, and the cunning girl called out to him in a miserable voice: 'I have quarreled with my husband, and now I have run away from home to kill myself. Could you fasten the noose for me, my friend?'

" 'If she is going to hang herself, then why should I kill the woman?' thought the drummer, and he tied a noose to the tree. He stepped on his drum, put his head through the noose, and said, 'This is the way to do it.' The same instant Siddhikarī kicked the drum to pieces—and the drummer himself perished in the noose. But at that moment the merchant came looking for her, and from a distance he discerned the maid who had stolen his entire fortune. She saw him come, however, and immediately climbed up the tree and hid among the leaves. When the merchant came to the tree with his servants, he saw only the drummer dangling from the tree, for Siddhikarī was nowhere in sight.

" 'Can she have climbed up the tree?' the merchant questioned, and immediately one of the servants went up.

" 'I have always loved you, and here you are, with me in a tree!' whispered Siddhikarī. 'Darling, all the money is yours. Take me!' And she embraced him and kissed him on the mouth and bit the fool's tongue off with her teeth. Overcome with pain the servant tumbled out of the tree, spitting blood, and cried something unintelligible that sounded like 'la-la-la.' When he saw him, the merchant thought that the man was possessed by a ghost, and in terror he fled home with his servants. No less terrified, Siddhikarī, my pupil, climbed down from the top of the tree and went home with all the money."

The nun's pupil entered just as her mistress finished, and the nun presented her to the merchant's sons.

"But now tell me the truth," resumed the nun, "which woman do you want? I shall prepare her for you at once!"

"Her name is Devasmitā," they replied, "Guhasena's wife. Bring her to bed with us!" The nun promised to do so and gave the young men lodging in her house.

The wandering nun ingratiated herself with the servants at Guhasena's house by giving them delicacies and so on, and thus she gained entrance to the house with her pupil. But when she came to the door of Devasmitā's chambers, a dog which was kept on a chain at the door barked at her, though never before had the bitch been known to bark. Then Devasmitā saw her, and wondering who the woman was that had come, she sent a servant girl to inquire and then herself conducted the nun into her chamber. When she was inside, the nun gave Devasmitā her blessing, and after courteous amenities for which she found a pretext, the wicked woman said to the chaste wife: "I have always had a desire to see you, and today I saw you in a dream. That is why I have come to visit you. I see that you are separated from your husband, and my heart suffers for you; if youth and beauty are deprived of love's pleasures, they are fruitless."

With such talk the nun gained Devasmitā's confidence, and after having chatted awhile she returned to her own home. The next day the nun took a piece of meat covered with sneezing powder and went to Devasmitā's house. She gave the meat to the dog at the door, and the animal at once swallowed it. The sneezing powder caused the dog's eyes to run, and the animal sneezed incessantly. Then the nun entered Devasmitā's apartment, and once she had settled down to her hostess' hospitality, the shrew began to weep. Pressed by Devasmitā she said, as if with great reluctance: "Oh, my daughter, go and look outside at your dog; she is crying. Just now she recognized me from a former life when we knew each other, and she burst out in tears. Pity moved me to weep with her."

Devasmitā looked outside the door and saw the dog which seemed to be weeping. "What miracle is this?" she wondered for the space of a moment. Then the nun said: "Daughter, in a former life both she and I were the wives of a brahmin. Our husband had to travel everywhere at the king's orders as his envoy, and while he was gone, I carried on with other men as I pleased, to avoid frustrating the senses and the elements. Our highest duty, you know, is to yield to the demands of sense and element. That is why I in this present life have the privilege of remembering past existences. But she in her ignorance guarded her chastity, and so she has been reborn a bitch, though she does remember her other life."

"What kind of moral duty is that?" thought Devasmitā, who was clever enough. "This nun has some crooked scheme afoot!" Then she said: "Reverend Madam, how long I have been ignorant of my real duty! You must introduce me to some handsome man!"

"There are some merchant's sons from the Archipelago who are staying in town," said the nun. "I shall bring them to you if you want."

Overjoyed the nun went home. And Devasmitā said secretly to her servant girls: "I am sure that some merchant's sons have seen the never-fading lotus which my husband carries in his hand, and out of curiosity they have asked him about it when he was drinking. Now the scoundrels have come here from their island to seduce me and have engaged that depraved nun as their go-between. Fetch me immediately some liquor loaded with Datura drug and go and have a dog's-paw branding iron made." The maids did as their mistress told them, and one of them, at Devasmitā's instructions, dressed up as her mistress.

Meanwhile the nun selected one of the four merchant's sons, who each commanded to be taken first, and brought him, disguised as her own pupil, to Devasmitā's house. There she bade him go inside and went away unobserved. The maid who posed as Devasmitā gave the young merchant with all due courtesies the drugged liquor to drink, and the drink (as though it were his own depravity) robbed him of his senses. Then the girls stripped him of everything he wore and robed him monastically in air. Thereupon they branded the dog's-paw iron on his forehead, dragged him outside, and threw him in a cesspool. In the last hours of night he came to his senses and found himself sunk in the cesspool—the very image of the Avīci hell which his own wickedness had brought on! He got up, bathed, and, fingering the mark on his forehead, he returned naked to the nun's house.

"I won't be the only ridiculous one!" he thought, and so he told his brothers in the morning that he had been robbed on his way back. Pretending a headache from his long night and deep drinking, he kept his marked forehead wrapped in a turban's cloth.

The second merchant's son who went to Devasmitā's house that night was manhandled in the same way. He too came home naked and said that, despite leaving his jewelry at home, he had been stripped by robbers as he came back. And the next morning he too kept his head bandaged, supposedly because of a headache, to conceal the brand on his forehead. All four of them, though they dissimulated everything, were castigated, branded, plundered, and put to shame in the same fashion. Without disclosing to the nun how they had been maltreated ("Let the same thing happen to her!"), they departed.

The next day the nun, who thought that her plan had succeeded, went with her pupil to Devasmitā's house. With a show of gratitude Devasmitā courteously poured them drinks with Datura, and when the nun and her pupil had passed out, the chaste wife cut off their noses and ears and tossed them outside in a sewage pit.

But then Devasmitā began to worry. "Might those merchant's sons now kill my husband in revenge?" She went to her mother-in-law and told her everything that had happened.

"Daughter," said her mother-in-law, "you have done well. But something bad may now happen to my son."

"Then I shall save him as Śaktimatī once saved her husband with her presence of mind!"

"And how did she save her husband?" asked her mother-in-law. "Tell me, my daughter."

"In my country," Devasmitā began, "we have a great Yakṣa who is famous under the name of Maṇibhadra. He is very powerful, and our ancestors have built him a temple in our town. My countrymen come to this temple, each with his own presents, to offer them to Maṇibhadra in order to gain whatever it is they wish. There is a custom that any man who is found in this temple at night with another man's wife is kept with the woman in the sanctum of Maṇibhadra for the rest of the night, and the next morning they are brought to court, where they will confess to their behavior and be thrown in jail.

"One night a merchant named Samudradatta was caught in the act with another man's wife by one of the temple guards. The guard led the merchant away with the woman and threw them into the sanctum of the temple where they were securely chained. After a while the merchant's faithful wife, Śaktimatī, who was very ingenious, got to know what had happened. Immediately she took an offering for pūjā worship and, disguised, went out into the night to the temple, full of self-confidence and chaperoned by her confidantes.[1] When she came to the temple, the pūjā priest, greedy for the stipend she offered him, opened the gates for her, after informing the captain of the guard. Inside the temple she found her husband who was caught with the woman. She dressed the woman up to pass for herself and told her to get out. The woman went out into the night in her disguise, and Śaktimatī herself stayed in the sanctum with her husband. When in the morning the king's magistrates came to examine them, they all saw that the merchant had only his wife with him. The king, on learning the' fact, punished the captain of the guard and released the merchant from the temple as from the yawning mouth of death.

"So did Śaktimatī save her husband that time with her wits," concluded Devasmitā, and the virtuous wife added in confidence to her mother-in-law, "I shall go and save my husband with a trick, as she did."

Then Devasmitā and her maids disguised themselves as merchants, boarded a ship on the pretext of business, and departed for Cathay where her husband was staying. And on her arrival she saw her husband Guhasena—reassurance incarnate!—in the midst of traders. Guhasena saw her too, from a distance, and drank deep of the male image of his beloved wife. He wondered what such a delicate person could have to do with the merchant's profession.

Devasmitā went to the local king and announced: "I have a message. Assemble all your people." Curious, the king summoned all citizens and asked Devasmitā, who still wore her merchant's disguise, "What is your message?"

"Among these people here," said Devasmitā, "are four runaway slaves of mine. May it please Your Majesty to surrender them."

"All the people of this town are assembled here," replied the king. "Look them over, and when you recognize your slaves, take them back."

Thereupon she arrested on their own threshold the four merchant's sons, whom she had manhandled before. They still wore her mark on their foreheads.

"But these are the sons of a caravan trader," protested

[1] Pūjā worship is a particular rite for an icon or image.

the merchants who were present. "How can they be your slaves?"

"If you do not believe me," she retorted, "have a look at their foreheads. I have branded them with a dog's paw."

"So we shall," they said. They unwound the turbans of the four men, and they all saw the dog's paw on their foreheads. The merchants' guild was ashamed, and the king surprised.

"What is behind this?" the king asked, questioning Devasmitā in person, and she told the story, and they all burst out laughing.

"By rights they are your slaves, my lady," said the king, whereupon the other merchants paid the king a fine and the virtuous woman a large ransom to free the four from bondage. Honored by all upright people, Devasmitā, with the ransom she had received and the husband she had rejoined, returned to their city Tāmraliptī and never again was she separated from the husband she loved.

Gomukha's
Escapade

In the country of the Vatsas, on the river Kālindī, lies the city of Kauśāmbī, which is the heart of the world. There reigned King Udayana. If one tried to enumerate, however briefly, the virtues of this land, this city, and this king, the story would never begin. If a traveler sets out on a journey to the seven oceans and continents of this world and begins his voyage by counting the jewels of Mount Meru, when will he ever have time to see the world?

King Udayana had many wives, but none did he love so much as Vāsavadattā and Padmāvatī. One day when the king held court, two young men prostrated themselves before him. The king interrogated them concerning their petition, and they explained their case as follows. Their father, a merchant, had been lost on the high seas, and their eldest brother, moved with filial piety, set sail to search for his father. He never returned. When his two brothers thereupon proceeded to take possession of the family fortune, their widowed sister-in-law stubbornly refused to surrender it. Now they implored the king to see to it that their father's legacy, which should legally fall to them, be restored to them by their brother's widow.

The king sent his lady chamberlain to the widow, since, he observed, patrician women find it painful to appear in person in court. The lady chamberlain went and returned. The woman had received her exceedingly well, she said, and confirmed her brothers-in-law's story. However, the woman remarked that, though her husband's ship was reported lost, the reports had been silent about her husband himself. Many a time have travelers returned to their hearths after their ships foundered, and, since it was very possible that her husband one day would return, she refused to regard herself as a widow. Moreover, she was with child and already in the tenth moon. What would happen if her brothers-in-law inherited the family fortune, left her, and a son were born to her or her husband came home? She prayed the lady chamberlain to present her considerations to the king.

The king said to the merchants, "This lady knows the customs that govern the family, and she is right. If a nephew is born to you or if your brother comes back, either one of them inherits. If the child is a daughter and the merchant does not return, it is We who by law must inherit."

Even as the king was speaking, a loud tumult was heard of music and voices, and suddenly a concubine of the lost merchant appeared smiling in court, carrying gifts of robes and perfumes. She saluted the king with great ease of manner and testified that the merchant's wife had given birth to a son.

Thereupon the king marveled, and he thought, "Aho! How clearly is the blessing of a son here shown before us! Behold, one drop of seed is born that bears the name of son, and all these people here, friends or foes, are beside themselves with joy or despair, crying, 'Now he shall be the guardian of the merchant's fortune!' But when We die, who shall be the guardian of our fortune and of the orb of the world? Who but our son?"

Thus the king sat musing and became concerned to have a son. He ordered a general observance of penance and fast in honor of Kubera, excusing among his women only the *frail Padmāvatī from taking part in the mortifications. Queen Vāsavadattā dreamed that Kubera appeared to her and gave her a jewel that suddenly changed into a lion's whelp and entered her body. The son thus conceived was felicitously born and received the name Naravāhanadatta, Kubera's Gift. The king's four ministers were also blessed with sons who were to be the newborn prince's companions.*

The prince grew in years, beauty, virtue, and wisdom until he reached the age when he was to be consecrated Young King of the Realm. At the grand royal reception that preceded the ceremony, a great lady came to court with a young girl, her daughter. The prince was enchanted by the girl, who was called Madanamañjukā.

Now the ceremony was over, and one of the prince's companions, Gomukha by name, began to behave in an extraordinary fashion: he absented himself continually and became absent-minded in the presence of his friends. He explained his strange behavior by his intensive study of the Upaniṣads.

The king had proposed an outing to the prince and his friends, a drive in the Nāgavana Park, which Gomukha supported strongly. As they were being driven around, the conversation turned to the hierarchy of factors that influence people's actions. Gomukha declared that desire is man's main motivation. This desire, as he understood it, was known only to him. According to the Kāmaśāstras, he added, there are four kinds of people: those who are loved and in love, those who are loved but not in love, those who are in love but not loved, and those who are neither loved nor in love. He put himself in the first category, the prince in the second, the others in the last.

His friends pressed him to reveal the name of the girl who loved the prince, but Gomukha refused until the embarrassed prince himself ordered him to tell his story. And Gomukha began.

When Your Royal Highness had been invested with the title of Crown Prince, for the greater honor of the title, I went to the Royal Seraglio to congratulate both the king's consorts. There I saw a painting such as even spirits have never seen, which equaled the king's realm in the pure harmony of its colors.

"What are you looking at, Gomukha my boy?" asked Queen Padmāvatī.

"Your Majesty," I said, "at three things at once!"

"Which three?" the queen asked, and I explained.

"Your wealth, the painters' art, and the abundance of the world's wonders!"

The queen smiled. "Gomukha is really sophisticated!" she said. "Who but a sophisticate could think of such an answer?"

But at the queen's remark, doubt invaded my mind: is it a virtue to be sophisticated, or is it a vice? However, despite my doubts, I did not dare to ask the queen for fear that she would think me naïve and unsophisticated.

Wondering who could explain to me what sophisticated meant without my having to ask him first, I walked out of the Royal Palace and wandered vaguely around. Then I saw a carriage with two splendidly plumed and caparisoned Arabian horses which stood stamping and pawing the ground. Holding a whip, the coachman politely folded his hands at his forehead and addressed me.

"Your Honor," he said, "may I ask you a favor? I am a hereditary servant at the Royal Palace, and it is my task to look after the king's mounts. Now the king has ordered me to turn these saddle horses at short notice into coach horses. So I have hurriedly trained their withers to the yoke, as far as I could, but I cannot be sure of them before an expert has tried them. Please ride the coach and examine them just as a student of words, sentences, meanings, and criteria would examine his books!"

I deliberated for a moment and lowered my head. "That is certainly a service he asks!" I thought. Then I noticed a scribe who wore a trailing robe and a cultured air, with inkpot and pen ornamentally stuck behind his elongated ears.

"The king certainly has thrown us in a lot of trouble," he complained. "A curse on the wretched dog's life we call our living! Now I am to take a census of all people in the country and list whether they are prominent and sophisticated or unsophisticated nonentities. And I can't find even one person who really qualifies as a sophisticate, but the unsophisticated are rocking the world!"

A second scribe, who carried two census registers in his hands, pointed his finger at me and said in amazement, "Did you notice how gauche that fellow is over there? For all his genteel looks he is just like a penniless quack who pursues the medical profession for profit! He ought to be number one in the register of unsophisticates if he refuses to get on the coach at such a courteous invitation. Anyone who would jump on, even without an invitation would have to be listed at the top of sophisticates with our congratulations!"

Eager to prove myself a sophisticate and fearing that somebody else would forestall me, I ran and landed with a long jump on the coach.

Riding along on the speeding coach, I saw an elephant in our way, just in front of us; attendants were humoring the animal with soothing words. My coachman reined in and shouted at the elephant's mahout, "Get your elephant out of the way. Don't detain the coach of a sophisticate!"

"Let your sophisticate's coach go by another way," replied the mahout. "I don't want to go against the whims of my elephant. His rutting ichor has not started to run yet, but it will if we coax him along. I am sorry we cannot force him against his will."

I said to my coachman, "If the mahout refuses to make way, you had better take another road."

"As you please," he said and turned the coach. Then he added, "I shall now drive you into the quarter where the sophisticates live."

"Long live the elephant!" I thought. "By barring my way he will introduce me to the world of sophistication!"

I saw a large bazaar, entirely paved with long stones, where mostly such merchandise as perfumes, jewelry, incense, and the like were being sold. Passing by the bazaar I saw a landscaped avenue of charmingly terraced villas which looked like architects' dreams come true. At one place I saw how disgracefully behaved young women, the worse for liquor, accosted equally intoxicated young men who turned their backs on them. At another place I saw a boy pursue a girl who scolded him at once harshly and gently: "Ah, go away, little scullery boy! Must you lay hands on me, unlucky girl? Canoodle with a kitchen maid who has been callused by scullery boys like you!" Somewhere else again I saw a girl who played the vīṇā lute with undulating fingers and another who sounded the seven-stringed lute at the touch of a plectrum.

While I was driving around in the carriage, which now moved slowly, I noticed a class of young girls who with great concentration were reading a manuscript aloud. I wondered what work they were studying, and, straining my ears, I heard distinctly from a distance: "After intercourse has taken place, the woman must not doze off or leave her man when he is asleep but must endeavor to harmonize her breathing with his."

"What kind of girls are these?" I thought. "They are studying the Libertine's Handbook!" Then I realized that the coachman had lured me into the District of the Prostitutes.

"I'll be blessed!" exclaimed a rake who was circumambulating the temple of the God of Love. "I can get some sleep now. That is Gomukha himself, who has become bored with the pretense of morality and has plunged into the District to reap the reward of his masculinity."

I said to the coachman: "This is disgraceful! Turn the coach back at once!"

"Don't be terrified by the District," he said. "It is not a pariah colony. And nobody loses his virtue just by looking. We have almost passed the main street, and there is only a short distance to go. Shall I turn back now, or may I drive on?"

"Drive on," I consented, and the coachman drove the carriage fast ahead.

Then I saw a big mansion, as high as Mount Mandára and not unlike the Royal Seraglio in appearance. Guards were posted at the gates, and throngs of women and eunuchs mingled with persons of quality. Young girls ablaze with pearls and jewelry came out and surrounded our coach, challenging the fresh beauty of a lotus pond. Then one of them, a proud young woman, folded her hands at her forehead and spoke.

"Your Honor," she said, "I was told to invite you to enter."

"Aho!" I thought. "A curse on the power of virtue! Queen of the world is she, but she must choose her words as if she were an errand girl. Perish the dumb rewards from unremembered lives, perish her servile I-was-told! Reincarnation has made a slave out of this Goddess of Beauty, and her humble manner betrays it. . . . But now, should I enter or shouldn't I?"

While I was deliberating for a moment, the lotus-like faces of the girls around me faded in distress, and they looked toward the mansion. Following their gaze, I saw a window with open shutters which blazed with the precious stones that adorned the trellis. And in the window I discerned an excitedly quivering fan of three palm leaves that were reddened by the glow of the fingers of their nervous bearer. And I saw a long neck belonging to a face that remained hidden behind the leaves—like a water lily on a high stalk disappearing between the wavelets in a pond. And I saw an outstretched hand with a beckoning forefinger—a hand like a blossom torn loose from its tree and now floating on a gentle breeze.

"Someone is beckoning to me! Who is she?" I wondered, and before I knew it I had leaped to the ground.

"A kind person," remarked the coachman, "will of course reciprocate a kindness. Your Honor must enter, and during the time that you remain inside, I shall rest the horses. They have become very tired indeed."

Thereupon, like a wild elephant lured into the stockades, I was led by the courtesans through the heavy doors into the first enclosure; and there I saw a young cow elephant, point perfect at the lip of her trunk and everywhere else, which was being put through training exercises. Entering a second enclosure, I saw a tiny lady's carriage and coach and a well-designed palanquin which bespoke the skill of its artisans. In a third enclosure were horses from all countries, perfectly built and excellently trained, which shook their bridles and harness. The fourth contained an arena of cages full of shrieking cakoras, parrots, and blackbirds and paraded by a troop of crowing cockerels. In the next enclosure I saw highly skilled metalsmiths work gold and silver and copper into various forms and shapes. In the sixth enclosure I saw expert perfumers impregnate with incense and perfumes the materials which, in the seventh enclosure, were tailored by specialists into garments of all descriptions—ribbons, veils, silken shifts, and so forth. In the eighth enclosure I watched the jewelers bore, cut, and set pearls and precious stones which glittered brilliantly. And in all eight enclosures the masters and their apprentices barred my way to sing the praises of their own skills. And wherever we entered, the girls who guided me, aglow with beauty and jewelry, said, "Your high fees have spoiled your judgment! Come on, this noble gentleman has arrived with a purpose, and there is no reason why he should be detained by miserable braggarts who talk shop!"

Women appeared with golden bracelets on their arms and white veils over their hair, and they proffered a guest-gift of jewels and flowers.

"Your Lordship be blessed!" they said. "Like the Stone of Wishes, you adorn, protect, and purify this household! Now meet sophisticated people and become their leader, for the qualities of a distinguished person emerge in the company of his equals!"

Thereupon the girls formed a procession and conducted me to a staircase the steps of which were paved with crystal tiles that glowed in the darkness. I ascended the stairs to the terrace, and there I beheld a wonderful picture like a silent, motionless vision of the world which one sees in dreams: surrounded by her lady-companions, like the intellect surrounded by the beautiful arts, stood a young girl whose beauty exceeded the bounds of comprehension. Inference and Comparison were left far behind, and even Perception could not help one to describe her indescribable form. For as soon as his eye beholds her, a man is robbed of his senses by sudden bewilderment and petrified by unconsciousness; so what would he perceive by Perception? Neither the God of the logicians, nor the Law of the Buddhists, nor the Matter of the realists, nor the Atoms of the naturalists, nor Time, nor World-Soul could easily produce such beauty as was hers.

But let me desist from describing her appearance. I could not do her justice without also enumerating her qualities at length. You yourself will be able to study both at leisure! Raising my folded hands to my head, I stood there speechless for a moment, contemplating her beauty in astonishment. Then she raised her head to regard me with eyes that opened like lotus buds, and she addressed me first.

"Live long, Gomukha!"

"Aho!" I thought, "she may look like an innocent girl, but she must be a loose woman if, with perfect equanimity and without a trace of shame, she dares to invite me in. Damned be my presence of mind and my voice, which were surprised off guard; and praised be my hands, which went through the motions of greeting! I am nothing but hands—mind and tongue have perished on me. For only the vigilant live, and he who is found off guard is already dead!"

While I was thinking, she offered me a seat, the legs of which were carved out of dwarf elephant tusks, and I sat down. After I was seated, she inquired, "From where has Gomukha come?"

"From the Royal Palace," I explained.

"Is the king in good health?" she asked. "And both the king's consorts and their women? And Rumaṇvat and the other ministers and their families? And the pr——" She started to say something but mumbled inarticulately and fell silent. For a moment she sat motionless, staring at the tip of her nose, but then she inquired after the health of Hariśikha and the others. I replied that all were in good health, and again she questioned me.

"I know very well," she said, "how all of you exercise your minds, but, tell me, in what particular arts does each of you excel?"

"His Highness the prince excels in the training of elephants and in the musical arts—an ocean which mere men can hardly plumb! Hariśikha excels in political science, Marubhūtika in scholarship, and Tapantaka has reached the top in the arts of riding, driving, and racing. As for myself, well, I have nibbled at all arts, as a donkey nibbles at the green tops of vegetables, and have learned a few tidbits I wanted to know."

"How much time do you spend in the pursuit of your studies, and what recreations do you have?"

"We get up after the third watch of the night, worship our deity, and dress ourselves properly. Then we study the epic. When our physicians allow us, we have a perfumed oil bath and take exercises in the use of arms and mounted combat. Then we have a bath, eat our noon meal, and rest for an hour. The remaining hours of the afternoon we spend in reading and discussing political handbooks and poetry, and at nightfall we retire to a white-stuccoed hall which is brighter than the full moon and amuse ourselves as we like, playing pleasantly on lute and flute."

She darted a glance at a girl sitting nearby and then looked back at me. With a tantalizing air of reluctance, the girl rose and, weaving the burden of her buttocks to where I sat, dropped down beside me. I did not even look at her. The same thing happened with a second courtesan, for whom I did not care a straw.

Then a third approached, a most beautiful girl, a goddess of beauty. She said: "What a dilemma! How am I to reconcile the strict instructions of my mistress with the honors that are due to a guest? What am I to do?"

"Even to goddesses are mistresses masters," I said. "So your mistress' masterful command ought to be obeyed!"

Her mistress said: "You certainly will not regret it if you do not see your friends today. Padmadevikā here will make you forget them!"

But Padmadevikā read my mind and looked embarrassed. "It is not proper," she said, "for servants to sit down without their master's permission. Your Grace may be pleased to enter this little room where a couch is made up and take a rest from the tiring trip in the rocking coach."

So at her invitation I entered and stretched comfortably on the magnificent couch whose golden frame was studded with gems. Padmadevikā remained standing at my feet.

"Who would be eligible," she asked, "to massage your feet, an honor hardly to be aspired to by persons of little merit?"

"Splendid," I said. "Someone ought to massage my feet. Anyone. I would not insist on any particular masseur."

But when she took hold of my feet with both her hands, I thought: "I am an innocent man! Why has this poison-girl been set on me? I have lost control of my senses, what has become of my mind I don't know, and my body is trembling all over. A curse on the harlot!"

When she had massaged my feet for a while, she asked, "How may your slave-girl now serve your weary chest?"

"Shameless and scandalous woman!" I thought. "She has touched the soles of my feet with her hands, and now she wants to touch my chest with the same dirty hands!" But she read my thoughts and smiled.

"Who would be so feeble-minded as to dream of touching your chest with her hands?"

"She must be a goddess who commands the divine lore!" I thought. "Sensuous mortals don't have the power to read minds."

"There is a blameless technique of massaging a chest that has been strained by the rocking of a carriage," she said. "It is called 'pressing the breasts.' If you are pleased with me, or if your chest is very tired indeed, allow me to show you. For women submit to their masters!"

"She is determined and pitiless," I thought, "and she will wait unperturbably until she receives my permission." So I said: "I am powerless, my girl, you can be sure of that. Any expert masseur who is in control of himself may go ahead." And she began massaging my chest with her exquisite breasts, which trembled as mine shuddered. . . . But stop, I am digressing into pointless detail, and if one has an interesting story to tell, he will never be boring if he sticks to the point.

When I emerged from our place of dalliance, I walked up the verandah, where after a moment Madame joined me. She looked at me with amazement when I was about to depart with a casual good-bye, and, hiding her displeasure under a smile, she said sweetly: "Please feel always at home in my house. One gets used even to a snake if it is around long enough." Padmadevikā pulled at the hem of my cloth. "I have something to tell you," she said, "but not today. . . ."

And so, with Padmadevikā living in my heart, I mounted the coach and returned to the palace of the prince, where I found Your Highness waiting for me and refusing to dine without me, and where I found our Marubhūtika making jokes at me.

The next day, after having waited on Your Highness for a little while, I went out to Madame's establishment and devoted myself further to Padmadevikā. Afterward Madame said to me: "Your friends must be worrying about you. Therefore it is better if this episode never reaches their ears." And when I was leaving, Padmadevikā asked, "Have you forgotten about *it?*"

"Certainly not!" I replied.

"I shall explain the next time when you come. For a secret that is kept keeps its charm."

When I arrived at Madame's house the next day, I found all the girls in tears and speechless sorrow, and I saw Padmadevikā clinging with both hands to a pillar, her face averted, and crying with long soft sobs.

I asked, "What cause of grief can there be so long as the king of Vatsa reigns gloriously in his realm and the crown prince flourishes?" But I received no reply, however often I repeated my question, and I was so overcome that I fainted and fell.

When I came to, one of the girls, wiping away her tears, said: "Why should anyone feel sorry for Padmadevikā, despicable girl, who at least has a protector, you! But see how her mistress is 'while the crown prince flourishes!' Miserably she suffers; but where help should appear, peril threatens. See our mistress whose companions must suffer equally while friends like you, such as they are, look on!"

She explained to me where to go, and I went to the garden, where I found Madame on the bank of a lotus pond. She was lying on a bed of water lilies, śaivalas, blue lotuses, and Nelumboes which faded under her burning sighs and restless tossings. Resting her feet on the lap of a little slave-girl of ravishing looks, Mudrikālātikā, she dreamed of her idol.

Nervously I drew near and greeted her.

"Honor me, my lady, by giving me your grief to share!" I said.

"It would be too much," she replied, "for a man who enjoys such great happiness to listen to my hopeless story which would only make him sorry and ashamed. Is there a lover indeed who, while free to walk with his beloved in paradise, would wade into the river of hell, unfathomable and haunted by monsters?"

Mudrikālātikā tried to comfort her mistress. "But the man of whom Madame will not cease thinking is not exactly despicable! If Madame cannot bring herself to tell the story, permit me to tell it. Courtesans are tough!"

"Let it be told," she replied. "No one can gratify a great desire without violent emotions. And nobody could be worthier than Gomukha to hear it, for only an envoy who is equally dexterous at conflict and reconciliation will be entrusted with an embassy."

So Mudrikālātikā took me aside and began her account. "Please attend to me for a moment," she said.

"Once there was a king named Bharata who had attained full mastery of the three aims of life.[1] This king summoned all the lovely virgins in the land, some from as far as the seacoast. By marrying them all at once and then singling them

---

[1] The pursuit of Virtue, the pursuit of Wealth, and the pursuit of Love.

out for secret assignations, he thought he would make the
pleasures of love flow continually. But the very first girl whose
hand he took, a virgin of such beauty as is only obtained
through the purest karman, satisfied him entirely. So he divided the remaining girls, temptresses of the eyes and seduc-
tresses of the mind, into eight groups which were all of a kind
to arouse a man's passion. To the queen of each group, who
would wear clashing ornaments as her regalia, the king
granted the royal privileges of throne, umbrella, and yak-tail
plumes. Since these queens themselves belonged to the group,
yet were superior to the other women, the king bestowed on
them the title of Mistress. The others were graded in ranks,
down to the rustic wenches whose hips were callused by the
chafing of the water pails they carried.

"This division of hereditary harlotry is still in force today
as it has been since the time Bharata established it. Our
present queen is Kaliṅgasenā, the Royal Concubine, and she
is directly descended from an unbroken lineage of queens, like
a lotus in a lotus pond. She has borne a daughter who puts
the perfect beauty of goddesses, demonesses, serpent-maidens,
and mortal women to shame—Madanamañjukā, none other
than Madame our Mistress.

"One day Madame saw her mother going to the Royal
Palace, and she cried, 'I want to go too, mother!' Mother knew
that her darling daughter was a very stubborn girl; so she
gave her some jewelry to wear that suited her age and took
her along to the king's residence.

"I saw her when she came back from the Royal Palace: her
eyes were brilliant, her lips radiant, her cheeks glowing—she
was perfectly happy. She stood and sat, walked and sat down
again, and for the rest of the day she did not stop telling her
companions, who crowded around her, all that had happened
at the king's audience; and she did not sleep a wink all night.

"The next morning she eagerly put on her most beautiful
jewelry, and when she saw her mother depart to wait on the
king, she came out too.

" 'Where are you going?' asked her mother.

" 'Where you are going!'

" 'But one cannot go to attend on the king without the king's
express permission, my daughter! Kings are men of little love.
You had better go back, my dear. You may go as soon as you

have obtained permission. Impudent women are always dis-
liked, even if it is love that leads them.'

"So the girl turned back at her mother's words, which,
gentle and appropriate though they were, she found harsh and
impossible to comply with. Like a poor merchant's wife who
had found a treasure and lost it again, she collapsed on her
bed, desperate, unable to sleep or eat or talk.

"One day when her girls were entertaining her with stories,
she snapped, 'I want to sleep, girls. Go away.'

"When they had gone, a suspicion of the truth dawned on
my mind: why should she send her friends away without a
reason? Before this she had never been able to sleep without
their company! There was something wrong here. So I stayed,
and hiding behind a window I spied on her by means of a
mirror. She was putting on her jewelry, I saw. Then she
turned toward the direction of the Royal Palace, folded her
hands in a gesture of salutation, and said aloud, 'I pray that I
be a bride to him in another birth at least!' Thereupon she
tied a piece of silk into a noose, put her head through it without hesitation, and promptly hanged herself from a clothespeg
in the wall.

"Swift as an arrow I ran to her and cut the noose which had
almost taken her life like the noose of Death. I carried her to
her bed, and with a fan dipped in water I fanned cool air
over her and forced her consciousness to return from the
mansion of the king of the dead. At last she opened her eyes
slowly and turned her bloodshot gaze on me and looked away.

" 'He alone can be called a friend who saves his friend
from a terrible fate; but, bringing me back to my fate, you
have shown yourself my enemy! When I tried to abandon this
life which had become the meeting ground of all miseries, you
had to prevent me. But why? There was no reason! After all
the time we spent together in perfect harmony, you suddenly
betrayed your hatred and spoiled my plans. It is true what
people say, entirely and unalterably true, that there is no way
to escape from a friend who is really an enemy!'

"To these unreasonable accusations I replied, 'My Lady,
undoubtedly you have the power to crush me with abuse, but
tell me this: did ever fortune or misfortune befall you which
you did not confide to us? You must have become very unhappy indeed if you turn away your servants and secretly try

to do away with yourself to be happy again! Tell me the cause of your grief, and if it is possible to cure it, we shall live. And die if we fail.'

"She remained silent for a while. Then she began softly to speak. 'Must I tell you, even you who share my body and my soul? You know already, but you want me to exhibit my shameless conduct by telling it myself. Who is crueler than a woman! Well . . . I went to the Royal Palace, and His Majesty graciously summoned me and lifted me on his right thigh, hard as a bludgeon! On his left thigh the crown prince was seated, and when I saw him, he entered my heart irresistibly. Even fire will dwell within the wood from which it is drilled without burning it, but he, coldly beautiful like the moon and pure, wants to devour me without smoke. He is the cause of my misery: I have seen him once, and today again I heard him mentioned. You ask why I complain?'

"The story she had told me left me in a state of utter confusion. To find a way out, I thought, was as easy as to dry up the ocean. But concealing my despair, I laughed out heartily and comforted her with meaningless assurances.

" 'Don't worry, my Lady,' I said. 'I could bring the King of the Spirits himself to fall in love with you, let alone a mortal prince! However, if you are too rash, you will not obtain the results which you crave, for kings know not only how to apply the principle of friendliness but also how to employ enmity and punishment! Try to keep your own counsel and restrain your volatile mind; you must suffer the next few days without being found out by the others.'

"As is the way with people who long for something, she thought she had already got what she longed for, and her blooming face bespoke her inner contentment. And she passed the following days safely because I held out hopeful prospects with well-intentioned but untruthful reports on the success of our affair. But then she realized that she was being deceived with empty promises, and I suspected her again of harboring thoughts of suicide. I hastened to her mother, and in collusion with her I resorted to an intrigue. Gomukha, I thought, is the alter ego of the prince, and somehow he must be enticed into the District, soon! His friendship with the prince will enable him with tempting tales to bring his friend to the District as the kokila bird brings spring.

"The mother of our Mistress, Kaliṅgasenā, told the story to Queen Padmāvatī, and the queen addressed you as a 'sophisticate.' We employed a number of blackguards to inveigle you into the District, and three girls were procured for you. From among them you chose the sweet Padmadevikā, like the tonestring on a three-stringed lute. However, Padmadevikā, having established an interest of her own, hesitated to serve the interests of her friend and, fearing that her own interests would suffer, failed to inform you. And look at our Mistress now! She cannot find another way; she is unable to restrain her long sobs; she is desperate! Now that this intolerable misfortune has befallen us and the sequel depends on you, please help us out!"

"Why!" said I. "This straw can be cut with a mere fingernail, and you insist on using a hatchet."

I went back to the Mistress and said spontaneously, "Dry your tears; you have gained your end! Your Ladyship longs for the prince, the prince loves truth and quality, and Gomukha is your go-between—a marvelous combination indeed! This won't be any trouble to me, for the royal swan, longing for the beauty of autumn, himself seeks out a lotus pond! But enough now of this confusing web of talk. In any case, I shall personally see to it that the prince pays his respects to Your Ladyship soon."

"Nothing is impossible for a man of the world like you," she said. "But please try to find a suitable opportunity so that success is assured. For if an enterprise is undertaken at an inopportune moment, it will go awry by annoying the masters."

I took my leave and returned to your gardenhouse, my prince, where I appropriated sweets and other delicacies which you had left there and brought them to her with the message that they had come from the prince's own hands.

"Even if it is a deception," she said, "it revives the spirits of a woman in love. Even the deer will take new hope for an instant when they see the mirage of an oasis."

I revived her further with garlands, sandalwood paste, betel, perfume, jewelry, and incense, which I said had been sent by Your Highness. Every day I resolved, "I shall tell him today, or at any rate tomorrow," but I failed to find an opportunity and wasted all this time.

Then one day Mudrikālātikā said to me in the presence of

the Mistress: "Well, well! We ought to be grateful to the great man of the world! You bragged that you would personally see to it that the prince paid his respects. Why do you deceive a credulous woman with flowers, herbs, and fruits? You wait here! I am going to get him myself. I am clever enough to arrange a meeting even if he is hostile."

Her harsh words mortified me. "Judge by results," I said, and kept watching for an opportunity.

Then, when this pageant took place, I found occasion, despite the presence of Hariśikha and the others, to make you do whatever I could under the circumstances. You saw the coach that passed us on the road? Her Ladyship was in it, like lightning contained in a thundercloud. And the half-revealed face which you saw, with the fingers folded at the forehead, was hers: she showed it in greeting to be greeted in return. And when I mentioned to you that your diadem had slipped a little and should be straightened, I did it on purpose: the women interpreted your gesture as a courtly salutation in honor of their beautiful Mistress.

Your Highness, Mistress Madanamañjukā loves you as the Goddess of Fortune loves a king of men who breathes wisdom and courage! Like a fresh garland of jasmine she is offered to you, a bouquet of lovable qualities, without any effort on your part, and she does not deserve a refusal. She has been bitten by the snake of love; so hurry and attend her! For those who are consumed by the burning poison will not survive for long.

*Two Tales
of Destiny*

*I arrived with my friend Gomukha in the city which is cele-
brated as the brilliant ornament of our Lady Ganges, the city
where temples and sanctuaries are strung together in unbroken
rows—Benares. At the outskirts of the city we found an
abandoned building and installed ourselves in one of the sheds,
which had decrepit beams and discolored plaster.[1]*

*Gomukha kept me company for a while until I had rested.
Then he said, "Stay here for a short time and don't lose your
patience. I shall come back as soon as I have found a place
for us to lodge."*

*He hurried off, but after sixteen or twenty steps he stopped,
deliberated a moment, and came back to me. "Let me take
the precious jewels which you are wearing," he said. "It's not
safe to keep them here. Benares is infested with tripod as-*

[1] Prince Naravāhanadatta, the object of the intrigue in the preceding
story, is narrating this episode.

cetics,[2] ash-streaked mendicants, and other heretics who behind their disguise of sanctity are really robbers, the usual
vultures that prey on a place of pilgrimage. If they find you
here alone with all your jewelry on and without arms, some
dangerous individual might try an assault."

"Go ahead," I said to humor him; and he took all my jewels
and walked hurriedly off into the city.

Scarcely had he gone when two persons entered, a mendicant
and a brahmin student who, weary from their round of begging, seated themselves in my barn.

"One is a heretic," I thought, "and the other a thief. I am
alone and unarmed, and of course they will want to rob me.
But even if there were thousands of them with daggers, I
would not care more than I would for a herd of boisterous
cows. The real coward is he who ruthlessly uses his knife on
ascetics: after all, they are shielded by their sacred vows, even
if they carry a dagger on the hip."

While I was thinking this, the mendicant looked me over
and turned to the brahmin student.

"Sāṃkhya, Yoga, and the other systems," he exclaimed like
a man who has awakened from his illusions, "are nothing but
sophistry, all of them! But the books trapped me, and so I
left a pleasant life and started out on the road to—of all
things!—Salvation. . . . And what do all the efforts we spend
on Salvation really amount to? A man might as well take infinite trouble to locate a blade of grass or the lotus in the sky!
If Salvation is as easy to find as a blade of grass, it is useless
to waste any energy on it. And if it is as impossible to find as
the lotus in the sky, then those who try are lost anyway.

"What is the proof that there is another world? The Word
of God who is omniscient, they say. But how do they prove
that there is an omniscient being? From the five divine attributes, including omniscience! So the argument by which
they prove his omniscience is vitiated by a host of illogicalities,
lack of conclusiveness, self-contradiction, etcetera etcetera. I
am tired of the florid verbiage of parasites and orators. Let us
enjoy life as we please!"

The student retorted heatedly: "Why do you expose a vicious circle which is really irrelevant? Let us leave aside the

---

[2] So called from their practice of carrying three sticks which were
tied together and could be used to form a tripod.

*question whether the thesis, ground, and illustration in the
syllogism proving the existence of God are completely correct.*[3] *You are defeated by the simple fact that all schools of
philosophy are unanimous in assuming that God exists. If you
argue with arid logic that the other world cannot exist, you
certainly are to be pitied; for you must be plagued by the dull
routine of hairsplitting debates and fault-finding disputations.
Or let us leave this too for the moment. Tell me first, how do
you know that the Books of Traditional Thought are rhetorical
fictions of parasites?"*

"Well," replied the mendicant, *"I am generally informed
about the science of palmistry, and I know the physical marks
of all kinds of people as described in such treatises as
Nandīśa's. Now, do you see that fellow there, a traveler with
dirty feet? According to science he is destined to become the
emperor of all aerial spirits! When I then see this 'emperor'
occupy a decrepit barn, I conclude that all sciences are as
meaningless as a vicious circle in logic. It is admissible to in-
fer from the existence of meaningful books, Gāruḍa's treatise
for instance, that there must also exist meaningless books, by
the same token as we conclude from the existence of beggars
that there must exist charitable donors. Thus, from the fact
that palmistry is a mere fiction, we are at liberty to conclude
that comparable sciences—Revelation, Tradition, Antiquities,
etcetera—are likewise fictitious."*

The student retorted: *"What we call 'destiny' is defined by
the learned as the good or bad results that are the outcome of
a man's actions in a previous existence. And the physical marks
from which we divine a man's future are nothing but the outward signs of the past acts which we term 'destiny.' But
destiny will not come to pass unless a man cooperates. God
himself needs for His creation of the world the cooperation of
all the causes operative in creation, time, space, and so forth.
That young and amiable man there who challenges the beauty
of gods and spirits has brought himself down with his laziness
and indolence to the mental level of a frog or a rhinoceros. Unless it is aided by a man's personal efforts, destiny is like a*

[3] These are the first three steps in the five-part Indian syllogism.
Thesis: the mountain is on fire. Ground: because it has smoke. Illustration: things that have smoke have fire, for example the kitchen.
Application: the mountain is such a thing. Conclusion: the mountain
is on fire.

bow without an archer, a seed without a sower: it merely exists
as a possibility."
"But destiny is stronger than a man's efforts!" said the
mendicant. "And I shall illustrate my point with a story I
have heard. Listen."

Destiny Triumphant

On the banks of the Indus is a village called Brahmasthalaka. There lived an eminent brahmin, Vedaśarman, who knew
all four Vedas. This brahmin had a pupil who was extremely
industrious at his lessons and so earned from his fellow scholars the nickname Dṛḍhodyama—the Grind. Vedaśarman had
instructed him always to collect his food and clothing from a
certain householder, Tamobhedaka, and he had lodgings in the
house of an avowed follower of the Pañcarātra sect whose
name was Bhinnatamas.[4] So while he lived in these circumstances, Dṛḍhodyama mastered all four Vedas in ten years,
thanks to his ardent faith and keen intelligence.

Late one evening when the crowds had dispersed, Bhinnatamas and Dṛḍhodyama sat discussing at length the four
classes of society and the four periods of life, and in the course
of their discussion Bhinnatamas said: "Not only do I own a
large homestead with many cattle, buffaloes, pastures, serfs,
and women, with guards to protect it against robbers and animals, but I also lead a monastic life, the first requirements of
which are study and meditation. Nevertheless, being destined by
birth to lead the life of a farmer, I cannot even aspire to the
repute I deserve. . . . However, with advancing age a certain weariness has settled on me, slackening the vigor of
speech and body, a sure sign that the afterworld is at hand.
The sages of old have prescribed that those who have elected
to establish a household should go on a pilgrimage to the holy
places when they become lax in the performance of their

---

[4] The members of this sect were subject to certain rules of conduct, as, for example, never to sleep more than five consecutive
nights in the same place.

duties. The Vedānta school of thought holds that one should be guided by Brahman the Saviour. Thus if a man aspires to liberation, he should not omit Avimukta near Benares from his itinerary. Therefore I have decided to depart for Benares tomorrow morning, for the religion of the Buddha has a reputation for efficiency.

"You on the other hand," he continued, "recognize the authority only of Revelation and Tradition, and these prescribe that marrying a woman and begetting a son is obligatory at your stage of life. To do his duty as a family man, one needs property, cows, and so on, and what more effective way is there for a brahmin to acquire property than by marriage? However, there is a fortune waiting for you to pick it up, a vast fortune honestly come by, including serfs and their women —mine. You can take it!"

"If you were to order me to commit a crime," said the student, "a man in my position could hardly disobey—much less a demand so eminently legal! But now that I am a householder, I shall have to say farewell to *both* the men who took my father's place, not only my teacher, who gave me knowledge, but also you, who have given me life! When I have passed the night, I shall do what you demand."

The night passed, and Bhinnatamas, who was impatient to start on his travels, had to wait a long time for the student to come and say farewell. When it was noon and the boy still had not come, the old man himself went out to look for him. He found the student in the yard of Tamobhedaka's house, slowly walking back and forth while repeating softly some memorized Vedic formula.

"Why have you stayed here all this time? Tell me the reason—which is no doubt unreasonable!"

"For some reason every servant in the house appears to be busy and keeps running around," said the student. "And every maid I ask what is going on tells me to think of something that brings luck! So far I have not had a chance to take leave of Tamobhedaka, who is all upset. That is why I could not come to you before."

Bhinnatamas smiled.

"I'll tell you why everybody here is so upset," he said. "Tamobhedaka's wife is about to give birth, and all the servants are busy, here and there and everywhere. It will be a girl, and you will marry her. She will be ridden by passions and misconduct herself wickedly!"

Upon this prophecy he turned and went his way. Dṛdho-dyama was shaken with fear, and he thought: "If the brah-min's wife really bears him a daughter, that means that Bhinnatamas' words will come true! It is as with the Veda: when a *stobha* formula has proved to be effective in a rite to cure poisoning, one concludes that all other formulas possess comparable powers." [5]

Even as he was thinking, Tamobhedaka came out of the house, looking very disappointed and swearing under his breath: "Ha, the devil of luck!" And almost instantly a pierc-ing noise, suggesting the kennel, came from inside the house like the wailing of a cat which is caught by dogs. Several women, dressed for the event, appeared through a side door, covering their heads in shame and gesturing their despair with upturned hands. They were followed by a group of servants and a throng of mourning relations who grieved, "What can one do if fate is against him?"

When this tumult went on in the house, Dṛdhodyama was gripped by fear, for obviously Bhinnatamas' prophecy had been fulfilled. And he thought: "The monk's words may have come true—but now let everyone watch how one man's effort will change fate! I shall leave Sindh to wander from country to country and steer clear of this dangerous woman!" And with such thoughts in mind he took flight at once, without even asking the advice of knowledgeable brahmins, and in one day left ten leagues behind him.

For ten years he wandered about the earth and its islands. Then one day he came to the banks of the Ganges in order to worship at the holy places. Sunburned and thirsty he entered a house in a brahmin village to seek shade and water. A brahmin lady was sitting on the verandah, and her yellow-powdered hair shone like flames of fire.

"Mother, please give me water!"

Anxiously the woman called out: "Halé, Tamālikā! Come at once, daughter, and bring a stool and water."

A girl appeared from the house with a footstool and a waterbowl; she was dressed in a black robe and her endless

[5] A *stobha* formula consists of meaningless sounds, like dādā, hoī hoī, etc.

braids were powdered yellow. Peering everywhere at once from squinting eyes, she walked laboriously up to Dṛḍhodyama with the heaving and limping gait of a cripple.

"Sit down," said the cripple, and confusing the waterbowl with the stool, she dropped the bowl before his feet.

"Please conduct yourself properly!" cried the old lady. "Get another bowl to offer the water."

Pretending she was horrified, and trembling all over, and biting her lips so as not to burst out laughing, the girl did as the old lady told her.

When Dṛḍhodyama had rested, the old lady asked him: "From what country do you come? And where are you bound for?"

"There is no country on earth where I do not come from," he replied, "but I shall answer your question as to where I am going. I am going to some brahmin village to spend my days happily tutoring the children and enjoying village life."

"The proverb is right," said the old lady. "One cannot forge hot iron with cold! I have two grandchildren, both boys, who are now ready for school. They need you and you need them, and thanks to your good karman you have found one another. You want to teach, they want to learn; so both of you can join like a chariot that has lost its horses with horses that have lost their chariot!"

Dṛḍhodyama complied. And so for the next two years he remained in that village to teach the two brahmin boys and a group of other pupils.

Then one day the relatives of the old lady came for a visit and asked her: "Why don't you marry off Tamālikā to Dṛḍhodyama? Of course, any suitor will at least have one of the virtues that make a good son-in-law, but look if you find even one virtue *lacking* in Dṛḍhodyama. He is a rarity, and he is at hand! Let us take him; for who would be willing to set a wild elephant free when it is already trapped in the stockades?" The old lady was won over, and she prayed her honored relatives to put the question to Dṛḍhodyama.

"Wanderer," they said, "you have learned the Veda and the Traditions during your years of study and celibacy. But now you are under the obligation of marrying a purebred wife lest the breath of your chest, throat, and lips remain barren.

Therefore consider Tamālikā. She is of perfectly pure descent and will make you a wife like three Vedas incarnate in the best part of the best state of life!"

Dṛḍhodyama considered their proposal for a while. "These brahmins are right," he thought. "What can one say against it? Besides, my old master Tamobhedaka who was contaminated by that bewitched daughter of his is as distant as the western seacoast, and it is unlikely that I would find him here. But if fate has brought that same girl here all the way from Sindh, then who can ever escape fate? As if a thread would fall and fall straight through the eye of a needle!" So when he had thought it over, he accepted the proposal and married the girl.

A year went by; and one day in the very early morning when the three watches of the night had passed and his wife betrayed with a yawn that she was awake, Dṛḍhodyama asked her: "Say, Tamālikā, tell me, who is the head of your family? What is that old lady to you, and who are the two boys?"

With a deep sigh which told of endless misery, she began to speak, stammering and shedding many a tear. "This old lady once had a good and kind husband who with his knowledge and his wealth satisfied pupil, priest, and beggar alike. He had a daughter whom he bestowed on a student who knew the entire Veda by heart and possessed those qualities of the soul—self-control, tranquility, and so on—which make for salvation. So the pupil became his son-in-law; but if before marriage that student was so forbearing that he would forgive you when you kicked him, as a son-in-law he proved as irritable as a black cobra. He detected insult in even the most courteous treatment and made his parents-in-law's life, as well as his own, needlessly unpleasant.

"One day his brother-in-law said jokingly: 'My friend, you are as difficult to please as Durvāsa himself!'

" 'Ah, if that is so,' he drawled, 'why try to please an ill-bred boor at all?' and he left the house with his wife.

"Ignoring the reproaches of her parents and his friends, he turned his back on his homeland and moved to Sindh. There he settled in a village called Brahmasthalaka where henceforth he dedicated himself to ritual. There too his wife bore him a daughter of ill omen, frightful like Doomsday Night, and also twin sons, who were the Yama and Kāla of the family.[6] I am the daughter, and your harelipped pupils are my brothers. We knew our parents only when we were small children. At that time the Indus—which can be tremendously powerful and impossible to check—had flooded and ravaged a large part of Sindh country. My parents were so concerned about it that they decided their children should go and stay with the parents of the mother and———"

Pierced by the arrow of panic, Dṛḍhodyama cried, "Never mind the rest of your story; it is all too plain!" And he thought to himself: "That all-seeing sun of mendicants was omniscient! Truly is he called Bhinnatamas, for he dispelled the darkness of ignorance![7] Two of his prophecies I have now seen come true, and I shall leave the country to defy the third."

For twelve years he wandered in the Archipelago, until at last, when his hair was already greying, he thought dejectedly: "In all the time now passed, that possessed witch must have committed the sin which the mendicant prophesied. I have not followed the precepts of Veda and Vedānta, and my life has trickled away as through leprous wounds. . . . Now I shall go to Benares to worship at the sacred places and spend my last days accumulating the merit which at least will gain me a sojourn in heaven."

So he crossed the ocean to the Bay of the Ganges and journeyed upstream to Benares without once leaving the river. Just as he was entering Benares he encountered a mahāpāśupata mendicant who wore the skulls of his order; he swayed as he walked and slurred his words when he spoke. Behind him trailed a woman who wore curious necklaces and ornaments mostly of glass. Her squinting eyes were bloodshot with liquor, and she staggered and swayed so cumbrously that she doubled the length of the road, lurching like a snake that wriggles out of its old skin.

The skull worshipper said: "Hurry up, Sister of the Skull, before the Hour of the Incense passes at Avimukta. I shall praise the greatest God of the Trinity with *hūm! hūm!* and then find myself some liquor in the taverns!"

Then, in the midst of her degradation, the woman saw

---

[6] Yama and Kāla are gods of death.
[7] Bhinnatamas means "He Who Pierces Darkness."

Dṛdhodyama. After staring at him for a long time, she threw
herself at his feet with a piercing scream.

"Leave that traveler alone. He is a brahmin!" cried the skull
worshipper. "Come on, the joke has lasted long enough. Leave
him be, mad woman!"

"He is my husband; the gods have returned him to me!"
she cried. "Brute! Lecher! Why did you desert me?"

The street filled with a huge crowd, including monks and
brahmins, curious to witness the scene.

"You, a scholar of all four Vedas, have thrown away your
Veda completely!" the woman said. "Will any man who abides
by the Veda ever come to grief if he follows its precepts? You
did not beget sons, you did not perform the daily *agnihotra*,[8]
you did not worship the ancestors with funerary oblations—
you simply went off like the wind! You have deserted me,
Dṛdhodyama, me the wretched Tamālikā who now has to
wander from hearth to hearth as a mendicant nun. How many
young women are to be found who, deserted by their husbands,
remain virtuous and faithful to their hearths? You have done
evil, Dṛdhodyama, by deserting your lawful wife, and you
must expiate your evil by taking her back to you!"

Then the brahmins questioned Dṛdhodyama, who was
blinded with shame and despair: "Tell us the truth about the
accusations of this nun!" And, surrounded by a crowd of
brahmins and other people, he told his and her story from
their life in Brahmasthalaka onward.

Thereupon the brahmins insisted: "Brahmin, take this
brahmin lady back, for it is not the way of the just to desert a
loving wife. And whatever ill she has done while she had no
protector must be expiated with the severest of vows!"

"But Reverend Sirs," replied Dṛdhodyama, "though you
may know what expiations are prescribed for which sin, do you
know precisely which sin she has committed? Of course, some
wicked women whore with the lower castes, but look at the
man she has followed. He may be a blackguard, but at least
he is a brahmin. Therefore she must remain with the man for
whom she left me, our illustrious and everlasting lord of the
skull, collector of small pleasures!"

Deeply ashamed, the woman exclaimed: "No! I shall remain with you for the rest of my life!"

[8] A daily oblation to the sun.

Then one of the brahmins said to Dṛḍhodyama: "I have a
pretty daughter, brahmin. Marry her. I am rich as Kubera,[9]
and she is my only child. You will have both a wife and a
fortune!"

Dṛḍhodyama thought, "No need to worry now about what
will or will not be, for that woman has fulfilled the mendicant's
prophecy entirely." So he consented and received from the
generous brahmin his daughter in marriage; and her shoulders
were decked with a fortune. Tamālikā shaved her head, clothed
herself in a penitent's red tunic, and spent her days living
near Dṛḍhodyama's house. Dṛḍhodyama himself remained in
Benares to worship our Lady Ganges who sports in Śiva's
hair,[10] and he performed with regularity the rituals of the
brahmins.

*"Thus," concluded the mendicant, "in spite of all his stren-
uous efforts, it was impossible for Dṛḍhodyama to prove
Bhinnatamas' prophecy false. Indeed, the mighty elephant
of Human Effort has found its powerful master, the Hunter
who straddles Fate!"*

*With a faint smile the brahmin student said to the mendi-
cant: "Now listen how human effort gets the better of fate!"*

Destiny Conquered

1

There was a merchant in Ujjayinī whose fortune was considerable. His name was Sāgaradatta, Gift-of-the-Ocean, and
his character was as unfathomable as the sea.

Once when this merchant's ship was under full sail on the
ocean, he sighted another vessel with a streaming pennant
atop. "Heave to alongside that ship," he commanded the crew,
and soon the two ships met.

[9] The god of riches.
[10] The Ganges is said to flow in heaven before it falls to earth.
Śiva, whose seat is on the Himalayas, catches the river in his hair
to break the fall which otherwise would shatter earth.

Sāgaradatta asked the master of the merchantman: "Tell me, sir, who are you and from where do you hail?"

"I am the merchant Buddhavarman from Rājagṛha. And you, sir," he asked in his turn, "who are you and from where do you come?"

Thus their acquaintance began, and together they continued their voyage. Whiling away their time with poems and tales, music and song, liquor and dice, they penetrated the vastness of the unplumbed ocean. They sailed to Sumatra, where they acquired an enormous load of gold bullion and returned with their load to a port on the mainland.

Then Sāgaradatta said to Buddhavarman: "Let us perpetuate our friendship! When I departed from home, my wife was heavy with child, and in the meantime she must have given birth to a child, a boy or a girl. If it is a daughter, I shall marry her to your son; and if it is a boy, you must marry your daughter to him."

"Oh, wonder!" exclaimed Buddhavarman, "that is just what I myself had in mind. But what is so strange? We have the same nature!"

So the two merchants contracted the alliance, embraced each other, and parted, each returning to his home town with a caravan of camels. There they paid their respect to their rulers, one to the Rājā of Avanti, the other to the Rājā of Magadha, presenting to them a profusion of gifts, and then repaired to their homes. There each of them, one in Ujjayinī, the other in Rājagṛha, spent the day feasting the brahmins and the monks and being themselves feasted by their relatives.

When at last Sāgaradatta was at leisure on his couch, a baby girl was put in his arms, a girl garlanded with jasmine blossoms. "Whose is this jasmine-garlanded girl?" he asked his wife, and she whispered shamefacedly: "But yours, whose else?"

"Lucky the parents who have a son as beautiful as Jasmine!" he said. "My love, do not worry too much if you now are a daughter's mother. Knowledge, which bore Fortune as her daughter, has never yet been blamed for her issue!"

When he had consoled her with such kindly words, he told her about his meeting with Buddhavarman on the high seas and the friendship that had ensued. And because her father had asked, "Whose is this jasmine-garlanded girl?" his daughter was henceforth known as Jasmine.

Buddhavarman meanwhile had interrogated his wife too. "Tell me, what have you borne me?" But she remained silent. Then she brought him a one-eyed, hunchbacked son, a skinny, potbellied dwarf with protruding teeth and a drooping underlip.

"Why have you given birth to this useless dromedary!" he cried. "Why did you not consult a fortuneteller and abort the child? Now this deformed goblin has voided the contract I made with Sāgaradatta. If he sends a message that he has a daughter, am I to reply that I have a son?" Then he added to his wife: "If a messenger arrives from Avanti, let no one mention this dromedary!" At the first sight of his son, the father had called him a dromedary, so thereafter the townspeople called the boy Dromedary.

After some time Buddhavarman received a letter from Sāgaradatta, which he read in private.

Hail the Honorable Buddhavarman at Rajagrha!
Sāgara of Ujjayinī embraces you happily and begs to inform you that a child has been born to your friend, a daughter, favored with prospects of excellent fortune. No woman on earth will match her beauty! If your wife has borne you a son, luck is with us; and if it be a daughter, a contrary fate has robbed us. For a friendship which is not strengthened by an alliance will remain without foundation; and beauty seconded by masculine strength will prove everlasting.

After seeing to it that the messenger who had carried the letter was well looked after, Buddhavarman asked his wife, "Now that the matter has come to this stage, what are we to do? Advise me!"

"Women have but two fingers of sense," she said, "so what can they know? But as long as you ask me, I shall speak: a woman like me takes courage from questions!

"A merchant's business is the compromise between truth and falsehood, and no merchant should neglect his business. For to desert the duty to which one is born is censured as misconduct. Now, you have really got a son, and there is no falsehood in that at all. But you must lie about his defects and call them virtues. All things in the world have fictitious names; there is even a deadly poison they call a 'sedative'!

If a man gets involved in a difficult matter, truth is useless. That is the rule, and there is good authority for it: did not even the Pāṇḍava lie that Droṇa's son Aśvatthāman had been killed? [11] The allurements of riches prompt merchants like you to penetrate the frightful Milky Sea (which resounds with the grumbling of Death) as though it were a pond in a park. Well, the daughter of this prince of caravan traders will not enter your house without a treasure of riches which the ocean has yielded. Don't scorn a treasure which the poor can hardly hope to find; and this treasure, prize of a hundred privations and efforts, is now yours to pick up without trouble!"

"Well spoken!" praised Buddhavarman, and he gave the messenger a reply for Sāgaradatta. "Tell my friend: 'We too have been favored—with a son of a shape that defies description. And as to his physical and intellectual endowments, you shall judge for yourself. Why should I try to describe them?' " With this highly equivocal message he sent the messenger off, properly reimbursing him for his travel expenses.

For eight years they exchanged messages until at last one messenger told Buddhavarman bluntly that he had been ordered by Sāgaradatta and his wife not to return before he had seen their prospective son-in-law. "So if you want me to return to Ujjayinī," the man said, "you must show me the boy and his qualities." Instantly Buddhavarman made up his mind and replied with perfect presence of mind: "He is staying with his uncle in Tāmraliptī, where he studies."

Another four years went by while the matter remained at this stage. Then a delegation of three or four messengers arrived, shrewd diplomats all. Without respect for the respectable Buddhavarman they declared: "Listen what your friend and his wife have to tell you. 'Thirteen or fourteen years have passed now, and still we have not seen what our son-in-law is like. Is it possible that you have never heard the proverb, 'Two trade with the merchandise in full view'? Your claim that he is studying in Tāmraliptī is a most unimaginative pretext. Even those whose business and vocation

[11] In the great war between Pāṇḍavas and Kauravas, which is the subject of the *Mahābhārata*, the hero Droṇa who sided with the Kauravas is told by his enemy that his son Aśvatthāman has been killed. When Droṇa thereupon lays down his arms, he is decapitated.

it is to study the Veda according to the prescribed rules have only a limited time set for their studies. But it is hardly natural to believe that your son has given up all his other duties to devote his whole life to learning. Stop this joke, which frightens us as the laughter of Yama, and whether here or in Tāmraliptī show us the boy!"

"My good sirs," countered Buddhavarman, "rest for a moment." Then he sought his wife and said to her in consternation: "Without even thinking of the bad things that were in store, wretch that I am, I was lured by distant hopes and followed the advice of a woman! Have your son's many defects—his protruding teeth, his single eye, and so forth—disappeared in the meantime? Of course not! When a man's body grows, his defects, like his arms and legs, grow even faster! Show the messengers your son, who looks like a creature of Śiva, or your wisdom be pleased to think of another way out!"

"As a matter of fact," she said, "I have already thought of one. If you approve, we must start on it at once."

"Speak!" he said, and she whispered in his ear.

"Marvelous!" he exclaimed and got to work on it.

He had a private meeting with a friendly brahmin who lived on his charity, and when he had disposed him to be kindly by a hundred flatteries, the merchant begged him dejectedly: "You know the character and the appearance and the nature of my son, who has been nicknamed White Crow; there is no need to tell you about his defects. You know about the agreement between Sāgaradatta and myself and the exchange of messengers. Your friend is lost! Prove that your friendship is enduring. But, bah, I don't need to be so embarrassed about it; after all, it is in your own interest. Your have a handsome son, Yajñagupta, who is not only learned in Revelation, Tradition, and all sacred lore but quite competent in the worldly arts to boot. Let him marry Sāgaradatta's daughter, bring her here, and turn her over to my son, but intact! You shall have a share of the dowry she brings—gold, jewelry, everything."

He fell silent, ashamed of his proposition. But the other, greedy for his share, replied eagerly: "Should gentlemen like you have to beg us? Command us!" Then he called Yajñagupta and in the presence of Buddhavarman told his son the entire story.

Yajñagupta said: "Children and pupils must obey without reservations their masters' orders, whether proper or not. I shall do as you say."

Buddhavarman waited for a few days and then showed Yajñagupta, who had been dressed as a groom, to the family's delegates. "My son has just returned from Tāmraliptī," he said. "Judge his appearance and qualities for yourselves!"

"The jasmine is most fortunate to meet the young spring!" they exclaimed. "There is no need to inquire after his qualities, for no untalented young man could ever strike such a figure or display such poise. Only, his name is most inappropriate: Dromedary indeed! It is not fitting to call the Tree of Wishes by the name of a deformed bush. Yet, there are even deities with unspeakable names: the moon is called 'tumor,' and the wind is even referred to as 'his mother's dog'! But a bad name has no effect if what it names is good: it is the inadequacy of the bearer which affects his bearing! In any case, today the wife of caravan trader Sāgaradatta has gained another child. And the affection which exists between the two of you has now become truly supreme and everlasting. Let us go quickly and congratulate Sāgaradatta's wife, who has lost both sleep and appetite in her anxiety. And you, sir, start the Groom's Procession on an auspicious day; for now there is nothing that stands in the way of the marriage."

Thereupon the delegates left with magnificent presents, and Buddhavarman sent off the Groom's Procession with Yajñagupta as the bridegroom. The merchant dressed his son, the real Dromedary, in the style of a brahmin and sent him along ostensibly as the companion of the supposed groom. In this guise, the hunchback carried the gold for the groom's gift to the bride's family.

At last the Groom's Procession reached Ujjayinī, capital of Avanti, which was so splendidly decorated for the event that it resembled the City of the God of Riches when his kobolds come marching in. The party lodged in the official guesthouse on the banks of the Siprā in enchanting public gardens which spring had decked with splendor. Bypassing Mahākāla's famous statue,[12] the townspeople arrived in procession, curious to see the prospective bridegroom, and they could not stop looking. The groom himself passed some time with

[12] Ujjayinī's famous phallic icon of Śiva Mahākāla.

the accredited wits, poets, and pundits of Ujjayinī as well
as with the city's accomplished lute and flute players.

Then his brother-in-law arranged a magnificent banquet
and announced, "A simple meal is ready for you. Please be
seated and serve yourself!" When Yajñagupta saw that there
was one common dining room with many seats, he asked his
brother-in-law, "Who is going to eat here?"

"Please sit there in the middle on the gilt chair with the
high coral legs that is covered with a sparkling clean cloth.
The eldest and the youngest of your brothers-in-law will sit
on both sides of you on those cane chairs, and this long row
of seats on either side will be occupied by your other brothers-
in-law."

The bridegroom considered a moment; then he said to the
other: "I cannot eat and drink with you. We have a custom
in our family that we do not drink or take food with others
before we have married. When after my marriage I come back
here, I shall have my father's permission to do so; but now,
especially without my preceptor's sanction, I cannot do so."
With his father-in-law's consent the bridegroom dined sep-
arately and ate a pure meal; but the family was piqued.

The next morning, as soon as the last watch of night had
passed, the bridegroom was taken in procession with loud
music to Sāgaradatta's house to be married. He took the bride's
hand which glittered with gold, but his own was bare of
ornaments according to his preceptor's instructions. And when
he had ceremonially made the solemn circumambulation of
the sacred fire, a piercing pain made him grip his stomach
with both hands, and he fainted and fell. His breath stopped,
his eyes closed, and he let out a roar of pain that could have
silenced a wild bull.

Seeing the state her son-in-law was in, the bride's mother beat
her breast and head and shrieked at Jasmine, who had fainted
with her husband. "Aah, you are lost, you are dead! A curse
upon you, devil in disguise; you have murdered a husband
more beautiful than Pradyumna himself![13] Why aren't you
dead? Why am I not dead, I who now must share your misery?
Now I shall have to live with you all my life, alive with the

[13] A son of Kṛṣṇa who also passes as the reincarnation of the God
of Love, who, according to the legend, had been burned by Śiva's
third eye.

dead. . . . How is a woman to live who is widowed while
still a girl? A husband is far, far more important to women
than their life. And the mother who can bear seeing her dearest daughter, as beautiful as she is virtuous, become a young
widow—ai, she is the eldest sister of death!"

Shrieking, the mother collapsed. Then there was a faint
movement in the bridegroom's chest and stomach, and at this
sign of life the air was filled with the laughter and happy
shouts and yells of the people. Slowly he began to breathe,
his lashes quivered slantwise, and he opened bloodshot eyes
under his heavy lids. Thereupon Sāgaradatta celebrated a
feast so huge as to be beyond the means of an aged king who
is blessed with the birth of a son.

The physicians asked what had happened to him, and he
replied that he had suffered an attack of acute indigestion.
The worried physicians prepared a medicine for indigestion,
and he was carried to a bedroom. Somehow he passed the
night, now and then dozing off in spite of his stomach pains,
while his bride sat up with him. Drinking nothing but ex-
tracts of nāgarā, ativiṣā, and muṣṭā herbs and eating small
portions of fatless foods, he grew thinner every day. Jasmine
was so busy concocting medicines that she forgot the becoming shyness of a bride, so sick she was with worry for her
husband's health.

While she was sitting with her husband, the hunchback
came visiting, and playfully he dared to caress her body that
was limp with anxiety. "Leave this tradesman, this impotent
libertine, and be good to me," he urged. "I am your lover.
The gods themselves have presided over our wedding!"

She jumped up from her place and sought protection behind her husband's bed. "What kind of vulgar joke is this?"
she asked her husband.

He smiled. "Don't be so provincial! No civilized woman
minds a clown. The rich usually keep a wretched fool for his
prattle. Nobody will keep a *dumb* parrot in a cage. Don't
mind this foul-mouthed buffoon if he teases you or touches
you, silly girl!" But Jasmine, who came from a proper family,
ignored his advice and contemptuously told the hunchback
that the lowest and fiercest kind of whores would do for him.

It occurred to Yajñagupta that the best course for them
was to leave before the moron could give the secret out. And

so when the physicians, whose care had been useless, asked him what he would like to eat or drink or to divert himself, he said in a very faint voice: "I have been wishing to see my dear parents for a long time; they love me dearly." The physicians reported to Sāgaradatta, "This is what your son-in-law says, and let it be done. All the treatment a doctor can give for indigestion has failed in his case. Perhaps when he goes to his home town, he may recover. Seeing one's friends is a universally recognized medicine."

And so the merchant sent off his daughter with the bridegroom—like a dark night with a waning moon—and he sent her servants, headed by her nurse, along with her, as well as an escort to protect them and a caravan of camels laden with the treasures of the ocean.

2

Calculating the stages of the bridegroom's journey to Rājagṛha, the merchant prince sent along a group of trusted servants so that at each stage two of them could return to Ujjayinī with the latest tidings of his son-in-law. The first two returning runners reported a slight improvement in the health of the bridegroom. And with every further stage he traveled, he parted with more and more of his illness. The last two servants, who returned from the last stop before Rājagṛha, reported to Sāgaradatta that the bridegroom had regained his full weight and was in high spirits. At this news the merchant, blinded by joy, passed out veritable treasures to everybody without regard to their merit, from the most learned brahmin to the lowliest pariah.

But the next morning the false bridegroom threw off his pretense, donned his brahmin garb, and continued the journey on foot. Freed from the glittering guise which was out of character, he was splendid in the beauty that was truly his, like the moon which emerges from a rainbow-hued and lightning-girt cloud. The blackguard Dromedary contentedly dressed himself up as the bridegroom and mounted the groom's carriage where Jasmine was seated. And Jasmine shuddered at the sight of the misshapen man who outdid Śiva's monsters in grotesqueness, and she closed her eyes.

All the people in town left their work and ran out with

great curiosity to see the bride and bridegroom. And when
the townspeople saw the ill-matched couple—a pearl in a cast-
iron setting—they raised their hands and cursed the Creator.
"Even Love, whimsical as he is, could hardly be praised for
this latest feat—should we praise you, Creator of proven decency? To have joined together so ill-suited a couple, a sylph
and a goblin, makes you the recognized patron of all crooks!"

Buddhavarman had come out at the head of his entire guild,
and he conducted the girl, who had conquered all Rājagṛha
with her beauty, to his house. There he embraced his daughter-
in-law and said to his wife, "She shall be both a son and a
daughter to you!" Rites of honor were performed, bards
chanted the praises of the house, actors and dancers performed until the day passed with the sun. Then Jasmine entered
with the hunchback and Yajñagupta into a bedroom which
enchanted eye and heart. Jasmine sat down on a beautiful
chair near the bed, and the bridegroom and his friend seated
themselves on a high bench beside her. All three were lost
in their thoughts, their minds blank with confusion. Lower-
ing their heads, they each traced meaningless figures with
their fingers on the floor. In this painful situation Jasmine
thought, "Why doesn't the brahmin go away now that he has
surrendered me?" And Dromedary too, who wanted his love-
making to be private, was thinking, "Why doesn't he get out
of the bedroom?"

Yajñagupta was aware of their tacit hints, which indeed
suited the occasion, and decided that he had better go. He
made a move to leave, but Jasmine cried out in despair as
she saw him rise. "Do you run away and leave your wife in
disaster?"

"Don't talk of disaster when you are close to the man for
whom fate has destined you! Let him share your kisses and
embraces. Mine is a bitter law, and what I receive from it
is but a burden to carry. . . ." And he departed with the remaining servant girls.

Dromedary, that peasant, tried to drag the struggling girl
to him, but, calling for help with the loud clang of the ornaments at her girdle and ankles, Jasmine ran out after the
brahmin. She could not find him in the overcrowded hall
where the townspeople were wildly drunk and the servants
were dancing. "There he goes, there he goes!" she thought,

but, deceived by a resemblance, she pursued a stranger. She struggled her way out and crossed over to the king's highway, frightened by the savage music in honor of Durgā that came from a potter's shed. Then she saw a Brother of the Skull who lay sleeping soundly along the road, unconscious with drunkenness. "Yes, that is how I shall be perfectly safe!" she decided.

Having made up her mind, she unfastened her costly jewels from her body and, true to the familiar practice of merchants, tied them securely inside her robe. She appropriated the skull-worshipper's paraphernalia, skull-staff, and so forth. Then, disguised as a Brother of the Skull, she staggered as if in drunkenness out of the city and walked to a nearby village.

There she noticed a white-haired brahmin lady who was sitting on the verandah of her house carding cotton. Although alone, the woman was muttering imprecations upon fate in a sad voice. Then she exclaimed angrily, "Bah, what a cad, Buddhavarman!"

"But he is a good man," said Jasmine, "without any pretenses. What wrong has he done you, good woman, that you curse him?"

"Brother," answered the woman, fooled by Jasmine's disguise, "you are either a crook or a fool if you have not heard of his crime, which is public enough! But you must hear about it from someone else. Natural modesty does not permit a lady of my station to mention the unmentionable."

No sooner had she spoken than a proclamation was loudly heralded all through town with the beating of drums: "Hear ye! The king proclaims that any citizen who reports Buddhavarman's daughter-in-law will be relieved of his poverty. But anyone who foolishly dares shelter her in his house shall be parted with all his fortune and die a horrible death at the scythes!"

When the brahmin lady heard the proclamation, her eyes flowed with tears. Beside herself with joy, she laughed and wept at the same time. "Is it a wonder if a citizen of Ujjayinī refuses to put up with such scoundrels, who are a match even for Mūladeva? [14] Bravo, bravo, Jasmine, noble and clever girl, for having tricked that baseborn Buddhavarman and his hump-

---

[14] This wizard, who appears in the story of "The Man Who Changed Sexes," is the prototype of the wily crook.

backed son! If you are to live happily here in Rājagṛha, stay my child, but as Yajñagupta's bride!"

When Jasmine heard her speak in this fashion, she thought that the selfless old lady would give her shelter if she revealed her identity. Quietly she told her all that had befallen her. The old woman was delighted. She embraced Jasmine warmly and led her into the house. Then she made her take off the skull-worshipper's garb and rest her weary body. She massaged her, bathed her in agreeably warm water, and at last made her lie down on a soft bed with a thick cover of flower petals.

The next morning Jasmine put on her gruesome string of skulls and entered the city, where the people ran around in excitement. "Why is everybody rushing around so excitedly?" she asked a citizen.

"The chief of the merchant guild here in town, Buddhavarman, has a son called Dromedary who is as misshapen as his name implies. An impotent brahmin, no better than a greedy pimp, gave the cripple his own wife whom he had just married. But the same evening the girl deserted Dromedary to look for the brahmin and has been gone ever since. That is why everybody is so excited."

Hiding a smile she said, "Friend, bring me at once to the house of that impotent brahmin!"

Charmed by the pleasant-spoken stranger the citizen took her to Yajñagupta's house, which was bare of decorations save for the hushed sound of holy recitations. She saw Yajñagupta sitting at the door of the hall where the sacred fires were kept. He was surrounded by pupils to whom he was explaining a treatise.

She put the skull-staff down and sat down cross-legged. "What is the book you are explaining?" she asked in a grumble.

"Your Reverence, it is the Laws of Manu. At this point the four stages of life and the four classes of society are described."

"Why do you lie to me? This is no book of law. I am sure it is the kind of hedonist work that attracts unprincipled people. Manu's Laws are a far cry from your own lawless behavior. A physician who knows his medicine does not eat meat when he has a skin disease. You, a brahmin who pretends to explain Manu, have sinned against your class by marrying a girl of another caste. And you, an able-bodied, accomplished, and handsome man, have passed the girl off to a one-eyed imbecile eunuch! I ask you, Śivaite, why have you committed such a lawless deed? Or if it was right, tell me how!"

"Let us leave the question whether it was right or wrong," he said. "A man who is still under his father's authority must follow his master's irrevocable word. For example, Rāma-of-the-Hatchet could not transgress his father's word and so beheaded his own mother.[15] What do you have to say to that, sir?"

"The deeds of divine persons are not proper examples for ordinary men. Brahmins do not drink liquor because Rudra did.[16] And an intelligent person should not do everything his master tells him. What might his master not tell him to do when he is unhappy, or angry, or vexed with something? If a father says, 'I have a piercing headache, son; cut off my head!' should the son do as he is told? Besides, when Rāma cut off his mother's head at his father's orders, he had the power to put it back at once. You don't have divine powers. How can you undo the wrong you did? Now you will have to stay married to your wife. You have done what your master told you, and the deed is done."

Yajñagupta had no answer: what has a debater to say if his opponent's argument is sound? She sat for a while; finally, when the sun had reached the zenith, she rose up to take leave of him, pretending that it was her time to go begging.

He stopped her. "This house is yours with all its riches," he said. "Your Reverence must have his meal here every day."

She smiled. "The food of a heathen like you is too unclean even for a skull-worshipper! Only if a man repents of the great sin he has done and collects himself again will his food be pure enough to share."

At this she departed and returned to the brahmin lady's

---

[15] This ancient hero, later elevated to an incarnation of Viṣṇu, beheaded his mother after she had irritated his father. When his father, pleased at his obedience, granted him a boon, he asked that his mother be revived.

[16] A vedic storm god, predecessor of Śiva.

house, where she threw off her disguise and took a bath. In the evening she again dressed up as a skull-worshipper, went to Yajñagupta's house and spent the rest of the day there. For many days thereafter she spent the meal hours and the nights at the brahmin lady's and the remaining time at Yajñagupta's.

One day a thought occurred to her. "If this brahmin committed his crime because he was in the power of greed, then it must be possible to goad him on by arousing his greed." If the means are available, the intelligent person does not stray from his task. Jasmine had a pink pearl necklace that fairly blushed with splendor, and this she told the old brahmin woman to sell. The coined and uncoined gold and silver from this sale she put into two copper pitchers which she buried just outside a nearby village at the edge of the woods. Then in the course of a leisurely discussion on metallurgy and mining she said to Yajñagupta, "A hermit must live one night in a village for every five nights he spends in town; you know this practice of wandering mendicants. All this time, my boy, I have been staying in Rājagṛha; my affection for you has made me break the hermit's rule. Since even householders are in peril when they are chained down by love, the greater the peril for Aspirants who have renounced the world and who despise even their own bodies. Therefore I now intend to go to Benares, for we of the Somasiddhānta sect are beholden to visit the sacred places.

"One other thing, though. I know a book on how to detect hidden treasures. It is called the Book of Mahākāla, and it is the perfect medicine for the disease of poverty. One day when I was tired of meditating and strolled along the edge of the woods, I noticed certain signs of glittering on the ground which told me that someone had buried a treasure here. If you have any liking for me, take this treasure. Encounters with good men like you will bear fruit."

Together with her and his more reliable and solid pupils, Yajñagupta unearthed the treasure and secretly brought it home. Happily he told his father about the find and the skull-worshipper's knowledge of the Book of Mahākāla.

"Give up the Vedas; they are useless," said the father. "You'd better learn from the mendicant his great science, the Book of Mahākāla. This Book of Mahākāla matches clairvoyance if it can make you see through the treasure-filled earth! For the sake of the Book of Mahākāla you must try hard to ingratiate yourself with that mahāpāśupata as if he were Mahākāla himself!" [17]

At the prompting of his father, who coveted the Book of Mahākāla, Yajñagupta said to Jasmine when she was about to depart, "I shall follow you, sir, on your pilgrimage. For such as I the sacred waters, however unstable, are the source of bliss both seen and unseen."

She pretended to try to dissuade him, using words that lacked conviction. Hoping to acquire Mahākāla's wisdom, however, he refused to turn back.

When they arrived in Benares, she gave Yajñagupta a gem. "It is not worth too much," she said, "but you can live comfortably on what you receive for it. However, don't be tempted by your age to consort with the courtesans. Nine times out of ten an inquisitive student like you falls a victim to harlots and inevitably becomes impotent with his own wife. Harlots are like witches; they suck all the blood of your body, and it is a miracle if you save your life. But where is virtue, where your good name and a happy life?"

He promised that he would do as she said; and so he did. For the words of the master they seek to flatter are not wasted on fortune-hunters who know the rules.

3

They spent four or five months in Benares, after which they left for Naimiṣa. From there they traveled to the Gate of the Ganges, then to the Kurus, and from the Kurus to Puṣkara, where they spent the rainy season. At the end of the month of Kārttika they visted Mahālaya, a very sacred place.

Then, one day, Jasmine said: "I shall unearth a rich treasure and give it to you. You must take this treasure, which will bring you all things seen and unseen, and return to your home. For those who are still in the stage of householder must strive toward the three goals of life. It is only ignoramuses who don't know their texts, fools, cripples, or penniless wretches who devote themselves entirely to pil-

[17] It must be kept in mind that the fake ascetic was assumed to know the book by heart, not to carry the manuscript around with him.

grimages in order to acquire merit. I myself shall now go on to Ujjayinī, for the city of Avanti is as much a haunt of skull-worshippers as it is of courtesans. The followers of the great Lord of Cattle who come to Ujjayinī on pilgrimage come only for the fights: they fight one another with their sharp-toothed tridents. A brawny brother of the skull may kill me this time. . . . Yes, the jugglers of the basket and the sword may face death when they expect it least. And the crime you have committed in Ujjayinī makes you as unwelcome there as a brahmin-killer in heaven. If you go there, you will find nothing, I fear, but misery. Therefore return home with your treasure and see how your parents are."

He thought: "The feet of this holy man are graciously disposed to me. This is my opportunity to lay hands on the Book of Mahākāla. For when people fear for their lives, they will give up anything, even their wealth, to save their life, let alone a useless book. This man does not even care about his life, and I have danced attendance on him for a long time now. Why should he then refuse me the Book of Mahākāla? And the crime I have committed in Ujjayinī at my father's instructions—well, it is as easy as anything to conceal that. I shall hide in temple corners, put on dark clothes, let my hair grow wild and dirty, and nobody will notice me."

Having decided that this was the right thing to do, he said to Jasmine, "Is it proper for pupils to desert their master in danger? Wherever you are bound, I shall go with you. As the full moon goes, so go its spots." Jasmine allowed him to come with her.

When they reached Ujjayinī, she said to Yajñagupta, "Rest here for a while in Bhadravaṭa, my boy.[18] I shall come back here as soon as I have found a buried treasure. Don't worry if you do not see me for some time. Treasures are hard to come by in Ujjayinī, and I am afraid I shall have to look around for quite a while. Old people, fathers of large families, and orphans, they are all the same: no man from Ujjayinī will bury a sizable fortune."

After giving this and other advice she went on to the bank of the river Siprā. She took off her skull-worshipper's garb and cleaned her immaculate body. And dressed as a Sister of the Skull in a robe as white as jasmine, with glittering

[18] A sacred grove near the temple.

ornaments of shell and crystal, she glowed like the autumn sky crowded with brilliant stars. Then, her breasts straining against her bodice like pumpkins in a net, she walked away with her little begging bowl. The skull-worshippers in full paraphernalia, drinking and drunk, crooked their fingers at her and shouted, "Come on, come on, girl with the roving eyes. Take the brother who pleases you most and celebrate with him the drinking rites as the creed commands!"

Even in that crowd the girl kept her natural wit, which was greater than theirs. Walking on hurriedly, she retorted, "Better stop looking, my reverend sirs. I am a girl to poison your eyes, enchanting to look at but dreadful to touch. My husband is a Gandharva. He is crueler than an ogre . . . and he is jealous . . . and he never stops watching me! Like Yama himself, he must have killed off at least a million like you who were smitten with love and laid hands on me!"

"This goddess of beauty surely does not exaggerate," they said. "There have probably been even more. Where the whole universe suffers from insomnia at one glimpse of her beauty, it is a miracle that Brahmā, Viṣṇu, and Śiva are not dueling. So let her favor her Gandharva, or the handsomest man in the world, with her looks of love!"

Ploughing a furrow to the city through a crowd of heretics who kept following her, she went to her father's house, which buzzed with prayers and benedictions. Reaching her goal at last, she entered in high spirits the seven-storey mansion and at the door of her mother's apartment asked for alms. A servant girl appeared from the house with a gift and looked Jasmine over from head to toe. At last she recognized the girl and, beating her breast and head, rushed inside and nervously addressed her mistress in a whisper.

"You are lost, you are ruined! You have fostered at your bosom like a trembling garland of sirīṣas your jasmine-garlanded daughter, and there she is, waiting at your door, her body defiled with the skull-bearer's garb! Look for yourself!"

The mother went outside and saw her daughter as she was. But forgetting respectability, she tore her daughter's headpiece off, broke the skull in pieces, and shattered her bowl and shell and glass jewelry. She ripped the bodice in shreds, purified and cleaned her with benedictions and a bath, and finally took her into the women's apartments. Only then did she speak.

"Tell me, my dear, speak freely. What is the meaning of all this?"

"How could you be so mistaken, mother? Would your virtuous daughter ever really adopt the vows of the skull, even if she happened to be thrown in with sinners? But my story must wait until father has been called. I have a difficult task with which I need his help."

As soon as Sāgaradatta was called, he came and set eyes on his daughter. He cried, "What is this? Why——" and fell in a faint. When Jasmine saw that her father had lost consciousness, she embraced him and greeted him, laughing merrily to reassure him.

When he had regained his composure, she said, "Your son-in-law is staying in the Bhadravata enclosure. Tell your sons to bring him here."

So he did, and Yajñagupta was forcibly captured by his brothers-in-law. "You are caught, kidnapper," they taunted. "What do you seek here, scoundrel? Get up. Get where you belong. The king has summoned you!" they added, grinning.

Then he recognized them, and expecting imprisonment and death he prayed *mā nas toke* . . . and tied his hair in a brahmin's knot.[19] He begged them, "Please wait for a moment, until my friend, a skull-worshipper, comes back."

Laughing, they said. "The friend you are waiting for is ahead of you. He is the one who ordered us to arrest you. Those whose affections are selfless and who speak as they think become disenchanted with blackguards like you, even if they have been friends!"

With great jolliness they seized the speechless and desperate man and, piling abuse on him, took him to their house where his in-laws were happily assembled. Sāgaradatta, all gooseflesh with excitement and love, embraced and reassured his son-in-law. He bade him welcome with the proper offerings and, when Yajñagupta had finished eating, made him sit on a couch which had been set up in an enchanting garden house. The parents, the brothers-in-law with their wives and children, the authorities, the guild leaders, and the merchants sat down around him. Then entered the daughter herself with the sweet sound of ornaments: she was like a clean-washed

[19] *Ma nas toke* is a stanza from Rig Veda 1. 114.8, which is used as a ritual prohibition: "Thou shalt not injure us in our seed, nor in our life, nor in our cattle and horses. . . ."

autumn sky echoing with the call of flamingos. Her elders she greeted with her head, her contemporaries with her voice, and Yajñagupta with frequent glances that were heavy with mascara and love. Then she sat down on a low seat at her parents' feet and related all her adventures, beginning with her wedding. Meanwhile Yajñagupta thought, "A curse, a curse on my useless erudition; I have been tricked by a well-born girl with two fingers of sense! If that is what women can do, their wit is sharper than kuśa grass. Is there anything more astounding than the way in which this girl managed to change her appearance, her walk, even her voice? If anybody wonders how the dim-witted Pāṇḍavas could have lived in disguise at Virāṭa's court, she furnishes an excellent case in point! [20] At any rate, she has released me from my private hell, the great feat I did at my father's bidding. . . ."

When the king heard of the story, he delightedly sent for Jasmine and her husband. He gave Yajñagupta a grant of many large villages with much gold, then said, smiling: "You had better take care in your wisdom, my girl, that your husband does not neglect his duties as a brahmin!"

Thus driven by a singleness of purpose which overrode her jealousies, this merchant's daughter succeeded in making her husband marry her: for those who wish to live do not defy the inviolable decree of the lord of the realm. And the brahmin cherished Jasmine, the vaiśya bride, for the joys of love, for the birth of sons, for happiness, and for faithfulness. And he lived a life of a hundred years crowned by the fruits of continuous good works.

"And so a merchant's girl who had been betrothed by fate itself to a cripple conquered the husband she wanted," resumed the student, *"by the clever contrivance of many tricks. The Mountain of Destiny, so beloved of creatures whose characters have been ruined by contentment and so humbly revered by cowards, is uprooted by the fierce storm of the Will of Man."*

And when they had told each other their stories, mendicant and student went their way.

[20] The Pāṇḍavas, as the result of an unfortunate gambling match, were compelled to withdraw to the jungle for twelve years and to live the thirteenth year in disguise at the court of King Virāṭa.

The
Perfect
Bride

In Tamil Land in a city called Kāñcī lived the millionaire son of a merchant prince. His name was Śaktikumāra, and when he was about eighteen years old, he began to worry.

"There is no happiness without a wife," he reflected, "nor with a wife if she is disagreeable. But how to find a wife who has all the wifely virtues?"

Distrusting the purely accidental aspect of marriage with a wife taken at the recommendation of others, he became an astrologer and palmist and, tucking two pounds of unthreshed rice in the hem of his garment, wandered through the land. Everyone who had daughters displayed them before him, saying, "Here is a fortuneteller!" But however well marked and suitable the girl was, Śaktikumāra would ask, "Are you able, my dear, to prepare a complete meal for us with these two pounds of rice?" Thus he roamed from house to house, entering only to be laughed at and thrown out.

One day, in a hamlet on the southern bank of the Kāverī

in Sibi country, an ayah showed him a young girl with but a few jewels, who, together with her parents, had gone through a large fortune of which only a decrepit house was left. He stared at her.

"Here is a girl," he thought, "with a perfectly proportioned figure—not too heavy, not too thin, neither too short nor too tall—with regular features and a fair complexion. Her toes are pink inside; the soles are marked with auspicious lines, of barley grain, fish, lotus, and pitcher; her ankles are symmetrical and the feet well rounded and not muscular. The calves are perfectly curved, and the knees are hardly noticeable, as though they were swallowed by the sturdy thighs. The loin dimples are precisely parallel and square and shed lustre upon buttocks round as chariot wheels. Her abdomen is adorned by three folds and is slender around the deep navel, even a little caved. The broad-based breasts with proud nipples fill the full region of her chest. Her copper-red fingers, straight and well rounded, with long, smooth, polished nails like glistening gems, adorn hands which show the happy signs of abundance of grain, wealth, and sons. Her arms, which start from sloping shoulders and taper to the wrists, are very delicate. Her slender neck is curved and bent like a seashell. Her lotus-like face shows unblemished red lips that are rounded in the middle, a lovely and unabbreviated chin, firm but fully rounded cheeks, dark brows that arch a little but do not meet, and a nose like a haughty Sesamum blossom. The wide eyes, jet black, dazzling white, and reddish brown, are radiant and tender and profound and languidly roving. Her forehead is shapely like the crescent moon, her locks darkly alluring like a mine of sapphires. The long ears are twice adorned, by a fading lotus and a playful stalk. Her long, abundant, and fragrant locks are glossy black, every single hair of them, and do not fade to brown even at the ends.

"When her figure is so beautiful, her character cannot be different. My heart goes out to her. However, I shall not marry her before I have tried her: for those who act without circumspection inevitably reap repentance in abundance."

So he asked with a kindly look, "Would you be able, my dear, to make me a complete meal with this rice?"

The girl gave her old servant a meaningful glance; whereupon the woman took the two pounds of rice from him and placed it on the terrace before the door after sprinkling and scrubbing it thoroughly. Then she washed the girl's feet. The girl then dried the sweet-smelling rice measure by measure, repeatedly turning it over in the sun, and when it was thoroughly dry, she spread it on a hard, smooth part of the floor, threshed it very, very gently with the edge of a reed-stalk, and finally took all the rice grains out of the husks without breaking them.

Then she said to her ayah: "Mother, jewelers want these husks; they use them to polish jewelry. Sell it to them and, with the pennies they give you, you must buy good hard firewood sticks, neither too dry nor too damp, a small-sized pan, and two shallow bowls."

When the servant had done that, the girl placed the rice grains in a shallow mortar of kakubha wood with a flat, wide bottom and began pounding them with a long, heavy, iron-tipped, smooth-bodied pestle of khadira wood that was slightly recessed in the middle to form a grip. She tired her arms in a charming play of raising and dropping, picking up and picking out single grains, which she then cleaned of chaff and awn in a winnowing basket, washed repeatedly in water, and, after a small offering to the fireplace, dropped in boiling water, five parts water to one part rice.

As the grains softened and started to jump and swelled to the size of a bud, she lowered the fire and, holding the lid on the pot, poured out the scum. Then she plunged her spoon in the rice, turned the grains with the spoon, and, having satisfied herself that they were evenly boiled, turned the pot upside down on its lid to let the rice steam. She poured water over those firesticks which had not burned up entirely, and when the fire had died and the heat was gone, she sent this charcoal to the dealers: "Buy with the coin you receive as much of vegetables, ghee, curds, oil, myrobalan, and tamarinds as you can get."

When this had been done, she added two or three kinds of spices, and once the rice broth was transferred to a new bowl placed on wet sand, she cooled it with gentle strokes of a palmleaf fan, added salt, and scented it with fragrant smoke. Then she ground the myrobalan to a fine lotus-sweet powder, and finally relayed through her servant the invitation

to a bath. The old nurse, clean from a bath herself, gave
Śaktikumāra myrobalan and oil, whereupon he bathed. After
his bath he sat down on a plank placed on sprinkled and
swept stones. He touched the two bowls that were placed on
a light, green banana-tree leaf from her own garden—a
quarter of one leaf was used—and she set the rice broth
before him. He drank it and, feeling happy and content after
his journey, let a sweet lassitude pervade his body. Then she
served him two spoonsful of rice porridge and added a serving of butter, soup, and condiment. Finally, she served him
the remaining boiled rice with curds mixed with mace, car-
damon and cinnamon, and fragrant cool buttermilk and fermented rice gruel. He finished all the rice and side dishes.
Then he asked for water. From a new pitcher with water
that was scented with the incense of aloe wood, permeated
with the fragrance of fresh Bignonia blossoms and perfumed
with lotus buds, she poured out an even thin stream. He held
his mouth close to the vessel; and while the snow-cold spatter-
ing drops bristled and reddened his eyelashes, his ears rejoiced in the tinkling sound of the stream, his cheeks tickled
and thrilled at the pleasurable touch, his nostrils opened to
the fragrance of the lotus buds, and his sense of taste delighted in the delicious flavor, he drank the water to his
heart's content. With a nod of his head he indicated that she
stop pouring, and she gave him, from another vessel, fresh
water to rinse his mouth. When the old woman had removed
the scraps of the meal and had cleaned the stone floor with
yellow cowdung, he spread his ragged upper cloth on the
ground and took a short nap.

Highly satisfied, he married the girl with proper rites and
took her with him. Once he had brought her home, he ignored
her and wooed a courtesan; the bride treated even that woman
as her dear friend. She waited on her husband as if he were a
god, untiringly. She did the household chores without fail and,
wonder of tact, won the affection of the servants. Conquered
by her virtues, her husband put the entire household in her
charge and, depending body and soul on her alone, applied
himself to the pursuit of Virtue, Wealth, and Love. Thus, I
say, a wife's virtue is a man's happiness.

The Buddhist King
of Taxila

On the bank of the river Vitastā was a city called Takṣaśilā.
Its rows of whitewashed mansions were so brilliantly mirrored
in the waters of the river that a subterranean city seemed to
have risen to gaze upon the splendor of a rival. A devout Buddhist king by the name of Kaliṅgadatta ruled there; and all his
subjects were zealous votaries of the flourishing Buddha, the
Consort of Tārā. His city was crowded with splendid gems of
Buddhist sanctuaries which seemed to raise the horns of pride
and boast that no city on earth could match Takṣaśilā. And
not only was the king a father to his subjects in protecting
them; he also imparted to them as a teacher the sacred knowledge of the faith.

Now there lived in Takṣaśilā a rich merchant, a Buddhist
who was devoted to the monks. His name was Vitastādatta,
and he had a son, Ratnadatta, who was in the prime of youth.
And the son always abused his father and called him a sinner.

"Why do you scold me, son?" asked the father.

"You have forsaken the religion of the Veda to follow a false faith," said the youth, "for you always honor the Buddhist monks and ignore the brahmins. But what concern of yours is the Buddhist religion, which is practiced only by lowborn people who abandon the discipline of daily baths and purifications, who feed themselves greedily at all hours of the day, and who not only give up the prescribed tuft of hair but shave off all their hair and content themselves with a mere loincloth?"

"There are many forms of religion," said the father. "There is religion which is concerned only with this world, and there is religion which is concerned with all the worlds. And that which they call the brahmin way also means restraint of passion and hatred, faithfulness to one's word, compassion for living beings, and abstention from vainly abusing one's relatives. . . . Besides, you have no right to blame an entire religion for the fault of one, a religion, moreover, which allows all creatures to live in peace. There is no difference of opinion about the morality of good works. And my good works consist in giving safety to all creatures. If I am too much attached to a faith which gives security and leads to salvation, is my faith therefore a false one?" [1] But the merchant's son stubbornly refused to give in to his father's words and only blamed him more.

In his grief the father approached King Kaliṅgadatta, who was a preacher of the faith, and told him all. The king summoned the merchant's son to his court on some pretext, and when the youth appeared, the king acted as though he were exceedingly angry.

"I have heard that this merchant's son is a wicked criminal," he said to his executioner. "He must be killed without delay, for he corrupts the whole country!"

At the king's verdict the father pleaded for mercy, and the king postponed the execution for two months so that the son might better his life. He committed him to his father's care on the condition that after two months he be brought to court again.

The father took his son home, and the youth, thoroughly alarmed, kept thinking, "What crime have I done to the king?" Expecting an undeserved but certain death at the end of two months, he got no sleep day or night, lost all appetite for food, and wasted away.

After the two-month term had expired, the father brought his son, pale and emaciated now, before the king again. When

---

[1] This tale was written by a non-Buddhist.

the king saw the desperate state he was in, he asked, "Why have you grown so thin? Did I forbid you to eat?"

"I forgot myself in my terror," said the merchant's son. "Could I think of food? From the moment I heard Your Majesty's verdict, I have not stopped thinking, day after day, of the ever-approaching hour of death."

"Yes," said the king, "I used an artifice to teach you the fear of death. All creatures fear death as I have made you fear it. Now tell me, is there a greater faith than that which undertakes to save all creatures from death? I have taught you a lesson for the sake of your religion and your salvation: for a wise man, fearing death, will seek release. Therefore do not blame your father for following this faith."

The merchant's son bowed deeply before the king and said, "You have awakened in me a desire for release. Instruct me, Sire!"

The king granted his request. When a festival was celebrated in the city, he gave the youth a bowl brimful of oil and ordered him, "Go and carry the bowl through the city, and beware lest you spill one drop of oil. If one single drop is spilled, my men will kill you on the spot."

Thus he sent the merchant's son away to make the rounds of the town, and he put his men behind him with swords drawn. In his terror the boy religiously guarded himself from spilling a drop of oil, and when he had gone around the town, he made his perilous way back to the king.

When the king saw that he had brought back the oil without spilling any, he asked, "Whom did you see today when you were walking through the town?"

"In truth, my Lord, I have neither seen nor heard anything. All my attention was given to the oil, and I tried to keep from spilling any of it for fear the swords would strike."

Thereupon the king said, "You did not see anything because your mind was fixed on the oil before your eyes. With that same concentration you must contemplate the highest good. A man who is so concentrated that his outer senses no longer function will see the truth, and once he has seen the truth, he is no longer trapped by the net of karman. Thus I have taught you in brief the way to release."

With this the king dismissed him; and the merchant's son prostrated himself before the king's feet and thereafter returned in joy to his father's house, sure of his goal.

The Brahmin
Who Knew
A Spell

Long ago, when Brahmadatta was king of Benares, there lived in a village a certain brahmin who knew a spell called Vedabbha. This is a most potent and precious spell. If at a certain conjunction of the moon and the stars he gazed upward and recited this spell, seven jewels would rain from the sky.

To this brahmin came a bodhisattva to learn a craft.[1] One day the brahmin took the bodhisattva, left the village, and traveled toward the country of the Cetyas to do a certain job. Halfway, at a place in the wilderness, five hundred bandits ambushed the brahmin and the bodhisattva and seized them.

They were messenger-bandits, so called because when they seized two people, they sent one to bring back ransom. When they captured a father and son, they would say to the father, "Bring us ransom, and your son will go free with you." In the same fashion they would send the mother if they had seized a mother and daughter, the elder brother if they had seized two

[1] One who in a future incarnation will become a Buddha.

brothers, the pupil if they had seized a teacher and his pupil.

This time they held the brahmin and sent the bodhisattva.
The bodhisattva in taking leave of his teacher said, "I shall
come back in one or two days—have no fear. Now do what I
shall tell you. Today is the conjunction of the moon and stars
which brings the rain of riches; but do not in your impatience
recite the spell to make the riches fall. If you do, you will
come to grief, and so will these five hundred robbers." Having
admonished his teacher, he departed to fetch the ransom.

When the sun went down, the robbers fettered the brahmin
and laid him on the ground. That moment the full moon rose
from the western horizon. Watching the constellations the
brahmin thought: "Tonight is the conjunction that brings the
rain of riches. Why should I suffer? I shall recite the spell,
bring down the rain of jewels, give them to the robbers, and
go free."

He said to the robbers, "Bho robbers! Why have you seized
me?"

"For ransom, sir."

"If you want money, then quickly loosen my fetters and let
me wash my face, put on new clothes, rub myself with
scented oils, and deck myself with flowers."

The robbers did as he said. Seeing that the conjunction was
taking place, the brahmin recited the spell and looked up to
the sky. At once a shower of jewels dropped from above. The
robbers collected the treasure, secured it in their upper robes,
and departed. The brahmin went after them.

Thereupon another band of five hundred thieves captured
these robbers.

"Why do you capture us?" they asked.

"For money," they said.

"If you want money, take that brahmin. He looks at the
sky, and riches rain down. He has given us what we have."

The robbers let the robbers go and seized the brahmin.

"Give us treasure too!" they demanded.

"I shall give it to you. In a year there will be another
celestial conjunction which brings the rain of the jewels. If
you still want it then, I shall make it rain a rain of treasure
for you."

Angrily the robbers said, "Ah, wicked brahmin, you have
made a rain of riches for others, but us you let wait for an-

other year!" They cut him in two with a sharp sword, flung him on the road, and hastened in pursuit of the other robbers. They slew them all and took the treasure. Then they split into two parties and fought each other. Two hundred and fifty were soon killed. They went on killing each other until only two men were left. So a thousand people had perished.

The two who survived took the booty and hid it in a thicket near a village. One drew his sword and sat guard over it; the other took some rice to the village to have it cooked for them.

Indeed, cupidity is the cause of man's downfall. The man who was sitting near the booty thought, "When he returns, the booty will have to be divided into two parts. Therefore, as soon as he comes back, I will strike him down with my sword and kill him." He readied his sword and sat watching his return.

The other thought, "The booty will have to be divided into two shares. But no! I will put poison in the cooked rice, give it him to eat, and do away with him. Then I have the treasure all to myself."

So when the rice was ready, he first ate his own portion and then put poison in the remainder. He went back with the rice; and no sooner had he handed it over than the other cut him in two with his sword, hid the corpse, and sat down to eat. Then he too died on the spot. Thus because of the treasure all of them perished.

After one or two days the bodhisattva returned with the ransom. When he did not find his teacher in the same place and when he saw booty scattered about, he thought, "My teacher did not follow my words and has brought down the rain of jewels. All of them must have perished."

As he went about, he found his teacher cut in two on the road. "He died because he did not heed my words," the bodhisattva thought, and he gathered firewood, built a pyre, and cremated him. After paying homage to him with wild-flowers, he went on and found first five hundred robbers dead, then two hundred and fifty, and so forth until at the end he knew there could be only two left.

"A thousand men save two have perished," he thought. "There must still be two robbers. They will never be able to control themselves. Where might they have gone?" He took the booty and went on until he saw the track leading into the thicket. He followed the track, found the hidden treasure that had belonged originally to the brahmin, and saw one dead robber next to an overturned rice bowl. "That is what they did," he thought, and knew everything. Looking about for the other, he found him cut down in a hiding place.

"My teacher failed to do as I told him and with his contrariness killed himself and these thousand men. Thus all those misguided and undeserving ones who seek to better themselves will fall to perdition like my teacher." And after these thoughts he said a verse.

Whoever seeks treasure by improper means shall perish;
The Cetyas killed Vedabbha, and they all came to grief.

Mahosadha's Judgment

A woman took her baby boy to the pond of the learned Mahosadha to give him a bath. When she had bathed the child, she laid him on her clothes on the bank and wiped his face; then she went into the pond to take a bath herself.

That very instant a ghoul saw the child. Wishing to devour him, the ghoul changed herself into a woman and said, "That is a beautiful boy, my friend. Is he yours?"

"Yes," the mother answered.

"I want to give him suck."

"Do so."

The ghoul picked the child up, played with him for a little while, and then started running away with him. The other woman saw her. She ran too and took her child back, saying, "Where are you going with my son?"

"Why do you take my child away from me?" asked the ghoul. "He is my son!"

While they were quarreling, they passed the gate of Mahosadha's house. The learned man heard them quarrel and called to them. "What is this?" he asked and heard what the quarrel was about. He saw by the redness and unblinking steadiness of her eyes that one of the women was a ghoul. Yet he said, "You shall abide by my judgment."

"We shall abide," the women replied.

Whereupon he drew a line on the ground, placed the child on the line, and told the ghoul to hold the hands and the mother to hold the feet. "Both of you," he said, "try pulling the child to your side. He is the son of the one who can pull him to her side."

They both started to pull. As the child was being pulled, it felt pain and began crying. The mother, as though her heart had broken, let go of her son and stood weeping.

The learned man asked the crowd, "Is it the mother's heart that softens for her child, or a strange woman's heart?"

"The mother's heart, learned one."

"Is the mother she who has kept hold of the child or she who released him?"

"She who released him, learned one."

"Surely you know who the child-snatcher is?"

"We do not know, learned one."

"She is a ghoul. She seized the child to devour him."

"How do you know, learned one?"

"From the unwavering steadiness and redness of her eyes, from the absence of her shadow, and from her urgency and ruthlessness."

Then he interrogated her. "Who are you?"

"I am a ghoul, my lord."

"Why did you seize this child?"

"To devour it, my lord."

"Blind fool, you became a ghoul because of the evil you had done in a former life. Now you do evil again. Indeed, you are a blind fool." Thus he admonished her and made her firm in the five principles and dismissed her.

The mother of the child praised the learned Mahosadha, saying, "Live long, O lord," took her child, and departed.

The Prince
and the
Painted Fairy

On the western seaboard there is a city, Kānanadvīpa, where
the people are both rich and righteous, as in the paradise of
Indra. Not an Indra but a king ruled there, who was fond of
his subjects, and he had a handsome son named Manohara.
The prince knew everything there was to know, but he had a
special preference for the art of perfuming. (People have
different tastes, and somebody always likes something better.)
The prince had two friends, Bakula and Aśoka, and the two
were inseparable like aśoka and bakula trees in springtime.

One day when Manohara was with his friends in the
princely chambers, the footman came and announced with a
bow: "A certain Sumaṅgala wishes to see Your Highness. He
is an expert perfumer and a quiet-spoken cultured gentleman."

"Go and let him in," Manohara told the doorman and hurriedly scented himself and burned some incense.

Sumaṅgala was admitted, but the instant he entered the
room he buried his face in his hands, shuddered, and shrank

away. "The incense disagrees with your perfume and the scent of your flowers," he said, "and the smell makes my head ache!"

He took a perfumer's palette from his traveling bag and, studying Manohara meanwhile, mixed his own incense. Only then did he greet the prince formally. "Burn this incense instead," he said. "It blends excellently with the perfume and the flowers." The fragrance convinced Manohara and his friends that Sumaṅgala was a master perfumer, and he honored his guest accordingly. Sumaṅgala was received with great hospitality, and within three or four days he cleverly ingratiated himself with the prince.

One day Manohara went out with his three friends to visit the enchanting Fair of the Yakṣas.[1] As the prince strolled around looking at the wonders that were displayed, his eye was caught by a painting of a Yakṣa fairy. Though it was lifeless, it seemed to vibrate with life; mute, it seemed to whisper to him; and though the girl was only a painting, the prince fell in love with her and placed her in his heart, ignoring everything else on view, however enchanting to eye and heart.

He burned incense for her alone and worshipped her with flowers and perfumes. Indeed, his passionate love so distorted his judgment of what could be enjoyed and what not that he even tried to rip her robe off her hips. And that very instant she rose from her painting as once the Lotus Goddess rose from the lotus pond and sought Viṣṇu's breast in the dark expanse of the sky; and she spoke to the prince.

"I am Sukumārikā the Fairy. The Lord of the Yakṣas cursed me and condemned me to live in a painting. But Kubera's anger is brief, and his mercy for women great. When I implored him to set a term to his curse, he pondered awhile and then reassured me, saying, 'As soon as a mortal man attempts to violate your painted body, your curse will be ended, and the man shall be your husband.' Even the curse of the great ones is equal to a boon! If you love me, then come to the pleasance of gods and demons on Mount Śrīkuñja where the Yakṣas dwell."

The fairy vanished, and so did Manohara's reason. Bakula and the other friends were desperate when they saw his condi-

[1] Chthonic godlings associated with Kubera, the god of wealth.

tion. But they had heard what the fairy had said, and, when the prince regained consciousness, they said: "Enough! Don't despair, for Sukumārikā is easily found. If that mountain were inaccessible, she would not have spoken as she did, for she wanted your love."

One day when the prince with his friends went to visit his father at the court, he met a merchant who had just returned from sea. The merchant, whose name was Siddhapātra, had just presented precious stones of the first water to the king and was graciously received. The king asked, "What wonders have you seen, my dear sir?"

"Sire, is there a wonder you have not seen who live on the shores of the ocean? The sea is the treasure house of all wonders! Yet, once when my ship had been blown off course by a gale, I saw above me in the sky a mountain garlanded with lofty peaks that shone with the yellow lustre of solid gold. I asked one of the mariners what mountain that was, and he answered, 'The old people say that that is Mount Śrī-kuñja.'" The merchant related other anecdotes and at last went home.

The prince immediately bowed to the king and went after the merchant. In his consternation the merchant at once offered the prince all his possessions: what rich man does not tremble when the prince comes to his door? But the prince took nothing more than a garland of flowers, remarking that children of one father ought not to offer hospitality which insulted their brother's generosity. "However," he continued, "the story you told to my father's feet about Mount Śrīkuñja has made me curious. Please describe it more clearly."

Relieved at the kindly words of the prince, the merchant began describing Mount Śrīkuñja in greater detail with all the landmarks. "One day our ship sailed into a gale and, like a wild elephant in heat, lost its balance and got completely out of control. When the gale had spent itself and died down, and the ocean was again as smooth as the skies above, we began to meet curiously shaped water animals. Here we saw lions, tigers, panthers, rhinoceroses, bears, and antelopes— herds of them—jumping and diving for the sport of it. Farther on, we spied naked men and women consorting in pairs. Their yells, which pierced our ears, seemed to be their only language, and they behaved like beasts. Elsewhere, gigantic winged elephants flew up from the surface of the sea like restless mountains. Then, suddenly, a northern breeze wafted down a perfume so divine that I think the whole world would gladly become nose just to smell it. We looked eagerly for its source and saw in the distance a mountain whose jeweled peaks were peopled by demigods. 'What mountain is this?' I asked a sailor, and he said, 'The old people call it Mount Śrīkuñja.' "

The merchant went on describing the course, and the prince charted everything on a detailed map with all the directions and distances by sea. Then he had a ship readied and manned by a crew of reliable sailors and set sail on the high seas with Bakula, Aśoka, and Sumaṅgala.

Strong favorable winds sped the craft, and soon the prince reached his point of destination. The landmarks corresponded to those he had noted on his map, and he was certain that this was the place. And his thoughts, eyes, and body rushed alike to Mount Śrīkuñja.

The ship was moored at a quay from which rose sapphire-paved steps, wide as the firmament and lofty as hope, which were sprayed by the sea. Manohara left his companions on the ship and eagerly climbed the stairs to the summit, even as the just man ascends by the steps of virtue to the vault of heaven. While throngs of joyous Yakṣas and Fairies watched, he went about looking for Sukumārikā with the eye of love. As the fairies expressed it, "Lucky Sukumārikā, to have inspired such love in a man so divine! Is there anyone, god, demigod, or mortal, who would not be charmed by his handsomeness, by his talents and virtues, natural and acquired?"

Then Manohara saw his fairy: she was rollicking in the wide courtyard of the palace as she was in his own loving heart. With no more modesty than any woman who lives by her beauty, she rushed to meet him, took his moist and trembling hands in hers, and conducted him inside. In the palace he met her tipsy, ruddy, red-eyed, paunchy father, who was playing dice. He embraced Manohara and kissed him on the head. "Go and see your mothers-in-law," he said and dismissed the prince to the seraglio where the women were waiting. They were beautifully decked with karṇikāra garlands, and all were in the prime of youth, even the grandmothers of his parents-in-law.

He greeted them, and they returned his greeting. Then

they permitted him to leave, and in a passionate mood he entered the girl's chambers. Drinks of divine mead, music of divine lutes, and the embraces of a divine woman carried Manohara's mind away.

Hardly a moment seemed to pass before Sukumārikā said: "It has been five days now, prince, and you must return. It is a rule in the world of the gods that a mere mortal is not to stay longer than five days at a time. Besides, your crew might desert you. They never wait more than five days for the master of the ship."

When the prince heard this, his splendor darkened and darkened like the splendor of a godling who is cast out of heaven. But, seeing his condition, Sukumārikā added, "From now on I myself shall come to your house." This comforted him, and he returned to his ship, where he found his crew exasperated at his long absence. His friends were wearing divine jewelry, robes, and garlands. "Where have you passed your days and how?" he prompted them. "As you yourself have," they answered. "Sukumārikā sent Yakṣa girls who were quite glad to come, and they have pampered us like gods! Men may worship the Great Lord,[2] but they have to die before they can be united with Him: we worship you, O Lord, and become gods before we die!" So absorbed were they all in the discussion of their women that they crossed the wide, perilous span of the ocean without thinking of anything else.

When they entered their city, they found the streets empty and all business, whether in pursuit of Virtue, Wealth, or Love, completely stopped: the town was grieving over the absence of its prince. Then an old brahmin lady came out on some errand and saw Manohara, who had covered his face in respect. She recognized the prince, and in an ecstasy of bliss which made her stumble on the road, she hastened to the court and gladdened the king. The king ordered his ministers as well as the merchants not to ask the prince where he had been and thus to save him from embarrassment. The prince greeted the king shamefacedly, but father took son to his heart and brushed away his shame.

When the prince had returned to his own palace, he told Sumaṅgala: "Create the perfect incense which is the epitome of the entire art of perfuming! My mistress is coming tonight,

[2] Epithet for Śiva.

and she will bring her friends along. As they say, the most
important thing in making love is the perfume. Our most
exquisite perfume is called 'Yakṣa Mud,' and that is precisely
what it would be for such divine women—mud. Concentrate on
a rarer scent and reveal your mastery in the art. In the arts,
it is the result that counts: the whole point of the art of
archery is hitting the target."

Thus prompted by the prince as well as by his own interest,
Sumaṅgala prepared incense, bathsalts, perfumes, and what-
not according to his master's instructions. Meanwhile Manohara and his companions conducted themselves in the true
fashion of lovers and took to their beds of torture, as yet
empty of their mistresses.

The perfume that Sumaṅgala had created with such a great
care was suddenly, exquisite though it were, swept away by
another as a fresh wind blows away a cloud. Sukumārikā
entered and sat down on a couch. She smiled at Bakula and the
other friends and said, "I have brought my friends. Go and
enjoy yourselves!" They bowed and were gone.

Sukumārikā and the prince spent the night together as they
had yearned to spend it. In the morning the glowing appearance of the prince's boon companions sufficed to tell Manohara
their exploits of the night.

Apart by day but rapturously united at night, the couples
passed a year together, though the women soon made their
men lose track of time. Then, one night, Sukumārikā's face
streamed with tears as she said, sobbing: "You are your own
master, but you have consorted with servants. Starting today,
I shall have to wait on my master, God Kubera, for a year.
That means that I and my friends must spend the year in
chastity. But I shall be going home once a week to honor my
parents, and you must come too. Merely seeing the space
through which you have passed is enough to make me live; but
seeing you in the flesh is an elixir of life that shames the
nectar of immortality!"

With these words she left. Hardly was she gone when the
prince's companions came in and found him gazing up at the
sky and muttering, "She is gone!" But while the prince and
Bakula and Aśoka grieved, Sumaṅgala rejoiced. Stuttering
with excitement, he cried: "There is no reason to despair!
Come and embark on my ship. We know the way now, and we

can reach the mountain of the Yakṣas in no time. Let us spend the year there, dreaming of our loved ones and seeing them from time to time, and so enrich our lives with both hope and fulfilment!"

They set sail on the high seas in Sumaṅgala's ship. The vessel sailed into a gale, was thrown off course, and came to grief. The prince was so absorbed in his beloved, like a sorcerer in a spell that has worked, that he failed to notice the disaster which threatened him with a terrible death. Yet he made the shore safely. As he crawled onto the beach, a band of robbers seized him and robbed him of his jewelry. A cavalcade of horsemen appeared soon and surrounded the bandits, cut them down, strung them up, and hanged them from the trees.

One of the horsemen, a pleasant-looking gentleman, came forward, bowed deep to the prince, invited him to mount an elephant, and rode off at the head of the cavalcade. They had gone but a short way when they reached a city. Bards joined the procession, singing the praises of the prince's virtues and lineage as he rode into the city through squares that were carpeted with saffron flowers. Garlands and banners encrusted with precious stones bade him welcome, the stones as they struck one another making clear, tinkling music like swarms of iridescent birds voicing their sweet songs.

Then he entered the gates of the royal palace, of a splendor commensurate with the city's, and rode up to the king, who like an Indra was sitting in a magnificent pavilīon. The prince dismounted and saluted the king. The king hugged his visitor affectionately and studied him for a long time, his gaze wandering with admiration over the well-proportioned figure of the prince. "Ah," exclaimed the king, "who has eyes like Sumaṅgala?" The prince thought, "Could he mean the same Sumaṅgala? Has he survived the shipwreck as I have?"

"Go, my friend," resumed the king, "and refresh yourself."

The prince went inside the palace, and there he saw his own Sumaṅgala, who stood before him bowing. "Sumaṅgala," asked the prince, "are they safe, the friends whom you love as your life, Aśoka and Bakula, who are my right hands?"

"Aśoka and Bakula are safely on their way home," he replied. "Please hear how I myself have arrived here. This

is the city of Nāgapura, famed in romances for the greatness
of which you yourself are a witness now. The king is Puran-
dara. He has a son Jayanta, a handsome warrior and gifted
poet; he is the one who brought you here from the woods on
the beach. The king has a daughter Nālinikā who does not find
her match in the whole world of women. Nor did she find her
match in the world of men; and the king, searching for a suitable bridegroom, dispatched to all corners of the archipelago
a series of scouts who were perfect judges of beauty, talent,
and character. They never returned.

"Much time was lost as things took their course. Finally the
king summoned me and said with a sad smile: 'Sumaṅgala,
not only are you my superintendent of magistrates, you will
have to be my protector as well and rescue me from the danger
in which I have fallen. Find me a bridegroom who in lineage,
character, beauty, and years is a match for my daughter, and
take good care. Ignore the ones who are diseased with the
fascination of wealth, for however rich a man may be in
wealth and possessions, if he is destitute of the riches of
virtue, he is far more deplorable in the eyes of the just than a
poor man.'

"I drew a portrait of Nālinikā on my tablet and traveled
about the eighteen continents of the earth in search of a
bridegroom. When I failed to find the right one, despite all
my efforts, I was so discouraged that I sought to kill myself
and set sail on the seas. I came to Kānanadvīpa, and as I
walked about the town, I constantly met groups of respectable
people who talked of nothing but your virtues. My resolution
to kill myself, which had lent fortitude to my uncertainties,
was swept away by your fame, as light sweeps away darkness.
People had told me that you were addicted to the art of perfuming, and so I made it known to you that I too was a student of the art. Servants soon find favor with their master if
their interest and knowledge are the same, even though they
lack all virtue.

"You and your friends purposely burned an incense that
disagreed with your perfume and the scent of your flowers, in
order to try my knowledge. While I prepared a more harmo-
nious perfume, I studied the princess' portrait which I had
painted on my perfumer's palette. And as I looked at her and
then at you, I knew that I and the princess and the creator

had succeeded and that our existence had not been in vain. While you yourself carried me away with your virtues of goodness and charm, I was bent on my own design to carry you off. However well I was treated, I remained intent on my plan to abduct you, for servants who wish to please their masters don't draw the line at crime. Sukumārikā herself was driven off, under the pretext of palace service, by the powerful good karman of Nālinikā which made her union with you inevitable.

"Once I had found a way, I lost no time and by rigging the ship contrived to drop you into the sea. There has never been a shipwreck in that part of the sea where the waves carried our ship to its doom! Bakula and Aśoka were able to sail home on the same ship without being marooned. I reached the city in the same way as you did.

"Therefore, Your Highness, take Nālinikā to yourself, for the goddess of fortune, arriving in person, will brook no delay!"

Thus the prince received a bride who in all respects enchanted him; and he enjoyed her to his heart's content as an elephant enjoys a lotus pond.

Sumangala had told the princess, "Be sure never to sleep apart from your husband at night, for your husband's mistress the fairy may suddenly come and take him away." One night, nevertheless, the princess was angry with the prince, and, though she was wide awake, she went to another room and pretended to sleep. Unwittingly, she did fall asleep.

It was a year now since Sukumārikā had gone to attend on her master, and the term of her service was over. The fairy found her lover sleeping alone and carried him off. He was never seen again.

"*Your Majesty!* *

"*On the day when Your Majesty descended into the Demon's Cave to help that brahmin, all your friends started out
to search for you; and I too wandered over the earth, until I
came to the kingdom of Aṅga. From the conversation of a
crowd of pilgrims on the banks of the Ganges, just outside the
city of Campā, I learned that there lived a great saint called
Marīci who had acquired second sight by the power of his
penance. In order to find out from him where Your Majesty
had gone, I made my way to the place where he lived, and
thus my story begins.*"

* Prince, later King, Rājavāhana, who had set out on an expedition
of conquest with nine princes, was separated from them and disappeared into a cave. At their eventual reunion with him, the nine companions, among whom are Apahāravarman and Upahāravarman, tell
their adventures.

The First Prince's Story

In a hermitage I found an anchorite of troubled looks sitting under a dwarf mango tree. He received me with all honor due a guest, and after I had rested awhile, I asked: "Where is the Reverend Marīci? I wish to learn from him where a friend of mine, who departed overnight on an errand, may have gone. The saint, of course, is famous all over the world for his powers of clairvoyance."

The hermit sighed deeply and sorrowfully before answering. "Indeed, there once *was* such a seer here in this hermitage. Upon a certain day he was visited by Kāmamañjarī, the courtesan who is the splendid ornament of the capital of Aṅga. Oh, but she was in a sorry state: glistening tears twinkled like stars on her breast, and the hair that touched the ground in reverent homage was disheveled. After a moment her relatives, led by her mother, came running after her with loud laments and dropped down on their knees one after the other in unbroken sequence. The hermit, filled with compassion, reassured these people with kindly words and then asked the courtesan the reason for her distress. And she, so bashfully, so desperately, so respectfully, said: 'Reverend Sir, this person is unworthy of happiness in this world, but, looking forward to greater joy hereafter, she seeks refuge at the feet of Your Reverend, so munificent in spending grace on the distressed.' But at that point the mother, saluting humbly with folded hands and raising her gray-streaked head as fast as she lowered it to the ground, began to speak.

" 'Reverend Sir,' she said, 'what your servant tells you is all my fault, the fault of making her do her duty! For it is the duty of a courtesan's mother to look after her daughter's person from the moment she is born: to nourish her body with a diet which balances the humors, the digestion, and the basics, while cultivating the power of her personality, her physical strength, the fairness of her complexion, and her intellectual gifts. To make sure that from her fifth year on she does not see even her father too often. To hold solemn and festive celebrations on her birthday and luck-days. To teach her the science of love with all ancillary disciplines. To educate her adequately in the arts of singing, dancing, and playing the lute; in acting, painting, perfuming, and garland-making, as well as in such accomplishments as the art of writing and perfection of diction. To impart to her a working knowledge of Sanskrit grammar, logic, and philosophy. To acquaint her in profound detail with the vocational sciences, with the repertory of sports, and with the arts of gambling, both with live animals and with lifeless pieces. To make her apply herself thoroughly, under the guidance of experts, to the more refined arts of love. To maintain an elegant entourage and to increase her prestige, at processions, festivals, and the like. To promote her success at occasional musical performances by hiring professional applauders in advance. To have her fame publicized in all quarters by specialists in any of the arts she practices. To make astrologers, soothsayers, and their kind trumpet her excellent prospects. To have the beauty and charm of her physique, disposition, and accomplishments praised by hangers-on, libertines, wits, and Buddhist nuns in gatherings of sophisticated townfolk. To put the highest price on her as soon as she has become the center of young men's interests and then to turn her over to a gentleman of independent means—either naturally in love or seduced by the display of her tender affections—who is wellborn, handsome, virile, rich, influential, impeccable, generous, clever, resourceful, businesslike, conscientious, and elegant; or, failing such a paragon, to render her available for a lesser but publicly exaggerated price to a young man who has greater talents but lacks fortune, or to extort full payment from his parents by claiming a secret marriage of their dependent boy. To collect, if payment is not made, by captivating judge or jury. To force the daughter to remain faithful to her lover until, by various stratagems, the resources of the libertine—whatever remains after regular and occasional love-gifts—have been fully exhausted. To have a continuous quarrel going between her and a defaulter or a miser. To milk the spending capacity of a lovesick miser by threatening him with a rival. To embarrass and dispose of the impecunious with sarcasm and public censure, by keeping the daughter away from them, and by other means of putting them to shame. Finally, by concentrating on the problems of the relationship between fortune and misfortune, continuously to introduce the courtesan to free-spending, propitious, and irreproachable wealthy gentlemen.

" 'The courtesan should always be ready for her lover, but never eager. And even if she happens to be in love, she must never disobey the instructions of her mother or madam. Nevertheless, this girl, infringing her duty as set by the Creator, has spent three months in love (and at her own expense) with a nondescript brahmin youth without background whose only asset is his beauty. Besides, by curtly refusing them, she has infuriated candidates who were able to pay. And she has brought the family down. When I tried to restrain her and pointed out that it was all wrong, that it was not *decent,* she indignantly started out to live in the woods. If she cannot be made to change her mind, all these people here have no other prospect than to starve and die,' and the mother began to cry.

"Thereupon the hermit, filled with sympathy, addressed the courtesan: 'My dear lady, is life in the woods not uncomfortable? The reward of such an existence is either final Liberation or a spell in Heaven. Well, the former, being attainable only through superior insight, is generally impossible to achieve, whereas the latter is easy to achieve for anybody if he follows the duties of his class. Give up your impossible undertaking and follow your mother's advice!'

"But her pride flared up. 'If there is no refuge at the feet of Your Reverence,' she said, 'the Fire God of the Golden Seed will not refuse asylum to my misery!'

"Having pondered awhile, the hermit said to the mother: 'Go home presently. Wait a few days until this very fastidious girl who is accustomed to the joys and comforts of life becomes vexed with the privations of life in a hermitage and under our repeated admonitions returns to her normal self.'

" 'So be it,' said her family and departed.

"When they had left, the courtesan became very zealous in her devotion to the saint. Dressed severely in white upper and under skirts and not too much concerned with make-up, she watered the seedlings of forest trees, diligently gathered bouquets of wildflowers for the worship of God, performed many kinds of offerings, and with perfumes, garlands and incense, dances, songs, and music honored Śiva the Punisher of Love. And with all these devout attentions and with inti- mate discussions about the three goals of life and the nature of God, she succeeded in arousing the passion of the saint in a remarkably short time.

"When she noticed that the saint had unwittingly fallen in love, she remarked one day, half-smiling: 'Aren't people foolish to classify Wealth and Love with Virtue?'

" 'Now tell me, darling,' Marīci encouraged her, 'to what extent does Virtue outrank Wealth and Love in your opinion?'

"Softly and slowly from embarrassment, the girl began: 'As though Your Reverence would have to learn from such as I how the three goals differ in importance! Or is this another way of showing favor to a slave? However, please listen. Is it not true that without Virtue there can be neither Wealth nor Love? Yet Virtue alone, regardless of Wealth and Love, can become the means to the bliss of Extinction, to be realized merely by Introspection into oneself. Unlike Wealth and Love, Virtue does not require any external means to be achieved. And if Virtue is fortified by insight into the nature of things, Wealth and Love, in whatever ways pursued, can never impair it. Even if it happens to be impaired, it is restored with little effort; and since that sin too has then been conquered, the lapse has actually led to greater saintliness! Instances are many. Brahmā, the God Grandfather, fell in love with the nymph Tilottamā. Śiva committed adultery with a thousand wives of hermits. Viṣṇu sported with sixteen thousand wenches. Prajāpati made love even to his own daughter. Indra was Ahalyā's lover. The Moon God disgraced his teacher's couch. The Sun God covered a mare. The Wind God cohabited with an ape. Bṛhaspati chased Utathya's wife. Parāśara seduced a fisher-girl, his son bedded his sister-in-law, and Atri lay with a doe! And in all these instances the devilish treachery of the gods could not hurt and damage their virtue because of the power of their wisdom. No dirt can linger in a heart purified by Virtue, no more than in the sky! Therefore, in my opinion Wealth and Love hardly amount to even a hundredth part of Virtue!'

"Lust rose in the saint while he listened, and he said: 'Ayi, my pretty, you have observed well: the Virtue of those who have insight into the nature of things cannot be damaged

by sensual pleasures. However, from birth we have gone un-
instructed in the ways and means of Wealth and Love. I must
now know them. What are their nature, their accompanying
features, and their rewards?'

"She answered: 'To begin with Wealth—the point is to
acquire it, increase it, and preserve it. Its features are agri-
culture, cattle-breeding, commerce, diplomacy, and war. As to
its reward—it serves to promote charitable causes. Love, on
the other hand, is a certain incomparably pleasurable tactile
experience of two persons, a man and a woman, who are both
passionately interested in the object of this experience. The
circumstances of Love are all things that are charming and
beautiful. And its reward is an exquisite sharing of joy that
springs from a close-shared contact—sweet to remember and
bolstering one's self-respect—supremely, immediately, self-
evidently delightful. For the sake of Love men of the most
distinguished stations perform gruesome mortifications, make
huge donations, fight cruel battles, set out on terrifying
voyages over the seas.'

"Was it the power of fate? Was it her sagacity or his own
stupidity? However that may be," continued the hermit,
"when the saint heard her talk, he forgot his vows and made
love to her. Thereupon she drove the bewildered hermit, who
was already far gone, in her carriage to the city and rode
with him along the splendidly decorated highway to her home.
Criers along the way proclaimed: 'Tomorrow is the festival
of love.'

"The next morning, when the hermit had had his bath and
massage and stood beautifully groomed and garlanded, already adept at the ways of lovers without the least desire of
returning to his own ways but smarting when he was separated
from his beloved even for an instant, the courtesan took him
along the royal way to a festive crowd somewhere off in a
park, where, surrounded by a court of a hundred young girls,
the king was seated. With a smile the king said, 'Pray be
seated, my dear, with His Reverence.' She curtsied coquet-
tishly and sat down with a smile. Then a most beautiful lady
arose, folded her hands, and, prostrating herself before the
king, declared: 'Your Majesty, she has defeated me. Henceforth I shall be her slave.' A loud cry of amazement and delight went up from the bystanders. Pleased, the king honored

the victorious courtesan with costly jeweled ornaments, favored her with a large retinue, and dismissed her.

"While courtesans and townfolk crowded around cheering, the girl called out to the hermit before she started for home: 'Reverend Sir, my homage! You have favored this slave girl too long already. You may now return to your own profession.'

"As though struck by lightning, the saint leaped up and cried out with passion: 'Darling! What do you mean? Why this sudden indifference? What has happened to the beautiful love you bore me?'

"Smiling, she replied: 'Reverend Sir, the girl who just now confessed herself defeated in the presence of the king once in a quarrel sneered at me: "You brag as if you had seduced Marīci himself!" And that is what I set out to do: it was a bet, and the odds meant slavery. I won. It was very gracious of you!'

"So the fool was jilted by that harlot, and, rapidly repenting, he wandered off, totally empty. And that saint whom the girl made a martyr, that saint, sir, am I. By retracting the passion that had thriven by her power, the same harlot has inspired me to great feats of dispassionateness. Soon I shall have full control over myself and be able to accomplish what you wish from me. Meanwhile remain in Campā, city of the Aṅgas."

As though fleeing the darkness that was released from the hermit's heart, the sun took flight to its setting; the crimson love also freed by the saint now glowed as dusk; and the red lotuses of the day closed as though his narrative had moved them to give up their passionate hue. Agreeing to the hermit's request, I remained to spend the night with him, and after the twilight prayers we whiled away the evening hours with appropriate tales until we slept. On the morrow, when the red glow of the morning sun dawned ablaze on the mountain peaks of the sunrise, challenging the blossoms of the Tree of Wishes, I bowed to the saint and departed for the city.

In a solitary grove of aśoka trees outside a Jain monastery by the road, I discerned a wretched-looking Jain monk who sat there dejected, beyond the reach of the blessed state of Extinction, and consumed by disease—a true paragon of the luckless. And I saw how the tears, dropping from his face onto his chest, soaked through loosening layers of accumulated filth. I sat down beside him and said, "You mortify yourself, and yet you weep? If it is no secret, I should like to hear why you are grieving."

He said: "Listen, good sir. I am Vasupālita, eldest son of the big trader Nidhipālita in this city of Campā. But I am better known as Ugly, for ugly I am. There is also in the city a man nicknamed Handsome, who does justice to his name. He is long on looks but extremely short on cash. Between this man Handsome and me, a bunch of crooks who make a living out of quarrels cultivated a feud that originally started from his good looks and my good money. One day when there was a holiday crowd, those crooks heard us exchange insults which spontaneously rose from the bottom of our mutual contempt, and they proceeded to arbitrate.

" 'Neither looks nor goods make a man. A real man is one whose virility is sought after by the most knowledgeable ladies! Kāmamañjarī, of course, is the jewel among ladies. Therefore whichever one of you can arouse her affections will win the pennant of popularity.'

"We agreed and sent messengers to the courtesan. Now will you believe it, I was the one who infatuated her! When Handsome and I both sat waiting in her anteroom, she chose to join me, throwing around me a noose of sly glances like a wreath of water lilies, and made my rival hide his face in humiliation. Thinking that I was really lucky in love, I made her the mistress of my money, my house, my slaves, my body, and my life. All she left me was my loincloth. As soon as she had her hands on all I possessed, she threw me out. I was the laughingstock of the town, and, much too ashamed to bear the censure of the townsmen, I had a monk in this Jain temple explain to me the path of Liberation. And in a fit of renunciation I thought, 'This is the right kind of clothing for one who comes from a brothel,' and abandoned my loincloth too.

"But then, when the dirt had caked on my body, when I was smarting from the frenzied plucking of my hair, suffering badly from extreme hunger and thirst, and struggling like a newly caught wild elephant against the severe restrictions in standing, sitting, lying, and eating, I came to my senses. 'I am born high!' I thought. 'It is a sin for me to walk down the road of heresy! My ancestors advanced along the path prescribed by Revelation and Tradition, but I, miserable apostate,

abominably undressed, have to suffer terrible tortures even
now. And since I have to listen to constant vilifications of
Brahmā, Viṣṇu, and Śiva, I shall even hereafter reap the
torments of Hell. How could I ever start out on this road of
unrewarding treacherous heresy as if it were the true religion?' And with this summing-up of my failures I betook myself to this solitary aśoka grove to cry my heart out."

Full of sympathy, I said: "Friend, be patient. Stay here for
a short while. I shall try to make this harlot restore all your
wealth to you from her own coffers. There are certain ways."
And with this consolation I rose.

As soon as I walked into the city, I found out from the
talk of the townspeople that Campā was full of wealthy
misers; and in order to bring them to their senses by a practical demonstration of the perishable nature of things, I
decided to follow the path opened by Mūladeva, past master
of thievery. I entered a gambling dive and mixed with the
gamesters. I noticed with great satisfaction how clever they
were at all twenty-five varieties of the art which forms the
basis of sound gambling: their almost indetectable tricks with
the gaming boards; their sleight-of-hand; the oaths and insults
which these tricks excited; the impulsiveness with which they
put their lives at stake; the force and efficacy of their methods
and systems for gaining the confidence of the players; how
they flattered the strong and bullied the weak; the expert
skill with which they picked partners and the variety of allure-
ment with which they tempted them; how they argued differences of stakes; their generosity in distributing their gains;
and finally the all-prevailing hum from which everywhere
raucous voices emerged. When one player in a game somewhere happened to make a rather careless move on the chess-
board, I began to smile. But his opponent suddenly caught
fire and, glowering at me with eyes bloodshot with fury,
yelled: "Hey! You signal to him how to play by smiling! Let
this stupid wretch go. I'd rather gamble with you, if you are
so smart."

With the permission of the gambling boss I joined in. I won
16,000 dinars from the man. I gave half to the boss and the
players, kept the other half myself, and rose up. With me
rose the happy congratulations of the crowd. I accepted the
invitations of the boss and partook in his house of a most

excellent dinner. Meanwhile the fellow who had given me the chance to join in the game, a man called Vimardaka, became henceforth my second and more reliable self.

From his mouth I learned how the entire city was constituted according to wealth, professions, and morals. Then, in a darkness as black as the poisonous stain on Śiva's throat, I set out, wrapped in a dark-blue coverall and with a sharp sword buckled on, carrying the necessary equipment and tools: mattock, soft-sounding string instrument, tongs, dummy h∩ad, sleeping powder, trick lantern, measuring tape, hook, flashlight, box with large "fly-in-light" bugs, and so forth.[1] I found the house of a certain wealthy miser, made a breach in the wall, entered the house after having reconnoitered the interior through a small peephole, roamed unmolested around inside as if it were my own home, stole a large capital of merchant funds, and made off.

On the royal highway, which was dark as though smothered in a bank of black clouds, a light flashed suddenly like a streak of lightning. And, despite the disreputable hour, a charming young woman appeared with flashing bracelets and rings. She resembled Campā's guardian goddess outraged by the robbing of the city.

"Who are you, my sweet? Where are you going?" I asked pleasantly.

She replied in a tremulous, halting voice: "Sir, here in town lives a noble merchant named Kuberadatta. I am his daughter. When I was born, my father betrothed me to a rich merchant's son from the city; his name is Dhanamitra. Now, when this Dhanamitra inherited a fortune at his parents' death, he was so liberal with it that he bought poverty from a crowd of beggars, and in spite of his poverty the people admiringly called him by a name of honor—Lord Bountiful. He still wanted me for his wife when I became a woman, but my father refused to give me because he was penniless, and instead

---

[1] The mattock was used to dig a tunnel into the house; an instrument similar to the ukelele was sounded to find out if anybody was still awake; the dummy head was stuck through the tunnel or hole in the wall to catch the first blow if anybody was waiting for the thief to crawl through; the trick lantern could be adjusted to a tiny beam. The bugs, big suicidal insects, were released inside the house to extinguish all the lights. They would dive into the flame of an oil lamp and thus put it out.

promised to marry me off to a big caravan trader named, rightly, Arthapati, Lord-of-Riches. Knowing that this disastrous marriage would take place tomorrow at dawn, I arranged to meet my true love before it happened, eluded my servants, and went out by the road which I have known since childhood to keep my tryst with him, with the guidance and escort of the God of Love. Now let me go. Take my jewels." And she unfastened them and handed them over.

I felt sympathy for her plight, and I said, "Come on, my fine girl, I shall myself bring you to the house of your lover."

Before we went more than three or four steps, a patrol of town guards with sticks and daggers in their hands fell on us, dispelling the burden of darkness with the light of lanterns. The girl started to tremble, but, noticing her fears, I said: "Don't be afraid. There's a good girl. Here is my arm and my sword, its companion. But on account of you I have thought up a more humane scheme. I shall lie down and act as if I have been bitten by a snake and am convulsed by the poison. You must tell them: 'We entered the town by night, and my escort was bitten by a snake at the corner of the Council Hall. If there is a poison-charmer among you who has mercy on me, let him revive the victim and return my life, for now I am without a protector.'"

Since no other course was open, the girl did my bidding. Somehow she managed to walk over to them, trembling violently, her eyes clouded with tears, and stammered in terror her message. Meanwhile I was lying on the ground simulating the symptoms of poisoning. One fellow among them who thought himself a poison-charmer examined me, treated me with complicated manipulations, charms, thought-healing, etc., without the slightest result, and finished by saying: "He is gone. He was bitten by a black cobra; that is why his body is stiff and black, his eyes glassy, his breath stopped. Stop grieving, my pretty. We'll burn him tomorrow. Who can escape fate?" And he walked off with his comrades.

I got up, escorted the girl to Lord Bountiful, and said: "I, dear sir, am a thief. I saw this girl stealing away to you, in the sole company of her heart that had already gone to you, and sympathy urged me to conduct her to you. Here are her jewels." I handed him the gems, which with their radiant splendor dispelled the darkness of the night.

Lord Bountiful took them and replied with embarrassment, joy, and nervous courtesy. "Noble sir, tonight you have rendered me my love but robbed me of speech, for I do not know what to say. Should I say: 'Your conduct was extraordinary'? No! For how could your own character appear extraordinary to yourself? Or: 'No one else ever performed such a feat'? No! For a man's faculties are determined in each individual case, and the greed and lust of others will not be found in you. Perhaps: 'Today, sir, you have brought virtue to life'? No! For in its generalization this would do injustice to your former feats of nobility. Or: 'This day I have witnessed the very essence of greatness'? No! Such a conclusion, failing to take into account your true purposes, would be unjustified. Should I then say that you have bought me as your slave with your virtuous deed? I would insult your intelligence, for you would have bought too little for too much! Or else that my life is yours in return for the gife of my beloved? But you yourself have given me my life, for without her I longed for death! No! Only this much is apposite: 'Sir, as of today you have a slave in your care!'" With this he threw himself at my feet.

I made him rise and embraced him. "Friend," I said, "what are your plans now?"

He answered: "I cannot live here any longer if I marry her without the consent of her parents. Therefore I intend to leave the country this very night. But who am I? Your Honor, command me!"

"True," I said, "an intelligent man does not distinguish between native country and foreign country. On the other hand, this is a very delicate young girl, and the roads through the jungle are rough and dangerous. Your leaving the country without much purpose would seem to indicate a certain lack of determination of mind and character. So you had better stay quietly here with her. Come on, let us take her home."

Without a moment's hesitation he agreed, and at once we conducted the girl back to her home. And while she kept a sharp lookout, we stole everything out of her house except the dishes. Lord Bountiful and I made our getaway, but no sooner had we hidden the loot than we came upon a patrol of the guards. We mounted a must elephant which was sleeping beside the road and threw the mahout off. While by planting both feet firmly on his neck chain I prodded him to get up, the beast found a purchase for his tusks in the broad chest of the cast-off mahout, and with the man's guts swinging like garlands from his tusks he shattered the entire force of the guards. Then we crashed with the elephant into Arthapati's house and razed it to the ground. Thereupon we rode off into a neglected park and dismounted by catching the branches of a tree. Arriving home at Lord Bountiful's we had a bath and went to bed.

The disk of the sun rose from the sea like a ruby chip carved from the Mountain of the Sunrise, incarnadine like a cluster of golden blossoms on the Tree of Wishes. We rose, washed our faces, and, after we had done the morning rites, sauntered into town. There was great excitement over our exploits of the night before, and we listened to the goings-on in the houses of the supposed bride and bridegroom. Arthapati soothed Kuberadatta with money and postponed his marriage with Kulapālikā, the merchant's daughter, for one month.

I took Dhanamitra aside and gave him the following instructions. "Approach the king, my friend, show him in private this leather purse, and tell him this: 'Your Majesty surely knows me. I am Dhanamitra, the only son of Vasumitra the millionaire. I lost my fortune to a crowd of solicitors, and now I am held in contempt. When Kuberadatta decided to marry his daughter Kulapālikā, who had been reared for me alone, to Arthapati because I was now too poor, I disappeared into an old dilapidated garden near the city and desperately resolved to do away with myself. But as the dagger was balanced on my throat, a recluse appeared and restrained me. "What is at the bottom of this act of violence?" he asked, and I said, "Poverty, the sister of contempt!" Then he took pity on me. "My son, you are a fool. Nothing is so utterly evil as suicide. Brave people save themselves by themselves, without ever falling prey to despair. There are many ways to collect a fortune, but there is no way of joining a cut throat to regain life. Enough! I am a magician. By magic I have conjured this leather purse which can hold one hundred thousand gold pieces. I have lived in Assam for a long time, granting the wishes of my people with the help of this purse. But when old age became jealous, I repaired hither to enter in this kingdom a paradise on earth.

Take this purse. The guaranty that goes with it is that it
yields its gift, after me, only to merchants and to harlots.
But if one is to use it, one must first return whatever he has
illegally acquired from others, while all legal possessions have
to be donated to gods and brahmins. Then one must put it in
a sanctified place and worship it in the same way that one
worships a god. Thus one will find it replenished with gold
every morning. These are the instructions." With these words
he gave the purse to me while I stood with folded hands and
then disappeared into a cave in the rocks. Realizing that I
could not live on this miracle purse without first offering it
to Your Majesty, I have brought it here. Your Majesty is
the judge.' The king will doubtless say: 'My friend, I am
pleased. Go and enjoy your purse as you wish.' But then you
must say: 'Favor me with a guaranty lest it be stolen.' And to
that, too, the king will certainly agree. Thereafter you go
home, distribute gifts in the manner described, worship the
purse every day, fill it at night with the money you have stolen,
and show it full of gold the next morning to the people. As a
result Kuberadatta will not care a straw for Arthapati and be
eager to unite you with his daughter. Arthapati, proud of
his wealth, will be furious and sue Kuberadatta. And by
various means we shall see to it that he will end up with
nothing but his loincloth. The same scheme will keep our own
robberies well concealed."

Dhanamitra happily did what I had told him. The same
day at my bidding my gambling friend Vimardaka entered the
service of Arthapati and fed that rich man's hatred for Lord
Bountiful. Kuberadatta, greedy for money, threw Arthapati
over and arranged, with all due apologies, to marry his daughter off to Dhanamitra. And Arthapati started proceedings.

It was in these same days that Kāmamañjarī's younger sister Rāgamañjarī was due to give a song and dance performance
in the hall of the Five Heroes, and townspeople turned up in
crowds with great expectations. I myself was present, together with my friend Dhanamitra. When she began her
dance, my heart was her second stage. Under cover in the lotus
clusters of her seductive sidelong glances, the God of the
Five Arrows, more powerful than ever because of the emotions
and sentiments inspired by her performance, tormented me
intolerably. She looked like the patron goddess of the town

who, outraged by our thefts in the city, chained me with fetters of playful sly glances from eyes darkly lustrous like the
petals of blue water lilies. When she rose after her dance,
radiant in success, she, unobserved even by her closest companions, playfully winked at me again and again (was it
coquetry? love? chance? I wondered), smiled for no reason
(thus revealing the moonlike brightness of her teeth), and
disappeared, pursued by the eyes and hearts of her audience.
I went home, but an irresistible longing killed all appetite
for food, and I lay in a state of collapse on my solitary couch,
pretending that I suffered from a piercing headache.

Dhanamitra, who was very well read in the manuals of love,
came to my bedside and reported in confidence: "My friend,
fortunate indeed is the courtesan for whom your heart yearns
so tenderly. But I have observed the sequence of her emotions too; the God of the Odd Arrows will bed her soon on
a bed of arrows. A meeting could easily be arranged, since
both of you long for each other. But the fact is that this
courtesan has declared, with a noble-mindedness, my friend,
totally at variance with the expected behavior of harlots,
that her price is virtue, not money, and that short of matrimony
nobody is going to enjoy her best years. Her sister Kāmamañjarī and her mother Mādhavasenā repeatedly tried to dissuade her, but without success. Tearfully they besought the
king: 'Your Majesty, we had great hopes that your slave
Rāgamañjarī, whose character, wit, and accomplishments
are commensurate with her beauty, would fulfill our aspira-
tions; but our hopes have been cut to the root. For, ignoring
the duty she owes to her heritage, she is unconcerned about
money and intends to sell her young years only for quality.
Unperturbed she tries to imitate the behavior of wellborn
ladies! If Your Majesty would command her to return to her
station, it would be best for all.' To oblige them, the king
indeed ordered the girl to do so; but she still refused to obey.
Her sister and her mother again implored the king, weeping
uncontrollably: 'If a young playboy without our consent se-
duces the girl and ruins her, he must be hanged like a common
thief.' That is how things stand now: her family says 'no'
without money to show, and the girl will not accommodate
anyone who gives money. That is the problem to be solved."

"What is the problem?" said I. "I first conquer her with

my qualities, and then we satisfy her family secretly with money."

I ingratiated myself with Kāmamañjarī's procuress-in-chief, a Buddhist nun called Dharmarakṣitā, with presents of clothes and delicacies; and through her good offices I made the following arrangement with the harlot about the money: "I shall steal the miracle purse from Dhanamitra and hand it over to you if you render your sister Rāgamañjarī in return." When she agreed to the bargain, I accomplished her purpose and then took the hand of Rāgamañjarī, whom I had already seduced with my qualities.

The same evening, before rumor spread that the magic purse had been stolen, my spy Vimardaka, still passing as Arthapati's servant, started at nightfall to insult and threaten Dhanamitra in the presence of prominent citizens who had been assembled there under pretext of other business. Dhanamitra retorted: "My dear chap, what do you hope to profit by insulting me in somebody else's cause? I cannot remember that I have ever done you the slightest injury." But Vimardaka sneered. "That is a capitalist's arrogance for you! Tempting a girl's parents with money when another has already paid the price, to get her for yourself! And then you ask, What injury have I done to you? Don't you know what everybody knows, that Vimardaka is the alter ego of merchant Arthapati? Yes, I'd gladly lay down my life for him. Nor would I mind murdering a brahmin! Just by staying up one night I could cure you of the fever of selfishness you have caught from that miracle purse!" Before he could go on speaking, the elders indignantly shut him up and drove him off.

This story was conveyed to the king by Dhanamitra, who feigned great exasperation, along with the report that his purse had been stolen. The king summoned Arthapati for a private interrogation and demanded: "Tell me, sir, could a man called Vimardaka have anything to do with you?"

The foolish merchant replied: "Your Majesty, he is my best friend! Is there anything you could use him for?"

"Can you summon him here?"

"Certainly I can."

He went forth, but however carefully he searched his home, the brothel district, the gambling dives, and the market place, he failed to locate him. How could he indeed, the wretch!

For I had given Vimardaka your signet ring, my Lord, and
ordered him at once to Ujjayinī to search for you! When
Arthapati could not find him, he thought that Vimardaka's
crime would be blamed on himself and, whether from confusion or from fright, started to deny that any crime had taken
place. Dhanamitra remonstrated, and the king waxed angry
and ordered Arthapati chained and jailed.

About the same time, Kāmamañjarī the courtesan wanted
to milk the miracle purse in the fashion prescribed in the instructions, and in order to do so she secretly approached the
fellow called Ugly whom she had mulcted before and turned
into a nude Jain monk in the process. She restored all the
property she had stolen from him and withdrew with many
protestations of loving affection. Thus my gospel released
him from the grips of asceticism and he returned with great
joy to his own faith. In anticipation of her gains from the
magic purse, Kāmamañjarī gave away so much in a couple of
days that at last her entire fortune consisted of an oven.

At my instigation Dhanamitra thereupon told the king in
confidence: "Your Majesty, Kāmamañjarī, the same courtesan
who is so avaricious that she has earned from the people the
nickname Lobhāmañjarī, Bouquet-of-Greed, now indiscriminately doles out everything she possesses, including mortar
and pestle. I believe the reason is that she has acquired my
magic purse, for such is the instruction that goes with it. And
the magic warrant says that the purse yields only to merchants and harlots, and nobody else. For that reason I have
come to suspect her."

At once the king summoned the courtesan and her mother.
With a great show of exasperation I took the women aside
and told them: "Ladies, there is no doubt that your extravagant and overpublicized donations have brought you under
suspicion of possessing the magic purse. Therefore you are
now summoned by the King of the Aṅgas to account for it.
When you are subjected to continuous questioning, you will
inevitably betray that you acquired the purse through me.
And then I am sure to be executed as an example. When I
die, your sister will not survive me. And you yourself will be
penniless. And the purse will be restored to Dhanamitra. So
in all respects this emergency will start a chain of disasters.
How are we to meet it?"

The courtesan and her mother burst into tears. "Yes," they agreed, "our own foolishness has all but betrayed the secret. And if we are put under pressure by the king, we may deny twice, three times, four times, but eventually we shall lay the theft at your door. But if you are accused, our entire family is ruined. Now, Arthapati is disgraced anyway, as everybody knows, and the whole town is aware that the brute was intimate with us. We can therefore best protect ourselves by pleading that he gave the purse to us."

I agreed, and they went to the royal palace. At first when they were interrogated by the king, they repeatedly denied any knowledge. "It is against the rules of harlotry to betray a customer," they said; "people don't go to whores with honest money." But when the king hinted at cutting off their nose and ears, the shrewd bawds, horrified, accused Arthapati of the theft. The king was furious and raised his staff over the merchant's life. But Dhanamitra, raising his folded hands in supplication, intervened.

"My Lord, King Maurya has granted the merchants this privilege, that in such crimes as this their life is not forfeit.[2] If you are angered, confiscate the felon's property and exile him from your kingdom."

This intervention of Dhanamitra increased his reputation of generosity. The king was pleased, and Arthapati, he who once had been possessed by his money, now in sole possession of one tattered rag to clothe him, was banished from the city, as the whole community witnessed. At Dhanamitra's suggestion, the king graciously conceded that a portion of Arthapati's confiscated possessions be granted to Kāmamañjari the courtesan, who had been separated from her fortune by the illusions into which the miracle purse had inveigled her. On an auspicious day Dhanamitra married Kulapālikā. And I myself, having now accomplished what I had set out to do, filled Rāgamañjarī's house with gold and jewelry. In this city the class of the greedy and the rich was now so plundered that with a begging bowl in the hand they had to make the rounds of the same poor people I had enriched with their own money!

Nevertheless, no man, be he ever so cunning, can outwit the fate that is written on his forehead. For one day when I

[2] Maurya is the name of the dynasty that established the first Indian empire.

had amorously given Rāgamañjarī wine to drink to quench a lovers' quarrel, and time and time again tasted and sipped the wine now sweetened by the honey of her lips lovingly offered, I was gripped by intoxication. As you know, it is character- istic of intoxication and lunacy to make a man behave stupidly even in his most habitual actions. Thus, as my drunkenness mounted, I cried out: "In one night I shall rob the town empty and fill up your house!" Shrugging off the hundreds of pros- trations, protestations, and imprecations of my loving wife who was very upset, I burst loose like a rutting elephant from his chains, and, with no other weapons than my sword and followed by Rāgamañjarī's ayah called Śṛgālikā, I set out in a fury of violence. When I fell in with patrolling town guards, I fought them without thinking. Crying thief, they attacked; and, more playful than angry, I killed two or three of them before my sword slipped from my drunken hand and I col- lapsed with rolling bloodshot eyes.

Whining miserably, Śṛgālikā immediately rallied to my side, but my enemies already had me fettered. The emergency sobered me up, and my head cleared at once. Collecting my senses, I thought: "Aho! I am in dire trouble and only because of my own lunacy! Almost everybody knows that Dhanamitra is my friend and Rāgamañjarī my love, and through my fault they are now sure to be arrested tomorrow and thrown into jail. But here is a plan which can save them both, if fol- lowed to the letter, and eventually pull me out of peril as well."

Thus taking counsel with myself, I decided on a certain stratagem, and I said to Śṛgālikā: "Get away, old hag! You were the one who brought that greedy cunning whore Rāga- mañjarī together with my enemy Dhanamitra, who is crazy about his miracle purse and pretends to be my friend. Be cursed for that, woman! And now I shall have to pay with my priceless life for stealing that hooligan's purse and pinch- ing the girl's jewels!"

She was uncommonly clever and caught on at once. Weep- ing, sobbing, raising her hands, she prostrated herself before the guards and implored them: "Good men, please wait a moment till I have found out from him what he has stolen from us." They allowed her to go ahead and she turned again to me.

"Kind sir, pardon this one lapse of your wife. By all means, let Dhanamitra who has seduced your wife be the target of your hates, but you must forgive your slave Rāgamañjarī if you remember for how long she has served you. For a girl whose stock in trade is beauty, jewelry is capital. Tell me, therefore, where her jewels are cached." And she prostrated herself.

As if moved by pity I said: "You are right. What is the use of carrying on my quarrel with her in the shadow of death?" And pretending to explain about the jewels I whispered my instructions in her ear: "Contrive to do thus and so." She, in her turn, acted as if she had gained her end and exclaimed: "Live long, my lord. May the gods show mercy to you; may His Majesty the King of the Aṅgas, who knows how to value courage, release you, and may these good men have pity on you." She scurried off instantly. I myself was led off to the dungeon at the orders of the captain of the guards.

The following day the warden, a man called Kāntaka, put in an appearance. He was a very conceited fellow, very conscious of his handsome figure and convinced of his appeal to the ladies. He had recently come into his post at the death of his father and, what with his boyish cockiness, was far from mature in his job. He threatened me a little and declared, "If you do not return Dhanamitra's magic purse or if you refuse to make reparations for all you have plundered in the city, you will go through all eighteen degrees of torture and finish by facing death!"

My smiling reply was: "My dear chap, even supposing that I returned everything else I have stolen since the day I was born, I would still refuse to return the magic purse of my enemy and so-called friend Dhanamitra, the fellow who stole Arthapati's wife. I would prefer to suffer myriad tortures rather than return it. That is the best I can offer." Every day in this way the warden proceeded with his interrogation, which was mainly a matter of threats and promises. Meanwhile I had adequate food and drink, so that after a few days I recovered from my wounds and was as healthy as ever.

Then one day at the hour when daylight dies in the yellow glow of Viṣṇu's cloak, Śṛgālikā arrived beaming in a beautiful dress. Leaving her companions behind, she embraced me and said: "My Lord, I congratulate you. Your beautiful scheme has succeeded. I went to Dhanamitra and said, 'Sir, your friend has come to grief in thus and such a way. He instructs me to tell you: "I have been jailed today because I was drunk, a mistake hardly avoidable if one lives with a harlot. You must at once without delay address the king as follows: 'Your Majesty, the magic purse stolen by Arthapati was, thanks to Your Majesty's gracious intercession, recovered. However, I cultivated an acquaintance with Rāgamañjarī's husband, a gambler, because I found him very accomplished in arts, letters, and manners. Consequently I also cultivated his wife by sending daily some dresses, jewelry, etc. Being the low-minded gambler he is, the fellow became suspicious and in his fury stole both my magic purse and her jewelbox. When he was once again abroad thieving, he happened to be arrested by the town guards. In his predicament he kept faith with his old affections and told Rāgamañjarī's ayah, who followed him in tears, where he had hidden her jewels. If somehow he could also be persuaded to return the magic purse, then Your Majesty may find cause for pardon.' And when the king has taken notice of this, he will not only spare my life but also try by little blandishments to persuade me to return your property. That will stand us in good stead." '

"As soon as he had heard your message, Dhanamitra followed instructions—without undue concern, for he trusts you implicitly. To continue, I myself gained Rāgamañjarī's confidence with the help of your token, and when I had received from her the necessary sums of money, I ingratiated myself in the fashion indicated by you with Māṅgalikā, the ayah of Princess Ambālikā. By taking advantage of my influence with the ayah, I succeeded in cultivating a close friendship between Rāgamañjarī and Princess Ambālikā. Bringing new presents every day from my mistress and entertaining the princess with stories rare and ravishing, I too came to share very largely in her favor. One day when the princess was in the roof garden, I told her that a flower in her hair was drooping (it was perfectly straight), and while straightening it I let it drop to the floor. I picked it up, and, spying a pair of coupling pigeons, with a loud laugh threw it to frighten them away—and deliberately missed. Actually, I threw the flower so that it landed on Kāntaka, who for some reason or other had entered the palace garden near the royal seraglio. The fellow thought that he was being favored and tilted up his head to smile at us, while I myself acted out a rather clever pantomine which made him believe that the high spirits of the princess, who was really laughing at my antics, were inspired by her love for him. The God of Love drew his bow and struck with a poisoned shaft; the fool scarcely had the power to walk away. In the evening I went to Kāntaka's residence with a girl who carried for me a basket filled with perfumed betel mixture, a set of silk clothes, and some jewels; the basket was sealed with the princess' signet and was meant for her friend Rāgamañjarī, but I told him that his beloved had sent it to him. Sinking in love's abysmal sea, he welcomed me as ecstatically as a marooned sailor welcomes a ship. By describing in great detail the terrible stages of lovesickness the princess was going through, I made the fool mad with love. He asked for more, and the next day I brought him used betel, left-over lotion, and dirty clothes of my own, telling him that his beloved had sent them. I took his own presents along for the princess and threw them away where they would not be found.

"When the fire of his passion was ablaze, I advised him confidentially: 'My Lord, there can be no doubt about the future which is foretold by the lines of your body. In fact, an astrologer and palmist who lives next door to me declares: 'This kingdom will fall in Kāntaka's hands—so his marks foretell.' Thus it is fitting that the princess is in love with you. She is the king's only child, and though he will be angry when he hears that you have been carrying on with his daughter, he won't put an end to it, for fear that his child may not survive the separation. On the contrary, he will invest you with the dignity of crown prince. So the one thing follows perfectly on the other. Then why not help things along, my son? If you cannot think of a way to enter the princess' palace . . . well . . . is the distance between the prison wall and the wall of the palace courtyard more than three fathoms? If you order a prisoner who is clever with his hands to dig a tunnel of that length, you can enter the garden, and from there on you will be in our protection. For the servants of the princess are very much attached to their mistress and will not give out the secret.'

" 'A splendid idea, my good woman,' replied the warden. 'In fact, there is a burglar here who is good enough at digging to pass for a son of Sagara.[3] If I can use him, the work will be finished in a moment.'

"'Which one? And why don't you use him?' I asked.

"He mentioned you: 'The one who stole Dhanamitra's purse.'

"'If that is the one, go ahead. Swear that you will see to it by various means that he is released as soon as the work is completed, and when the job is done, put him in manacles again, send word to the king that this thief has been approached in every way but is so incurably insolent and hopelessly resentful that he refuses to show where the magic purse is hidden, and then have him executed as an example. In this way your end is achieved and the secret won't leak out.'

"He agreed happily and instructed me to coax you into taking the job. He is now waiting outside. You must plan what to do from here on."

I was pleased. "My instructions were but few, and your schemes went much further," I said. "Let him come in."

She brought the warden in, and he swore that he would release me, while I swore never to betray the secret. I was freed from my manacles, and after I had enjoyed a bath, a meal, and a lotion, I began work on the tunnel with a curved-blade mattock, starting from a corner of the outer wall of the dungeon, which was in perpetual darkness.

Then I thought: "The man swore to release me while he was planning to kill me. But if I kill him, I am not guilty of breaking my word." So as he stood with his hands stretched out ready to chain me the moment I reappeared from the tunnel, I kicked him down with my heel on his chest and, when he was down, cut his throat with his own dagger.

Thereupon I asked Śṛgālikā: "Tell me, dear woman, how the chambers of the princess are laid out, so that this hard work is not entirely wasted. I shall steal something before I leave jail."

She explained to me the plan of the building, and I crept into the princess' chambers. And there by the light of gem-encrusted lamps, surrounded by her companions, who slept

[3] A legendary king who had 60,000 sons. Once, when in preparation for a Horse Sacrifice he let a horse run unmolested for a year, the animal was abducted to one of the lower hells, and his sons dug their way to the bowels of the earth to recover it.

soundly after the fatigue of their many games, I saw the princess. She was resting on a couch with ivory legs that were carved in the shapes of slumbering lions and beautifully inlaid with priceless gems; the couch was covered with bedding and pillows of swan's down, and flower petals were strewn over it. The instep of her left foot arched under the heel of her right. Her graceful ankles were slightly flexed. The calves snuggled close to each other. The delicate knees were bent a little. The thighs curved slightly. One graceful arm had charmingly crept across her hip, and the other arm was bent to rest her hand like a flower on her cheek. The nightgown of sheer Chinese silk followed to perfection the tender curving of the hips. The rather slender abdomen was not too vaulted, and the firm budding breasts trembled with the heave of her deep breathing. Her shapely neck, curved a little to one side, displayed a necklace of rubies set on a string of twice-molten gold. One earring lay hidden under the tip of a half-visible ear, but the other jeweled ring, in the ear that was turned upward, heightened the sheen of her carelessly tied and all but loosened wealth of hair with a net of golden rays. So fair shone her complexion that one hardly noticed the white splendor of the teeth between the slightly parted rosy lips. The blossom-like hand which had crept up to her cheek replaced the hidden earring, and the reflection of the magnificent floral canopy over the couch, mirrored on the smooth surface of her upturned cheek, did duty now as a beauty spot. The eyes, like lotuses of the day, had closed for the night, and the pennant of her eyebrows was no longer astir. The mark of soft sandal paste between the eyes floated on minute droplets of the moisture that fatigue had brought to her brow. The ivy of her hair strove up to the moonlight of her face. Trustingly she slept, and, with one side all but immersed in the sparkling white coverlet, resting at last after her long and heedless play, she looked like the lightning slumbering at the bosom of the last cloud of autumn.

When I set eyes on her, I stood for a moment undecided, ablaze with passion, quivering with desire, and forgot all plans of plunder, for my own heart had been stolen from me. I reflected: "If I cannot win this lovely girl, the Friend of Spring will not permit me to live. But if I touch her without her expecting it, this very innocent girl will surely cry out in

terror and kill my desire; which will be the end of me. Then
only this can be done." I took from a peg a wooden tablet
covered with a soft paste, lifted a painting stylus from a
jewelry casket, and drew her as she slept, putting myself in
the picture with folded hands prostrate at her feet. And I
added the verse:

> His hands are raised, his face lies prone,
> An urgent slave imploring you:
> Sleep when my love has devoured you,
> But nevermore, my love, alone!

Then I took from a golden basket a vītaka nut wrapped
in perfumed betel leaves, a piece of camphor, and some coral-
gum, which I chewed; and with the lacquer-red juice I spat
on the white stucco of the wall a pair of billing birds. Finally
I exchanged our rings and somehow tore myself away. I returned to the dungeon through the tunnel, and there I told
one of the prisoners, an eminent citizen called Siṃhaghoṣa
whom I had befriended in my prison days, how I had killed
Kāntaka and how he could effect his release by reporting the
secret. Then I walked out with Śṛgālikā.

On the royal highway we ran into a troop of the guards and
were about to be arrested.[4] I reflected: "I could easily run off
so fast that they would never catch me, but the old woman
would be caught in any case. Then this is indicated," and
capriciously I walked straight into their arms, put my hands
behind my back, turned around, and stood quietly waiting
for them to fetter me. "Come on, my good men," I said. "If
I am a thief, you must tie me up. That is your job and not
this old hag's!"

From the little I said she guessed straightaway what I had
in mind, and with respectful bows she came toward the guards,
wailing. "Oh, kind gentlemen, my son here is possessed by
the wind, and he has been treated for it a long time. But yes-
terday he seemed calm, as if he had become normal again.
So I took new hope and allowed him out of his confinement,
gave him a bath and a lotion, dressed him in brand-new clothes,
fed him rice porridge, and let him free to wander or to lie.
But in the middle of the night he was again possessed by the
wind, and, yelling 'I'll kill Kāntaka and sleep with the prin-

[4] Use of the royal highway was restricted.

cess,' he ran as fast as he could to the king's way. When I saw his condition, I ran after him, till this very minute. Please be so kind as to fetter him and turn him over to me."

But the moment she finished, I cried out: "Old woman, who could fetter the Wind God? Could these crows catch me, Eagle? Heaven forgive you!" and I started to run. Weeping and scolded and abused by the guards ("You are mad yourself to let a madman run free as if he were sane!"), she started in pursuit. I went to Rāgamañjarī's house, where I spent the rest of the night, consoling her in many ways for the sorrows of our long separation. In the morning I was reunited with my friend Dhanamitra.

Thereupon I paid a visit to saintly Marīci the hermit, who had now recovered from his vicissitudes with the courtesan and through the power of renewed mortifications had regained his divine faculties. He told me the circumstances under which I would meet you again, my Lord. In the prison, meanwhile, Siṃhaghoṣa had revealed warden Kāntaka's crime, and the king rewarded him graciously by appointing him to the warden's post. The new warden assisted me in returning frequently through the tunnel to the princess' quarters, and I visited the princess, who, on hearing from Śṛgālikā's lips all the reports, had fallen in love with me.

It was in these days that a neighboring king, Caṇḍavarman, infuriated by King Siṃhavarman's insulting refusal of the hand of his daughter, made war on him and laid siege to the city of Aṅga. While the enemy was closing in fast, King Siṃhavarman could not bear to wait for his rapidly approaching allies. He himself breached the city walls, made a sally, and in a violent battle with a numerically superior enemy was wounded and forcibly taken captive. Caṇḍavarman abducted Princess Ambālikā and brought her to his own quarters to force her into marrying him. He donned the ceremonial cord for the wedding, which was to take place at dawn.

So did I don the ceremonial cord for the wedding, in Dhanamitra's house, and I gave Dhanamitra the following instructions: "My friend, an alliance of kings is approaching to succor the King of Aṅga. Collect the city elders and bring the relief force in with the greatest secrecy. As soon as you arrive, you will find the enemy has lost his head." He promised to do as I said.

In a crowd of well-wishers I managed to enter the doomed
enemy's encampment, which was in festive confusion with
all the preparations for the wedding going on; and in the
throngs of people coming in one way and going out the other,
I could keep my dagger hidden. Then at the very moment that
Caṇḍavarman stretched out his arm to take Princess Ambālikā's blossom-like hand which was ceremonially bestowed
on him by his own house-priest before the sacred fire, I cut
his arm off with my dagger and stabbed him in the chest. A
few men jumped on me, and I sent them to hell too. Hunting
through the chaotic and quickly emptying quarters I found
the lovely princess, trembling and wide-eyed, and I carried
her off into an inner apartment to enjoy the delights of her
embraces. But at that very instant, my Lord, roaring like
the thunder at the onset of the rainy season, I heard your
voice.

*And King Rājavāhana, who had listened with amusement,
said, "Why, in ruthlessness you have outdone Mūladeva himself!" Then he glanced at Prince Upahāravarman and said,
"Now it is your turn to tell us a story." And the prince bowed,
smiled, and began this narrative.*

The Second Prince's Story

I Upahāravarman also traveled around, until one day I came
to the land of Videha. Before I entered the capital, Mithilā,
I went into a little hermitage thereabouts and rested for some
time on the verandah while an ancient woman recluse brought
me water to wash my feet. For some reason she could not
restrain her tears from the instant she set eyes on me.

"Tell me, mother," I coaxed, "what is the reason for this?"

She told me a sorry tale. "Your Worship," she said, "you
must have heard that we had a king in Mithilā whose name
was Prahāravarman. Our king's best friend was the Rājā of
Magadha, Rājahaṃsa; they were like Bala and Saṃvara,
and their beloved queens too were as close as friends can be.

Therefore when Queen Vasumatī of Magadha had given birth to her first child, Priyaṃvadā of Mithilā came with her royal consort to Pataliputra, the City of Flowers, for a congratulatory visit.

"At this time it so happened that Mālava waged a big war against the Rājā of Magadha, whose power was obliterated to the last trace. His friend Prahāravarman, the visiting ruler of Mithilā was spared, however, through the intervention of the victorious king of Mālava, and our king set out for his own country. But on receiving reports that his own kingdom had meanwhile been infiltrated by his nephews, Vikaṭavarman and the other sons of his eldest brother Saṃhāravarman, he changed his course to Suhma, where he hoped to obtain troops from the king, who was his sister's son. So he plunged into jungle country, and he was set upon by hunter tribes and robbed of all his possessions.

"I myself was in the king's train and carried his younger son. Under the tribesmen's arrows which rained down on us in torrents, I panicked and fled alone with the prince into the forest. I ran into a tiger which struck me down with one blow of its claws. My little charge tumbled out of my arms and rolled under the paunch of a dead cow. As the tiger tugged at the carcass, an arrow sprang from a bow and took its life. The little prince was carried off by boys from the tribes.

"I fainted, and a cowherd carried me to his hovel and took me in. When my wounds had healed under his merciful care and I had fully recovered my health, I wanted to start out again to rejoin my master the king. And while I was reduced to despair at having to set off without companions, my own daughter arrived at that desolate place with a certain young man. She was weeping pitifully. When at last she stopped crying, she told me that on the dispersion of the king's train the older prince, whom she was carrying, had fallen into the hands of the aborigines. Her own wounds had been healed by a woodsman. When she recovered from her injuries, the man had sought to marry her; but, disgusted at the thought of intermarriage with that lowly race, she harshly refused him. Unable to suffer her insults, the fellow attempted in a lonely spot to cut off her head, but the criminal was killed just in time by a young man who was passing by; and she married him instead.

"I questioned the young man. He was in the service of our king but had been delayed for some reason and was now following our trail to rejoin the king. Together with him we made our way to our master and scorched his ears and Queen Priyaṃvadā's with the bad news about his sons.

"The king warred for a long time with his nephews whose treachery I have mentioned, and after an all too cruel battle into which he was forced because he could no longer hold out, he was taken captive with the queen. Wretch that I am, I was unable to do away with myself even in my old age, and I put on the hermit's cloth. But my daughter, seduced by the temptations of her accursed life, even entered the service of the usurper Vikaṭavarman's wife, Queen Kalpasundarī. Had the two princes grown up without misfortune, they would by this time have reached your age; and had they been here, the king's nephews would not have acted with such brash violence." And she cried all the harder.

I too wept bitterly at the story of the poor woman. Then I said confidentially, "If these are the circumstances, mother, have courage. For did you not ask a certain hermit to rear the prince? He adopted the child and brought him up. It is a very long story. Why go into it all—I am the prince! And I shall be able to put Vikaṭavarman out of the way if by some device I can get to him. But he has too many younger brothers to succeed him, and the people of this town and country make common cause with them, while nobody here knows me for the prince. My own parents would not know me, let alone strangers. However that may be," I concluded, "I shall find a way to deal with the matter."

The old woman embraced me, weeping for joy, and she kissed and kissed me on the head, and her breasts began to flow. "My child!" she stammered, "live long, my dear child. The Lord who disposes has shown you His grace! Today the land of Videha has returned to its true king, Prahāravarman, for today you are here with your powerful arms to help us cross the shoreless ocean of sorrow. Aho! What a blessing for Queen Priyaṃvadā!" Supremely happy, she waited on me with a bath, a meal, and all other amenities.

At night I was lying in the little hovel on a straw mat, and I thought, "This job cannot be done without cheating. . . . Women are the source of all deception. . . . So I must find out from this woman what is going on in the king's harem and contrive some trick there."

I was still deep in thought when the steeds of the sun, emerging from the vast ocean, brushed the night away with the force of their panting breath and the sun itself arose with only a mild gleam as though it were still numb after its sojourn in the ocean womb. I rose up, and when I had completed the morning rites, I spoke to my old nurse.

"Mother," I asked, "do you know anything about the situation in the harem of our headstrong king?"

Before I could go on with this questioning, a woman appeared. When my nurse saw her, she cried out in a voice muffled by tears of joy. "Puṣkarikā my daughter, behold the prince! He is the child whom I had to abandon pitilessly in the wilderness, but he has returned to me!"

Overwhelmed by her joy the woman could not stop crying and babbling. When she had calmed down, her mother ordered her to describe the conditions in the king's harem. She said, "Kalpasundarī, who is the daughter of the king of Assam, surpasses even the celestial nymphs in beauty and artistry, and she has complete ascendancy over King Vikaṭavarman. The king, however numerous his harem, loves no one but her."

"Approach the queen in my name," I said, "and bring her fragrant garlands. Arouse her hatred for her own husband by blaming him for his viciousness and so forth. Make her sorry she married him by describing the perfect husbands of Vāsavadattā and other heroines of note. Be quick to detect and broadcast the king's indiscretions and attentions to other ladies at the court and foster the queen's pride.

"You too," I continued to her mother, "must concentrate on the queen in the same manner. And you are to report to me daily on the situation in the women's quarters. And your daughter must follow Kalpasundarī about like a shadow, exactly as I have told her, so that our efforts be crowned with sweet success."

The two women fulfilled their tasks to the letter. A few days passed. Then my nurse said to me, "My child, the queen has now reached the stage where she pities herself like a mādhavī creeper on a common nīm tree! What are we to do now?"

Meanwhile I had painted a self-portrait, and I told her,

"Take this portrait of me to the queen. When she has studied it, she is bound to ask whether any man can be as beautiful as that. Reply with a question: 'What if there were one?' Report her reply."

The old woman promised to do just so, and she went to the royal palace. Soon she returned and told me, "My boy, I showed your portrait to the queen, and she looked mad with desire! As she studied the painting, she exclaimed, 'At last the world has a master! Even the god who shoots with flowers does not possess such splendid beauty! The picture itself is a marvel. I don't know anyone in this country who could paint a portrait like that. Who is the painter?' She seemed very amazed.

"Smiling, I said, 'Your Majesty's judgment is quite understandable: it is hard to imagine that even the gods could be so handsome. However, the sea-girt world is wide—perhaps somewhere the power of fate has been able to create even beauty as splendid as this. But then, if there were a young man of such beauty, and of talents to match in art, manners, science, and philosophy, and nobly born—what would he gain?'

" 'What indeed?" she exclaimed. 'For what could one say? My body, my heart, my life itself are cheap trifles to offer. What would he gain? But if this is not a trick, please contrive that my eyes fulfill their destiny by seeing him!'

"To strengthen her decision, I said, 'Indeed, there is such a person, a prince traveling in disguise. At the spring festival, when you were diverting yourself with your companions in the city gardens like Love's mistress Lust come to life, his eyes happened to fall on you, and at once he became the sole target of Love's arrows. He came to me. And the rare beauty and excellent accomplishments of both of you so clearly suited you to each other that I have been prompted ever since to honor you with the wreaths, garlands, and ointments which he himself prepared. And he painted his own portrait and sent it you to show the depth of his devotion to you. If your mind has decided, nothing is impossible for this man whose superiority in intelligence, character, and vital strength is truly supernatural. I could present him today. Grant him a rendezvous!'

"She thought a little. Then she said, 'Mother, I can no

longer keep it secret, so let me tell you. My father, the King of Assam, felt great friendship for King Prahāravarman, and my mother and Queen Priyaṃvadā were old friends. Even before either of them had children they made a contract: if one had a son, he would marry the other's daughter; and if she had a daughter, the other's son would marry her. But, as fate would have it, when I was born and Vikaṭavarman proposed to my father, he agreed, for he thought that Priyaṃvadā's son had died. My husband is an uncouth man, brutal to his uncle, unprepossessing in appearance, inept at the niceties of love, and hardly interested in poetry, drama, and the arts. He is immoderately proud of his bravery, but he is a foolish braggart and liar, and he favors the wrong kind of people. No, I am not too pleased with him, especially not recently. In the garden lately, failing to notice that Puṣkarikā, on whom I rely completely, was around, he plucked with his own hands the flowers of my mādhavī which I had grown myself like a baby, and then he used them to adorn that little dancer of his, Ramayantikā, who does not know her place and is jealous of me, as if she could be a rival! And promptly he took her to the jeweled couch where I had just rested myself and had his way with her! That this man, worthless as he is, should slight *me!* Should I care about him? Fear of the world to come disappears in the face of misery in this world. For it is misery, unbearable misery, for a woman whose heart has become a quiver to Love's arrows to face the torture of living with a man she hates. Bring your man to the mādhavī bower in the garden, and I shall meet him! For what I have heard of him is enough to make my heart love him beyond reason. I have a fortune, and I shall use it to put him in his rightful place; I shall live again serving him forever!'

"I agreed to her proposals and came back to report. Your Highness must decide what we do next."

I had her describe to me the plan of the harem building, the posts of the guards, and the arrangement of the garden. Meanwhile the disk of the sun had turned crimson as though it bled from the shock of collision with the summit of the sunset mountain; the darkness which filled the sky yawned like a mass of smoke that was released by the fiery embers of the sun falling into the western sea. The moon rose to lead the planets—heralding his ancient abduction of his teacher's wife as though he wanted to act as my guide in seducing another man's wife. The flower-shooting god, reaching out for the conquest of the world, kindled his fierce splendor on the smiling face of the moon, which, resembling the lotus-like counte- nance of Queen Kalpasundari, shone eagerly in its powerful longing to set eyes on me. As suited the hour, I sought my bed.

And I considered. "The matter is practically done with. Nevertheless, my virtue may possibly suffer if I sin with another man's wife. Still, the authorities condone this sin if it is necessary to gain wealth and love. Besides, I shall commit the transgression with the ulterior purpose of finding a way to set my parents free from captivity. This surely takes all the wrong out of it and may even add a little virtue into the bargain. Yet, what are King Rājavāhana and my friends going to say when they hear about it?" While I was thinking, sleep came upon me.

I woke feeling amorous and spent the day dreaming of the opportunities which my rendezvous with the queen would afford. The next day the god of love, unoccupied elsewhere, showered a rain of arrows upon me. When the lustrous lake of the sun had dried and the black mud of the night appeared, I started up. Wrapped in a dark cloak and tightly girt, I set out, sword in hand and well equipped with the necessary tools, to the moat of the royal castle, keeping in mind the indications and signs which my old nurse had given me. In the moat the water stood to the brim, but nearby I found the bamboo pole which Puṣkarikā had placed at the door of her mother's cabin. I laid it down and crossed the moat, stood the pole up straight, and scaled the wall. By way of a brick staircase which climbed to the level of the gateway tower I descended to the ground. Having reached the ground, I first passed a row of bakula trees, then followed a campaka lane for a short distance until to the north of me I heard the plaintive calls of a pair of cakravāka birds. Thereupon I turned north, along a path lined with Bignonia trees the white blossoms of which masked the wide white-plastered palace wall, which was within easy reach. I followed this path for the length of a bow shot and then turned east along a sand road, which on both sides was bordered with clumps of aśoka and banyan trees. Soon after I came to a mango grove which faced south.

By the light of my lantern, which blinked a single beam from a tiny opening, I reconnoitered a shady arbor of jasmine vines in which a jeweled couch was set. I entered the bower and at one side discovered an inner chamber whose walls were formed by rows of amaranths thickly covered with yellow blossoms. I opened the door, which was made of low-hanging red aśoka boughs aquiver with fresh blossoms and tender buds and which shone pale red with a sheen of newly budding sprouts; and I entered this inner bower. Inside I found a bed of flowers, several baskets of lotus leaves which were filled with the delights that add spice to love, a fan of carved ivory, and a slender vessel of scented water. I was tired and sat down for a while, inhaling the delicious fragrance.

Soon I heard the soft sound of footsteps, and at once I left our place of rendezvous and hid behind a red aśoka tree. The queen with graceful brow, cool flame of desire, approached stealthily. When she did not see me, she shook violently and, like a maddened flamingo, gave forth a beautifully impassioned choked cry. "Ah, it is clear I have been deceived! I cannot live. . . . Ayi, my heart, how could you decide that the impossible was possible and yet tremble now because it cannot be? O Lord of the Five Arrows, what sin have I committed against you that you burn me so fiercely yet do not permit me to turn to ashes?"

At this moment I revealed myself with the lantern. "My little fury, have you not sinned many times against the god of love? You have slighted the god's mistress, who is his very life, with your beauty; his bow with your eyebrows; his bee-string bowstring with the splendors of your dark locks; his arrows with your glances; the saffron-colored silk of his banner with the red incandescence of your lips; his bosom friend the sandal-scented southern breeze with the fragrance-laden breath of your sighs; the song of his cuckoo with the sweet music of your voice; his flowered flagstaff with your arms. The ritual pitchers filled at the start of his world conquest you have surpassed with your breasts; his garden pond with your round navel; the wheels of his battle chariot with your hips; the two columns that prop the jeweled gate to his palace with your thighs; and the lotus that playfully swings from his ear with the shapeliness of your feet. Indeed, the god is right to make you suffer. But I am guiltless, and it is to his

shame that he tortures me! Be gracious, my lovely, and return
my life with your glance that can cure the poisonous bites of
the snake of love!"

I took her in my arms. As her passion mounted, her body
relaxed and her eyes expanded, and I made love to her. Her
upturned eyes became slightly tinged with red; little spoors
of perspiration drew wrinkles on her cheeks; she groaned
softly without restraint and employed on me her reddening
teeth and nails. When I saw her body go completely limp as
though she were suffering, I knew that she had attained satisfaction, and I too surrendered control of mind and body. We
lay for a while, at once separated and united, indulging in the
concluding rites of love and savoring an intimacy more profound than if we two had long been friends.

When it was time for us to part, I sighed deeply and hotly
and after a last embrace drew away with a sad look. Her eyes
filled with tears as she raised her hands to bid me farewell.

"If you go, my lord, trust my life to go. . . . Take me with
you! If not, your slave will be useless."

"Innocent girl," I said tenderly, "no sensible man refuses
to welcome a woman who loves him. If you are firm in your
love for me, then do without hesitation what I am going to tell
you.

"Show the painting that bears my likeness to your husband
and ask him, 'Is this not the ideal of masculine beauty?' He
will surely say that it is. Then go on to say, 'If that is what
you think, listen. I know a saintly woman who in the course
of her wanderings abroad has learned boldness. She has become a mother to me. She showed me this portrait and told
me, "There exists a magic charm by which your husband can
be changed into this form. To do so, you must go alone on
either a new-moon or full-moon night to a secluded place
where priests have sacrificed in a fire and afterward abandoned it, and there you must offer in the same fire a hundred
sandalwood sticks, a hundred aloe sticks, a few handfuls of
camphor, and many silk robes. Thus you shall obtain a new
body. Then ring a bell to summon your husband. When he
has come, he must tell you all his secrets, close his eyes, take
you in his arms, and your new body will pass to him; you
yourself will have the same shape as before. If this is agreeable to you and your loving spouse, you must perform the

spell exactly that way." Therefore, if you wish to change your body, you must first consult with your friends and ministers and younger brothers and subjects and then, with their consent, apply yourself to the ritual.'

"Your husband will certainly agree. The house-priest must ritually kill and sacrifice an animal in a fire here at this crossroads in the garden, and when he has gone, I shall enter this grove under the protection of the smoke and remain here. When nightfall approaches, you must whisper teasingly in your husband's ear, 'You ungrateful blackguard! With the handsome figure you will owe to my kindness, a figure to delight the eyes of the world, you intend to make love to my rivals! Well, I am not going to conjure up a specter for my own downfall. . . .' Listen to what he replies and come here to report it. I shall know what to do next.

"And have Puṣkārikā wipe out all trace of my footsteps in the garden."

Cherishing my every word as though it were scripture, she reluctantly made her way back to the harem. I left too and returned home by the way I had come.

My mistress, madly in love, did as I told her, and her fool of a husband followed her completely. The astonishing news was bruited about town and country.

"King Vikaṭavarman is going to exchange his body for a new one, worthy of a god! The queen has a magic spell to work it."

"Are you sure this is not an illusion? It would be most fortunate!"

"And there can be no question of any failure through negligence: the first queen is doing it personally in the garden of her own palace."

"Yes, the ministers themselves have consented, and they are as wise as the minister of the gods."

"If this really works, it will be the miracle of the age!"

"There is no imagining what spells, stones, and herbs can't do!"

As the gossip spread and spread, the day came. When evening fell and darkness gathered, a dark cloud, blue as the poisoned throat of Śiva, rose from the garden of the seraglio, and the smell of burning milk, butter, curds, sesamum, white

mustard, fat, flesh, and blood oblations was carried by the
wind and wafted in all directions.

When the smoke suddenly stopped, I had entered the palace
gardens, and the queen, full of poise, came to meet me. She
embraced me and said smiling, "My clever man, your wish is
done, and the victim is done for! To tempt him further I said
to him in the way you described: 'Scoundrel, I am not going
to make you more handsome! Even the dancing girls of heaven
will be yearning for you, let alone mortal women. And a heart-
less connoisseur like you, faithless by nature, will flitter away
like a bee.'

"He threw himself at my feet and implored me, 'Darling
with your lovely legs, forgive my indiscretions. I won't even
think of other women any more. Hurry and finish the work
you have started.' Then I hastened to you in this wedding
dress. If I was already married to you by the god of love,
who was our chaplain before the holy fire of passion, now my
own heart celebrates our marriage before this fire of sacrifice!"

As she spoke, she stepped with her toes on the instep of my
feet, lifting up her heels, and encircled my neck with the
lianas of her arms, the soft fingers intertwined; and pulling
my face down playfully and raising her lotus-like face up to
mine, she kissed me passionately with darting wide-eyed
glances.

"Stay here in the amaranth shrubs," I said, "while I go to
do what is still left to be done," and I released her. I walked
over to the place where the sacrificial fire was burning and
rang the bell that hung from an aśoka branch. The bell rang
out like the harbinger of death summoning the victim; meanwhile I began the oblations of sandal, aloe, and other incense.
The king approached. Surprise, mixed perhaps with suspicion,
made him stop and hesitate.

"Tell me the truth once more," I said, "and let the holy fire
be your witness. If you will promise never to make love to my
rivals in your new body, I shall allow you to enter it now!"

My words clearly convinced him that it was the queen and
no one else who spoke. He was ready to swear an oath. Smiling, I said, "Why swear at all? There will be no mortal
woman to succeed me, and if you want to go about with the

nymphs of heaven, by all means do so. . . . Now tell me what secrets you have, and when you have told me, your old body will depart."

"I hold my father's younger brother Prahāravarman imprisoned," the king confessed. "I have consulted with my ministers and decided to poison his food and announce that he died of dysentery. I intend to give my younger brother Viśālavarman the command of an army to attack Puṇḍra. Then, I have been secretly advised by the eminent Pañcālika and by Paritrāta the merchant that a Greek by the name of Khanati has a diamond for sale that is worth the earth but can be had cheaply. Then there is Śatahali, the superintendent of villages and a great man in the country; he is a close friend of mine, and he has agreed on my behalf to order the magistrates not to interfere in our scheme to have Anantasīra, that arrogant, treacherous and malicious landlord, assassinated by popular fury. These are the various secret designs that have been considered recently."

When I had heard everything, I said, "Your life is over. Meet the fate that suits your deeds." I cut off his head with my sword and threw head and body in the fire and sprinkled butter over it to make it blaze high. Soon he was ashes.

The love of my heart was only a woman, and she was a little upset. I comforted her, took her by the hand, and made my way to the palace, where with the queen's consent I summoned all the ladies and permitted them to pay their respects. They were quite astonished. I spent some time with the concubines and finally dismissed them. I passed the night with the queen in the seraglio and learned from her the customs of the late king's family. At dawn I took my bath, and after I had performed the morning rites, I held a meeting with the ministers.

"Gentlemen," I said, "not only my outward form has changed but my character as well. I plotted to poison my uncle, but now I shall release him again to take in hand the kingdom that is truly his. We shall act with all the obedience which a son owes his father. There is no greater sin than parricide."

Thereupon I called the late king's brother Viśālavarman and instructed him. "My dear boy, the Puṇḍras are close to starvation. Their despair may blind their minds and tempt

them to attack our prosperous country. You shall march when
there is a chance to devastate their seed corn or their crop. At
present an expedition is useless."

To the city elders I said, "I shall not buy a valuable gem
for too little money. I shall protect the law and pay its real
worth."

Then I had superintendent Śatahali called in. "This
Anantasīra," I said, "was supposed to be assassinated because
he sided with King Prahāravarman. But now that Prahāravarman has been restored to the throne, there is no reason to
have the man killed. Don't make any attempt now."

My complete knowledge of the secret plots convinced them
that I was really the king, and in great amazement they acclaimed me and the queen and glorified the power of incanta-
tions. My parents were released from prison, and their kingdom was restored to them. I had my nurse inform my parents
secretly of all that had been done, and when I threw myself
at their feet, they reached the very pinnacle of joy and consented that I be created crown prince.

My mind was now at peace, and I enjoyed the pleasures of
life, which were marred only by my distress at being separated from Your Majesty. Then I received a letter from
Siṃhavarman of Campā, an ally of my father's, saying that
Caṇḍavarman was attacking Campā. I decided that I had a
double duty, to defeat an enemy and save a friend, and I
marched to his rescue with a large army that was easily
raised. And the battlefield became the pleasure-ground where
I celebrated my good fortune to look once again upon the
splendor of Your Majesty's feet.

*King Rājavāhama smiled. "Behold!" he said, "adultery
aided by trickery has become a legitimate means to ensure
and enhance both virtue and fortune. In your hands it could
cause your parents to be freed from the evils of captivity,
help destroy a wicked enemy, and restore a monarchy all at
the same time! Is there any means that is not justified by the
intelligence of the person who uses it?"*

The Travels of
Sānudāsa
the Merchant

"*In the city of Campā,*" began Sānudāsa,* "*there lived a merchant named Mitravarman. He was a good man. He had no enemy in the world. No one even felt indifferent toward him. This merchant had a wife whose name Mitrāvatī, the Befriended One, described her to perfection. She was the very incarnation of her husband's spirit of kindliness and would have wished even his enemies well. Yet this virtuous couple failed to have a son to share their virtues, and all the people of Campā, even those who had sons, felt themselves bereft of sons.*

"*One day a wandering mendicant of the Naked Jainas presented himself at the door to beg food. Emaciated by a three-day fast, he was like an apparition of the great Vardhamāna*

* At a musical competition in the house of the merchant Sānudāsa, Prince Naravāhanadatta has won the favors of a beautiful and mysterious damsel named Gandharvadattā. Sānudāsa thereupon tells the prince how he found her.

himself.[1] *The mendicant, whose name was Sānu, was so pleased by the devotion of the merchant and his wife that even without prompting he proceeded to expound on Ṛṣabha's Truths. Thereupon, being learned in the Books of Questions and Answers, he divined their thoughts; and in an unambiguous manner he predicted that they would have a son, a son of many virtues.*

"And so when a son was indeed born, his father the merchant declared: 'He was prophesied by Sānu, and therefore he shall be Sānu's Slave.' Thus he named him Sānudāsa.

"Though an only son, and the more beloved by his father for the anxiety he had suffered in begetting him, Sānudāsa was so thoroughly instructed in all the sciences that he grew up wholly ignorant of the pleasures of childhood. And so energetically did his teachers discipline him that he treated his own bride with as much circumspection as he might have shown a stranger's wife. This excessive and unworldly morality could not fail to disquiet his king, his friends, his wife, her parents, and everybody else. And Sire," announced Sānudāsa, "this paragon of virtue whose birth had been prophesied by Sānu to the exemplary merchant and his wife is no other than your servitor, myself!

1

I had a friend called Dhruvaka in whose constant companionship I delighted. One day he said to me, "Please do what I am going to ask you, my friend. Just now all your friends are out with their wives at the lotus pond in the city park where they have been sporting in the water, and they are now supping and drinking there. You must come along with me and bring your wife too and enjoy for once the rewards of your beauty, your age, and your life! Pleasure is the reward of virtue and success, and if you refuse the fruit, you frustrate its cause; which is a sin. So? No sensible person forgoes the legitimate pleasures of this life merely by such an increase of virtue to secure pleasure in the next life. Moreover, I am not inveigling you on personal grounds. No less an authority than Bhīma himself declared: 'To forgo the

[1] The last of the twenty-four Jaina saints. Ṛṣabha was the first of the line.

pleasures which present opportunity offers and hold out for future pleasures is not the policy of the wise.' " [2]

I smiled. "But Bhīma was really discussing the wisdom of finding pleasure in things that do not matter for good or for evil. It does not matter by itself whether people drink or do not drink wine with their wives. It is the ubiquitous urge of passion that counts. In all creatures passion catches fire spontaneously. It does not take much to set it afire, my friend, but it takes a master to extinguish the blazing butter of concupiscence with the water of moral exhortations! If this kind of pleasure is indeed, as you claim, the reward of virtue, it puts an effective end to all virtue—and that means also to pleasure, its reward! I do not even look at my own wife when she eats or takes her ease, because the Law forbids it: could I then permit myself to be cuckolded? When a man's wife is in the company of his friends and her senses are befuddled by drink so that she becomes delirious and falls in a poisonous coma, she is adultery itself! You go and do as you please. I shall not, nor shall I subject my wife to mixed company."

When Dhruvaka saw that my mind was made up and that though I smiled I stood firm by my decision, he pleaded in despair. "But before I came here, I swore to all my friends that I would produce Sānudāsa and his wife. Can you bear to think of my face turning pale before the noisy ridicule of my friends because I had to break my promise? Do me the favor. Leave your wife at home if you must on principle, but prove that I am as good as my word and come by yourself. If it is sinful to drink, don't drink but just watch your friends drink, and their wives and children."

So I went with Dhruvaka to the pond in the city park, where I met my friends and their wives. Their colorful company, outdazzling the hues of the rainbow with the flamboyant splendor of their flowers, jewelry, and gowns, formed a lotus bed on land which outshone the radiance of its water-borne model. Dhruvaka gave me a seat that stood high off the ground, with a canopy of mādhavī and cūta blossoms on a frame of flexible mango branches and lianas. From it I watched my friends proffer drinks to their loves and then themselves drink deep from the mead which their women held out with cupped hands. Somewhere I heard the melodious

[2] Bhīma is one of the heroes of the *Mahābhārata*.

tune of a spring song accompanied by flute and strings, and
the sweet sound so humbled the kokila birds that they whimpered. The bees, as though charmed out of their sense of smell
by the inviting resemblance, deserted the flower cups of the
amaranth to bury their faces in the flowers that adorned the
ears of the women. Tilaka, aśoka, and kiṃśuka trees blos-
somed from root to crown; for a dried-up tree is like a dissi-
pated actor: only the most potent juices revive it.

Suddenly a swimmer emerged from the pond. He was drip-
ping and smeared all over with mud, and his clothes were
covered with algae. In his hand he held a cup of folded lotus
leaves which seemed to contain something.

"Halā," he shouted joyfully, "I have found the honey mead
of the blue lotus!"

Someone tried to silence him. "Idiot, stop shouting it from
the roofs! You have found no lotus mead, or you will be
ruined! If all your friends drink it, their share will not
amount to a drop the size of an atom. And if you present this
mead, which even princes find it difficult to procure, to our
king, he will ask you for more, for kings are greedy of
treasures. Flatterers who have his ear will insinuate that
there is more where this came from. You may say that that
was all, that there is nothing left, but is there any way of
proving nonexistence? And when the king has acquired a
taste for it, he may be prodded by mischief-makers into con-
fiscating all our possessions. So you'd better not let the king
have it. Lotus mead has a delicate flavor and does not contain
alcohol; Sānudāsa can drink it!"

Both the rareness of the wine and the insistence of my
friends who assured me that it was not intoxicating persuaded me to taste it. While I was drinking, I discovered that
it had none of the six known flavors: it could not be classified
as sweet, sour, salt, bitter, astringent, or pungent, nor could
I even try to define its composition. The omniscient gods
themselves would have found it impossible to distinguish any
particular single flavor. "This delicious taste must be a
seventh flavor," I thought. "Once a man has tasted it, even
nectar is insipid."

The taste and the bouquet of the mead as well as my thirst
got the better of my modesty, and I whispered to Dhruvaka
that I was very thirsty. I drank whatever he gave me, and my

mind went mad, and I staggered through the park, which seemed to spin around me like a wheel. It was then that I heard the touching sound, like the sound of the wind playing at dawn on a long bamboo reed, but wistful and languid, of a young woman crying. I went in the direction of the sound and saw a woman sitting in a garden house of vines, like the sylph of the vine incarnate. And not even in tales or romances or poems or plays had I ever seen so lovely a woman depicted.

Tenderly I said, "Young lady, tell me why you are so distressed, if there is no harm in telling me."

She whispered—whimpered almost—"But you yourself are the cause of my insufferable grief. . . ."

Embarrassed, I bowed my head. "If I am the cause of your grief," I said softly, "don't cry, my timid girl. Wealth is mine without measure, and I don't care a straw for it. I shall be happy to expend my body on whatever I shall be called to do!"

At this she began to smile, and her eyes filled with tears of joy. "It is your body that I need," she said. "For I am Gangā, Fairy of the Air, daughter of a Yakṣa, and the God of Love has begotten in me a yearning for you. Come into my house, if your promise is true, and your body will be called upon!"

She took hold of my hands and tugged at them temptingly. And I entered her house, which was a prince among houses, as palatial as the seraglio of a Spirit. Inside the house I was met by a fat, gray-haired woman who was light-skinned but creased with wrinkles; she was dressed in a dazzling white robe of sheer silk. The old woman did the honors, kissed me respectfully on the head, and said, "You must be tired from your walk, son. Rest a bit." Thoughtfully she gave an order to her maids: "Sānudāsa is thirsty. Bring sweet lotus mead, quick!" I thought, "Gangā *must* be a fairy: how else could she have lotus mead in the house when mortals find it so hard to obtain?"

I entered an inner apartment which was perfumed with the bouquet of lotus mead mixed with the scents of spring flowers. And after I had drunk the mead in the company of my happy mistress, I sacrificed my body as I had promised. At the same time that I abandoned my body for her sake, she tendered her own in return. "The merit I acquired by surrendering my body for my neighbor's good," I thought, "has been punctiliously rewarded by the gift of a girl's body!"

I stayed long. At last I asked, "My love, what are my friends doing now?"

"If you want to see them, come with me, and see how they have got drunk on a surfeit of mead. If you hold my hand, nobody will be able to see you, and you can watch them without being seen yourself."

So I went with her to the park, and, holding hands with my mistress, I regarded my friends, who averted their grinning faces. Then one of them said with a straight face, "I don't see Sānudāsa. Where could he have gone?"

"But don't you see that unseen miracle?" said another. "Sānudāsa has conquered an unconquerable fairy. Look at him: in the midst of his friends he walks invisible, our virtuous Sānudāsa, because he is holding her hand!"

"But," said I to Gangā, "if I am really invisible, my dear, how can he tell them to see how invisible I am?"

At that the merrymakers were no longer able to contain their mirth, and, like a river in spate, their laughter suddenly overflowed. One of them danced around, keeping time by clapping his hands, and cried, "Hail Thee, Invisible One, Lord of a Fairy! But where is your lotus mead? Where is your unconquerable fairy girl? You have drunk the wine of grapes and conquered a harlot! At last your incurable virtue has been cured by the expert surgery of your friends. Your Worship has now recovered and is free to take Gangā home. And so are your friends free to go—now that their trick has come off!"

Indeed, the trick of the lotus mead had come off quite successfully, but I was not angry with my friends, for now I had become acquainted with wine and with a beautiful girl. "They are wise indeed," I pondered, "who after becoming accustomed to women and wine are able to reject the sweetness of their touch and wander off in quest of salvation. I for one, now that I have acquired the taste, cannot break with them. A curse on my debasement!"

The sun repaired to Sunset Peak, birds retired in swarms to the trees where they nested, the merrymakers, heavy with wine, withdrew to their homes, and I with my mistress to hers.

And there I spent my time serenely with wine, a pleasing mistress, and the pleasantries of Dhruvaka and my other friends. With every ten days that passed, ten thousand pieces passed through my hands. I had a great time, and I spent a great fortune. Then, one day, one of our maidservants called and took me home. My mother told me the news no man should ever hear: my father had died.

While I was mourning his death bitterly, the king summoned me. "My son," he said, "I shall take Mitravarman's place for you. From now on you will have to conduct yourself as a wellborn son. For only such a son can bring a mortal man happiness in the afterworld." Thereupon, after I had been ceremonially anointed, garbed, and adorned, the king bestowed on me my father's position of guild leader and dismissed me.

A short time later Dhruvaka arrived. He looked miserable. "Gangā," he said, "is in a wretched state. Go and console her!"

"No," I said. "My youth, brief as it was, has gone for good. Another age has come now with the misery of carrying the burdens of a household. Proper care for one's family does not agree with a predilection for prostitutes: baby monkeys are not yoked to pull a cart. And Gangā's childhood too has passed away. Let her now follow the path of her mother and grandmother. A courtesan who like a wellborn wife is faithful to one man for a long time is remiss: the righteous don't approve of an outcaste who studies the Veda. Dutiful people should never abandon the duties to which they are born, however criminal they may be: thus spoke Viṣṇu, and let Gangā accept His word."

"Certainly," said Dhruvaka, "householders are forbidden to cultivate courtesans, but they are not forbidden to be civil to a woman in distress. My advice is that as soon as you have consoled her and her mother, you return home at once. Don't be cruel!"

My passion for the girl was rekindled, and, pressed by the insistence of my friend, I was persuaded to go to her house in spite of my misgivings. She had grown thin from our separation and her grief, and only with great difficulty was I able to revive her in the midst of her tearful companions. When she had bathed, we performed together the ceremonies for the dead: we sprinkled a handful of water for my deceased ancestors and put a bowl filled with wine in the courtyard. Then Gangā's mother appeared with a winecup in her hand. "Drink your fill, my son," she said, "and drown your sorrow."

I thought to myself, "The entire situation looks all wrong. Surely she hopes that I am fool enough to be trapped. She is clever with words, but I am not without talent, and this goddess of fortune seems clumsy! This is all very suspicious. But inevitably I shall lose my fortune to Gangā anyway. Birds of a feather nestle together. . . . At the same time, Gangā is an honorable cause for my charity, since one should bestow his gifts where his heart is pleased."

So I thought, and so I decided. And while my heart sipped fear, I sipped the drink, which tasted spicy.

"It does not do to drink only once," said the mother. "Three times is proper." I solemnly agreed. And as my drunkenness mounted, my grief over my father, however severe, subsided. I gave orders to my servants to fetch liquor from the taverns regularly, and both Gangā's servants and mine, seeing that I was cured of my sorrow, sang and laughed, though there were some who wept. And while the women made me forget my mourning, I spent the days in sole pursuit of liquor and love.

Until, one day, a girl was sent by the courtesan's mother. "Your mother-in-law lets you know that you are chafed," she said. "You must massage your body with oil. Gangā's skin also has become rough since she ran out of lotion. She too should rub oil on her body!"

She gave me a towel that was soaked through with oil and rubbed my shoulders with the bracing lotion. Then she said, "I shall now massage my mistress for a while. In the meantime you must go downstairs."

So I went down the stairs from the top storey, and on the next floor I watched the craftsmen who were busy designing and fashioning jewelry. They greeted me nervously with folded hands and said, "You are an expert, O son of a guild leader, and you embarrass us. In the presence of one so skilled in all the sciences and arts and crafts, even the hands of the omniscient tremble and refuse to move. Please proceed to the fifth storey, noble sir, for this jewelry job has to be completed quickly."

In every workshop the same thing happened: the painters on the fifth urged me down to the fourth, and so did the others, with various excuses, urge me onward and downward, until at last the serving girls and the scullery maids threw me out of the compound, shouting, "You have been soaked with cowdung oil!" And from the roof-terrace came the voice of a herald who recited loudly this couplet:

Conquer, O Lion among Kings, the alliance of your rivals!
Already stands the herd of your slanderers chastened:
You are radiant with the splendid halo of virtues
Which shine with the glorious fullness of the moon!

3

"A libertine must have come in, I am sure," I thought, "and now the heralds are singing the praises of that son of a whore. Could the fellow have any virtue at all? He must have devoured even his own modesty, the pimp, if he has his praises sung!" Grumbling, I made my way homeward, hiding my face in shame as the townspeople swore at me. If I ran into a friend, he would merely stare at me and say, "Bah, what do I see?" Whether I passed by the yard of an acquaintance or a stranger, people would pour cowdung water on the street to purify it. Everybody showed his disgust in a similar way. Finally I came to the gate of our house. A man I had never seen before stood guard. I was about to enter, without giving it a thought, by mere force of habit, when the watchman halted me angrily. "Stop, man, stop!"

My natural embarrassment gave way to my anxiety, and I said, "I don't understand this at all, my dear man. Tell me, what is the matter?"

"The matter is that you had better not try again to enter another man's house casually when the watchman is around!"

I grunted. "Is Mitrāvatī dead?"

"Ah, would you be Master Sānudāsa?" he asked. I had spoken rudely, and when he replied in this friendly tone, I was ashamed and kept my tongue.

"Your mother Mitrāvatī is alive, my dear sir," he continued. "But even alive she is dead. She, a mother of a son, now

wishes she had remained childless. One passionate love affair
with the wrong woman, and all the old established merit and
wealth that properly belonged to your family were wasted.
Your mother was left without funds and had to sell her
house. Without a man to protect her, she left for some place
with her grandson and daughter-in-law. Your old carpenter
is working in the first hall. Ask him where Mitrāvatī has
gone."

I went in to see the carpenter, and after a while he recognized me. Then he stammered loudly and sorrowfully: "Oh,
terrible disaster! Your sins have robbed your mother, and
poverty has forced her to seek quarters for herself and her
daughter-in-law in the colony of the poor."

"Where is the colony of the poor?"

"South of the city, close by the pariah settlement."

Slowly I trod along the road to the village of the poor, and
I looked at the dispossessed, wasted by consumption, more
dead than alive. Then, under a common nīm tree, I saw my
little son Dattaka. He was surrounded by a band of children.
He was the king and the others his ministers and subjects,
and he was sharing with them the little balls of half-ripe
barley which he had brought. One of the boys who played
the chamberlain snatched the ball that was reserved for the
king and swallowed it hungrily. Dattaka, robbed of his single
piece, began to scream for his mother. He ran to a little cabin,
the front yard of which was littered with rubbish. A fence of
straw mats ran around the place, but it was rotten and loose,
and the roof let sun and moon in through an infinite number
of holes.

I followed Dattaka to the front yard. A servant girl recognized me and went in to tell Mitrāvatī. My mother came out
in great confusion and embraced me, even in the state I was
in. She held me tight and did not move or even breathe, as
though at last she had found rest in a deep sleep. The poor
woman who had lost her husband and only today had found
her son washed me with her tears which were neither hot nor
cold. Then I saw my wife. She was hiding in a corner of the
hut and—— But why enlarge on the misery of it all? She
was the image of poverty itself.

By rubbing my skin carefully with kodrava grains still in
the husk, my mother removed the stuff which that malicious

wench at the brothel had smeared on me. A water pitcher had
to be borrowed next door to give me a hot bath; it was full
of holes patched with lac, the brim was chipped, the neck
cracked. The servant who was giving me my bath broke this
miserable pitcher in a moment of carelessness, and the woman
who owned it beat her breast and screamed wildly. "Ayi, my
little pitcher, my princess of a pitcher, now you are gone
and the world is empty and my mother dead. Mother got you
as a present from her family when she married, and I cry
over you as my second mother. . . ."

My heart grew weak with compassion for the woman who
was weeping so pitifully; and I cut my cloak in two and gave
her one half. Like elephants who drink the water in which
they have bathed I ate a soup of kodrava seasoned with rice
gruel; but it took effort. Enough! You have heard too much
already about life of the poor, and hearing more can only
upset a man of your sensibilities.

Somehow I got through a night that lasted a hundred thousand years. An inescapable gloom came over me, and when
morning broke, I said to my mother: "I shall return to your
house with four times more than I have wasted—or I shall
never return. You, mother, you must pass your days as if you
had never had a son or as if your son had died, with whatever
distraction your misery and your labor can provide."

"Don't go, my child," she begged. "I shall do the meanest
kind of work to keep you alive and happy with your wife and
son."

"Praised be the life of the talented man who lives on the
wretched labor of his old mother! Stop worrying about me,
mother. Are you not the wife of a man whose mind was as
lofty as the Meru?"

My insistence won out, and I bowed to my mother and departed from that terrible colony of the poor as from the in-
ferno itself. My mother followed me a long way, giving me all
kinds of good advice. "Go to Tāmraliptī, son. My brother
Gangadatta lives there, and when a man is in need, his
mother's people are his only refuge. An intelligent man leaves
his father's relations alone, for they are his born enemies!"

She gave me a bowl full of rice cakes, and with a last word
of advice she turned back. I went on and took the road that
goes east. On the road I saw a company of travelers from

foreign parts. Their umbrellas and sandals were worn, and they carried old leather haversacks and cooking pots slung over the shoulder. They looked exactly as I did; but when they saw me, they said to one another in pitying voices, "Aho, look at the cruel workings of fate! Who would have thought to see the upright Sānudāsa in this state? But why should we pity him? He has not lost his fortune yet: for so long as a man of character has not lost his talents, he has lost nothing!"

To me they said, "We are all your servants, sir! Don't fear that you have to travel alone!" While we were traveling, they entertained me with diverting stories, and a good part of our road was behind me before I felt that I was tried.

When the shade of the world had shrunk away from the spreading glare and the sun had mounted its zenith, I reached a very wide pond. I stole away, bathed at a distance, and ate my meal of kodrava (without butter or salt, but it tasted like nectar). My companions were calling me worriedly with cries that ended on a long high note: "Sānudāsaaa, Sānudāsaaa!" Though they called all the time, they found me only after I had finished bathing and eating.

"Oh, fools that we are to have been so careless!" they exclaimed. "You have tricked us neatly, sir! We made enough food in the pot for every one of us, and now that you have not eaten your share, it must go to waste. But you could still have a little? If you don't, we shall fast!" So I ate a little food as they prayed me and again took to the road with them.

At nightfall we reached a village called Siddhakacchapa. While I was walking on the main street, a householder saw me and bowed. "Come to my house," he said. I consented and with my fellow travelers entered his house. In spite of my protests he insisted on washing my feet himself, and after a bath and a massage with fragrant oils and rest had restored my tired body, he presented to me a turban cloth and a robe made of sturdy washable material dyed with vermilion. When I had eaten a hearty meal of rice porridge and was sitting on a bed with linen coverlets, the householder addressed me.

"I know the whole story, my friend. When the sun is eclipsed, can anyone fail to notice it? Thanks to the favors of your father Mitravarman, whose wealth was as vast as the Meru's or the ocean's, thousands of agents like me have grown rich ourselves. I am a merchant, one of your father's re-

tainers; my name is Siddhārthaka. Therefore all that I have
is yours: let it be the seed from which you will grow new
fortunes! All the branches of the tree serve only the greater
being of the tree itself.

"In a few days," he continued, "a caravan is leaving for
Tāmraliptī, and you shall come with me. Meanwhile you must
rest."

I thought it over and decided that his advice was good. So
I continued my voyage with that caravan and with Siddhārthaka.

On the road I heard a band of fierce-looking vagrant saints
who were boasting to the rollicking clank of all kinds of
weapons: "Hear ye! I am Broken-Shield, and we are shaven
pāśupatas all; and we have sworn with the firmness of mountains to break up any ambush that is laid for us. If I don't
send a thousand brave bandits to heaven in the first skirmish,
may I go to hell myself! If we encounter any robbers, O holy
Goddess, we shall offer you fresh blood of buffaloes and
goats!"

Meanwhile we had come into deep forest, and we halted at
a river in a steep ravine, as the souls of sinners halt at the
terrifying Vaitaranī in the underworld.[3] And then it was as
though the night of doomsday was upon us: black like the
moonless night and without a sound to warn us, a gang of
Pulindas fell on us, irresistibly. With one glance at the robbers the boastful pāśupatas fled, leaving their arms, their
bags, their glory, and their pride. The caravan broke up; I
had nothing to lose but my life, and I fled and ran until I had
lost all sense of direction. I even lost the caravan leader, who
ran away from me, thinking that I was one of the robbers, and
vanished in the jungle.

Toward evening I reached a village in the forest. When I
walked through it, an old woman threw herself at my breast
and started weeping in a voice that croaked with age. "Oh,
my son, you were cruel to go abroad and desert your poor old
mother who had lost all her relations and all her possessions!
The sin that a man incurs who deserts a poor mother like me
is not diminished even if he makes a pilgrimage to Prayāga.
Now you will have to atone for your sinful pilgrimage and
stay at home, propitiating me instead of God!"

[3] The Indian Styx.

"Oh, bother," I thought, "another piece of bad luck. This
is misfortune come to life to visit me! People like me may be
thoughtless, but our ill luck is alert and visits us unceasingly,
just as fortune visits the clever."

Meanwhile the woman was studying me carefully. Then she
said in embarrassment, "Sir, you look so much like my son
that I mistook you for him. Still, you are a son to me!" and
she took me to her house. There she rested me from my
fatigue with a massage, a meal, and other comforts, and
when morning came I said farewell. "Come to Sānudāsa's
house when you are in Campā, mother!"

Resting whenever I was tired and asking my way when
necessary, I finally reached the city of Tāmraliptī, which
surpasses the city of the gods in splendor. Every person whom
I asked for the address, saying, "Please, Your Worship, tell
me where Gangadatta lives," had the same reply: "Brother,
there are smarter people than you in Tāmraliptī. Very provincial to play the buffoon!" Discouraged because nobody
answered my question, I sat down in the market place. A merchant with a gray head asked me, "You look irritated and out
of sorts, sir. What is the matter?" I told him, since he seemed
to take pity on me.

He laughed and said, "The people of Tāmraliptī would
only think that you were trying to be funny. Ordinarily no
one would ask where Gangadatta lives. Only a man who would
not know where to find the full moon would not know where
to find Gangadatta—or he must be a joker. You see that dazzling white mansion where Virtue, Wealth, and Love crown
the roof in full glory? That is Gangadatta's house. Come
along, stupid." He took me to Gangadatta's door, which was
crowded with happy beggars.

When I had introduced myself, word was passed from doorman to doorman until it reached my uncle, who was in his
private apartments. And a loud and low tumult of lamenting
voices burst from the house like the thunder of the Ganges
falling from heaven in the desolation of the Himalayas.
Thereupon my uncle appeared from the house with his wife
and servants and made in the Ganges the funerary oblation
of water for my deceased father.

I spent a while at my uncle's, enjoying the very easy life
with a troubled heart, like nectar with an admixture of poison.

Then one day when I was completely rested from my journey, my uncle said to me: "Nephew, I implore you to do what I am going to ask you. All the immense and unalloyed wealth which you see here had its origin in the wealth of virtue and gold that was Mitravarman's. Consider it your own and, as you have vowed, take four times as much as you lost back to your mother, who is desperate in your absence. When the money is gone, more shall come to you: the Himalayas, source of the Ganges, never run dry. When one has limitless resources at one's disposal, it is disgraceful to start again from the bottom. Would a scholar who knows the Vedas and the sciences start again learning the alphabet?"

Gangadatta went on lecturing me in the same vein, but I said, "I have made up my mind firmly, uncle, and it is a matter of importance. Don't try to dissuade me. A young man's elders should, if need be, even force him to apply himself to his duty; but if he does so by himself, who are they to keep him from doing it? You ask me to let my family live on your money, but that is the wrong thing to tell a man who has both his hands and feet. A man who lives with his mother on the money he gets from his uncle is simply kept alive by his mother and uncle as a weak character."

His conversations with me convinced my uncle that I was a man of character, and he ordered his trusted servants to keep a careful eye on me. But I knew the proverb, Who can guard a man who flies or a man who dies? and I had but one thought —to escape. So when a certain merchant was about to set out on the seas, I went to see him, undetected, and greeted him courteously. I gave him a full description of my superior talents—is there a crime which a man enslaved to the whore of greed shies away from?

"I am the son of Mitravarman of Campā," I said. "I am an expert in a great number of arts, and among other things an expert on precious stones. I want your protection, noble sir, for even a man without a protector is the best protected of men when he is your protégé!"

When the merchant heard the name Mitravarman, he was overjoyed and credited me at once with omniscience, a quality usually hard to prove. "In the old days," he said, "Mitravarman was our protector, but now it will be his son. Let us start, my friend!"

On a promising day which abounded in good omens the merchant paid homage to the gods, the brahmins, and his elders and weighed anchor. The merchant set sail, but were the ocean and the ship more than appearance? It was as though we rode the eternal and infinite skies, blue as Śiva's throat, in a flying machine, encircled by the asterisms of shark and dolphin, on the waves of the clouds.

4

Who would not think of a flying machine? Our craft moved with the speed of thought, and in the blinking of an eye we had done five hundred leagues. Then a whale emerged from the deeps and hit us. The joints burst asunder, and the ship broke to pieces. I repeated in my mind the prayer, "O God in whose locks are the clouds and the rivers . . . ," but luck was with me. I got hold of a plank and was washed ashore.

After a moment's rest I wandered about in a daze on the seashore, without any sense of direction, yelling, "Haa, what has happened?" The coast was cut by lagoons which were lined on all sides by rocks and cliffs and wooded with sandal, camphor, aloe, clove, and lavalī trees. Wild elephants roamed in forests where plantains, coconut palms, and other such trees bore fruit in abundance.

Then somewhere in the opening of a cave under a rock formation I saw a woman. The front of her body was hidden behind the rocks. She looked at me with unblinking, wide open eyes, and the unwavering directness of her glance unnerved me.

"Is it a nymph," I thought, "or a goddess? Never have I seen such beauty in a mortal woman. Or is she a famished ghoul who, seeing me here alone, has put on the shape of a goddess like a jacket? They say that ogresses assume the form of beautiful sylphs to strike at the weaknesses of un-cautious men like me, and that is what has happened. I must get away from this dangerous country!"

With this thought I started, but the same moment she spoke: "Have no fear, my good man. I am not a ghoul. I am just a mortal woman who was marooned when our ship was wrecked."

When I heard this, my consternation increased, and, all

gooseflesh, I invoked Pārvatī and Śiva, the Saviors of the world. "Now I am quite sure," I thought, "she is superhuman. Not only does she not blink her eyes, but she can read a man's mind! If she is really a ghoul, where is there escape for me?"

So I decided to turn back to her. Now *she* was frightened. "If you are in truth a mortal woman," I said, "come out of the cave and show yourself. And if you are a goddess, protect me!"

Shyly she half closed her eyes, in which tears had appeared, and lowered her glance to the front of her body, which was only half concealed by the rocks. Seeing that she really could close her eyes, I thought, "She must be a mortal after all, and, poor girl, she has no clothes!" Keeping my eyes averted, I cut my own robe in two pieces and threw her one piece to cover herself. As far as possible she covered her body with her hair, her arms, and the half of my robe and sat down on a rock, which was favored by the intimacy of her touch.

I did not venture too close, for I was afraid that she might be another man's wife, and I kept my face averted when I asked her, "Good woman, whose wife are you, and who are you?" Having met a mortal in a region where mortals were scarce, her confidence returned, as though she had found a relative in the jungle, and she told her story.

"In the city of Rājagṛha," she began, "where the houses are like the palaces of the king of kings himself, there lived a caravan trader Sāgara who was as great in virtue as he was in wealth. This merchant had a wife from the Greek countries—she was called the Ionian—who worshipped her husband like her god, though she was a very popular woman. They had an elder son Sāgaradinna who emulated his parents in virtues, another son Samudradinna, and a daughter with the same name, Samudradinnā.

"The father promised his daughter to the son of the worshipful Mitravarman, the ornament of Campā. The son's name was Sānudāsa. This Sānudāsa was widely acclaimed as Smara's equal in beauty and as a master of all the arts. Only he was less ingenious than ingenuous: could an ingenious man have acted as he did? All the merit and wealth he possessed was taken by a harlot, and he was killed in a caravan raid by bandits who wouldn't distinguish even a brahmin from a

pariah. When Sāgara received the news of Sānudāsa's unspeakable end, he departed with his family to the Greek countries. The ship foundered, and all perished in the ocean—as
all men will at the end of the world. Only the girl Samudradinnā was too ill-favored, and the sea, cruel as it is, refused
to accept her. This ill-fated girl whom Sāgara had destined
for Sānudāsa and whom the ocean rejected—this girl am I.
I have been here ever since, clinging to my life, and with
worry as my sole diversion: what to do, where to go, what had
happened, what was still in store for me. I fed my useless
body with oysters I found on the shore, cooked with fire that
I took from forest fires, and with the fruits and roots that I
recognized. But greed comes natural to me—I am the daughter of a merchant!—and I have collected mother-of-pearl
from the beach and saved a big pile in a hidden corner. That
is my story. Tell me yours!"

I hesitated to reply, as she must have hesitated to confide
in me. "If I tell her I am Sānudāsa," I thought, "she will
imagine even worse to come from me. But let her imagine!
How can I remain indifferent to her in her misfortune: she is
a woman, and I am a man! Besides, I clearly remember my
father saying that he had chosen her as my bride and that her
father had promised to give her; so it is pointless to hesitate."
So I told her that there lived a merchant called Mitravarman
in Campā who still survives in his fame; his wife was Mitrāvatī, and they had a son Sānudāsa. Since he was their only
son, they gave him a perfect education in all the arts. He
thought he was a genius and disdainfully turned his back on
the everyday world. Friends of his, expert practical jokers,
brought him together with a whore. Then I confessed that I
was Sānudāsa and related how the woman robbed me of
everything and, when she knew I was penniless, arranged to
throw me out.

At this point she interrupted me. "Let me ask you one
question, and please give me the answer: when the slave girl
brought that thick oil-soaked towel to you on the roof-terrace,
what did she say to you?"

"She said: 'I am going to massage the mistress for a while;
meanwhile you must go downstairs.' "

Again she asked, "What did the craftsmen on the sixth
floor, who were working on jewelry settings, say to you?"

"They said, 'You are an expert, and you embarrass us. Please go from this floor to the fifth.' "

She continued asking me every detail until I had told the entire story, ending with the destruction of my caravan. Withdrawn like a turtle, not touching my body, she modestly embraced me with a sidelong glance to which a sheen of love lent grace.

"Timid little girl, what are we to do?" I asked. She stretched her right hand, moist and trembling, out to me. And while the drum of the ocean beat softly, and the bumblebees hummed their sweet songs, and the peacocks danced to the clear beat of their mating calls, I took her hand, pink like an elephant's palate.

5

At once all the misery of the shipwreck was wiped away like the sin of a good man. In my newly found happiness I laughed at the householders and sectarians who worry so much about finding the far-off bliss of heaven and release. We fed ourselves with the invigorating meat of fish, turtles, crabs, and other denizens of the sea and supplemented this diet with coconuts and fruits. Lover and beloved, we strolled like two flamingos along the ocean sands which were covered with pearls and coral, and like young elephants we roamed along the wooded peaks of the mountains with their waterfalls and fruit-bearing forests. We treated our bodies to the rare luxuries that were always at hand—cloves, Areca, camphor, betel leaves, and sandalwood paste. Like hermits we slept in secluded garden houses made of lianas and covered ourselves with bark skirts; and like true mystics of love we meditated on the god who is born in the heart.

One day Samudradinnā said to me, "Darling, you must do what marooned merchants always do: raise a flag by day on the highest tree and light a fire by night from the highest point of the coast. Some day a sailor may sight one of our signals and take us back to our own country, for that is the custom of the merchants." I realized that she was right and did as she told me; for the advice of a reliable person carries authority, even if it be a woman.

At dawn one day a sloop appeared, dancing on the crests of

the waves like a row of seagulls. There were two sailors on
board. I stepped into the sloop and sailed briskly, like a cloud
swept by an eastern breeze, a long way offshore, until I saw
a ship that stood firm on the unsteady seas like a man of
steady character in a crowd of cowards. On board ship I met
a merchant, a man of great wealth who, like Mount Kailāsa
in the Himalayas, was the very pinnacle on which grew the
lotus of fortune.

He studied me searchingly while I greeted him; and with
tears in his eyes and throat he cried excitedly, "I don't have
to ask you, my friend, for your caste or your parents. You
must be Mitravarman's son! How did you get to this
country?"

I told him my adventures in full detail, and he said, "You
are my son as well as my son-in-law, for I regard both
Sāgaradatta of Rājagṛha and Mitravarman of Campā as my
own self! Go ashore in the sloop with a crew of sailors and
bring Sāgaradatta's daughter back with your pearls. Another
point: my expedition was a failure. Don't you see that my ship
is as empty as a dried-up pond? For me it is just an empty
ship to sail home, but for you it holds a fortune. We can join
forces in a most happy way like a man without horses and a
man without a chariot! We shall share the profit equally between us, but you can set the price. That is the custom of
merchants."

We loaded the mother-of-pearl, and it filled the ship.
Samudradinnā bowed to the feet of the merchant, and he gave
her clothes and ornaments by thousands and called her daughter and daughter-in-law. To make a long story short, a gale
overtook our craft, and like the first one it foundered. When
the ship was sinking and my life with it, I despairingly tucked
a number of pearls in my tuft of hair and prayed to them,
"Goddesses, return to your devoted slave in his next life!"
Then, in the middle of it all, I saw my wife appear between
two waves, clinging to a plank. She was floating toward me,
and she called me and stretched out her hand to me, but a
wanton wave carried the powerless woman off. Raging at the
wave, I lost consciousness until I found myself rolling on
the beach. I had lost my love to the bliss of liberation, and,
desolate with grief over our separation, I wandered around
destitute, raving in the emptiness, "Hail thee, blessed lord

Unconsciousness who givest blessed oblivion, and a curse on senseless Consciousness, which is void of all sense of timeliness! And sea! Take the pearls; they are yours. But O kindly lord! surrender my beloved, the constant companion of my misfortunes!"

When I scratched my head, I felt the pearls which I had tucked away in my hair as the ship went under. They made up my entire fortune, and I estimated their value. But what did their value mean when they could not be seen by the experts? Still, while I was looking at them, my misery grew thinner, for verily money is life in hand. I tucked the pearls in the hem of my cloth and tied them securely with a series of knots. My heart took new courage from the comfort of possession, and I started down the coast.

Now I slipped in the mush of rotting bananas; then I quenched my thirst with coconut milk. Here my eyes were held by breadtree and betelnut groves laden with fruit, boughs intertwined with cardamom, pepper, and Areca vines; there I rested from my journey in a campaka bower peopled with long-tailed monkeys that were plucking the blossoms.

After several days of traveling I reached a village; the sun spelled the end of the day, and clouds of dust were thrown up by herds of cattle trotting home. When I asked some of the villagers for a night's shelter, they laughingly said, "*Dhanninum collid!*" Finally a householder who was bilingual took me to his home, and I was treated with kind hospitality like a well-liked son-in-law who had not visited for a long time.

At night when my host was sitting on his bed, I asked him, "What country is this, my good sir, and what is the name of the village?"

"This is the land of the Pāṇḍyas," he said, "which stretches along the southern sea. You are no more likely to find a poor man here than the lotus of fortune itself! From this village it is less than five leagues to Mathurā of the Pāṇḍyas.[4] Rest tonight, and you will be able to reach it tomorrow morning."

When I slept, I was with my love—when I lay awake, with money worries. So I spent the night in stretches either all too short or all too long.

The next morning, after a few miles' walk, I came to a

[4] The present-day Madura.

banana-tree grove where I saw a resthouse crowded with travelers. I saw foreigners there who were being shaved, massaged with oil and unguents, and clothed and fed with great hospitality; and I too was shaved and offered clothes and an excellent noon meal. I stayed the day. At night when I had retired to bed, the manager of the resthouse came to me and asked, "Have you seen anywhere a young, intelligent-looking merchant by the name of Sānudāsa? He is tall and swarthy, with copper-brown eyes."

"What about this Sānudāsa?" I asked. "What family is this Sānudāsa from?"

"Gangadatta's family. Gangadatta is the ornament of Tāmraliptī, and Sānudāsa, a talented boy who went to sea, is his nephew. His ship was wrecked in a gale on the high seas, like a rain-filled cloud torn apart in the sky. The news reached Gangadatta by circuitous routes like a poisonous snake seeking out its prey, and it crushed him. He has alerted all traveler's inns in all countries, in forests, at river fords, and in coast towns, hoping that some time a traveler somewhere may bring news to an inn that Sānudāsa has escaped alive from the wreck. If you happen to have seen the young man—a long life to him, and to you, sir!—please tell me so that his anxious relatives may breathe again."

I thought, "How far have I made good my promises so that I can show myself to my uncle unashamed? Therefore I must tell this," I decided and said, "Sānudāsa has boarded another ship and set out again."

The next morning I reached Mathurā of the Pāṇḍyas, a city of a hundred wonders, where every wish has come true as though the place possessed the stone of wishes. I installed myself in the bazaar where many-hued gems, like the ocean swallowed by Agastya,[5] wove a brilliant net of rays.

Two men, a seller and a buyer, approached with a piece of jewelry. They said to a jeweler: "You are an expert. Can you tell us the right price for this jewel?" The jeweler studied it for a long time and said finally, "No, I can't tell you."

I had given the jewel a hard look, and the two men said, "You have been looking at this piece with a close and interested eye. We think you know its value."

[5] A great legendary sage; he drank up the ocean to help the gods in their war with the anti-gods who had gone under water.

I opened my hands in a careless gesture and said, smiling, "It is not so difficult to tell. No reason for you to be worried. All expert jewelers know that a jewel like that is worth a million, more or less, depending on who buys it or sells it." The seller wept for joy. "If it is worth that much, I am a millionaire! I have always dreamed, 'Suppose it were worth a million,' and here is my dream come true!"

The buyer said, "I have my dreams too. I want to buy it for a million!"

They were full of praise for me: "Hail God of artisans! You must be a god, for what mortal man could know the inscrutable? One of us wanted to sell and the other to buy, and many a time we have gone around the town to get an estimate of the jewel's value. Somebody said, 'It is worth the world.' Another ignoramus thought, 'A farthing.' Still another estimated, 'Nothing at all!' The price you have set for it has made us both very happy; it was precisely what we had in mind." So they went on, ecstatically. They gave me ten thousand pieces of gold and costly ornaments and robes.

The matter reached the ears of the king. He sent for me courteously and told me to evaluate those precious stones in his treasury on which his experts would not commit themselves. He was quite pleased and gave me a mansion of many rooms with a large staff, valuable furnishings, and beautiful gardens.

After that I was established in the city as an expert on precious stones; and nobody asked me to do an expertise for charity! While I was living in these happy circumstances, I started wondering what merchandise could be had cheaply and yield a large profit. To judge by the talk of the town, cotton was an excellent investment. So I acquired a stock of cotton, seven piles of snowclad Himalayas. A curse on the story of the cotton—there is no sequel to it. A burglar broke into the warehouse and set my seven piles afire; only ashes were left. There is a law in Mathurā that a man whose house catches fire is thrown into the fire with his family, screaming. So I fled with nothing but my hands, and completely at a loss, without any sense of direction, I decided, "That is the way," and headed north. I did not stop running for the rest of the night and half the next day, until I was out of danger; and exhausted I fell asleep under a vaṭa tree.

The moon was shining when I woke up rested from the deadly fatigue, and I heard the loud noise of people talking close by. "Disaster!" I thought. "Now I am really lost. I'll be thrown in a blazing fire by the merciless Dravidians!" Then I saw that they looked like travelers, with patched clothes, worn umbrellas, and sandals and such, and the language they were speaking was Gauḍa.[6] "Oh, mother, I am safe!" Seeing them I breathed again. What man would not welcome men after escaping from demons?

The men set down their bags and made beds of leaves on the ground. They sat down around me and asked as they rested, "What country do you come from, sir, and from what city?"

"From the land of the Pāṇḍyas," I said.

Eagerly they asked, "Have you seen Master Sānudāsa, the merchant, in Mathurā? Tell us!"

"There is no merchant of that name in Mathurā," I said. "What do you want of him?"

They told me. "In Tāmraliptī lives a great merchant, Gangadatta, whose virtues even you cannot help knowing, sir. The man has not been born, unless he be already dead, who does not know Gangadatta's virtues. His fame has spread all over the world to the islands and to the farthest seas. Sānudāsa is his sister's son. He was marooned when his ship foundered, and he established himself in the cotton business in Mathurā of the Pāṇḍyas.

"When Gangadatta received reports of Sānudāsa from travelers, he called his friends and devoted servants and told them, 'Those of my friends who bring my kinsman from the South will be rewarded with treasure to their full satisfaction!' So Gangadatta sent us off to fetch his nephew, and if you have seen him, please tell us, sir!"

I thought, "I'd rather be thrown in the fire! I can't show my face to my mother before I have made good my promises." So I told him, "Poor Sānudāsa, the pitiless Pāṇḍyas threw him in the fire when his cotton caught fire."

They beat their breasts and wailed loudly for a long time. Then their speakers advised them, in voices thin with despair, "You have been implored by Gangadatta to bring Sānudāsa back. How will you be able to bring back tidings of his death? When they hear the news in Campā and Tāmraliptī, news

[6] The old language of Bengal.

ghastly like the mocking laugh of death, nobody will live.
Let us acquit ourselves of our debt to our master and give up
our lives. Gangadatta must hear the news from somebody
else." They set fire to a pile of logs, and, ready to enter the
fire, they made a ritual circumambulation around the pyre,
singing litanies to the gods.

"Aho!" I thought, "they have caught you, lamb! The wretches
have set up the net, and whatever you try, you can't get out
of it." Aloud I shouted, "Whoa! Stop this violence! I am
Sānudāsa, and I am at your disposal!"

Their spirits, which had been about to depart in despair,
were revived by the joy of finding me and returned to their
throats. Life was not over for them yet, and, again in possession of their spirits, they danced madly around, and the
wilderness shook with the beat of their clapping. Joyfully
they sang my praises, went in procession around me, like
Buddhists around Buddha, and saluted me with their heads.
They seated me in a palanquin, and, happy as if they had
found a treasure, conducted me in short stretches to Tāmraliptī.

It was as though the son of a king had come to be married.
In his joy my uncle himself came out to meet me in great
splendor. Even Vyāsa would not have been able to do justice
to the celebrations that followed.[7] I can only summarize it
—speech fails me. Not only did my arrival bring out matrons
of impeccable character on whom neither sun nor moon nor
wind had ever set eyes; even the naked Jains, poor dancers
at best, came out covered with vermilion paint to sing and
dance on the highways.

6

Through the brahmins, who deployed all their knowledge,
and by himself too, Gangadatta gave me a lecture which was
both sympathetic and to the point. It went as follows: "There
was a time when you could ignore your duties; for as long
as your father lived, and looked after his dependents, you
could argue, there was no reason for you to take any responsibility or exert yourself at all. But now you have obligations
—to your mother, your wife, your child, and your elders, who
simply must be supported and protected. You are the family's

[7] The Indian Homer.

provider, and when the provider is gone—I surely don't need to tell you that—they are like riderless horses. Therefore return home. Your family is anxious to see you again, my dear boy, terribly anxious, and you must relieve their anxiety."

One day I met a merchant by the name of Acera who was going to the Gold Countries with a large company of traders. I embarked with him on his ship, and when we had completed part of our journey on sea, we landed, beached our ship, and continued on land down the coast.

When the sun reddened at dusk, we halted in wooded country at the foot of a majestic mountain whose peak pierced the clouds. That night, after we had finished eating and were sitting on our beds of leaves, the caravan leader gave us instructions.

"Merchants, when we are climbing the mountain, tie your rucksacks with provisions tightly to your backs with three windings of rope and hang your leather oil-flasks around your necks. While climbing, use a flexible and sturdy cane stick, not too dry or brittle, and hold it firmly with both your hands. Any fool who uses any other kind of stick is bound to get killed on the mountain. They call this the Cane Trail. It is like the great Lord of Obstacles, and it seeks to frustrate all the efforts of those who are driven by the prospects of gold."

He sounded discouraging; but, devoured by our cupidity, we did as he told us. When one of our party had already climbed a good part of the way, the end of his cane broke; and, like a warrior whose bowstring is cut by a blade, he tumbled and fell to the valley. All the others in our party made it to the summit. We mourned our companion's death and made him a water oblation. We passed the night on the peak.

The next morning we traveled a long way until we found a river full of large rocks that were shaped like cows, horses, goats, and sheep. Acera, at the head of our column, stopped us from going any farther.

"Don't touch the water, don't! Hey, there, stop at once, stop! Any fool who touches this water is changed into stone. Can't you see for yourselves, friends? Now look at the bamboo trees across the river. There is a sharp wind blowing this way which bends the trees all the way across to this bank. Get a firm grip on one of these bamboos with both your hands, but it should not be too brittle, soft, rotten, or dry. When the wind dies down, the bamboos will straighten themselves and swing you, if you are careful enough, to the other bank. But if anybody holds onto the wrong kind of bamboo, he'll fall in the river and be turned into stone. This is the Bamboo Trail, and it is terrifying like the Last Trail itself. But with some agility and luck any one with courage can jump it."

Like the fool who entered the demon's cave at the sorcerer's bidding, we did what he wanted. One of us had got hold of a thin bamboo; it broke and he fell; and, abandoning his petrified body, he went to God's heaven. We climbed down our bamboos and left the river far behind. We made an oblation of water for his soul at another river where we camped.

The next morning when we had covered about five leagues, I saw in front of me an extremely narrow ledge which snaked along the side of a horrifying abyss. The bottom receded from sight in an intense darkness which even the sun was afraid to penetrate. Acera instructed the travelers.

"We must make a smoking fire with damp wood, leaves, and straw. The highlanders will come out when they see the smoke, to sell us their mountain goats which are covered with tiger skins. You have got to buy them, giving saffron, indigo, or śakala-dyed clothes or even sugar, rice, vermilion, salt, or oils in exchange. Mount the goats and carry bamboo poles with you, then ride on to the circuitous ledge, death's crooked eyebrow. . . .

"Now it is possible that on the ledge there will be another party of travelers returning with gold from the gold mines, and we may come face to face with each other halfway. And that means we die in the ravine with our gold or our hopes. The ledge is too narrow for a goat train to pass or to turn. Therefore we need a powerful man who is used to handling a spear and has a butcher's experience to ride at the head of our train. One man like that can kill off an entire row of enemies as long as he is not himself slain by the enemies. This terrible road is known as the Goat Trail. Those who don't mind the fall are sure to meet Bhṛgu!"

Acera was interrupted by the arrival of a band of tribesmen, armed with tall bows, who drove a troop of goats ahead of them. When the buying and selling was done, they departed. The travelers bathed and prayed in loud voices to Śiva and Kṛṣṇa. Thereupon the long train of goats carrying the travelers started along, moving fast enough, yet precisely balanced like a becalmed ship on the high seas. I was the seventh from the rear, and Acera, immediately behind me, the sixth. As we were riding on, we heard in the distance ahead of us the loud clatter of bamboos striking against one another—zing zing!— and the cries of men and beasts—meh meh! and aah aah!— as they fell into the abyss of darkness and mud, terrifying even to a brave man's heart.

A moment later the ranks of the enemy were annihilated save for one man, and in our own ranks the seventh from the rear had suddenly become the first. Our leader prodded me: "Come on, what are you waiting for? There is only one enemy left. Send him to heaven!"

The man opposite me threw his bamboo stick away, folded his hands at his forehead, and, now that his entire caravan had been destroyed and he was left unprotected, sought my protection. "My family is perishing," he cried, "and I am the only one left to continue it. Don't destroy it completely by cutting down the last branch! My parents are blind, and I, their only son, their only love, am the stick to guide them. Brother, don't kill me!"

I thought, "Damn the life that is smeared with the filth of sin, thrice damn the gold that must be won by killing the living. Let the wretch kill me. He clings to his life, and his life means sight to the dead eyes of his parents."

Red with rage and pale with despair Acera sneered at me between clenched teeth in a harsh and hissing voice. "Ayi! stupid ass, have you no sense of time? This is not the time to use pity, but to use a sword. Bah, you and your theories: we know all about your pity in practice! Are you going to sacrifice sixteen for the sake of one scoundrel? Kill him and his goat, and at least fourteen lives are saved. If you don't, he and you and the goats and all of us will perish. A man's life is sacred and should not be sacrificed to save one scoundrel! 'One must always protect one's self, with one's wife as well as one's wealth,' " and so on and so forth. He read me a sermon as long as the Bhagavadgītā, prompting me to an act of cruelty as Viṣṇu prompted Arjuna. Deeply ashamed, blaming myself for the cruelty of my deed, I struck my enemy's goat very lightly on the legs. And as the animal sank like a ship in the ocean of darkness, the traveler who sailed it drowned with his cupidity. We came away from the perilous road like the survivors from the Bhārata wars: our thin ranks annihilated, seven saved their souls but lost their hearts.[8]

We continued our journey through the country until we reached a Ganges. There we offered a handful of water, mixed with our tears, to our dead. Soon our grief, bitter though it was, gave way to our appetite; for man knows no pain like the pain of hunger. We prepared our meal and lay down on a bed of leaves.

When the leader woke us up, our eyes were still heavy from too little sleep. "These goats," he said, "have to be killed. We shall eat the meat; the skins we turn inside out and sew up to form sacks. Then we wrap ourselves in these sacks—no room for squeamishness here, it will only delay us!—in such a way that the bloody inside is turned outside. There are birds here as large as the winged mountains of legend, with beaks wide as caverns. They come here from the Gold Country. They will mistake us for lumps of meat and carry us in their beaks through the sky all the way to the Gold Country. That is what we must do."

I said, "It is true what people say, 'Throw this gold away that cuts your ears!' How could I be so cruel as to kill my goat, this good spirit that has saved me from peril as virtue saves a man from hell? I am done with money and done with living if I have to kill my best friend to save the life he gave me."

Acera said to the travelers, "Everyone kill his own goat. And take Sānudāsa's goat out of the way." One of the traders took my goat somewhere and came back with a goatskin hanging from his stick.

"I swapped Sānudāsa's goat for another," he said. "Look, I have its skin here." But I recognized it: it was the skin of my own goat. "You did not take it out of the way," I cried, "you *put* it out of the way!"

Thereupon, taking our leader's word for it, we prepared ourselves for a voyage through the sky, which is more terrible than a voyage by sea because there is no way of escape. Soon all the heavens were filled with huge gray birds thundering ominously like autumn clouds. Under the wind of their

---

[8] The conflict described in the *Mahābhārata*, of which the *Bhagavadgītā* is a part.

wings the heavy tree trunks on the mountain were crushed
to the ground as though they were the mountain's wings being
cut by the blades of Indra's arrows. Seven birds swooped down
and carried the seven of us, each with his heart in his throat,
to the sky. One bird was left without its share, and, cheated
out of its expectations, it started to tear me violently away
from the bird that had got me. This started a gruesome fight
between the two vultures, each greedy for its own share, which,
like the battle of Jaṭāyus and Rāvaṇa, terrified all the inhabitants of heaven. I was torn between the two birds, passing
from beak to beak and sometimes rolling over the ground. I
prayed to Siva. Their pointed beaks and claws, hard as diamond points, ripped the skin until it was worn like a sieve.
I was dragged from the torn skin bag and tumbled into a
pond of astonishing beauty.

I rubbed my bloodsmeared body with lotuses and bathed.
Next I made a thanksgiving offering to the gods and the
fathers, and only then tasted the nectar of the pond. I sank
down on the shore and lay until I was rested. My eyes wandered over the woods that had been the scene of prodigious
adventures and forgot the anxieties of the battle between the
giant birds, forgot them like a man who has escaped from the
Hell of the Swordblades to stroll in Paradise. There was not
a tree with a withered or faded leaf; not one was burned
by lightning and brushfire or empty of bloom and fruit. The
blossoms of cadamba, malatī and kunda jasmine, and spring
creepers were thickly dotted by armies of bees. The ground was
covered with a carpet of grass four fingers high, blue-green
like Śiva's throat, and as soft as rabbit fur. Lions, tigers,
peacocks, snakes, and all kinds of game lived peaceably like
hermits on nothing but leaves, flowers, water, and wind. My
eyes did not tire of looking as I roamed in the woods.

Then I discovered a faint track, a path made by some man's
footsteps. Slowly I followed the track, which led me far into
the woods to a river with low banks and shallow bed; both
bottom and banks were covered with precious stones and gold-
dust. I crossed the stream, bathed, and paid homage to the
gods and my elders.

Near the riverbank I saw a hermitage surrounded by banana
trees where monkeys were crouching quietly. And within the
hermitage I saw a great hermit with a matted tuft of hair,

golden like a flash of lightning, who was sitting on a sheaf of
dwarf kuśa grass like the image of the sacrificial fire resting
in the womb of a pit, its base and kindling sprinkled with
butter oblations.

7

When I approached to greet him, he was like a rising moon
of graciousness, like a winter sun without summer glare. His
cheeks were moist with tears of joy as he spoke to me: "A
blessing to merchant Sānudāsa!"

I thought, "Then it is true that hermits have second sight,
for he sees what is hidden to the eyes of the flesh. My name,
which could have been anything, and the vocation that governs
my action—he has named them before he was told."

While I was thinking, he directed me to a grass cushion,
and I sat down slowly for I was embarrassed. But the recluse
smiled and said, "It is as you think, my boy. But the mere
mention of a name is none too miraculous a feat of austerity.
I know everything about you: how Dhruvaka and his friends
inveigled you into drinking spirits, how you met the harlot
Gangā in the park, and from there on until your escape
from the battle of the birds, the very mouth of death, and
your arrival here.

"Yes, you have seen ships wrecked and you have explored
inaccessible mountains, forests, and rivers. Why have you
toiled so tirelessly? Ah, your mother Mitrāvatī will tell you
that. You expended all that effort just to find gold. It is
within your reach now; don't despair any longer, for where
can the gold go? It is easy to find for people with energy and
intelligence, for a man of character like you who listens to
the counsel of one like me. Stay in my hermitage for a few
days; you will sleep in a hut of leaves and eat the fruits of
trees."

So I ate forest fare, nutritious, invigorating, and purifying;
and it tasted so good that I lost all taste for grown vegetables.
And as I slept on the bed of leaves I had made in a hut of
foliage, I learned to hate Gangadatta's house with its high-
legged couches. Yet, although these simple joys which are
outside a common man's experience made me oblivious of my
sorrows, I never forgot that my mother was living in a slum.

The misfortunes I had suffered so far till my abortive journey
through the sky I now regarded as blessings; for misfortune
that leads to the discovery of gold is fortune indeed!

One day I saw a celestial chariot arrive from heaven, splendid like Mount Meru; it had come for the sage, the incarnation of his merit. Heavenly maidens alighted, illuminating the
forest with their radiance, as flashes of lightning alight from
a beloved rainbow-hued cloud. They bowed before the prince
of hermits, made a circumambulation to honor him, and returned to heaven like the rays of the moon.

One girl had remained behind. The hermit raised her to
his breast, and with his eyes streaming and his voice stammering for joy, he said, "Gandharvadattā my daughter, you
must forget me and devote yourself to your father Sānudāsa!"

I thought that her meticulous attentiveness was merely
mockery, and I felt like a humble attendant of Śiva's whom
the great White Goddess is amused to greet respectfully. One
day I asked her, "Who is he? And who are you?"

"Listen," she said and told their history. "The sage, who
is the sitting stone of all hermits, is of the clan of Bharadvāja.
He is Bharadvāja of the Aerial Spirits whose science he has
sought to acquire. So powerful were his mortifications that
Indra himself was perturbed and worried lest he be thrown
off his mountain throne. Even as he lay in the arms of his
wife, Indra could not help thinking that there was a hermit
somewhere. When Nārada, the messenger of the gods, reported that this hermit was Bharadvāja, Viṣṇu summoned
Suprabhā, the daughter of the king of Gandharvas, the
celestial musicians.

" 'It is common knowledge in all the worlds,' Viṣṇu said,
'that you surpass even Urvaśī, however vain she may be of
her youth, her beauty, and her charms. Therefore, my lovely
girl, go to Bharadvāja and attend to him so that your beauty
and charm be suitably rewarded.'

"Suprabhā tried her best to seduce the saint with all the
stratagems of love, with words, glances, and meaningful
gestures, but the saint's mind remained fixed on truth. When
she failed, even though she spent years, she was so discouraged
that she became his handmaiden. She did all the chores so
well, plucking flowers, fetching water, sweeping the cell, that
the sage was pleased and asked her to choose a boon.

" 'Sir,' she said, 'your imperturbability has made a mockery
of charms for which the wives of all thirty-three gods envy
me. Beauty, ornaments, garlands, and ointments are valueless
to women unless their value can be measured by their power
to arouse the passions of their men. Therefore I pray you, if
you are pleased to grant me a boon, then may you, the greatest
man in the world, be a man to me! If a young girl's heart is
smitten with love, what greater boon is there than a husband
who charms her eyes and heart? Please, although you hate passion, submit to your mercy and love me so that you may restore my charm to me!'

"He was agreeable and gave her one daughter; for even a
contrary man will be won in the end by devotion. Suprabhā
took the girl to the house of her father Viśvavasu, and she
reared her there and educated her in the arts and sciences.
Then the king of the Gandharvas took his granddaughter to
Bharadvāja and asked him to give her a name. The name
the sage gave her was full of meaning. 'Let her be Gandharvadattā,' he said, 'the Gift of the Gandharva, for you have
given her to me.'

"So a girl was born to Bharadvāja and Suprabhā and given
the name Gandharvadattā. And I am this girl," she concluded.

One dark night I happened to notice that the trees on a
rocky hillock were aglow with a golden light. I thought,
"This hill must be pure gold ore. That is a piece of luck to
find gold here! It will bring me luck." What sense I had was
caught in the noose of greed, and I completely filled one
large hut with rocks. When Gandharvadattā the next morning saw the rocks, she asked me what they were, and I told
her. She told her father, and he called me.

"This is not gold ore, my boy," he said, "just rock. That
golden glow you saw in the darkness comes from the herbs.
Sunlight obscures it, but at night it spreads freely. You see
nothing but gold, even in rocks: thus a man with a jaundiced
eye sees the whole world yellow. At the right time I myself
shall arrange for your gold and your return to Campā. It will
be soon now. Now free yourself of your confusions!"

It took me a whole day of increasing misery to throw out
the rocks which had taken an hour of increasing contentment
to bring in.

Then one day the hermit handed me a lute made of tortoise

shell and said, "Hear what I am going to say and do as I
tell you. The story which Gandharvadattā has told you about
me is true; she is indeed my daughter. She is the future bride
of the future emperor of Aerial Spirits: the goddess that rose
from the ocean could never be any but Viṣṇu's bride. You
must take Gandharvadattā to Campā and give her to the emperor. I shall tell you how you can recognize him, and you
must plant the signs firmly in your memory. Every six months
you will assemble all the Gandharvas, and when they are assembled, Gandharvadattā will chant for them the 'Hymn to
Nārāyaṇa.' If one of the Gandharvas is able to accompany
her song on the lute and to chant it himself, you must give
him my daughter."

(*"Sire, he predicted exactly what you yourself would do
at the meeting of the Gandharvas, everything, including your
chanting the hymn and accompanying her on your lute!"*)

The sage continued. "Children, you have been bored for
a long time now. To relieve your boredom, start for Campā."

I threw myself at his feet; and my happiness made me so
nervous that the whole long night had passed before I fell
asleep.

When I woke up, I heard the divine music of two wooden
vīṇās and a flute, enchanting to ear and heart, and, interrupted
by the crowing of cocks, the loud benedictions and greetings
of heralds which at once dispelled my sleep. Wide awake now,
I found myself in a palaquin framed in gold and aglitter with
precious stones. It stood on a shining clean stone floor in the
center of a pavilion that was thatched with colorful silks which
were supported by polished golden tentpoles. Gandharvadattā
was sitting in the lap of a blue crystal bench under an awning
to bar the sun, and she was playing her vīṇā with great concentration. My pavilion was surrounded by a host of smaller
tents in flamboyant colors, and their beautifully dressed pro-
prietors happily moved between the sacks of gold that filled
their tents. Merchants were busily buying and selling such
costly wares as gold and jewelry, and all around the encampment crowded herds of camels and bullocks. But how could
a dumb man describe the spectacle? Impossible! No man has
ever seen such wealth in all his dreams.

I asked Gandharvadattā, "What is this miracle? Is it
fantasy, is it magic, is it a dream?"

"These are the fruits of Bharadvāja's austerities," she said, "which have become a very Tree of Wishes. For if rightly observed the mortifications of the just have a power that is beyond the imagination. You can spend as you wish, for your wealth has no limit. Spend it on anybody, worthy or worthless, but don't bury it in the ground. Don't worry how to gain; worry how to spend! You can draw forever on Bharadvāja's mountain of gold. And don't worry any more about when you will see your mother. Campā is only ten miles from this caravan camp." She was like wisdom whose soul is Certainty, and as she spoke, all my doubts about magic or dream dissolved instantly.

Then I saw Dhruvaka, the scoundrel. He did not dare to look me in the face, and he hung his head; and so did his friends around him. Getting up from my bed, I hugged him affectionately and gave him my own chair; his embarrassment vanished at once. Grandly he favored his friends with a gracious word or two, an embrace, and a seat, strictly according to seniority.

Soon after, all Campā's people came out dancing behind their dancers and surrounded the caravan. They were uproariously happy, so happy indeed that several of them lost their breath—one found it back in the end, but another died. I showered presents on the crowd: delicacies of food and drink, jewels, robes, garlands, perfumes, and liberal quantities of gold. And especially did I rescue from the hell of poverty those who had had to clean their streets with cowdung when I passed by on my way back from the brothel.

At last I said to Dhruvaka, "Friend, get my mother out of that ghastly slum and bring her to her own house. Give the owner a hundred times as much as he paid when he bought it from my mother. Perish the life of a man who can see his wealthy mother in a poor man's quarters and live!"

Dhruvaka smiled. "Madame poor? Who has seen the Ganges run dry? The house is her own and her wealth as solid as ever. But now that you have returned, she will bloom like a lotus pond in the moonlight."

Day and night passed like an instant, and early the next morning I rode into Campā, as Kubera into Alakā.[9] Preceded by a parade of all the different guilds, I went along the high-

[9] The residence of the god of wealth.

ways and avenues to call upon our glorious king. I prostrated myself before him at a respectful distance, but the king addressed me joyfully and embraced me without dissimulation. When he had honored me with costly gems and robes without end, he said, "Son, now go and see your mother." I filled the insatiable hellhole of royal cupidity with a mass of gold and precious stones that was worth Mount Meru and, surrounded by the king's boon companions and chanting brahmins, returned to my old house. It is a wonder I was not trampled by the townspeople who with the energy that only rapture can arouse danced wildly in the streets to the soft beat of drums. But when they saw my mother from a distance, carrying in her hand the little bowl with the water of hospitality, the crowd shrank away in confusion. For the masses of commoners are unnerved by the sight of a lady and disperse as darkness disperses before the full moon.

8

When I reached the door, I touched my mother's feet with my head, and she threw herself on me, water bowl and all. At last she breathed again, and she made me rise and took me by the hand into the house. I distributed large gifts to the gods, the brahmins, my teachers, destitute beggars, and of course my servants. After a while when I had seen to things and had finished my meal, mother bade me enter a very beautiful chamber.

I sat down on a couch and looked upon my first wife; she was sitting on the floor and hid her face in her arms. I wiped my eyes which had filled with tears of compassion; and when I looked up, I saw Gaṅgā the harlot clinging to a wall, her face averted. I did not honor her even with a word, if the truth must be told; for even the more venerable hermits cannot forget the humiliations they have suffered.

As I regarded this room, its floor carpeted with flowers, I thought of the little cottage of blossoming lianas on the seashore where I had lived so happily with Samudradinnā, staying home or going about or singing and dancing, in joyous intimacy. "It is better to suffer bitterly than to turn my heart away because my dearest has gone. . . . But she always knew how to find my weaknesses, and now she has found my heart empty of sorrow and entered it, pitiless and irresistible. Yes, she entered my heart as though it were her chamber—but let her, for my love is hopeless. The very moment she cried out to me, 'Save me!' the cruel sea stretched his hand and a wave dragged her away. . . ."

These gloomy thoughts made me ill with grief, but suddenly there she was, entering the room, overcoming her modesty, and rushing at me to embrace my body that thrilled to hers. But even as I saw her, and never was a reunion more unexpected, I could think only of her floating on the crests of the ocean waves; and oblivious of all that had happened since, so total was my absorption, I shouted encouragingly, "Don't be afraid, darling!"

Now she did look frightened. "But you are home now," she said. "You are no longer adrift in the sea!" My mind came back from the terrors of the sea to the present; and I looked at the house around me, and I looked upon my two wives. Recalling the etiquette that governs a man's conduct in the presence of co-wives, I refrained from returning Samudradinnā's embraces. In this situation, which was somewhat delicate with two wives present, my mother walked in without warning, an apprehensive look in her eyes. I seated her with Samudradinnā on a bench, and the others sat on the floor, while I remained on my feet with a trace of confusion.

To tell the truth, I was a little irritated with my mother. Even a mother can be insulting to her son if she is tactless. My mother smiled at me.

"Don't think I am tactless," she said. "Remember, I am the wife of Mitravarman, who knew almost everything. If I had not walked in on you and your wives, a matter of grave importance would have been endangered. Let me have your attention.

"You were born, son, to your father and me after hundreds of prayers. Your father brought you up and educated you in the four sciences, but you followed the scriptures of the Mendicants, Buddhists, and Jains with such devotion that people began to cast aspersions on your life as a family man. We consulted with the king and his ministers as well as with our religious counselors, and in collusion with us Dhruvaka and his friends enticed you, made you drink spirits, and brought you together with Gaṅgā. Your yourself know best what she

did with you. The trick she played on you to throw you out
and bring you home was planned by the king himself, who
told Gaṅgā's mother. And that village of the poor where you
spent one day and one night was set up by the king and his
courtiers for this single occasion. You know full well that
there is no poverty in all of Campā. Has anybody ever seen
the full-moon night soiled with darkness? For as long as our
puissant ruler reigns, generosity reigns. That same night
when you were sleeping with us in that horrible place, Gaṅgā
was sleeping at the foot of my cot. Ever since that terrible
night, until last night in fact, she has been sleeping on the
floor at the foot of my bed. All the money you had given her
she returned to your coffers, and everything is accounted for.
The girl was in love with you and hoped to see you again. If
she humiliated you, it was only appearance; don't let your
resentment induce you to humble her! She is a sensitive girl,
and had you humiliated her in the presence of your wives because she was a prostitute, she would have taken her life.
That was the matter I had on my mind when I burst in on
you. What does tact matter when you have a duty to do and
important matters are at stake?

"That is the story of Gaṅgā. Now listen how Samudradinnā came here. The travelers whom you joined as you came
out of the slum were sent by the king, and so was merchant
Siddhārthaka at the village of Siddhakacchapa. It was Siddhārthaka who kept us abreast of the terrible happenings when
your caravan was raided and of the rest of your journey until
you reached Tāmraliptī. The adventures that followed, how
after the shipwreck you were marooned and wandered along
the seacoast, how you took Samudradinnā's hand and, after
a second shipwreck, came to the city of the Pāṇḍyas, the fire
in your cotton, and your return to Tāmraliptī—all these adventures were reported to us by merchant Gaṅgadatta, who
kept messengers going.

"That was before Acera took you along with him. I have
had no news from you since then. I did not know what had
become of you, and I was so senseless with despair that I
hoped for my death.

"Thus matters stood when the doorman announced visitors,
and Samudradinnā entered with her two brothers. I welcomed
them and extended the hospitality of our house, and after a

brief rest the men addressed me, but they avoided looking at me.

" 'Our father,' they said 'had promised this girl to your son, but your son with the foolishness of the young let himself be possessed by Gangā; and when she had dispossessed him of all he owned, he departed to see his uncle in Tāmraliptī. We dare not tell you what fate he met at the hands of the Pulindas, but when our family heard of the unspeakable end of Mitravarman's son, we lost all hope and left the city of Rājagṛha for the Greek countries. After worshipping gods and brahmins we boarded a ship and sailed out to the high seas where disasters and wrecks are to be expected. And, indeed, our fast sailing craft was overtaken by a fierce hurricane, as a lion overtakes an elephant, and broken to pieces. But fate is stronger than death; riding the swift arrows of the waves on drifting planks, we were thrown on the beach. Only your daughter-in-law was lost among the capricious waves of the ocean, like the crane that wanders off into the cloud-swept skies. We abandoned all hope of regaining Samudradinnā or of recouping our fortunes and continued our tearful journey to the Greek countries where my mother's father lives. And like a swarm of swans that finally reach the pond they have long been looking for, our family found the comforts of luxury to which they had hopefully traveled from far away.

" 'Some time passed. Then one day father said to the two of us, "How can you sit idle here like two old men? You are both young, able-bodied and healthy, and capable in the skills of your profession. Do you then allow people to say that you are living on your parents? Take a capital of pearls, coral, and other products of the sea and cross the ocean!"'

" 'We promised to do so, and so we did. While we were at sea, we sighted a woman floating on a plank, and she was shouting. We ordered our sailors to take her aboard in a sloop but not to touch her with their hands since she might be another man's wife. When she was on board our ship, we questioned her in a low voice, without looking her in the face, for she might have been a married woman.

" ' "Mother, whose wife are you?" we asked. "Who are you?"

" ' "I recognize your voices. I know them so well!" she cried. "You are the sons of Sāgaradatta!"

" 'We recognized her voice too. "Could you be Samudradinnā?" we asked, facing her. With a loud cry she threw herself at our feet and embraced our legs with both her arms, the right leg of one of us and the left of the other.

" ' "Aah, father," she cried. "Oh, mother who loved your children so much, I curse the evil sea which has taken you away! Oh, my husband, where have you gone? Had your love died that you abandoned me? No man of honor would desert his wife in danger if he loved her!"

" 'The word "husband" aroused our apprehensions, and we said brusquely, "Stop screaming, girl. Your parents are safe. But who is the husband you are talking about?"

" 'At the news that her parents were still alive, grief left her heart. "Don't be afraid," she said and told us her vicissitudes. "I was marooned on the seashore, and as I was wandering about the coast, I saw the man to whom you had given me. He too had been marooned. When we had heard each other's stories, he took my hand; for even in calamity there can be joy if one's destiny ordains it. He was so good at comforting a young girl that as he comforted me I forgot even father and mother, however dearly I had loved them. Today we boarded a ship that happened to come our way and set out for his home town, but that ship too was wrecked like the first one. Just a moment ago a cruel wave carried your sister's husband away before my very eyes. I shouted for help, but he vanished behind the waves, as the sky vanishes behind the wind-swept clouds. Then suddenly you had to become my enemies and save me! But I shall yet cool this burning body in the cold sea and quench the fire of separation. Let me go!"

" 'The neat propriety of it all convinced us that she had spoken the truth, and in our joy over the happy outcome of what could have been a disaster we embraced each other joyously. We sought to divert her gloomy thoughts by telling her that if fate had arranged a meeting by marooning both of them, it would certainly hold an even stranger reunion in store. This reassured her entirely. Then we crossed the ocean and multiplied a thousandfold our capital of pearls, coral, and so forth which we had brought with us.

" 'Here is Samudradinnā, and here is our capital which has grown to a fortune. We give you both; accept our gift. Samudradinnā's experience shows how people may survive after their ships are wrecked and be reunited with their families: so will your son. Sānudāsa survived once before when his ship foundered, and he may return again. Don't despair, madame.'

"So the two brothers left their sister and her dowry with me; and after they had been honored with all due hospitality, they departed as they had come. That is how Samudradinnā has come to your house, my son, as Fortune comes to a man of noble birth who is blessed with courage and luck.

"Son, I have been a mother to your wives, and I have protected their honor and their virtue as it was my duty to do. To wish that you who put the God of Wealth to shame with your celestial riches be equal to your father would be to curse you. Therefore let me wish that as you enjoy your wealth and enjoy it in accordance with the law, you will acquit yourself of the debts that you owe to the gods and your ancestors."

ᶜᴀ ᵉᴺote on the Sources

For the translations from the *Bṛhatkathāsaritsāgara* (KSS) the editions both of H. Brockhaus (2 vols.; Leipzig and Paris, 1839–62) and of Parab and Durgaprasad (Bombay, 1889) have been utilized. The selections from the *Bṛhatkathāślokasaṃgraha* (BKŚS), here translated for the first time into English, are based on Félix Lacôte's edition (Paris, 1908–29), and I owe much to his French translation (Books I–XX) and the continuation by Louis Renou (Books XXI–XXVIII). For the *Daśakumāracarita* (DKC) I have used M. R. Kale's edition (Bombay, 1917); for the two Pāli selections Dines Andersen's *Pāli Reader* (London, 1901). The sources of the individual stories are as follows:

THE KING AND THE CORPSE. KSS, 75–99 (*Vetālapañcaviṃśatikā*, 1–25); the introductory story, KSS, 75. 21–58; the concluding story, KSS, 98. 57–75; 99. 1–41.

"The Faithful Suitors," VetP. 2
"The Transposed Heads," VetP. 6

"The Three Fastidious Brahmins," VetP. 8
"The Three Sensitive Queens," VetP. 11
"The Man Who Changed Sexes," VetP. 15
"The King and the Spiteful Seductress," VetP. 17
"The Son of Three Fathers," VetP. 19
"The Boy Who Sacrificed Himself," VetP. 20
"Four Who Made a Lion," VetP. 22
"The Rejuvenated Hermit," VetP. 23
"The Insoluble Riddle," VetP. 24

THE TALE OF TWO BAWDS. KSS, 57. 54–175.
THE MAN WHO IMPERSONATED GOD VIṢṆU. KSS, 12. 78–136.
144–94.
THE CITY OF GOLD. KSS, 24. 19–81. 200–232; 25. 1–73. 297–
98; 26. 1–193. 254–83.
THE RED LOTUS OF CHASTITY, KSS, 13. 54–194.
GOMUKHA'S ESCAPADE. BKŚS, 10. 30–265.
TWO TALES OF DESTINY. BKŚS, 21. 21–172; 22. 1–312.
THE PERFECT BRIDE. Tale of Gomini in DKC, 6.
THE BUDDHIST KING OF TAXILA. KSS, 27. 10–54.
THE BRAHMIN WHO KNEW A SPELL. "Vedabbha-Jātaka"
(Jātaka 48; Fausbøll, I, 253. 4, 256. 27).
MAHOSADHA'S JUDGMENT. "Comm. on Mahāummāga Jātaka"
(Fausbøll, VI, 336. 31, 337. 15).
THE PRINCE AND THE PAINTED FAIRY. BKŚS, 19. 62–199.
TWO KINGDOMS WON. DKC, ucchvāsa 2, 3.
THE TRAVELS OF SĀNUDĀSA THE MERCHANT. BKŚS, 18. 4–702.

vaidagdhyakhyātilobhāya mama naivāyam udyamaḥ
kiṃtu nānākathājālasmṛtisaukaryasiddhaye

KSS, 1. 12